A CONCISE INTRODUCTION

TO PHILOSOPHY

CONSULTING EDITOR:

V. C. Chappell

UNIVERSITY OF CHICAGO

A Concise
Introduction to
PHILOSOPHY

William H. Halverson
The Ohio State University

RANDOM HOUSE New York

TO MY PARENTS
Arthur William Halverson
and
Clara Helena Halverson

PREFACE

IT HAS LONG been my practice, in teaching introductory courses in philosophy, to attempt to involve students as swiftly as possible in the active discussion of important philosophical problems. The chief task of the beginning student, as I see it, is not to acquire a collection of historical information about what some people called "philosophers" happen to have said, but to learn to participate intelligently in that exciting venture of the mind that is philosophy. The focus of the student's attention should be *important philosophical issues* rather than the "big names" in philosophy. And the issues, moreover, should be presented to him in such a way that he is encouraged to think of himself not as a spectator but as a participant in the discussion of these issues.

The teacher who wishes to teach his introductory course in this way—and there are many—has had thus far to choose between two types of textbooks: the single-author text and the anthology. The chief advantages of the former are (a) that the book (if it is well-written) has a certain logical progression and coherence which it is almost impossible to achieve in an anthology and (b) that a suitable technical and semi-technical vocabulary is established as the discussion proceeds, so that the student is not subjected to the terminological confusion which sometimes results from having the same matters discussed in different terms by different writers. These advantages of the single-author text, however, are counterbalanced by at least one serious defect of most such texts: they tend to be more or less biased in favor of the personal philosophical views of the author. It is exceedingly important, I think, that a student in philosophy be allowed—indeed, encouraged—to face each issue

vii

squarely and to make up his own mind—or, if he prefers, to suspend judgment for a while. The single-author text rarely allows the student to do this: it leads him to a conclusion, namely the author's conclusion, and the student's own struggles with the problems (assuming he has begun to engage in some struggle) tend to get short-circuited.

A well-planned anthology is a valuable teaching tool precisely because it overcomes this defect. Such a textbook is able to give a fair hearing to a variety of views and need not give preferential treatment to any one philosophical tendency or school. But this advantage is purchased at a price, and the price is a substantial decrease in just those qualities that constitute the chief advantages of the single-author text.

A Concise Introduction to Philosophy is an attempt to combine the advantages (and to eliminate the disadvantages) of both types. It possesses, I hope, the logical progression and coherence and the terminological consistency that only a single-author text can have. At the same time I should like to think that it also exhibits the openness and lack of bias of a good anthology. This, if it has in fact been achieved, has been done in the following way: each chapter setting forth a view on this or that philosophical problem has been written *from the point of view of a convinced advocate of the view in question.* I have tried at all times to present just as strong a case for those views with which I disagree as for those with which I agree—and on some of the problems discussed I am, in fact, far from having made up my own mind. Only in the introductory section (Chapters 1-4), in the introductory chapter of each succeeding section, in the two "retrospect" chapters, and in the concluding chapter, do I write, so to speak, "in my own name." All the remaining chapters might be termed "pseudonymous": they should be read as if they had been written by many different authors.

It is both a pleasure and a duty to express my sincere thanks to the many people who have assisted me in various ways in the writing of this book. Because the book is necessarily very broad in scope, it would be tempting—and altogether appropriate—to record here my appreciation and indebtedness to all of the many teachers and colleagues who have contributed in one way or another to my own philosophical education. This temptation I shall resist.

Special thanks are due, however, to Professor Vere C. Chappell of the University of Chicago, Professor Kaith Ballard of Bucknell University, Professor George F. Thomas of Princeton University, and Professor Herbert Reinelt of the University of the Pacific, all of whom made valuable suggestions regarding various portions of an earlier version of my manuscript. Their efforts, as I trust they will recognize, have resulted in a far better book than I should have been able to produce without their kind assistance; though it is I alone who am responsible for whatever defects may remain. Not least of all, however, thanks are due to the students at Augsburg College and at the University of Minnesota with whom I have had the privilege of "talking philosophy" these past several years. I hope they learned something in the process; for my part, I know that I learned a great deal. Should some of them chance to read this book they will find, I suspect, quite a few things that we learned together.

WILLIAM H. HALVERSON

Princeton, New Jersey

CONTENTS

xi

PART III: **The Problem of Induction**

CHAPTER

The Philosophical Enterprise

Chapter 1

PHILOSOPHY AND THE MODERN WORLD

IF WE WERE to attempt to construct a list of the ten or twelve men who have most strongly influenced the thinking of Western man during the past fifty years, whom might we choose? Einstein? Churchill? Kennedy? Should John Steinbeck, or James Joyce, or Ernest Hemingway, or T. S. Eliot appear on our list? Who have been the chief determiners of the thought and outlook of man in the modern world?

No doubt we are raising a question to which one cannot give a definitive answer. A good case could certainly be made for a considerable number of candidates, and it is unlikely that we could reach complete agreement as to which candidates were in fact most influential. But there is one point on which I think we might all agree, and that is that the chief determiners of thought in the modern world have not been professional philosophers. The men who have made the greatest impact on the thought of our day have been scientists, statesmen, novelists, historians, and theologians. Philosophers have not been very prominent. Their influence, it appears, has been largely confined to that relatively small group of college students who take a course or two in philosophy. Beyond the confines of the college classroom, they are virtually unknown.

Looking back over a somewhat longer span of history, however, it becomes evident that prior to the present century, philosophers did have a considerable influence on the thinking of their contemporaries. Consider, for example, the importance of Socrates, Plato, and Aristotle for the thought and outlook of the ancient world. Or consider the importance of St. Augustine and St. Thomas Aquinas with respect to the intellectual life of the medieval world. The seventeenth century had its Descartes, the eighteenth century had both Hume and Kant, the nineteenth century had Mill and Hegel. What, then, has become of philosophy in the twentieth century?

What, in fact, is the view of "the man on the street" regarding philosophy and philosophers today? Let us ponder this question for a moment. For although philosophers are not prominently influential in the intellectual life of our day, people are aware that there is such a thing as philosophy, and they do have some impressions of philosophy and philosophers. What are those impressions? How have they been formed?

Common Impressions

Many people understand the term "philosophy" to mean a general theory about something, particularly a general theory about how to approach some broad kind of undertaking. Thus, for example, it may be said that "Hubert Humphrey and Barry Goldwater have some fundamental disagreements in *political philosophy*," or "public education has recently had to come to terms with a radically different *educational philosophy*." A moment's reflection makes it evident that in either of these cases we could substitute the term "theory" for the term "philosophy" without changing the meaning of the statement. Hence, it is clear that in these instances philosophy means, simply, "theory." And since this is one of the most common ways in which people who are not professional philosophers hear and use the term, it is one of the strongest impressions which people have of philosophy.

It may be of some importance to note in this connection that "philosophy," when it is used in this way, always has a very practical orientation: it is a theory about how to *do* something in a given area of human concern. Indeed, the broader the area, the more appropriate it seems to speak about activity in that area as being guided by some "philosophy." We do not hesitate to talk about a man's "political philosophy" or his "educational philosophy"; it would seem very odd to talk about a man's theories regarding gardening or house painting as his "gardening philosophy" or his "house-painting philosophy."

Not too far removed from this impression of philosophy is the idea that philosophy means a general view of life, or a general theory about how one ought to go about the living of one's life. Here, too, "philosophy" is understood to have a very practical orientation—only the activity which is envisioned in this case is not restricted to this or that area, but includes the whole of life. A man can live for gain, or he can live to serve: it depends, we sometimes say, on his "philosophy of life." And a "philosophy of life" would presumably include views on such things as the nature of man and man's place in the universe, some convictions as to what things are worth living for, etc. When the term "philosophy" is used without a qualifying adjective (political, educational, economic), most people probably understand it to mean "philosophy of life."

It also seems to be a very common notion that philosophy has to do with matters that are very abstract and/or profound. People by and large are of the opinion that philosophers are very wise and learned men—though they may not have any very clear idea what it is that these men are so learned about, or how they acquired their peculiar wisdom. Students very often approach their first course in philosophy with a kind of secret fear that, though they may do very well in other fields, they may not have what it takes to master so forbidding a field as philosophy.

Perhaps one reason for this impression regarding philosophy is that, as already noted, the term "philosophy" is often understood to mean "general theory." People do know in a general way what is meant by "political philosophy," or "philosophy of education," or "philosophy of life," but very few people have a specific and detailed knowledge in any of these areas. Indeed, it is almost axiomatic that a theory must be somewhat mystifying before we are willing to dignify it with the name of "philosophy"; hence we readily acquiesce in the view that someone who has worked out the details of a "philosophy" of something must be a man of almost super-human wisdom. We can all easily understand how to paint a house, or thread a needle, or raise a garden; hence we do not call views on these things "philosophy." But a theory about how to organize an economic system, or how to go about the business of education, or how to pursue the business of living, is a different matter. Here the perspectives are so broad, the content so vast and mystifying, the categories so obscure: this we call "philosophy"!

Another reason for this impression, perhaps, is that we have often heard it said when someone makes a vague or general statement about something that he is "getting philosophical." It is not clear in such cases whether it is the broad generality of the statement or its vagueness that makes it "philosophical"; but "philosophical" is what it is called. And so, many people have gotten the impression that, at best, philosophy is concerned with matters that are very profound, beyond the understanding of most men, or, at worst, that philosophy is simply vague and imprecise.

There is another fairly widespread impression regarding philosophy, namely that it is dangerous. Well-meaning people sometimes warn college students (in the words of St. Paul) to "see to it that no one makes a prey of you by philosophy and empty deceit" [1]—the inference being that all philosophy is nothing but "empty deceit" that will "make a prey" of the unwary. Not uncommonly, perhaps, philosophy is regarded as a threat to religious faith, to morality, and perhaps to citizenship; and the conclusion is drawn that for this reason it ought to be avoided by anyone who values these things.

It is interesting to note that this impression regarding philosophy is very old, dating in fact from the earliest days of the Western philosophical tradition. The most notable example of the "bad press" from which philosophy has long suffered is, of course, the trial and conviction of Socrates on grounds of "impiety" and "corrupting the youth." Socrates, in making his defense to the Athenian court, is quite explicit about the fact that the court's opinion of him is prejudiced because of their negative opinion of philosophy. He tells the court:

> I have had many accusers complaining to you, and for a long time, for many years now, and with not a word of truth to say.
> . . . These . . . got hold of most of you while you were boys, and persuaded you, and accused me falsely. . . . These, gentlemen, who have broadcast this reputation, these are my

---

[1] Colossians, 2:8.

dangerous accusers; for those who hear believe that anyone who is a student of that sort of lore must be an atheist as well.[2]

Whether or not this reputation is deserved—that is, whether or not philosophy really is dangerous, or potentially dangerous, to the generally accepted values of society—is a question which the student will have to decide for himself after he has acquired a sufficient acquaintance with philosophy to be entitled to an opinion. The point is indisputable, however, that philosophy is regarded by many people in this way, and one result is that students who register for their first course in philosophy often do so with a strange, uneasy feeling.

Finally, it is not unusual to hear it suggested that philosophy is a waste of time. The indictment might read like this: "Scientists and technologists do things that help to provide the necessities and comforts of life; doctors and dentists work to alleviate human suffering; athletes and musicians provide enjoyable entertainment —but what do philosophers do for their fellow men? They speculate and dream and talk nonsense and undermine the faith of men. Anybody who wants to amount to anything will do well to leave philosophy alone!"

It cannot be denied that all of this adds up to a rather consistently negative attitude toward philosophy on the part of those who share these impressions. In some respects, perhaps, these impressions derive from the actual character of the philosophical enterprise; in other respects, they show a total misunderstanding of that enterprise. The student will be able to assess their accuracy for himself as soon as he has developed some understanding of what the philosophical enterprise is about. For the present, it may be of some value to make a few generalizations about philosophy that relate to the popular views which we have just discussed.

A Preliminary Characterization

It is just as well, when undertaking a study of philosophy, to be aware from the very outset that philosophy, as distinguished from

---

[2] Plato, *Apology*, W. H. D. Rouse, ed., *Great Dialogues of Plato* (New York: New American Library, 1956), p. 424.

many other fields of study, is "impractical" in the sense that a mastery of it is not primarily a means to some vocational goal. In this respect, the study of philosophy is similar to the study of literature; an appreciation of it is valuable in and of itself, and this is the justification for spending one's time on it. One can, of course, teach literature, just as one can teach philosophy; but this would be quite pointless if the study and appreciation of either were not worthwhile in itself.

It must be admitted that the values which have guided the thinking and behavior of our society in recent years have not been conducive to the flowering of philosophy, literature, or the arts. Our society tends to value what pays and to devalue what does not pay. We are, so to speak, consistently "commercial" in our values. Thus works of art, for example, are considered "art" if people are willing to buy them. Music may be a "worthwhile" field of study for one who "has what it takes" to become a successful performer, or composer, or teacher of music. An English major, if he is really talented, may eventually make a handsome living as a novelist, a writer of short stories, or as a member of the editorial staff of some periodical; at the very least, he can become an English teacher. In any case, he is not in any great danger of being left unemployed.

What is missing in this very commercialized account of what used to be called the "liberal arts," however, is any appreciation of the intrinsic and non-saleable value of developing a genuine capacity for appreciation in these areas. If an acquaintance with, and an appreciation of, art or music or literature is not worthwhile in itself —if the cultivation of such an appreciation does not justify itself simply on the ground that it makes life richer and broader and more human—then the teaching or promotion of these things is wholly unjustified.

Because of the commercialization of values in our society, it is necessary to remind ourselves from time to time that there is a difference between education and job training. Education is concerned with the development of one's capacities as a human being —one's capacities for understanding, for appreciation, for interpersonal relationships, for creative participation in the ongoing common life of man. Job training is concerned with the preparation for some particular kind of employment. To forget this distinction and to think only in terms of the latter, is to render irrelevant a considerable part of what is typically included in a college or university program of study.

Philosophy, like literature and the arts, belongs essentially to what we have called education rather than job training. Unlike the others, however, it is almost impossible in the case of philosophy to make the mistake of regarding it, or rather the study of it, as a preparation for a career. The major in philosophy is not, by virtue of his major, prepared to do any particular job (though he may, of course, go on to graduate school and become a professor of philosophy).

Why, then, should anyone study philosophy? Simply because, in ways that will shortly become apparent, it is an essential part of becoming a truly educated person. Do not approach the study of philosophy—or, for that matter, of history, or music, or literature, or art—with the expectation that in this study you will acquire some saleable knowledge or skill. Chances are that you will not. Approach it rather with the hope that it will enhance your understanding, broaden your horizon, increase your self-awareness, and enrich your appreciation of the powers as well as the limits of the human mind: then you will not be disappointed.

The beginning student in philosophy would also do well to bear in mind from the outset that philosophy is by its very nature critical of the status quo, unwilling to accept as unquestionable even the most widely held beliefs. It was Socrates who said, "The unexamined life is not worth living." [3] Philosophy ever since has taken its cue from him. Do not be dismayed, therefore, if you encounter in your study views which seem preposterous—as you undoubtedly will. The beliefs that are called in question may indeed be true; the philosopher's point is simply that their truth ought not to be taken for granted.

We shall have more to say on this point in connection with our discussion of the critical side of the philosopher's task. For the present it is enough to note that the suspicion with which many people regard philosophy derives in large part from the fact that philosophers almost invariably stand in a critical, questioning rela-

---

[3] *Ibid.,* p. 445.

tion to prevailing modes of thought. It is not strange that people regard with suspicion an enterprise whose main business often seems to be the raising of embarrassing questions.

It would also be well to say a few words here about the kind and degree of precision that one should strive for in the study of philosophy. A physicist once remarked in a public lecture (departing from his prepared text), "If you want to evaluate any proposal made by a physicist, don't pay any attention to the blah-blah-blah: just look at his equations." Translation: talk does not make any difference; it is only equations that count. But the philosopher, except when he is engaged in formal logic, does not have any equations, and that leaves him with—at best—*talk!* The result is that philosophy commonly lacks the precision—both in its methodology and in its conclusions—that most of us have learned to demand of the natural sciences.

This unavoidable imprecision of language must not, however, be used as a camouflage for fuzzy thinking. "It is the mark of an educated man," Aristotle once remarked, "to demand that degree of precision in each field which the nature of the subject allows." [4] Philosophy does not allow the perfect precision of pure mathematics, nor even the high degree of precision found in mathematical natural science; but neither is it the case that philosophers place a premium on ambiguity. Every philosopher tries to find language that will express his thoughts clearly and unambiguously. The technical and semi-technical language of philosophy has been developed precisely in order that certain ideas may be discussed with greater precision than would otherwise be possible.

The greatest temptation for the beginning student in philosophy is to be satisfied with *less* precision than the subject allows. Not a single idea in this book is so difficult (or "profound") that, with reasonable effort, it cannot be grasped. Do not be content, then, with anything less than complete mastery of the ideas here discussed. Language is not a perfect tool, but it is the best tool available to us for the purpose of thinking and conversing about the world in which we live.

---

[4] Aristotle, *Nicomachean Ethics,* Book I, Chap. 3, Richard McKeon, ed., *The Basic Works of Aristotle* (New York: Random House, 1941), p. 936.

Study Questions

1. Can you name any philosophers who have lived all or part of their lives in the present century? Have any of them, in your judgment, had a strong influence on the thinking of our day? If so, how has that influence been exerted? Where and by whom has it been felt?
2. What prior impressions about philosophy do you bring with you to this study? How have you gotten these impressions?
3. Write four or five sentences in which it seems natural to you to use the term "philosophy." In what sense or senses are you using the term?
4. How widespread, in your judgment, is the view that philosophy is "dangerous" and "a waste of time"? As far as you can judge, do the people who hold these views know enough about philosophy to be entitled to an opinion?
5. Do you think it is fair to say that our society is quite consistently "commercial" in its values? With what sort of evidence could you either support or oppose such a statement?
6. Can you see any possible value in questioning beliefs that most people just simply take for granted? Would it not be better to leave such matters alone and to concentrate all our efforts on attempting to find solutions to the social, economic, and political problems that plague mankind today?

Chapter 2

THE TWO SIDES OF
THE PHILOSOPHICAL TASK

WHEN ONE APPROACHES the task of reading a book purporting to introduce a field of study with which he is not previously acquainted, or with which he has at most a very casual acquaintance, he brings to that task certain legitimate expectations. He expects, for example, that his study will yield him some kind of overview of the field in question rather than a study in depth of some one aspect of the field to the complete exclusion of others. He expects, further, that in the course of his study he will be exposed to some of the most representative thinking in the field— lest his initial understanding of the field be grossly inaccurate. And very importantly, he expects (and rightly so) that what he will encounter in an introductory text will represent the consensus of scholars in the field. He does not, at this stage, wish to be subjected to novel or untried proposals: these can wait until he has achieved some perspective from which to evaluate them. What he needs first is a distillation of the best knowledge available in the field, an intelligible account of the common ground upon which all, or most, of the practicing scholars in that field stand.

Unfortunately, it is not possible at the present time to state anything that might be called a consensus among philosophers as to what it is that constitutes the task of the philosopher. There is, in fact, substantial disagreement among men who call themselves philosophers as to just what it is that they are, or are supposed to be, doing. There are reasons for this uncertainty, and before we proceed to outline our own proposal for a definition of the philosopher's task, it may be helpful to look briefly at a few of these reasons.

Reasons for Uncertainty

One development that has played a role in the creation of the present crisis in philosophy is the progressive taking-over by the special sciences of various areas of inquiry formerly belonging to philosophy. Aristotle, for example, included in his "philosophical" inquiries a large number of matters that are now customarily divided among biologists, physiologists, psychologists, zoologists, political scientists, literary critics, and so on. For Aristotle, "philosophy" was virtually a collective name for the quest for knowledge—in whatever area, by whatever means. But since the time of Aristotle, and particularly during the past three or four hundred years, the quest for knowledge has been carried on by a wide variety of specialists who have developed to an incredibly fine point the methods of investigation appropriate to this or that area of inquiry. What, then, remains for the philosopher to do? Philosophers—i. e., men who occupy professorships in philosophy in colleges and universities—are not quite sure how to answer this question. This, then, is one reason for the current turmoil over the nature of the philosophical enterprise.

There exists also another reason, closely related to the first. For a long time after the advent of modern science, with its division of labor among the various special sciences, there was a widely held view among philosophers that the peculiar domain of the philosopher, as distinguished from the several sorts of natural scientists, was *metaphysics*. The relation of metaphysics to the special sciences was a matter of some dispute, but for a time everyone seemed happy with the arrangement whereby philosophers concentrated on metaphysics and scientists claimed the various kinds of merely "factual" inquiries as their own.

During the eighteenth century, however, questions were raised about the validity of the whole idea of metaphysical knowledge. David Hume and Immanuel Kant, in very different ways, both asked, in effect, "But does the emperor (in this case metaphysics) really have any clothes at all? Is there anything to the claims of philosophers, or are their speculations really empty?" Hume recommended consigning all such treatises to the flames. Kant, more gentle, only called on metaphysicians to suspend their labors until they had answered a few questions. In both cases, however, the enterprise that had become the central business of the philosopher was radically questioned, and it could only be a matter of time until philosophers would have to give some kind of answer to this challenge.

At length, after about a century or more, the strictures of Hume and Kant sank in. Led by G. E. Moore, a group of philosophers in England became convinced that metaphysics was indeed an impossible sort of inquiry, and that whatever the proper business of the philosopher might be it certainly was not that. About the same time a group of young philosophers in Vienna (the so-called "Vienna Circle") came to a similar conclusion. Presently a loosely organized movement became discernible, the most obvious features of which were (a) a common abandonment of metaphysics and (b) a common affinity for the empirical methods of the natural sciences. This does not mean that Moore and the Vienna Circle philosophers attempted to transform philosophy into an empirical enterprise—a quasi-science, so to speak. But their affinity for the empirical methods of the natural sciences was one of the prominent causes of their disenchantment with traditional metaphysics. As a consequence, they attempted to define the philosophical task much more narrowly than it had been defined before.

But what, then, remains for the philosopher to do? If the several natural sciences have taken over the empirical inquiries which were once a part of the philosophical enterprise, and if metaphysics is abandoned as unwarranted and/or empty speculation, does there remain anything for the philosopher to do? This is a question that haunts present-day philosophers, and the many conflicting statements that are made about "what philosophy is" give some idea of how far the discussion remains from anything like a consensus.

There is quite general agreement among philosophers on one point, however, and that is that at least one part of the traditional philosophical enterprise remains the sole property of the philosopher, namely *logic*. Some philosophers are of the opinion that logical studies, broadly conceived, constitute the whole of philosophy; others believe there must be something more to philosophy, but are uncertain what that "something more" might be. And still others, of course, retain the belief that metaphysics is still possible, even though it is presently "out of style."

The Nature of the Question

Perhaps we may take a small step toward the formulation of a defensible proposal if we clarify the nature of the question that we are asking when we ask, "What is the proper task of the philosopher?"

Let us note first that our question is not a *moral* question. We are not asking, "What *ought* philosophers to be doing?"—as if there were some prescribed task that they had been assigned to perform, in such a way that their non-performance of it (or their non-performance of it to the best of their ability) would be blameworthy. There is, admittedly, a kind of common agreement about the sort of competence that a man should have if he claims to be a chemist, or a physicist, or a mathematician, or a philosopher, and it would certainly be misleading for a man to call himself any of these things if he were lacking in the appropriate competence. But it clearly is not the case that any person or agency or group has "assigned" this or that sort of inquiry to scholars of a given designation. It may be misleading for a man to call himself a philosopher if he does not, in fact, engage in a certain kind of enterprise, but it does not by any means follow that he is morally culpable because of this fact. Our question is not a moral question.

But neither is our question an arbitrary verbal one, a matter of simply assigning some useful meaning to the phrase, "the philosophical task." This is why it is not helpful to say, as has sometimes been said, that "Philosophy is what philosophers do." We could, of course, assign some random function to a group of men— basket weaving, for example—and say, "That is what we shall hereafter call 'philosophy.' The task of the philosopher is to weave baskets." But this would obviously be confusing. The question concerning the task of the philosopher is not answered by making an arbitrary assignment and calling it "philosophy." And the reason the question is not satisfactorily answered in this way is that we are not asking an arbitrary verbal question.

The question is, rather, a historical question. It might be re-phrased like this: There is, as everyone knows, a tradition of thought that began in Greece in about the sixth century B.C., and that has included such men as Socrates, Plato, Aristotle, St. Augustine, St. Thomas Aquinas, Descartes, Kant, and many others. Is there some common enterprise in which all of these men were engaged by virtue of which they are all called philosophers? If so, what is that enterprise?

Our question is, however, a bit more complicated than this re-phrasing might suggest. We have noted, for example, that Aristotle engaged in a number of inquiries which today belong to such specialists as biologists, physicists, literary critics, and so on. Furthermore, a number of men who regard themselves as philosophers today are convinced that what some philosophers in the past regarded as the unique task of the philosopher is an unperformable task. Taking account of these qualifications, we may re-phrase our question thus: Is there not some task which (a) has traditionally been performed by men who have called themselves philosophers, (b) has not been taken over by any of the special sciences, and (c) is still performable? If such a task can be identified, it is that task that is most appropriately designated "the task of the philosopher."

The Critical Task

In the previous chapter mention was made of Socrates, the great Greek philosopher and martyr who lived and worked in Athens during the fifth century B.C. (469-399 B.C.). Socrates, as we learn in the *Apology,* was convicted by the Athenian court of "atheism" and "corrupting the youth" and was condemned to die. The death of Socrates is beautifully and movingly described by Plato in the concluding pages of the dialogue entitled *Phaedo.*

What was Socrates doing that led to his being haled into court on these charges? Evidently it was not his deliberate intention to promote impiety or to corrupt youth. What was his intention, then, and how did he go about pursuing it?

According to the *Apology,* which is considered to be a fairly accurate account of the historical Socrates, the facts are these. A friend of Socrates—Chairephon—inquired of the oracle at Delphi whether anyone was wiser than Socrates and received the reply that no one was. Hearing this, Socrates—who, as he says, knew in his conscience that he was *not* wise—proceeded to test the oracle's statement by interrogating some of his fellow-citizens who were generally regarded to be wise and learned men. Socrates commented as follows on his testing:

> I approached one of those who had the reputation of being wise for there, I thought, if anywhere, I should test the revelation and prove that the oracle was wrong. . . . But when I examined him, . . . and when I conversed with him, I thought this man *seemed* to be wise both to many others and especially to himself, but that he was not. . . . After that I tried another, one of those reputed to be wiser than that man, and I thought just the same; then he and many others took a dislike to me.[1]

Socrates took it to be his unique task to interrogate his fellow-citizens to see whether or not their opinions could stand up under close scrutiny. Wherever Socrates found people holding opinions, or making truth-claims, there he went to work. Does Meno claim to know whether or not virtue can be taught? "Well, Meno," says Socrates, "What is virtue? Do you really know what virtue is?" Or does Euthyphro claim to know for sure that his father is guilty of impiety? "Euthyphro," says Socrates, "I do not even know for sure what piety and impiety are. Could you instruct me in this?" The critical examination of opinions, the testing of truth-claims—that was the task in which Socrates was engaged.

This picture of Socrates going about questioning the men of Athens as to the soundness of their opinions symbolizes what we may call the *critical* side of the philosophical enterprise. We all take many things for granted, and we live and think and work on the basis of what we take for granted—on the basis, that is, of our assumptions. Very often, perhaps most of the time, we are scarcely aware of what our assumptions are. But the philosopher is tremen-

---

[1] Plato, *Apology*, W. H. D. Rouse, ed., *Great Dialogues of Plato* (New York: New American Library, 1956), p. 427.

dously interested in the assumptions that underlie various kinds of supposed knowledge. He wants to know what those assumptions are and whether or not they are reasonable. And so, like Socrates, he examines them.

Socrates, of course, went about his business in a very informal and very personal way. He queried individuals and examined their claims to knowledge, claims which usually did not stand up under close scrutiny. Since Socrates' time, however, the whole business of knowledge and learning has been more or less institutionalized— and so also has philosophy. This has had the effect of making philosophy a more formalized, but less personal, undertaking. The questions which the philosopher raises in this context are directed not so much at individuals as at fields of learning. The philosopher asks his questions not of the scientist, but about the truth-claims of science; not of the religious person, but about the truth-claims of religion; and so on. Philosophy is, so to speak, the "gadfly" in the curriculum of a modern college or university, just as Socrates attempted to be a "gadfly" to his fellow-citizens in ancient Athens.

The Constructive Task

Philosophers, however, do not engage in this critical task just to make a nuisance of themselves. Indeed, the central aim of philosophers has always been a positive one. What, then, is this positive aim, this constructive task of the philosopher?

The answer suggested by a careful scrutiny of the work of many generations of practicing philosophers is this: the positive goal of the philosopher is to construct a picture of the whole of reality, in which every element of man's knowledge and every aspect of man's experience will find its proper place. Philosophy, in short, is man's quest for the unity of knowledge: it consists in a perpetual struggle to create the concepts in which the universe can be conceived as a *uni*verse and not a *multi*verse. The history of philosophy is the history of this attempt. The problems of philosophy are the problems that arise when the attempt is made to grasp this total unity.

It cannot be denied that this attempt stands without rival as the most audacious enterprise in which the mind of man has ever engaged. Just reflect for a moment: Here is man, surrounded by the vastness of a universe in which he is only a tiny and perhaps insignificant part—and he wants to *understand* it, to conceive the whole thing in his mind, in such a way that no reality that confronts him, no event that occurs, no fact that he discovers, is beyond the categories of his understanding. Audacious indeed; but what are the alternatives?

One alternative, perhaps, would be to make no effort to understand anything. Perhaps, if he tried hard enough, man could learn to control his propensity to ask questions and could just gape at the world, responding to it only as might be necessary for the preservation of his species. Apparently other species of life do no more and survive rather well in the struggle for life.

In all seriousness, however, it does not appear likely that man ever could or would do this, even if it were desirable. It seems to be characteristic of man, as Aristotle said long ago, that he "by nature desires to know." [2] Moreover, although a part of man's quest for knowledge appears to stem from a desire to control his environment, it has deeper roots as well. Man desires to know not solely in order that he may more effectively manipulate his environment, but simply and purely for the sake of knowing. The total abandonment of the quest for understanding is not a promising alternative to constructive philosophy.

Another alternative would be for man to be content with piecemeal knowledge—to establish what can be established in each of the special sciences, and to make no attempt to discern the features of the "total picture" of which each of these fragments is presumably a part. This view is occasionally expressed in statements like, "It is better to know one thing well than to know a little bit about everything," or "It is better to be a good chemist than a poor philosopher."

But here, too, is a problem, and it is one that makes it impossible to hold such a view except in the half-jesting mood that is reflected above. For as we focus our attention on first one area, then another, we are sometimes driven to conclusions that appear to be in conflict with one another. One of the by-products of such "compartmentalized" thinking is what we may call "apparent incompat-

[2] Aristotle, *Metaphysics*, Book I, Chap. 1, Richard McKeon, ed., *The Basic Works of Aristotle* (New York: Random House, 1941), p. 689.

ibles," and these a healthy mind does not easily accept. How, we insist on asking, do these apparently conflicting truths fit together? How, for example, can man be free in the sense that ethics seems to require if, as appears to be the case, the whole universe is subject without exception to causal law? If all knowledge comes to us through experience, and if experience yields only probability, how does it come about that in mathematics we are able to establish our conclusions with absolute certainty? These and other questions thrust themselves upon us, almost in spite of ourselves. It is out of such tension—tension between the various elements of our piece-meal knowledge—that much philosophical thinking arises. For to ask such questions is precisely to ask for the wider concept, the total picture, in which what is legitimate in each of these competing truth-claims can be given its due.

Philosophy, on its constructive side, is nothing more or less than the systematic quest for the unity of human knowledge. Reality discloses itself to man in a wide variety of ways. The philosopher asks, "How does it all fit together? How can I conceive of reality as a whole?"

Many philosophers would grant that the quest which we have just described—the quest for the unity of human knowledge, for the "total picture"—was indeed the quest that motivated the great philosophers of the past. And it is apparent to everyone that this task has not been taken over by any of the special sciences. But, many would say, the task which has just been described simply is not performable; therefore, it cannot be a part of the philosopher's present task.

How are we to understand such an objection? If, as we have already argued, the only alternatives to such a quest are either (a) to abandon altogether the quest for knowledge or (b) to be content with piecemeal knowledge, and if neither of these is a practicable course to follow, then it would appear that somebody must continue to pursue this task within the household of learning. Who should it be if not the philosopher? On what grounds, or for what reason, could a present-day philosopher forswear this task as being "unperformable" in the modern world?

The answer to the puzzle, one suspects, is something like this: Those philosophers who decline to embrace the traditional philosophical quest for the unity of man's knowledge recognize that any proposals that they might make with respect to "the total picture" cannot exhibit either the precision or the empirical probability of a scientific hypothesis, and they are reluctant to commit themselves to any proposals that do not meet these qualifications. Their objection, in effect, is that the traditional philosophical task is not performable *with the same degree of precision* as are the several tasks of the special sciences. This is indisputably true, and its truth should be a warning to any philosopher to make his proposals with considerable caution if he nonetheless elects to pursue this quest. But if our previous reasoning was sound, this consideration ought not prevent pursuit of this quest with such precision as the nature of the inquiry will allow. Ours is indisputably an age of science, and we are all captivated by the precision and the power of the scientific method; but not all questions are scientific questions, and where other sorts of questions are asked, other sorts of answers must be expected and other methods must be employed in searching for them.

One thing, at least, seems clear: the quest for "the total picture," the struggle to discern the unity that we instinctively believe must somehow lie behind the apparent inconsistencies of our little fragments of knowledge—in short, the constructive philosophical quest —will go on, with or without the cooperation of professional philosophers. It may turn out that those philosophers who of late have found their profession somewhat sterile and unchallenging will find a renewed interest in their work if the quest for unity comes once again to be accepted as the *raison d'être* of the philosophical enterprise.

Study Questions

1. What, precisely, do you understand to be the "critical" task of philosophy? What are some of the questions that a philosopher might ask in attempting to pursue this task?

2. Are you convinced that the *only* alternatives to "constructive philosophy" are (a) giving up the quest for understanding altogether or (b) settling for "piecemeal" knowledge? How might one go about trying to refute this claim?

3. Are you inclined to agree or to disagree with the following statement: "The constructive task of philosophy is a task that cannot be
avoided: the only question is whether it is to be pursued carefully
and systematically or informally and haphazardly"?

Chapter 3

PHILOSOPHICAL PROBLEMS AND PHILOSOPHICAL SYSTEMS

THE HISTORY OF philosophy, we have observed, is the history of man's quest for a comprehensive picture of reality, in which every element of man's knowledge and every aspect of man's experience finds its proper place. The problems of philosophy, we suggested, are the problems that arise when one pursues this quest. But when is a problem a philosophical problem? How does an answer to a philosophical problem relate to this "quest for the total picture"? And how does all of this relate to the so-called "philosophical systems" about which we hear from time to time?

Although it may not always be convenient to do so, it is always possible to state a problem in the form of a question. It is seldom convenient to do so in the case of, say, an arithmetical problem. It is much easier (because shorter) to write "$7 + 5 = ?$" than to ask, "What is the sum of seven and five?" But in the case of most philosophical problems, we do not have a precise symbol system in which to abbreviate our problems. The best that we can do is to state our problem in terms of a precise question. Let us ask, then, "When is a question a philosophical question?" i. e., "When does a question express a philosophical problem?"

Characteristics of a Philosophical Question

Consider the following questions: (a) "At what temperature does pure water freeze, assuming sea-level barometric pressure?" (b)

"What is the name of the capital of India?" (c) "Who held the office of President of the United States in 1797?" (d) "Is the atomic theory helpful in explaining the process of photosynthesis?" (e) "What is religion?" (f) "Is moral responsibility compatible with the determinism assumed in most scientific inquiries?"

Of these six questions, the first three are obviously not philosophical questions. Anyone who is remotely familiar with how the labor of inquiry has been divided up among the several academic fields will readily recognize that question *a* belongs to physics, question *b* to geography, and question *c* to history. If we wanted an answer to any of these questions, we would turn, respectively, to the physicist, the geographer, and the historian for our information.

Question *d* may puzzle us for a moment. Is it a question for the botanist to answer, or is it one for the physicist? We are not sure. But note this: we do recognize it to be a scientific question, our reason for hesitation being only that we are uncertain as to which of the sciences is competent to handle it. Such questions we shall call "intra-scientific" questions; they arise because of the particular ways in which the several natural sciences have marked out the boundaries of their inquiries.

Questions *e* and *f* present some new features. First, there is evidently no existing science that is competent to handle either question. Consider, for example, question *e*. One could imagine a number of scientists having opinions about the answer to the question, "What is religion?" Freud, for example, who was a psychologist, felt strongly enough about his opinion regarding this question to write a book about it. But it is not, strictly speaking, within the competence of the psychologist *as a psychologist* to answer this question. The same must be said about the sociologist, the anthropologist, and the archaeologist: each of these scientists, pursuing his own proper inquiries, may discover some important facts about religion (this is within his competence), and each may go on to form an opinion as to "what religion really is." But in forming such an opinion, the scientist is no longer speaking *as a scientist*—i. e., as a psychologist, a sociologist, an anthropologist, or whatever. All may indeed contribute something to the answer, but none is competent within the limits of his own academic specialty to answer the question. A moment's reflection will make it evident that the same holds true for question *f*.

This, it will be found, is one of the defining characteristics of philosophical questions. Philosophical questions are questions which do not fall within the competence of any of the special sciences, or even within the competence of any combination of the special sciences. Philosophical questions, in short, are neither straightforwardly scientific nor "intra-scientific": this is part of what one is saying when one calls them "philosophical."

A second feature of questions *e* and *f*, and a second defining characteristic of philosophical questions, is that one cannot readily imagine what sorts of evidence, if any, would be relevant to answering them. There is something bewildering, something puzzling, about such questions. With respect to question *e,* for example, one supposes that some of the findings of psychologists, sociologists, archaeologists, anthropologists, and historians would be relevant. But which? And how to collect the relevant data? These are baffling questions, and it is characteristic of philosophical questions that they leave us baffled in just this way.

Third, philosophical questions are questions whose possible answers appear to have far-reaching consequences for one's whole world-view. Philosophical questions have a kind of multiple relevance: any answer that is given has implications that touch many areas of human concern. If, for example, one decides with respect to question *f* that determinism is not compatible with moral freedom, and that determinism is true, what are the consequences for one's view of man's moral responsibility? for one's view of the significance of one's own "decisions"? for one's understanding of the penal system? for the status of law? for the conduct of international diplomacy? for one's estimate of one's own conduct, and of the conduct of one's fellow-men? It would be possible to go on and on finding areas of human concern to which any answer to this question is directly or indirectly relevant, and one could make the same point by using as an illustration any one of dozens of philosophical problems that have been discussed. But let our single example suffice; a philosophical question is one any answer to which has profound and far-reaching consequences for a total world-view—

and, therefore, for a view of many matters of which one may not be aware when the problem is initially raised.

These characteristics of philosophical questions all derive from the fact that the over-all goal of the philosophical quest is, as we have said, to achieve a "picture of the whole," an all-inclusive concept of reality in which no truth fails to receive its proper due. Every philosophical problem is, in fact, an integral part of this broader project, and it is only because (or perhaps insofar as) we are interested in the larger project that we find ourselves interested in the particular problems. Students of philosophy whose only impression of philosophy is that of a group of loosely related or unrelated problems would do well to explore the many relations among problems that become evident when they are viewed in the context of the broader philosophical task.

Types of Philosophical Questions

Any question exhibiting the three characteristics mentioned will, then, be a philosophical question. During the long span of time in which Western philosophers have been discussing questions of this sort, however, philosophical inquiry has come to assume a fairly well-defined structure, as a result of which it is possible to speak of various "departments" of philosophical inquiry and, accordingly, of various "types" of philosophical questions. There is, of course, nothing final or definitive about this typology, but it is of value, nonetheless, as a kind of system of points of reference when one is attempting to get a bearing in a new and strange field of inquiry.

Many philosophical questions are what may be called "logical" questions. That is to say, they are questions that arise in that department of philosophical inquiry known as *logic.* It is not easy to define logic in a way that does justice to the wide range of problems with which logicians are concerned. A definition acceptable to most logicians, perhaps, would be "inquiry concerning the principles whereby one may distinguish between correct and incorrect reasoning." Some representative problems of this type would be: What is the relation between words and things? What constitutes the "meaning" of a proposition? What does it mean to say of an argument that it is "valid"? How does one test the validity of an argument?

Some philosophical questions are what may be called "ontological" (or metaphysical) questions. These are questions that arise in that department of philosophical inquiry known as *ontology* (or *metaphysics*). Again, it is difficult to give a definition that would be acceptable to everyone concerned. Ontology has been defined as "[the science of] being *qua* being" [1] and as "[an investigation concerning] the character of everything that is insofar as it is." [2] It is assumed that simply to *be*—not to be a man or a house or a tree, but simply to *be*—a thing must have a certain "structure." Ontology is the attempt to ascertain what that structure is. Some philosophers, though they allow that the metaphysical proposals of the past are appropriate subjects of historical study, would maintain that it is not possible to pose an intelligible question of this type, much less to give an intelligible or, at any rate, a defensible answer. The student may wish to reserve judgment on this until he has had an opportunity to reflect on the questions raised in Parts IV, V, VI, and VIII.

A third general type of philosophical questions consists of a group of questions commonly called "epistemological." *Epistemology* is that department of philosophy in which the attempt is made to ascertain the nature and limits of human knowledge. Under what conditions may we properly be said to "know" so-and-so? Does all knowledge of the real world arise out of experience, or do we have some knowledge which is in some degree independent of experience? If all knowledge does arise out of experience, and if experience can only yield varying degrees of probability, how is it possible to achieve the absolute certainty which we do achieve in logic and in mathematics? These are only a few of the epistemological questions in which philosophers are interested.

A fourth type of philosophical questions is technically called "axiological," although the terms "axiology" and "axiological" are

[1] Aristotle, *Metaphysics,* Book IV, Chap. 1, Richard McKeon, ed., *The Basic Works of Aristotle* (New York: Random House, 1941), p. 731.

[2] Paul Tillich, *Systematic Theology,* Vol. 1 (Chicago, Ill.: The University of Chicago Press, 1951), p. 163.

not very commonly used among philosophers at the present time. Instead, philosophers speak of "theory of value" and of questions that arise in this context as questions concerning the nature of value. Some typical questions of this type would be: Are beauty and goodness qualities that are objectively present in things, or are they not? If so, how is their presence or absence ascertained? If not, are they simply sentiments in the mind of the person who judges that something is good or bad, beautiful or ugly? And if this is not the case, what *is* the status of beauty and goodness? That branch of axiology that is principally concerned with the nature of *non-moral* values (particularly beauty, and whatever other values are of special relevance for the arts) is called *aesthetics.* The branch of axiology that deals with the nature of (and fundamental principles governing) good and evil, right and wrong—i. e., *moral* values—is known as *ethics, or moral philosophy.*

It may be that all philosophical questions can be reduced to one of these four types. In philosophy of science, for example, philosophers typically ask logical and epistemological questions arising out of their reflections on the methods and theories of the various natural sciences. In philosophy of religion they commonly ask questions of all four types concerning the presuppositions and claims of religion; and so on. Be this as it may, it is at least the case that *most* philosophical questions (i. e., questions possessing the three defining characteristics discussed above) belong to one of these four types; and at times it can be helpful to clarify a philosophical question by determining just what type of question is being asked.

Philosophical Systems

In view of the fact that the philosophical quest has been going on in the West for over 2,500 years, it is not surprising that by this time a considerable number of proposals have been made. To make such a proposal—to suggest that such-and-such are the key elements in the total picture of reality, in terms of which every element of reality can be understood—is to offer a philosophical "system." That is what a philosophical system is: a view of the whole which purports to do justice to every element of human knowledge and every aspect of human experience.

There is considerable hesitation among philosophers today to talk about philosophical systems, just as there is a certain reluctance to accept the quest for unity as we have described it as the central task of the philosophical enterprise. The day of system-building, in the view of many philosophers, is past; it came to an end when—within the memory of some philosophers still living—it was concluded that constructive metaphysics is an impossible undertaking, a building of castles in the air.

In actuality, however, one need not be convinced of the possibility of metaphysics in order to hold that philosophical systems are not only possible but necessary—any more than one needs to hold to the possibility of constructive metaphysics in order to acknowledge that the proper business of philosophy is to seek the total view. The truth is that every human being (including philosophers who do not like systems) carries on his thinking within some kind of a philosophical system. To say that one's philosophy constitutes a "system" is a perfectly innocuous statement: it is only to say (a) that one's views on various matters (whatever matters one *has* views on) are logically consistent with each other and (b) that they are interdependent. Not everyone, of course, is explicitly aware of the "system" with which he operates, and even fewer people are sufficiently confident of the superiority of their system to recommend its adoption by others. But an intelligent being with no philosophical system whatsoever is unthinkable.

Lest one be completely overwhelmed by the sheer number of philosophical systems which one may encounter in the study of philosophy, it is helpful to think of philosophical systems as belonging to one or the other of two "families" of systems, that is, the naturalist family and the transcendentalist family. A philosophical system may be said to be "naturalistic" if it affirms (a) that there is only one order of reality, (b) that this one order of reality consists entirely of objects and events occurring in space and time, and (c) that this one order of reality is completely self-dependent and self-operating. A system may be said to be "transcendentalistic" if it asserts (a) that the world of space and time depends for its existence on a reality that transcends space and time, (b) that reality is therefore *not* limited to objects and events occurring in space and time, and (c) that explanations of even spatio-temporal phenomena may, therefore, take thought beyond the spatio-temporal world to the dimensions of reality that transcend it. As a matter of historical fact, the dialogue between proponents of these two great "families" of philosophers has provided much of the impetus for philosophical discussion all through the long and sometimes tortuous history of Western philosophy, and many philosophical controversies which would otherwise be trivial take on profound importance when viewed in the context of this dialogue.

All philosophical thinking is implicitly "systematic" in character. This is why philosophers defend so passionately their views on what sometimes appear to be relatively trivial matters. Because of the systematic character of all philosophical thinking—because, therefore, of the multi-dimensional relevance of all philosophical questions—no philosophical question is trivial. Every philosophical problem is, so to speak, a test case: one's whole world-view (the entire "system" in the context of which one attempts to understand the complex array of data that come before one's consciousness) is at stake. The position one adopts with respect to a given philosophical problem inevitably limits the options available on other problems, problems of which one may not even be aware.

Would it not be the part of wisdom, then, simply to suspend judgment—to refuse to commit oneself on any point until one can see its relevance to all the rest? Ah, but we are forgetting: *as rational beings we have no alternative but to philosophize.* One can, of course, suspend judgment on some points some of the time—but not on all. At the very least, we must think and act *as if* we had decided about a vast number of things; and this "as if" is as near as makes no difference to committing oneself to certain positions in relation to which all else that we hope to understand must be understood.

Study Questions

1. Review the three characteristics of philosophical questions suggested in this chapter. Can you think of any questions—questions that may

have puzzled you—that are "philosophical" according to these criteria? What are they?

2. Consider carefully the questions you have formulated in response to the previous question. Can you identify them as belonging to one or another of the four types (logical, ontological, epistemological, theory of value) discussed in this chapter?

3. If it is true that "an intelligent being with no philosophical system whatsoever is unthinkable," then (presumably) every reader of this book has such a system. What are some of the elements of your "system"? What are some of the ways that your philosophical system is different from that of, say, an uneducated member of some primitive society or an educated member of an advanced non-Western society?

4. As far as you understand these matters at present, does it seem to you that the philosophical system with which you operate is "naturalistic" or "transcendentalistic"? Does this strike you as being an important question? Why?

Chapter 4

FIRST STEPS IN PHILOSOPHY

GETTING BEARINGS IN philosophy, like getting bearings in any new field, is not easy—but neither is it too difficult. The key, as in all fields of study, is to employ a method of approach that is appropriate to the field which one is attempting to master. The purpose of the present chapter is to suggest a method which will enable the beginning student to make maximum progress toward a mastery of philosophy.

The student should take encouragement from the fact that he has on many occasions, probably without knowing it, concerned himself with philosophical problems. Very often in the study of philosophy one finds oneself involved in a rigorous and systematic discussion of a problem encountered before, but not pursued for lack of direction. This is one of the great rewards of studying philosophy, and the fact that everyone who comes to the point of studying it has already been introduced to philosophy in this informal way makes it much easier to "establish a beachhead" in the field than would otherwise be the case.

Alternative Approaches to Philosophy

There are basically two ways to approach the study of philosophy, and each has its peculiar advantages and disadvantages.

One way to approach philosophy is via the historical route, i. e., by taking a course (or doing some reading) in the history of philosophy. This approach has two unique advantages and two serious disadvantages. The advantages are that one becomes acquainted, hopefully to some extent firsthand, with the thought of the greatest philosophical thinkers, and one sees the intimate relation that always obtains between the philosophical reflection of a given period and other elements of the culture of that day. The disadvantages of making a first approach to philosophy via the historical route are, however, extremely serious. It is very confusing to spend several weeks or months studying the history of something whose essential nature is not understood. (Question: What is the history of philosophy the history of?) And, second, there is a semantic problem which is not readily resolvable through a purely historical approach. Different philosophers, unfortunately, frequently use different terms to express the same idea; and the student who studies their work without some prior systematic orientation to the field is often bewildered by the sheer profusion of terms which are used to discuss ideas with which he is also unacquainted.

Many teachers of philosophy, therefore, prefer what may be called a *systematic* approach to philosophy. This approach has three distinct advantages over the historical approach. The first is that it greatly minimizes the semantic problem by providing an opportunity for the student to build up his philosophical vocabulary step by step in the context of philosophical discussions which, with reasonable effort, he is able to clearly understand. The second advantage is that it provides the novice in philosophy with a more familiar starting point, namely problems and concerns which he has already encountered, and which therefore do not seem so strange and unfamiliar as would, for example, the theories of Thales and Heraclitus (two early Greek philosophers). Third, the systematic approach enables the student to identify with the philosophical enterprise, and to participate in philosophical discussion far more readily than does the historical approach. To really understand a philosophical problem—almost any philosophical problem—is to see its relevance for many areas of concern which previously may not have seemed at all related.

These remarks are not meant in any way to disparage the study of the history of philosophy. The point is, rather, that as a first introduction to philosophy the systematic approach has a great deal to commend it, and the study of the history of philosophy is considerably enriched if one comes to it with the kind of prior understanding and equipment that the systematic approach is intended to provide. There is no substitute, however, for a firsthand encounter with the writings of the great philosophers; the student who does not go on to participate in this encounter is depriving himself of one of the most enriching experiences which a liberal education has to offer.

The present book, in any case, uses the systematic approach. This means that we shall be considering, in succession, a number of philosophical problems, and for each of them we shall attempt to understand the possible ways of solving that problem. We shall, of course, refer from time to time to philosophers of the past and of the present who have addressed themselves in one way or another to the problems under discussion. Our purpose is not, except perhaps incidentally, to acquire historical information. Our purpose is to acquire a certain kind of understanding, and thus to enter into the philosophical arena as participants rather than as mere spectators. The suggestions that follow are intended to help the student in focusing his efforts in such a way as to make maximum progress toward the kind of understanding which is here envisioned.

Three Steps Toward Understanding

There are three distinct determinations to be made and understood with respect to any given philosophical problem. First, one should attempt to understand precisely *what the problem is.* Note well: *understanding a problem is not the same as memorizing some approved formulation of it.* There are undoubtedly some things that must be learned by rote, but there is very little in philosophy that can profitably be learned in this way. To understand a philosophical problem is to know what question you are asking, to know what sort of an assertion would count as an answer to the question. If you do not know this, if you cannot imagine anything that would qualify as a possible answer to your question, then you have not really asked a question: you have only made a little interrogative noise.

Most of us, unfortunately, are so much in the habit of deceiving ourselves (and others) about what we really understand and what we understand only in a general, hazy way, that it is necessary to apply some very strict self-discipline if we are to overcome this deception in our struggles with the philosophical problems that follow. The deception is rendered all the more difficult to get rid of by the fact that there is no sure method for determining when we are and when we are not guilty of it. The following may, however, be offered as a general rule: if you really understand something, it should be possible for you to vary the expression of it. If you cannot express an idea in more than one way (if you cannot vary the expression, confident that in so doing you have retained the original meaning), then you have not understood that idea.

It is impossible to overemphasize the importance of insisting on *understanding* if one is to make any significant progress in philosophical learning. We can memorize facts and words, but meanings and relations must be understood; and philosophy is concerned with meanings and relations. I know the *meaning* of the question, "Is New York City more populous than London?" Thus, I can ask the same question in a variety of ways: "Is the population of New York City greater than that of London?" "Are there more people living in New York City than in London?" "Does New York City have a greater population than the capital of England?" But I am not at all sure what people mean when they ask, "What is the meaning of life?" Hence, I cannot hope to make any progress in my reflections on this question until I am helped to understand what, precisely, is being asked; then, and only then, can I imagine what sort of assertion might count as a possible answer to the question. Then, too, I can re-phrase the question in a number of ways—but not before. Until I can do this I am not, strictly speaking, asking a question: I am only uttering an interrogative sentence.

The second step toward the kind of understanding which we seek in philosophy is to determine precisely what are the possible ways of answering the question that has been raised. If one has really understood the question that is being asked, this is not usually too difficult—since, as we have already noted, to understand a philosophical problem is to know what sort of an assertion would count as an answer to it. One may, however, have an accurate but limited understanding of a problem without being explicitly aware of *all* of the possible ways of answering it, and it is, therefore, of great value to make a conscious and determined effort in each case to ascertain *all* of the alternative ways of answering the question at the very outset of one's consideration of it. Then, and only then, can one weigh the arguments for and against the various positions—and perhaps make up one's mind on the matter—confident that one has not simply neglected to consider some position which, if examined carefully, might commend itself more strongly than any of those under consideration.

Some philosophical problems allow as few as two possible alternative "positions." An example of such is the epistemological problem discussed in Part II of this book. More commonly a problem will allow three or four possible solutions. In a few instances, however, it is not possible to state with certainty that such-and-such are the *only* possible positions to take with respect to a given problem. An example of such a problem will be found in Part V. Even in such a case, however, it is extremely important to make the attempt to "define the alternatives," since in so doing one may hope to discover *why* it is not possible to set a limit to the number of possible solutions. And one may, of course, be reasonably confident that one has considered all of the plausible alternatives, even though one has not surveyed all of those that may be logically possible.

If one pursues study carefully through these first two steps—demanding precision in understanding the problem, and precision and completeness in understanding what alternative positions are possible—one will have in hand a powerful instrument for organizing subsequent philosophical inquiry. Consider: if I have understood a given problem *P*, and if I have determined that positions *A, B,* and *C* are the only possible positions to take with respect to it, then nothing that anyone can say with respect to *P* can be completely novel to me. If Plato, or Aristotle, or Kant, or Bertrand Russell, or anyone else addresses himself to this problem, he must do so in behalf of (or in opposition to) position *A,* or position *B,* or position *C*—no matter what terminology he may employ. Hence, I can attend carefully to his arguments and can, so to speak, enter into the discussion with a clear understanding of what the discussion is all about.

The third step toward philosophical understanding is consideration of the arguments for and against the various alternative positions. To the making of arguments there is no end, and it is, of course, impossible to state with respect to any philosophical position that thus-and-so are *the* arguments for or against such a position. Practically all philosophical discussion consists in bringing forth arguments either (a) in favor of some position which one is attempting to establish or (b) in opposition to some position which one is attempting to refute. Step three toward philosophical understanding is, therefore, never completed: it is the arena of philosophical discussion into which one is qualified to enter as soon as steps one and two have been mastered (with respect to any given problem).

Again, there is no great value in memorizing a list of "approved" philosophical arguments—for example, three or four arguments in favor of rationalism, and three or four arguments in favor of empiricism (see Part II). Rather, one should ask: "What sorts of considerations would tend to support the rationalist thesis?" "What sorts of considerations would tend to refute it?" "What sorts of considerations would tend to support or to refute the empiricist thesis?" Then he will be in a position to assess any arguments which he may encounter—and, perhaps, to devise a few of his own.

There is one type of argument which appears with such frequency in philosophical discussion that it is advisable to become familiar with it as soon as possible. This is what is called the *reductio ad absurdum*. The *reductio ad absurdum* is a powerful form of argument for the purpose of refuting the position of one's opponent. It consists in showing that the position which one is attacking implies absurd consequences. Let us suppose that I wish to attack position *A:* if I can show that *A* implies *X, Y,* and *Z,* and that *X, Y,* and *Z* are absurd or contrary to fact, then I have shown that *A* is absurd; for from a true proposition you cannot validly deduce false consequences. This type of argument may also be used constructively in situations where there are only two possible positions on a given problem: if either *A* or *B* must be the case, and if *A* is shown (by a *reductio ad absurdum* argument) to be untenable, then *B* must be the case. (If there is more than one alternative to the position which one is attempting to establish, then separate arguments must, of course, be constructed against each of the alternative positions.)

In attempting to assess such an argument, two questions must always be asked. Do the alleged consequences really follow from the position in question? and, Are they really absurd? If the answer to either of these questions is negative, the attempted *reductio* is not successful.

The Importance of Terminology

At each step along the route to philosophical understanding it is important to observe one cardinal rule: maximum care must be taken at all times to establish the exact meaning of terms, and terms once defined must be used in just those ways that are appropriate to their definitions.

For the purposes of ordinary discourse we can often get on well enough without demanding absolute precision in the language that we are using. We can, for example, discuss the weather, and even agree that it is a "nice day," without being too picayunish about just exactly what qualities a day must have before it qualifies as a "nice" day. Anyone who is inclined to question whether or not we do operate with relatively imprecise language in our everyday conversation might try giving precise definitions to such phrases as "a nice day," "a good ball game," "a boring speaker," or "a snap course."

For some purposes, however, it is important that language be used with as near-perfect precision as we can possibly give to it. For the purposes of mathematical computation, for example, it is obviously important that the symbols which one employs have precise meanings and that those meanings remain constant throughout the course of computation. The ideas of "force," "mass," "velocity," and many others have been given similarly precise meanings in physics, and the calculations which physicists make would not be possible were it not for this precision.

In philosophy, unlike the natural sciences, it is seldom, if ever, possible to define terms mathematically. What one must do, therefore, is to define them in non-mathematical terms and to make the definitions just as precise as non-mathematical language will allow.

The technical and semi-technical language of philosophy—such terms as *a priori* and *a posteriori,* not to mention those interminable "isms" so often encountered in the study of philosophy—has been developed precisely to enable philosophers to discuss what they wish with greater precision than would otherwise be possible. The serious student of philosophy will make every effort to master this terminology as he goes along, for, however esoteric it may sound at first, its real and valid function is to enable us to think and speak precisely about matters which in everyday language remain obscure and imprecise.

More than this, however, one must learn to be on the lookout for ambiguities in everyday language which, if they are not detected, may mislead and confuse. If we, knowing that Socrates died in prison, hear someone say, "Socrates was a freer man on the day he died than those who brought about his imprisonment," the chances are that we shall find the statement extremely confusing. For in one sense of "free," Socrates clearly was *not* as free as his accusers: they were free to go about the streets of Athens and to spend time with their families in their own homes, and Socrates was not. What, then, does the speaker mean? Is he talking about some "inner state," which Socrates allegedly had on the day of his death in a greater degree ("freer") than his accusers? Or is the speaker suggesting that in dying Socrates is somehow "freed" from his body, and in this way he becomes "freer" than his accusers—or what? Clearly some critical thinking about the meaning of the term "free" is needed if we are to dispel the bewilderment which such a statement can create. And to think critically, carefully, analytically about the exact meanings of terms is to observe the rule stated above.

Learning by Doing

Thus far we have been talking *about* philosophy. Such talk has its place, namely at the beginning of a book whose purpose it is to introduce philosophy to the previously unintroduced. But it is now time to stop talking *about* philosophy and to begin engaging in philosophical discussion. And here, philosophy being what it is, the student must be prepared to play his appropriate role.

"Philosophy being what it is"—what do we mean by this? We mean that philosophy is an activity in which one can learn to participate, not a body of information which one can commit to memory. As with any skill, there are some points of information that must be mastered. In learning to ski, for example, there is a certain amount of information that one has to learn with respect to where one should put one's weight, what to do with the poles, how to use the edges of one's skis, etc., if one is to learn to execute the various maneuvers that constitute "skiing." But the point of it all is to learn to do something, not simply to acquire some information. And this is true also for philosophy: the point in studying it is to learn to philosophize.

What this means for the student is this: he should approach the discussions that follow not simply as a spectator, but as a participant. The first chapter in each part will provide him with his "ticket" to the arena: a statement of the problem and a description of the alternatives. These must, of course, be very carefully studied and thoroughly understood. Beyond that, it is altogether a matter of arguments: each "position" is allowed to speak for itself, to marshal whatever arguments it can in support of its own position and in refutation of all others. Not all of the arguments used are good ones, obviously, since for most philosophical problems there is room for only one "correct" position, and the arguments which allegedly "prove" some other position must, therefore, be unsound. But which position is "correct" in each case? And which arguments are unsound? Those, obviously, are questions that no one can answer with finality. Within the living dialogue that is philosophy there is room for differences of opinion on these matters. Indeed, it is these differences of opinion—differences which cannot but occur when honest men seek answers to questions that have long puzzled the greatest minds—that keep the dialogue alive.

And now, to the dialogue itself.

Study Questions

1. What is the history of philosophy the history of? Why is the philosophical reflection of any given period intimately related to the other elements of the culture of that day?

2. What is the difference between (a) uttering an interrogative sentence and (b) asking a question? Can you do one without doing the other?

3. Has your education thus far tended to obscure the difference between (a) understanding something and (b) memorizing some "recommended" or "official" verbal formulation regarding the subject in question? What sorts of behavior by parents and teachers might tend to obscure this distinction? What steps might you take to overcome whatever unfortunate habits of this kind you may have developed?

4. Give an example of a *reductio ad absurdum* argument (not necessarily relating to a philosophical question). On the basis of what has been said about this type of argument in the present chapter, what uses do you anticipate will be made of arguments of this sort in the discussions that follow?

For Further Reading*

Ayer, A. J., *Philosophy and Language*. New York: Oxford University Press, 1960.

Jaspers, Karl, *Way to Wisdom*, trans. Ralph Manheim. New Haven, Conn.: Yale University Press, 1951 (paperbound). See especially Chapters 1-3.

Krikorian, Yervant H., ed., *Naturalism and the Human Spirit*. New York: Columbia University Press, 1944. See especially Chapter 15, "The Nature of Naturalism," by John Herman Randall, Jr.

Merleau-Ponty, Maurice, *In Praise of Philosophy*, trans. John Wild and James M. Edie. Evanston, Ill.: Northwestern University Press, 1963. See especially pages 33-64.

Nagel, Ernest, *Logic Without Metaphysics*. New York: Free Press of Glencoe, 1956. See Part I, Chapter 1, "Naturalism Reconsidered."

Plato, *Apology*. Many editions. Plato's moving account of Socrates' defense—of himself and of philosophy—before the Athenian court.

Russell, Bertrand, *The Problems of Philosophy*. New York: Oxford University Press, 1959. See especially Chapter 15, "The Value of Philosophy."

Ryle, Gilbert, "Systematically Misleading Expressions," in *Essays on Logic and Language,* First Series, ed. Antony Flew. New York: Philosophical Library, 1951.

Sheldon, W. H., "Critique of Naturalism," *The Journal of Philosophy*, Vol. 42 (1945), 253-270.

Smart, J. J. C., *Philosophy and Scientific Realism*. New York: Humanities Press, 1963. See especially Chapter 1, "The Province of Philosophy."

Waismann, Friedrich, "How I See Philosophy," in *Contemporary British Philosophy*, Third Series, ed. H. D. Lewis. New York: The Macmillan Company, 1956.

* Dates given are usually for the most recent edition available, which sometimes differs from date of original publication. If books cited are available in paperbound editions, this is indicated. Books published abroad but distributed here are listed with the distributor.

The Meaning of Meaning

PART I

The Meaning of Meaning

Chapter 5

WORDS AND THINGS

PHILOSOPHY, WE HAVE said, is a dialogue, a conversation in which varying points of view are expressed about the questions that force themselves upon us when we try to conceive of the whole of reality in such a way as to make due allowance for every element of human knowledge and every aspect of human experience. The vehicle of this dialogue, as of all conversation, is language. It would seem, therefore, that a brief inquiry into the nature of language would be a logical starting-point in our study of philosophy.

There is, as a matter of fact, a very special reason for beginning our study at this point. Interesting philosophical questions are always controversial: they are questions to which there are at least two more or less plausible answers, both (or all) of which cannot be correct. Philosophical questions, therefore, are the occasion for disputes between the representatives of opposing positions. In order to have a real dispute, it is necessary that the parties to the dispute be in genuine disagreement as to what is the case: if they are in agreement about the facts, but are simply using certain terms with different meanings, then their dispute is not real but verbal. A real dispute can only be settled by determining what really is the case; a verbal dispute can only be resolved by securing agreement as to the meanings of the terms which are being used in different senses by the disputants.

Suppose, for example, that two men are arguing about the ques-

45

tion, "Are all men created equal?" *A* says, "All men are created equal. No one has a right to any special privileges by virtue of his race, religion, or social status. All men have an equal right to life, liberty, and the pursuit of happiness." *B* says, "I disagree with you: all men are not created equal. They differ in their physical and intellectual endowments by virtue of their differing heredity and in their privileges and opportunities by virtue of their birth into either wealth or poverty. To deny this is simply to blind oneself to the facts."

It is clear upon a moment's reflection that, although *A* and *B* are talking as if they were in genuine disagreement with each other, the dispute between them is really only verbal. *A* is arguing that all men have equal rights; *B* is arguing that they have unequal endowments and opportunities. What *A* is asserting, therefore, is not at all incompatible with what *B* is asserting, but this fact is obscured by the apparent incompatibility of the two statements, "All men are created equal" and "All men are not created equal."

Unfortunately, however, it is not always as easy as in this example to determine whether a given dispute is merely verbal or not. Language is an extremely complex phenomenon, and it is quite possible for intelligent and able men to debate long and hard over a question which, as they later discover, posed an issue that was merely verbal. Only if there is agreement on the meanings of the key terms employed in the discussion can it be determined whether or not there is genuine disagreement on a substantive issue. This is why, in a formal debate, one of the first steps must be to establish agreement on the meanings of crucial (key) terms.

It must be admitted that there is no method known to man that can guarantee the detection of verbal disputes. There have been philosophers who have maintained that all philosophical questions are merely verbal in character, but in the judgment of most philosophers this does not seem very likely. It is undoubtedly true, however, that the discussion of many philosophical questions of substance is frequently obscured by issues that are merely verbal, and it is, therefore, a sound principle to be on the alert for such confusion-producing issues.

There are some features of language which are fairly non-controversial, and it is helpful to be aware of these—both to enlarge one's capacity to recognize verbal disputes when they occur and also as a preparation to understand the philosophical question about language with which we shall be concerned throughout most of the present section. Consequently, we shall begin our discussion by calling attention to some important characteristics of language of which the casual user is seldom explicitly aware.

Some Facts About Language

Language is primarily a social phenomenon. If there were only one intelligent being in the world, there would be little need for language. But there are many intelligent beings in the world, and they have an evidently incurable desire to communicate with one another. Language is the principal medium for communication between intelligent beings.

Language consists of words. Words occur in two forms—spoken and written. Considered simply as an occurrence in the natural world, a spoken word is nothing more than a noise uttered by a human being. Similarly, a written word is simply a pattern of marks made on a sheet of paper or some other surface with a pen or pencil or some other instrument.

What distinguishes words from other noises or marks, however, is the fact that they have *meaning*. A shriek may be a noise uttered by a human being, but it is not a word. The symbol ZQJ is a mark on a sheet of paper, but it is not a word.

In one sense of "meaning," a mark or noise produced by a human being has meaning, and thus is what we call a "word," by virtue of the fact that it refers to (denotes) something other than itself. Most words denote objects, events, or properties in the world. Some words denote physical objects—for example, "book," "tree," "stone." Other words denote events—for example, "running," "walking," "eating." Yet others denote feelings, such as "cold," "tired," "bored." Those words which grammarians call adjectives usually denote qualities of objects, such as "red," "long," "heavy." Adverbs typically denote ways of doing things, such as "diligently," "carelessly," "quickly." Some words, like "within," "beyond," "above," and "behind" denote relations—especially, as in these examples, spatial relations.

Some words, however, do not denote anything in the world, and hence do not have the kind of meaning we have been discussing (*denotative* meaning). The most important of these are the logical connectives (*syncategorematic* terms)—words like "if," "unless," "all," "not," "or." It is characteristic of such words that there is nothing to which one can point as the *referent* of such words: they have meaning only in the context of the sentences in which they occur.

Since some words, such as those just mentioned, do not have a denotative meaning, and yet clearly do have some meaning, it is clear that not all meaning is denotative. Moreover, it is altogether possible that this other kind of meaning, which evidently attaches to syncategorematic terms, attaches also to words that denote. Let us call this the *connotative* meaning of words. Some philosophers call this the "intensional," or "sense," meaning of words. It is this kind of meaning that one ordinarily tries to express in a definition.

Among words that do refer to things, some refer to just one single thing. Such words are commonly called proper names. "Socrates" is the proper name of a man who lived in Athens 2,500 years ago; "Christmas" (meaning the birth of Christ) is the proper name of an event that occurred nearly 2,000 years ago. Proper names are commonly given to people, pets, important buildings (Buckingham Palace), and significant historical events.

Most words that refer to things, however, are class words: they refer not just to one person, object or event but to a vast number of things of a given type. The word "cat" refers to a large number of four-legged, furry creatures that say "meow"—some of which are now living, some of which are dead, and some of which are not yet born. The same is true of words like "red," "running," "above," "slowly," and very many others: they refer to objects, events, or occurrences of a given type, not to one particular thing. The overwhelming majority of the words in any language are of this kind.

There are at least three ways in which a person may be said to "know the meaning" of a word—or perhaps we should say rather that there are three ways in which one may demonstrate that he knows the meaning of a word.

One way is to give a verbal equivalent. Suppose that someone asks me, "What is the meaning of 'quick' in the phrase, 'the quick and the dead'?" and I reply, "living." I have then given a verbal equivalent of the term "quick," and I have thereby demonstrated that I know the meaning of the term. This is the way in which we typically learn the meanings of foreign words (*gut* means "good," *Mensch* means "man," etc.)—by learning what word in our own language is its equivalent. When two words in the same language are equivalent in meaning, they are called synonyms.

A second way in which one can demonstrate that one knows the meaning of a word is to point to, name, or describe, some of the things to which the word refers. What does "run" mean? Answer: it is what I do when a dog comes after me, what horses do when they feel the spurs, what baseball players do when they are trying to make a score. The whole class of things to which a word refers —in our example, all of the instances past, present, and future that are instances of "running"—constitute the *extension,* or *denotation,* of that word. To be able to specify some of the things which a word denotes is to demonstrate that one knows the meaning of that word.

One also may be said to know the meaning of a word if one is able to state a correct definition of that word. In the case of words that denote, one would normally do this by specifying the characteristics which a thing must have in order to belong to the class of things denoted by that term—i. e., by specifying *defining characteristics* of that term. (Example: "bachelor" means "an adult male human being who is not married.") Words that do not denote are most commonly defined in terms of their function. In both cases, however, one is attempting to demonstrate that one knows the meaning of the term by explicating its "connotative" or "sense" meaning.

Some words have denotations (extensions) and connotations (intensions) that vary from one occasion to another, depending usually on the context. Where the context makes clear which meaning is intended, no special problems arise. But sometimes it is not clear from the context which of several possible meanings of a term is intended by the speaker or writer of a given sentence. In such a case the term in question is said to be *ambiguous.* (Example: "Mr.

Jones has a good grip." Does this sentence say something about Mr. Jones' handshake or does it say something about his suitcase?)

Many words which we use frequently in everyday conversation, usually without any difficulties arising, cannot be precisely defined (i. e., in a way that accords with actual usage) in either intensional or extensional terms. Such words are said to be *vague*. The difficulty here is not that the same mark or sound has a different meaning in different contexts (that is what we have called ambiguity), but rather that common usage does not allow us to draw a precise boundary around the meaning of the term. We all know, for example, that neither a tubful of ice water nor a tubful of boiling water would constitute an appropriate preparation for a "warm bath." Evidently, then, water must be warmer than 32°F. and cooler than 212°F. for a warm bath. But exactly what temperature range would qualify? How cool could the water be without becoming a cool bath instead of a warm one? How hot can it be before it becomes hot instead of warm? We cannot say. Any answer that one might give would appear arbitrary: it would define the term more precisely than our actual usage of the term allows.

Normally when we employ language, we utter not single words but sentences. Sentences occasionally consist of a single word, but more commonly they consist of several words put together according to certain rules called *laws of syntax,* or *syntactic rules,* the details of which differ from one language to another.

Sentences serve a number of different purposes: for example, requesting information ("Where is my hat?"), conveying information ("The book is on the shelf"), directing behavior ("Please bring me my slippers"), or expressing feeling ("Hurray for the team!"). These may be called, respectively, the interrogative, the informative, the directive, and the emotive functions of language.

Informative sentences assert or deny that something is the case. That which is asserted or denied by an informative sentence is called a *proposition*. Some particular combination of words in which a given proposition is asserted or denied is called a verbal form of that proposition. The same proposition may be expressed in a variety of verbal forms—for example, "Some cats are black." "Some feline animals are black." "Some members of the cat family are black." A correct translation of any of these sentences into another language would yield yet other verbal forms of the same proposition.

Only propositions may properly be said to be true or false. A proposition is said to be true if what it asserts to be the case is in fact the case, or if what it denies to be the case is in fact not the case. If what it asserts to be the case is not the case, or if what it denies to be the case is the case, the proposition is said to be false. In common parlance, however, the sentences expressing propositions—i. e., particular verbal forms of them—are commonly called true or false according to the same criteria.

One of the surprising characteristics of sentences is the fact that their meaning evidently does not consist simply in the sum of the meanings of the words of which they are composed. In order to understand the meaning of a sentence, it is necessary to know not only the meanings of its constituent terms, but also the relevant syntactic rules of the language in which the sentence occurs. And this brings us, at last, to our problem.

The Problem of Meaning

A given language—French, German, English, or any other—consists of two distinguishable elements, namely (1) words and (2) a more or less complex system of *syntactic rules* which specify the ways in which words are combined to form sentences by the persons who use that language. If one knows a sufficient number of words in a given language (i. e., knows, in the case of most words, what sorts of things they refer to) and if one knows the syntactic rules of that language (i. e., is able to apply them, whether or not one is able to state them), one can use that language to communicate with (question, inform, direct, express feeling to) other people who, as we say, "know" that language.

But how does language acquire meaning? Is the meaning of language a matter of convention, or is there some "natural" or "essential" relation between language and reality, between words and the world? Or, to put the question even more precisely: (a) is the relation between language and reality such that the meaning of language is entirely the product of human decisions, or (b) is the relation altogether "natural," so that for any given state of affairs there is one and only one "correct" way of expressing it verbally, or (c) is it something in between?

The view that the meaning of language is purely a matter of convention we shall call the conventionalist theory of language—or, more briefly, *conventionalism.* In order to support this position, it is necessary to argue (a) that the meanings of words are assigned, not discovered—that certain words refer to certain things because a group of human beings has agreed to have them refer to these things—and (b) that the rules of syntax are invented, not discovered—that words are combined to form sentences in certain ways because a group of human beings has agreed to allow these rules to govern the word-combinations in this language. (The conventionalist does not, of course, claim that groups of people have explicitly decided—in a kind of mass committee meeting, so to speak—to use certain marks or sounds to stand for certain things, but only that the connection between a given mark or sound and its meaning rests on nothing more than the tacit agreement of people who use the language in which it occurs to use it in just that way. It is perfectly consistent with this view to hold, for example, that most words initially acquired the meanings they now have quite by accident, or that the actual circumstances surrounding the attachment of certain meanings to certain marks or sounds is altogether beyond our finding out.)

The view that the relation between language and reality is altogether "natural," so that for any given state of affairs there is only one "correct" way of expressing it verbally, we shall call the essentialist theory of language, or *essentialism.* To support this position it is necessary to argue that neither the meanings of words nor the rules of syntax are established by convention, but that both are "givens" that must be discovered if one is ever to speak correctly.

The view that the relation between language and reality is partly a matter of convention and partly a natural relation we shall call the modified essentialist view of language, or *modified essentialism.* To support this view it is necessary to argue that either the meanings of words or the rules of syntax are *in some degree* natural, i. e., they are not a matter of convention. Modified essentialism is, therefore, a mediating position: it allows that there is much in language that is purely conventional, but insists that in some respects language is independent of human convention. How the advocate of modified essentialism conceives this to be the case we shall see in Chapter 8.

It is evident that this third view is capable of a number of variations. An advocate of modified essentialism might hold, for example, (a) that the meanings of words are established by convention, but the rules of syntax are natural; or (b) that the meanings of words are natural, but the rules of syntax are established by convention; or (c) that the meanings of words and the rules of syntax are both partly established by convention and partly natural; or (d) that the meanings of words are partly established by convention and partly natural, but the rules of syntax are established by convention; or (e) that the meanings of words are established by convention, but the rules of syntax are in part natural and in part conventional. Since modified essentialism is defined as any view which affirms that the relation between language and reality is in part a matter of convention and in part natural, it is clear that all of the views just enumerated qualify as forms of this position. In the discussion that follows, two versions of this position will be defended corresponding, respectively, to the *c* alternative (Chapter 7) and *e* alternative (Chapter 8).

We turn now to a more detailed consideration of the alternatives that are available with respect to this question, beginning with the conventionalist theory.

Study Questions

1. Construct precise definitions for each of the following terms: language, word, proper name, denote, extension, intension, ambiguous, vague, sentence, proposition, assertion, statement.
2. Can you think of any functions which language serves in addition to the four suggested in this chapter? Does a single sentence seem to you to typically serve just one function or several?
3. Check your understanding of the problem posed in the latter part of this chapter by attempting to restate the problem in two or three different ways.
4. Does the problem posed in this chapter qualify as a "philosophical"

problem according to the criteria suggested in Chapter 3? If you are in doubt, which of the criteria do you think this problem may fail to satisfy?

5. The five forms of modified essentialism enumerated in this chapter do not exhaust the logically possible varieties of this view. Can you supply the missing alternatives?

Chapter 6

THE CONVENTIONALIST THEORY

LANGUAGE IS A tool invented by men for the purpose of communicating with one another. It consists of a system of signs which have been made, as a matter of convention, to stand for certain things. These signs—the noises and marks that we call words—have no closer relation to the things that they signify than green and red lights have, respectively, to going or stopping when one is driving. This is my view, and I propose now to set forth the considerations that have led me to adopt it.[1]

There are, as was pointed out in the previous chapter, two parts to this view. I maintain (1) that the meanings of terms are entirely a matter of convention and (2) that the rules of syntax are also established by convention. Since language consists only of words and syntactic rules, to affirm these two propositions is equivalent to affirming that the relation of language to reality is entirely a matter of convention.

The Meanings of Words

The meanings of terms are assigned by men and are thus purely a matter of convention. This is so evident that it is almost embar-

[1] The student is reminded that the "I" of this and of subsequent chapters is in each case a hypothetical advocate of the view in question. See the Preface, p. viii.

rassing to argue about it, to defend it as if there were a plausible alternative. Therefore, just four considerations will be cited to demonstrate conclusively that my view on this matter is correct.

First, there is the simple but, in this connection, very important fact that there are many different languages in the world, each with its own system of sounds and marks. Here is a two-legged creature which Englishmen call a *man,* Germans call *ein Mensch,* and Frenchmen call *un homme.* It would be silly to say that one of these sounds or marks is "right" and the others "wrong." Any sound or mark will do, provided only that those using it agree as to what it is to stand for. But if this is the case, the meanings of terms are not natural: they are a matter of convention, of mutual agreement among persons using that language.

This is evident, second, from the fact that whenever we find that we want to talk about something for which there is no word already in use to refer to that thing, the only recourse is to *invent* a word to stand for that thing. The meanings of terms, therefore, are not discovered: they are assigned. Most of us probably do not have very many occasions to invent terms in this way, and very few of us have enough influence on other people to establish a new term in common usage. But if we did wish to speak or write about something for which no term currently in use was available, it would be a waste of time to try to find out what the "right" term for that thing would be. Terms mean what people agree that they shall mean.

Third, the conventional character of the meaning of terms is evident from the fact that when we come upon a "borderline case"—an object or event concerning which there is some doubt as to whether or not it is to be included within the denotation of a given term—the only way to resolve the question is to decide whether it would be convenient to include it or not. Consider the following example. A dog is barking at a cow, and in so doing he goes around and around in a wide circle in the middle of which stands the cow. The cow, however, turns slowly around as the dog moves, in such a way as to keep the dog always in front of her. Does the dog go "around" the cow or not? It would be futile to study the meaning of the word "around" to try to find out whether, under these circumstances, the dog "really" goes around the cow or not. There is nothing to study. What is called for is a decision: shall we or shall we not call this an instance of "going around"? Whichever decision is made, that (if it is generally adopted) will be the "right" answer. But to say that the meanings of terms are established by the decisions of those who use those terms is precisely to say that such meanings are purely a matter of convention.

Fourth, the conventional character of the meaning of terms is evident from the fact that in general the meanings of terms are no more and no less precise than they need to be in order to serve the purposes for which those terms are most commonly employed. For purposes of ordinary conversation it is not necessary that phrases like "nice day," "warm bath," or "good driver" be precisely defined; hence, these phrases, as they are normally employed, are more or less vague. One can imagine circumstances, however, in which a more precise definition might be required—for example, an automobile association might want to set up precise criteria to determine which of its members should receive "good driver" awards. It would then have to define "good driver" precisely enough to enable it to determine who should and who should not receive such an award. The history of science furnishes a number of examples of words that have been given precise definitions for purposes of scientific descriptions—such words as "salt," "acid," "mass," "velocity."

This being the case, the most reasonable explanation would seem to be that language has been invented by men to serve certain purposes, and meanings have been assigned with only the precision that is necessary to serve those purposes. When communication requires more precise meanings than are currently attached to the relevant words (as, for example, in science and law), we then assign more precise meanings to those words—or, in some instances, we invent new words. In either case, however, the meanings of words are simply assigned by the makers and users of language. Words have meanings because we give them meanings.

A number of puzzling questions can be cleared up as soon as one realizes that words are nothing more than labels whose meanings are arbitrarily assigned to them. People sometimes ask questions of the form, "Is a ———— *really* a ————?" Is an hourglass really a clock? Is a big hill really a mountain? Is a foetus really a human being from the moment of conception? Is a man who makes music on a carpenter's saw really a musician? Does the vibration of air within the range normally audible to the human ear really constitute sound, even if there is nobody around to hear it? In these—and a thousand similar cases that could be mentioned—what is called for is not an investigation but simply a decision. All of the crucial words in these examples—clock, mountain, human being, musician, sound—are vague (in the sense defined in the previous chapter). For this reason we are in doubt about whether or not we ought to include this or that object or event in the denotation of the term. It may or may not be convenient to include it—that is what we must consider as we try to make a decision on the matter. But it is a decision that is called for: once we have decided, the question disappears.

The reason many people find this view of the relation between words and things implausible at first is simply that each of us is aware that the meanings of the words that we use were not assigned by us: they had been assigned by others long before we were born, and we had, obviously, to learn them in order to communicate with other human beings. Since each of us has had the experience of discovering meanings rather than assigning them, we (until we have had an opportunity to reflect on the matter) get the impression that certain sounds just naturally "mean" certain things. Our native language is, so to speak, a kind of "second nature" to us: we cannot conceive of the word "bird" referring to anything but the winged and feathered bipeds that we have learned to call by that name. But although we ourselves did not assign meanings to most of the words that at present comprise the English language, it is evident that those meanings have been assigned by the countless and for the most part unknown people who have participated in and contributed to the evolution of our language. Language, as Anatole France once said, is nothing but "the cry of the beasts of the forest or the mountains, complicated and corrupted by arrogant anthropoids." No doubt the complicated symbol system which we today call the English language reflects the efforts of millions upon millions of our human and pre-human ancestors; but if we today, in order to speak English, must learn the meanings that have thus gotten attached to certain sounds, it is equally certain that those

meanings originally got attached to those sounds because somebody or other attached them.

The Rules of Syntax

Anyone who has studied a foreign language is aware that there is
much more to learning a language than simply learning a vocabulary. Learning a vocabulary is, as a matter of fact, relatively easy:
it is only a matter of learning what sounds have been made to stand
for what things in that particular language. In addition to this,
however, there is the much more difficult and complicated matter of
mastering the system of syntactic rules which govern the ways in
which words may be combined in that language to produce intelligible discourse. I maintain that these rules—like the meanings of
the words whose usage they govern—are established by convention;
but their conventional character is not nearly so evident as is that
of words. Therefore, we must proceed very carefully in our scrutiny
of them if we are to avoid being misled.

Let us make no mistake about the importance of syntactic rules
in determining the meaning of language. The meaning of a sentence
is not merely the sum of the meanings of the words of which it is
made up. The sentence, "The boy hit the ball," contains exactly the
same words as the sentence, "The ball hit the boy," but the meanings of the two sentences are obviously not the same. "The boy hit
the ball" describes one state of affairs, and "The ball hit the boy"
describes a quite different state of affairs. The difference is due
entirely to the syntactic rules which prescribe the functions that
words may have depending, for the most part, on their position in
the sentence. We know that in the English language a noun standing near the beginning of a sentence and followed by a verb is normally the subject of that verb, and so we understand without
difficulty that in the one case it was the boy that did the hitting and
that in the other case it was the ball. Similarly, we know that in
English a noun following a transitive verb is usually the object of
that verb, and so we know that in the one case it was the ball that
got hit and in the other case it was the boy. Were it not for our
knowledge of these rules, we would only know, upon hearing these
sentences, that a boy and a ball were somehow involved in a case

of hitting; it is our knowledge of the relevant syntactic rules that enables us to understand who was hit by whom.

The chief reason for holding that syntactic rules are purely conventional is that these rules vary so greatly from one language to another. It would indeed be a remarkable thing if all of the many languages evolved by men, though differing profoundly in vocabulary, exhibited the same syntactic structure: then we would have good reason to suspect that there was some "natural" relationship between language and reality. But this clearly is not the case. The syntactic rules that govern English usage will not work for German. To make yourself understood in German, you have to learn the syntactic rules that the people who use that language customarily employ. And the same is true for every other language.

There are, of course, similarities among the syntactic rules of various languages. This is not surprising, for the many languages which men speak today have not developed in complete isolation from one another. There are, for example, great similarities among what are called the Romance languages, and these similarities—in both vocabulary and syntax—are easily explicable in terms of their common derivation from the same proto-language. When one compares one of the Romance languages (French, for example) with a Semitic language (like Hebrew or Arabic), however, the similarities are far less apparent than the differences—though there are still some parallels which probably go back to the language or languages of the Indo-European peoples who were the common ancestors of the present inhabitants of both Asia Minor and modern Europe. And when one compares a modern European language with, say, Swahili, or with one of the oriental languages, the similarities are almost non-existent.

In view, therefore, of the vast differences in syntactic rules that exist between various languages, and in view of the fact that similarities can be easily explained in terms of common derivations from the same sources, it seems evident that these rules owe their origin to nothing more than the common agreement of the makers and users of each language to observe such-and-such rules in the speaking (and subsequently the writing) of that language. The rules of syntax for any given language have, of course, evolved over many thousands of years, and in a living language they continue to change—though the changes may be so subtle that they are not even noticed by the persons who employ that language in their day-to-day efforts at communication. Those who use a language fluently do not, for the most part, even think of "applying a set of rules" when they are speaking. The rules are simply a description of the speech habits of a group of people who speak a common language: a child who is born into that group learns these habits, and in so doing learns to communicate with those who share them.

Should any doubt remain regarding the conventional character of syntactic rules, consider for a moment that it would be perfectly possible to invent a language employing any set of syntactic rules one chooses. It might be agreed, for example, that the subject of a sentence should always be indicated by the suffix *-is,* and a direct object by the suffix *-et.* Further, that the sounds "pok," "wot," and "rund" would stand, respectively, for the English words "boy," "hit," and "ball." To say "The boy hit the ball," one could then say either "Pokis wot rundet" or "Rundet wot pokis"; and to say, "The ball hit the boy," one could say either "Rundis wot poket," or "Poket wot rundis." But note: as long as the rules were agreed upon, there would be no difficulty in communicating with one another; and if this language were used every day, with consistency in the observance of rules, it would soon be spoken as easily and as habitually as any language now in existence.

I do not, of course, mean to suggest that a language created in this artificial way could begin to duplicate the beauty or the richness of the languages which are in actual use among the various peoples of the world. It takes a community of users of a language, thousands of years of actual use, and eventually a literature in that language, to establish the emotional associations and the subtle shades of meaning that make a living language the beautiful thing it can become. However, it still remains true that the rules of syntax which constitute the formal structure of that language are, like the meanings of its terms, purely conventional in origin. Thousands and thousands of people, by actually using the language in certain ways, have contributed to the formation of the rules that now govern the "correct" use of that language. But what they thus contributed was not a "discovery" about the relation of language to the world: it was an original gift.

Language as a Game

Although I offer it as nothing more than an analogy, I should like in conclusion to suggest that language may be rather accurately compared to a game and the speaking of a language to the playing of a game. In a game there are certain things you can and certain things you cannot do. In baseball, for example, you cannot run around the bases any time you please: you can run only when you get a hit, and you can advance only when a teammate gets a hit, or when the ball is being pitched to a teammate, or after a fly-ball has been caught, etc. If you do not observe these rules, then you are not playing the game of baseball, or, at any rate, you are not playing it "correctly."

It is the same with language. Every language, like every game, has its own peculiar rules. If you want to speak that language, you have to observe the rules. And if you do not know or do not observe the rules, then you are not speaking that language "correctly." The penalty is that those who hear you will not understand what you are trying to say. You will, as we say, fail to make your point.

But in language, as in baseball, there is nothing "natural" about the rules governing the play. They are what they are, in both cases, by the common consent of the interested parties. The rules governing the game of verbal discourse are much more complex than those governing the game of baseball, and it is, therefore, infinitely more difficult to bring about a change in them should one ever be desired. But their status, nonetheless, is in the last analysis the same: they rest upon the mutual agreement of men.

The implications of this theory do not seem, however, to be very important. After all, we are able to communicate rather effectively with our various languages, and some of us—poets, novelists, playwrights—are able by the skillful use of language to create literary works of surpassing beauty. We can also, as jurists and scientists in particular have shown, make language a very precise tool for communication when the need arises. It serves us, therefore, remarkably well, just the way it is. Why should we not be proud to admit that it is wholly and completely the invention of man—indeed, one of the very finest creations of the human mind?

Study Questions

1. What arguments does Conventionalist use to support his contention that the meanings of terms are purely a matter of convention? Do his arguments conclusively establish his thesis? Can you think of any additional considerations that might be brought forward in support of this position?

2. Conventionalist gives a number of examples of "puzzling questions" that can be cleared up as soon as one realizes the conventional character of the meanings of terms. Is he right about these? Can you think of any such questions (in addition to those which he mentions) that might be taken care of in this way?

3. Conventionalist seems to believe that a lot of people hold some sort of essentialist view regarding the meanings of terms. Is he right? If so, are you satisfied with his "biographical" explanation of this fact?

4. What arguments does Conventionalist use to support his second thesis—that rules of syntax are also established by convention? Is his case for this thesis stronger or weaker than the case for his earlier thesis? Can you think of any additional arguments that might be used in support of this position?

5. What do you think of Conventionalist's "game" analogy? Is it helpful, or is it misleading? More specifically, in what ways would you say that speaking a language is *like* playing a game, and in what ways is it *unlike* playing a game?

Chapter 7

AN ESSENTIALIST THEORY

ALTHOUGH I SHOULD like my view regarding the nature of language to be called an essentialist theory—in order to distinguish it as sharply as possible from the theory set forth in the preceding chapter—I am not willing to defend this theory in the extreme form in which it has been stated in the introductory chapter. I do not think it is possible to seriously maintain that the relation between language and reality is *altogether* natural, so that for any given state of affairs there is one, and only one, absolutely "correct" verbal expression of it. To hold this would commit one to many absurd conclusions. For example, it would imply that if an English sentence happens to be true, its equivalent in French or German would, nonetheless, not be true. Anyone who held such a theory would deserve, in my opinion, to be regarded as a fool.

It is interesting to note, however, that the position is considered (albeit not very seriously) in Plato's dialogue *Cratylus*. Cratylus (one of the three persons who appear in the dialogue) is there represented by Plato as holding the position, and Socrates goes along with the idea in a somewhat jesting way throughout much of the dialogue. It is clear, however, that Plato does not intend this view to be taken seriously, and its mention in the dialogue only serves the purpose of indicating one of the extreme limits of the spectrum within which any serious theory of language must be defined.

The theory of language which I do propose to defend is a version of what in the introductory chapter is called "modified essentialism." If an unqualified essentialism is an extreme and untenable view of language, the unqualified conventionalism to which we were introduced in the preceding chapter is, in my judgment, no less so. The truth in this matter lies between these two extremes—and much closer to the essentialist end of the scale than might at first appear to be the case. I propose to begin, therefore, by pointing out what seem to me to be the most serious shortcomings of the conventionalist theory. I shall then define somewhat more precisely the "strong essentialism" which I should like to put in its place and shall outline the considerations that have led me to this position.

A Critique of Conventionalism

The conventionalist theory of language, popular though it is among philosophers at the present time, seems to be inadequate in a number of ways.

In the first place, it is difficult to see how, on the conventionalist theory, there could ever be such a thing as knowledge. According to the conventionalist theory there are just two elements involved in what we would call an instance of someone's knowing something: (a) some state of affairs in the real world and (b) some verbal expression which, according to the rules of the language-game that a person happens to be playing, describes that state of affairs. However, the meanings of words constantly change; and rules of syntax, according to Conventionalist, also change, albeit perhaps more slowly. But how, then, can knowledge be prevented from constantly eroding away as a consequence of the subtle changes that are constantly occurring in language? How, indeed, can any statement be objectively true, if truth and falsehood are nothing but functions of the completely arbitrary rules of this or that language-game? If there is nothing that mediates between words and the world, if language is nothing but an arbitrary system of signs and conventional rules by means of which men communicate with one another, it is difficult to see how men could ever have any reason to believe that what they are communicating is true. And if they should by chance hit upon the truth, it is difficult to see how, in a language where nothing is fixed but all is in constant flux, that truth would not shortly be lost.

Second, the conventionalist theory seems to be inconsistent with the fact that it is possible, with a high degree of accuracy, to translate texts from one language into another. There are, admittedly, difficulties involved in translation, though these are seldom—as Conventionalist seems to imply—difficulties of a purely syntactic nature. Texts of a purely factual or scientific nature, for example, translate rather easily, regardless of the peculiarities of syntax of the two languages involved. It is rather such things as (a) idiomatic constructions, (b) expressions conveying emotional overtones that cannot be easily duplicated in the language into which the translation is being made, and (c) expressions connoting ideas or beliefs widely prevalent in the culture in which the original language has been nurtured, but not prevalent in the culture associated with the language into which the translation is being made—it is factors such as these that create the chief problems in translating texts from one language into another. But how is such a thing as translation possible at all if each language is only a collection of conventional signs that are to be manipulated according to a set of arbitrarily established rules? You cannot "translate" a play in baseball, say, into a play in football or a move in chess. And the reason for this is obvious: the rules of a game are not "about" anything except the game that is constituted by those very rules. But language is about reality. It has an essential relation to reality, without which it would not even be language. It is this relation which Conventionalist fails to satisfactorily account for, and indeed that his theory of language explicitly denies.

It seems clear, therefore, that however superficially plausible the conventionalist theory of language may appear to be, a closer scrutiny makes it evident that it is not adequate to explain many facts about language with which we are all more or less familiar. Somehow or other we must try to understand the wonderful phenomenon that is human language in such a way as to account for the remarkable facts that language can be made to embody and communicate *truth,* and that the truth that is expressed in one language can be re-clothed in the garb of another. The theory of language which can accomplish this is a strong version of what is called modified essentialism, and I want now to turn to an exposition and defense of this view.

The Case for Essentialism

Language, in my view, has arisen out of the encounter of the human mind with reality—an encounter that has continued throughout the many millennia of the existence of man and was foreshadowed in the encounter of man's pre-human ancestors with the world of their experience. The emergence of reason on our planet—and it is only reason that makes possible the existence of language—marks the emergence of a remarkable faculty that incorporates within itself the very rational structure of reality itself. What appears chiefly to distinguish the rational consciousness of man from the sub-rational consciousness of every other being known to us is the fact that man is capable of considering not only the particular data that he happens to encounter by means of his senses, but also the vast (indeed infinite) range of the logically possible. Because of this, man is liberated from the bondage of lesser beings to the tyranny of what is, and he is able to relate to his environment in terms of a conscious vision of what might be. Moreover, he is able to understand the world of his actual experience—that is, to view it not as an inexplicable, irrational something that surrounds him, but as an actualization of possibilities. In his awareness of the infinite range of logical possibility, man potentially understands all things; for even what is actual must, first of all, be logically possible.

There is, therefore, a kind of one-to-one correspondence between the rational structure of the human mind and the rational structure of reality. And this rational structure, which is the *sine qua non* of all knowledge, must therefore pervade and inform all human language as well. It is for this reason, for example—and not, certainly, because the users of a given language have made this one of the rules of the game—that no matter what language one is using, a statement that is true is not at the same time false, and one that is false is not at the same time true. Every language incorporates the rational structure which is at once the structure of the human mind (subjective reason) and the structure of extra-mental reality (objective reason). Were this not the case, the capacity of language to describe reality, and to communicate truths about reality, would be totally inexplicable. This is also the reason, incidentally, why the truths of logic are the same for all people, regardless of the language which they happen to speak.

The necessary conformity of language to the canons of reason has at least two important implications for a proper understanding of language.

It means, in the first place, that definite limits are set to the rules governing intelligibility. Whatever role the original users of a language may have played in giving it its unique form (and I do not deny that they have played a role), it was not open to them to establish rules of intelligibility which would violate the limits of logical possibility. The sentence, "Some circles are square," is unintelligible not because English-speaking people have thus far neglected to specify a use for the phrase "square circles," but because that phrase purports to denote a combination of qualities which are logically incompatible. Other examples might easily be given.

The other implication is that rules of inference—the principles stating the conditions under which one may validly proceed from premises to conclusions—are similarly grounded in reason, and thus independent of the whims of the framers and users of language. If all *A* is *B,* and all *B* is *C,* then all *A must* be *C*—not because that is the way the rules of the language-game happen to have been set up, but because it is logically necessary that it be so.

The logical structure that pervades all language constitutes, therefore, an exceedingly important essential relationship between language and reality, but it is not the only essential link between the two. The logical structure of language reflects, we might say, the human mind's awareness of the infinite realm of the *possible,* and it takes account of the relations that hold within that realm. But the encounter of the human mind with reality includes also an awareness of what is *actual,* of the world as it actually is; and this awareness of certain pervasive features of the actual world is also reflected in the structure of all language.

Students of linguistics are not in complete accord as to which features of language are absolutely universal, and thus, in all probability, implicit in the very nature of language, but there appears to be general agreement that there are some such uniformities in the structure of all language. Every language must have some way of indicating, for example, what is being talked about, and it must, therefore, have something corresponding to what we call "nouns." For comparable reasons—i. e., reasons that are implicit in the very functions for which language is employed—it would appear that every language must also have verbs and adjectives as well. Whether there is or could be a language without such other parts of speech as adverbs, pronouns, prepositions, and the like, we may leave to linguists to determine.

What is enshrined in these grammatical uniformities is man's awareness of the actual world as a world of things (designated by nouns) that have certain qualities (designated by adjectives) and engage in certain sorts of activities (designated by verbs). The syntax of any language must take account of these "natural" features of language. To that extent, at least, it is not a matter of convention.

Nor is this all. The actual world presents us with situations in which we want sometimes to say something about just one thing and sometimes about many. Language, therefore, must provide some way of distinguishing between singular and plural. We want sometimes to speak about events that occurred in the past, sometimes about events that are occurring in the present, and sometimes about events that will or may occur in the future. Language must, therefore, provide some way of distinguishing "tense." We want sometimes to indicate not that something is the case, but that it is not the case. Thus language must provide some way to deny as well as to assert—in short, some technique for negation. And so on.

It seems evident, therefore, that syntactic rules, far from being the purely conventional things they were asserted to be in the preceding chapter, are really the embodiment of essential features in the absence of which there would be no language at all. Human ingenuity has undoubtedly played its role in creating the syntactic variations which are, in fact, exhibited in the many languages spoken by the peoples of the world, but it has not created those variations out of nothing. They are, to use a metaphor that suggests itself quite naturally at this point, like so many variations on a single theme. Conventionalism focuses its attention solely on the variations, and wrongly concludes that they are the free inventions of each language community; but it is the underlying theme that is of greatest importance, for it is in this that the essential link between the syntax of language and the world about which language is conversant is to be found.

The Meanings of Words

Even individual words, however, are not nearly so loosely related to the objects and events which they denote as the conventionalist theory suggests.

The most serious error of conventionalism on this point consists in its failure to recognize the *rational insight* which is enshrined in the name that we give to an object. I said earlier that man, by virtue of his possession of reason, is able to view the world of his experience as a place in which possibilities are actualized. What I mean by this is that individual things appear to him not simply as so many diverse things that happen to have such-and-such common characteristics, but as the embodiments of what, with Plato, I should like to call universal forms. Reason is able to discern these forms—to see in Dick and Tom and Ned, for example, the actualization of rational animality. It is these forms that are expressed in our concepts, and it is these that we "mean" by the terms denoting these concepts. (It is for this reason, for example, that we recognize "rational animal" to be a better definition of man than "featherless biped"—no matter how accurately we might, with the latter definition, succeed in distinguishing the beings that we intend to denote by the word "man" from everything else in the world.)

The concepts that we express in our words are, therefore, far from being merely a matter of convention. They arise out of the mind's encounter with the world and consist in the apprehension by reason of the intelligible forms that are embodied in the particulars of experience.

Even individual words, however—the particular sounds that in this or that language stand for some particular concepts—do not seem to be entirely a matter of convention. I think it very likely, for example, that Socrates is right when he suggests (in the aforementioned dialogue *Cratylus*) that the primitive roots from which many of our present-day words have evolved were in the first instance a form of mimetic gesture. Many of the names of animals appear to be derived from primitive roots which were originally attempts to duplicate the natural sounds of those animals, and it may be that some words are remote descendants of what we might call the "natural cries" of primitive man—"ache" from a sound something like the German *"ach,"* "laugh" from the actual sound made by a person who is laughing, and so on. No doubt human inventiveness has also played a large role in the association of certain sounds with certain concepts, and the requirements of phonetics have so changed the words that were originally of more "natural" origin that today we can only guess at what that origin may have been; but enough has been said to make it clear that the relation of words to things is far from being merely a matter of convention.

Language, therefore, both with respect to the meanings of its terms and with respect to its syntactic rules, stands in a much closer relationship to the world than the conventionalist theory allows. In its logical structure, in the general features of its syntax, in its embodiment of intelligible forms, and even in the primitive roots from which many of its terms are derived, this relationship is evident. It is by virtue of this relationship that language is capable of serving as a medium of understanding and communication, and thus as the chief instrument for the enhancement of the life of reason that is man's highest dignity.

Study Questions

1. The author of this chapter (whom we shall hereafter refer to as SE— Strong Essentialist) employs two *reductio ad absurdum* arguments to refute the conventionalist position. Applying the tests for such arguments suggested in Chapter 4, do you think SE succeeds in his effort? How might Conventionalist defend himself against SE's attack?

2. What do you understand SE to mean by "the necessary conformity of language to the canons of reason"? As far as you understand him on this point, are you inclined to agree with him or to disagree with him?

3. What is SE's view regarding the status of syntactic rules? Are they

natural, conventional, or both? How does SE attempt to support his view on this point?

4. What "natural" elements does SE claim to find in the meanings of individual words? Would it be possible for Conventionalist to agree with him on this point without abandoning his conventionalism?

5. Is the sentence, "Some circles are square" *unintelligible,* or is it simply *false?* How does your answer to this question affect SE's argument?

Chapter 8

MODIFIED ESSENTIALISM

As an advocate of a more modest form of essentialism than that which is set forth in the preceding chapter, I cannot help but disagree with a number of the statements which my colleague has just made. My views, in many ways, are much closer to those of Conventionalist than they are to those of Strong Essentialist, and if I considered the matter worth arguing, I would be inclined to urge that the position which I represent be called modified conventionalism, or something of that sort, rather than (as is implied in the last chapter) simply a "weak" version of modified essentialism. But what is important, obviously, is to try to get clear as to what really is the relationship of language to reality, of words to the world; and if we can succeed in our attempt to do this, it makes little difference what name we choose to attach to the theory thus defined.

Since, as I have indicated, my own views on this matter are in many ways identical to those of Conventionalist, I cannot but regard the attack on conventionalism as an attack on my position as well. I want, therefore, to begin with a defense of those points in Conventionalist's position which seem to be valid. I shall then go on to formulate a critique of the strong version of modified essentialism which was advocated in the last chapter and shall conclude with additional remarks in support of what I trust will be seen to be the correct view on this matter.

Conventionalism Reconsidered

Conventionalist has argued that language, both with respect to the meanings of its terms and with respect to its rules of syntax, is completely the product of human invention and that it has, therefore, no closer relation to reality than the makers and users of language have assigned to it. Against this position it has now been objected (a) that it would render language incapable of communicating truth, and (b) that it is inconsistent with the fact that it is possible to "translate" intelligible discourse from one language into another. Let us see if we cannot separate what may be sound from what is patently unsound in these objections.

With respect to Strong Essentialist's claim that the conventionalist theory would render language incapable of communicating truth, I am somewhat uncertain as to whether it constitutes a sound criticism of Conventionalist's position or not. My uncertainty is due, I think, to the fact that I am not sure that I see clearly just what is the point of Strong Essentialist's argument. There is, I believe, a weakness in Conventionalist's position at this point, but I am not sure that Strong Essentialist has succeeded in locating it with the precision that one might desire. Let us try to improve upon his efforts.

There are three things that need to be distinguished when one is attempting to understand the notion of truth. These are (a) a state of affairs in the real world, (b) an awareness of this state of affairs by some rational being, and (c) a description of this state of affairs in some language. For a person to "know the truth" about something, it is not necessary that he enunciate, or that he be able to enunciate, a verbal description that is a correct description in that language of the state of affairs that exists in the real world. It is enough if his awareness (what he believes to be the case) corresponds to what really is the case.

Knowledge, therefore, it would seem, is in a certain sense independent of language. Our knowledge of the truth, insofar as we have such knowledge, does not consist in our assent to certain true sentences, but in our assent to true propositions, in our conceptual awareness that certain things are the case. Changes in the meanings of terms, and even changes in syntax (if they occur), do not in and of themselves alter this conceptual awareness. What these changes do is simply to alter the way in which we must *express* our knowledge if we wish to make ourselves understood.

It would seem, therefore, that the changes in language of which Conventionalist speaks would not in and of themselves lead to the "erosion of knowledge" which Strong Essentialist fears. To this extent, at least, his criticism of the conventionalist position does not appear to be sound.

It does seem, however, that Conventionalist is in error in suggesting that truth and falsehood are functions primarily of sentences, thus resting them on nothing more secure than the conventions of language. A true sentence may indeed become false, or even unintelligible, if the meanings of its terms or the syntax according to which it is constructed should change; but so long as there are men who retain an intellectual conception of the state of affairs which that sentence originally described, that bit of truth will remain in the reservoir of human knowledge. It is not with our lips or our pens, but with our minds, that we know the truth; and if we know the truth, no matter how much language may change we shall always find ways to express it.

The chief error of conventionalism is to be found, therefore, not so much in what it asserts as in what it fails to assert. There is such a thing as an intellectual comprehension of truth that is independent of the linguistic expressions in which that truth may be expressed. Conventionalism fails to take account of this, and because it does so, it appears to place truth itself, and our knowledge of the truth, at the mercy of a constantly changing system of linguistic symbols.

It is this same omission, surely, that renders plausible Strong Essentialist's suggestion that the conventionalist theory of language would render inexplicable the fact that what is said in one language can be "translated" into another. A translator clearly is not a person who simply transposes the symbols of one language into those of another and then re-arranges these symbols according to the rules of syntax of the second language. A good translator is, rather, a true master of the two languages with which he is working. He is able, therefore, to grasp the meaning of what is said in the one language and to express this meaning in the other. It is intellectual comprehension, once again, that constitutes the missing element in the conventionalist account; once this is supplied, the mystery about how translation is possible disappears.

A Critique of Essentialism

How much of the essentialist account of language ought we, then, to retain? Not a great deal, it seems to me.

Strong Essentialists's suggestion that some words derive from roots that originally had some "natural" relation to the things they denote (ache, laugh, etc.) we may dismiss at once. This may be so, but it clearly need not have been so, and conventionalism is, therefore, right in insisting that the choice of what sounds are to stand for what things in a given language is entirely a matter of convention.

The suggestion that language has an essential relation to reality by virtue of the fact that it embodies "intelligible forms" also appears, upon close scrutiny, to have little to commend it. There is a grain of truth in this doctrine, however, and it is important that we not lose sight of it. The grain is this: terms not only denote things, but they express concepts, and concepts do arise out of the encounter of the human mind with reality. Because the general features of the real world do appear more or less the same to people the world over, the vocabulary of concepts with which people operate are more or less universal, and communication is therefore possible. But it is, nonetheless, strictly because it is convenient to do so that we divide up the "booming, buzzing confusion" of the world of our experience in the way we do. Anyone who has had the experience of trying to translate materials from a language that belongs to a cultural situation very different from his own knows that, apart from names for everyday objects such as men, trees, and stones, there is very little to support the thesis that all language embodies the same "universal forms."

On the matter of parallels in syntactic structure among the languages of the world, I think Strong Essentialist is right in asserting that there are some such parallels, but he is wrong in claiming on this basis an essential relation between language and reality. Such parallels as there are derive for the most part from the fact that language has been developed to serve certain purposes, and those purposes would not be served, or at least would not be served nearly so well, if language did not have certain features. It is because it is convenient for purposes of communication that language distinguishes various parts of speech (nouns, adjectives, verbs, etc.), singular and plural, tenses, and the like. But to state this is not to assert that these features of language are not conventional. It is to say, rather, that the conventions which men have adopted are more or less similar because the purposes for which they have adopted them are more or less the same.

With respect to at least two of the four points at which Essentialist finds a "natural" relation between language and reality it seems necessary to conclude, therefore, that he is simply mistaken, and on a third point it would appear that he is more wrong than he is right. It remains now to consider whether he is right in what he says about the logical structure of language and if so what this means insofar as the relation of language to reality is concerned.

A Modest Proposal

The question as to how language is related to reality is an exceedingly complex one, and it is not strange if able men of good will have not been able to come to agreement on it. So many separate questions are involved, and so many answers to each of these questions may be given, that it is all but impossible to keep the whole range of issues in view when one is attempting to come to some defensible position on the general question that has been posed for consideration in these chapters. Precisely what, for example, is a "proposition," in view of the fact that it is apparently not identifiable with any single linguistic expression or any finite set of linguistic expressions? What is occurring when someone "believes" a proposition to be true? What are the conditions that must be present if a statement is to have "meaning"? What are the conditions that determine whether a proposition is true or false? An answer to each of these questions is implied in any view which one adopts on the larger question with which we have been dealing, and it is only insofar as one has been satisfied that a given view on each of these is correct that one can have any confidence that the view on the larger question is also correct. I have been able, in the space available, to do no more than touch on some of these matters as they relate to the question under discussion; but it is well, nonetheless, to be aware of these problems and to recognize that a complete answer to the general problem presupposes some view on each of these as well.

There is one point, however, where it seems that the several parties to the dispute about the relationship betwen language and reality ought to be able to reach agreement, and that is on the matter of the logical structure of both language and reality. I should like to conclude, therefore, by stating what I conceive to be the truth about this matter. The point is not, as I see it, susceptible of strict proof; I can only state what seems to me to be the case, and trust that others who consider the matter will be able to see for themselves that the account which I shall give is indeed correct.

It is a remarkable fact, as Strong Essentialist has correctly observed, that the truths of logic are the same for all people regardless of the language that they happen to speak. Languages vary from people to people, but a logical fallacy is a logical fallacy in any language, and a logical implication is equally valid whether it is expressed in English or in French, in Chinese or in Swahili.

It seems clear, therefore, that the truths of logic are not in any sense constituted by the rules governing the use of this or that language, but are prior to and independent of these rules. But—and this is the important point—language would not be language if it did not, in its very structure, conform to the canons of logic. An a-logical language is a contradiction in terms: if a system of sounds were to ignore the canons of logic, it would not be capable of serving as a vehicle of intelligible communication: hence, it would not be a language.

But reality, too, must and of course does conform to the canons of logic. What is not logically possible in the realm of concepts is not really possible in the actual world. What is logically necessary in the realm of concepts is really necessary in the actual world. If a given state of affairs logically implies certain things in the realm of thought, then those implications must find their counterparts in the real world as well. Not everything that is possible need be actual, that is clear. But what is actual must, obviously, also be possible, and logic has to do with the realm of the possible.

It is in the necessary conformity of both language and reality to the canons of logic that I find the one indisputable essential link between the two, and it is on this basis alone that I qualify as an adherent of what is called modified essentialism. All of the other features of language—the meanings of its terms, the details of its syntax—seem to me to rest upon no other foundation than the arbitrary conventions of men, guided perhaps by the requirements of convenience. But in one way or another every language conforms, and indeed must conform, to the general requirements of logic. In so conforming language is essentially related to a world which is also bound by the canons of that self-same logic.

The only way that anyone could dispute this conclusion, so far as I can see, would be to assert that the truths of logic are not independent of the conventions of language, but are established by those conventions. And this seems to be clearly false. We are left, therefore, with one essential link between words and the world; everything else that is to be found in language is a product of the remarkably fecund inventive genius of man.

Study Questions

1. Review the two *reductio ad absurdum* arguments used by SE against the conventionalist position. Does ME (Modified Essentialist) defend conventionalism against these arguments, or does his discussion tend to re-enforce SE's view?
2. Make a list of the points at which SE has asserted a natural (non-conventional) relation between language and reality. Which of these does ME disallow? For what reasons?
3. What does ME affirm to be "the one indisputable essential link" between language and reality? Is he right about this? What would Conventionalist have to say on this point in order to maintain his position? How might he attempt to support his position on this matter?
4. One of the sorts of things that language is able to express is *logical contradictions*. Is this fact compatible with ME's claim that language must conform to the canons of logic?

For Further Reading

Austin, J. L., "Truth," *Proceedings of the Aristotelian Society*, Supplementary Vol. 24 (1950), 111-128.

Ayer, A. J., *Thinking and Meaning*. London: H. K. Lewis, 1947.

Black, Max, *Language and Philosophy*. Ithaca, N.Y.: Cornell University Press, 1949. See especially Chapter 4.

Blanshard, Brand, *Reason and Analysis*. La Salle, Ill.: Open Court, 1962. Chapter 5.

Church, Alonzo, *Introduction to Mathematical Logic*. Princeton, N.J.: Princeton University Press, 1956. Pages 1-68.

Gellner, Ernest, *Words and Things*. Boston, Mass.: Beacon Press, 1959. See also the Introduction by Bertrand Russell.

Hospers, John, *An Introduction to Philosophical Analysis*. Englewood Cliffs, N.J.: Prentice-Hall, 1956. Chapter 1.

Jespersen, Otto, *The Philosophy of Grammar*. New York: W. W. Norton & Co., 1965 (paperbound). Chapter 3.

Ogden, C. K. and I. A. Richards, *The Meaning of Meaning*. New York: Harcourt, Brace & World, 1956 (paperbound). Chapters 1-3.

Plato, *Cratylus*. Many editions.

Russell, Bertrand, *An Inquiry into Meaning and Truth*. Baltimore, Md.: Penguin Books, 1963 (paperbound). Chapters 16 and 20-22.

―――, *Human Knowledge*. New York: Simon and Schuster, 1962 (paperbound). Part II, "Language."

Urban, W. M., *Language and Reality*. New York: The Macmillan Company, 1939. Part I. See especially Chapters 7-8.

A Priori Knowledge

Chapter 9

THE ISSUE BETWEEN RATIONALISTS AND EMPIRICISTS

WHATEVER IS THE correct answer to the question posed in the last section, it is clear that somehow or other language does have meaning and that by means of language we are able to think, speak, and write about things and events in the real world. This is obviously very fortunate, for it provides the possibility of communicating with one another—of reporting our feelings, asking questions, pooling our information, and so on. Were it not for the medium of language, each individual could at best know only those facts which happened to fall within his own particular experience. Language makes possible a sharing, and thus an increasing accumulation, of knowledge: each generation can learn (by means of language) what was known by the previous generation and can go on to increase the sum of human knowledge which will in turn be passed on to the succeeding generation. Each generation is, as Blaise Pascal once said, like a dwarf sitting on the shoulders of a giant; and the dwarf is able to see farther than the giant only because of the height to which he is raised.

Knowledge

But what does it mean to "know" something about the world? Suppose, for example, that we say "Johnny *knows* that if you put your hand into a flame you will get burned." Just what does this mean? It appears to mean three things: (1) It is the case that if you put your hand into a flame, you will get burned; (2) Johnny believes that if you put your hand into a flame you will get burned; and (3) Johnny has valid grounds for so believing. Let *p* be any statement about the real world, and let *A* be any person whatsoever. When *A* knows *p,* then (1) what *p* asserts is the case, (2) *A* believes that *p* is the case, and (3) *A* has valid grounds for believing that *p* is the case. If any one of these conditions were not present, we could not say that *A knows p.* If (1) were absent, we would say that *A* mistakenly believes *p.* If (2) were absent, we would say that although *p* is true, and *A* ought to know it (since he has valid grounds), he does not. And if (3) were absent, we would probably say that *A* just "had a hunch" or "made a lucky guess."

It is important to note that what we are talking about at present is knowledge of the real world, which accordingly is expressed in statements about the real world. A "statement about the real world" is one that asserts that something is the case, that some state of affairs obtains. If what it asserts really is the case, then it is a true statement; if not, it is false. Some philosophers speak of such statements as "statements asserting some matter of fact." Another common name for them is simply "empirical statements."

Statements about the real world should be clearly distinguished, however, from statements which only tell us something about the meaning of some word or phrase. The statement, "All bachelors are bald," is a statement about the real world: it asserts that something is the case, and it can be shown to be false by producing the appropriate evidence, that is, an unmarried adult male human being with hair on his head. But the statement, "All bachelors are unmarried," is not a statement about the real world: it is simply an elucidation of a part of the meaning of the term "bachelor." You do not have to produce a single spouseless adult male human being in order to support the statement that all bachelors are unmarried, for it is not a statement about human beings at all—it is a statement about the meaning of a word. Construed as a statement about the real world, it is vacuous: it says that all unmarried adult human beings are unmarried. Hence, we know better than to construe it in this way.

The Sources of Knowledge

It is evident that there are many statements about the real world which we know to be true, that is, we have a good deal of knowledge about the real world. How did we acquire this knowledge? What are the ways by which one may come to know something about the world?

One source of our knowledge, obviously, is our own experience. We have, in the course of our lives, seen and heard and touched and tasted many things, and on this basis we can say many things about the world. We know, in this way, many simple facts about ourselves: that we have two arms, two legs, eyes, ears, and so on. We know, moreover, many general truths about the world in which we live on the basis of our own experience: that unsupported objects tend downward, that fire burns, that rain makes things wet, etc. The list of things which each of us knows by direct experience would be very long indeed, and since every person's experience is in some ways unique, no two lists would be exactly alike.

But if each of us knew only what we ourselves had directly experienced, our knowledge would be vastly more limited than it in fact is. By far the greater part of what we know we have learned from others; we have listened to them and have read the books some of them have written. In so doing we have learned many things about history, geography, literature, and the sciences—things which in all probability we would never have been able to discover for ourselves.

In reality, however, there is not much difference between these two sources of knowledge. It is as if ten men set out together to inspect a ten-room house, and in order to save time and effort agreed to inspect just one room each and report to the rest. Each man, then, would know about one room by direct experience, and about the other nine by indirect experience. The information that we get from teachers and from books is what we might call "secondhand experience." If you trace this information to its source, you will inevitably find someone whose experience has taught him what he is now teaching us through language.

Rationalists and Empiricists

Apart from a minor quibble over whether what we have been talking about really deserves to be called "knowledge" or not (Plato, for example, called it mere "opinion"), most philosophers would have no quarrel with what has been stated thus far. It is obvious that we have some kind of cognitive rapport with the world by means of direct and indirect experience, and it is perfectly consistent with ordinary usage to say that what we acquire in this way is *knowledge* of the real world.

At this point there arises, however, one of the most controversial and important issues in philosophy. The issue is: Do we or do we not have any knowledge of the real world that is in any degree independent of experience? Is there or is there not such a thing as a direct apprehension of empirical truths? Is experience the whole and only source of our knowledge of the real world, or is the human mind capable of grasping truths about the world in such a direct way that experience functions only as the occasion for this insight? This is the central problem of epistemology.

Some philosophers hold that the human mind is capable of a direct apprehension of some empirical truths and that we in fact do have some knowledge of the real world that is in a certain way independent of experience. This view is called *rationalism,* and a person who holds this view is accordingly called a *rationalist.* Other philosophers deny this possibility and maintain that our knowledge of the real world arises entirely out of experience. Such men are called *empiricists,* and the position which they represent is called *empiricism.* With respect to this question rationalism and empiricism are the only alternatives, and they are mutually exclusive. You can be a rationalist or you can be an empiricist, but you cannot be both and you cannot avoid being one or the other.

In order to discuss this issue with maximum precision, however, we need a vocabulary that is somewhat more technical than the language we have been using thus far. Let us pause, therefore, to define a few terms and then attempt to state our problem in a more precise way.

We may begin by making a distinction between *analytic* and *synthetic* statements.

An *analytic* statement is one in which what is affirmed in the predicate is already contained in the concept of the subject. An example of such a statement would be "All circles are round." In order to test the truth of such a statement, it is not necessary to examine any circles to see whether in fact they are all round. Being round is part of what is meant by the term "circle"; consequently, we know without making any inspection that all circles are round, that if anything is a circle it must be round. We need only "analyze the subject" of the statement, and there we shall find the notion of roundness. To call something a circle and to deny that it is round would be to contradict oneself: it would be equivalent to saying that some round things are not round.

A *synthetic* statement is one in which what is affirmed in the predicate adds something to the concept of the subject. A house, for example, may be defined as an enclosure within which human beings live and find shelter. If, then, I say that "Some houses have pink shutters," I am uttering a synthetic statement: the idea of having pink shutters is not contained in the idea of a house. I cannot produce my statement simply by analyzing the subject (house); it is, rather, a synthesis of two different concepts (house and pink shutters)—in short, a synthetic statement.

Strictly speaking, the definitions of "analytic" and "synthetic" given here apply only to analytic and synthetic statements *of the subject-predicate type*. But if the distinction is understood, it can be easily generalized to apply to statements of other types. An alternative—and broader—definition of "analytic statement" would be: "a statement whose truth is determined solely by the meaning of its terms"; and of "synthetic statement": "a statement whose truth or falsehood is not determined solely by the meaning of its terms." A statement whose *falsehood* is determined solely by the meaning of its terms is said to be "analytically false."

The second pair of terms for which we shall shortly have use are the terms *a priori* and *a posteriori.*

Something is said to be known *a posteriori* if it is known on the basis of experience. How do we know that lemons are sour? We know it *a posteriori:* we have tasted them. How do we know that too long an exposure of skin to the sun causes sunburn? We know it *a posteriori:* we have been sunburned, or we have seen others who have been sunburned. All of the things we talked about a few moments ago—all of the things that we know by direct or by indirect experience—we know *a posteriori*. Experience (either our own or someone else's) is the whole and only source of such knowledge, and if such knowledge is challenged it is to experience, and experience alone, that we must appeal for confirmation. *A posteriori* knowledge is only as secure as the factual evidence upon which it rests.

With *a priori* knowledge the situation is different. Here factual evidence is not relevant—though some philosophers would say that many *a priori* truths are constantly exhibited in experience. What, then, is an *a priori* truth? It is a statement the truth of which is evident apart from the facts of experience. To know something *a priori* is to know it immediately, directly, without recourse to factual evidence. In a certain sense, it is to know something "prior to experience"—in the sense, namely, that all subsequent experience must conform to what is thus known. What is known *a priori* is seen, as Immanuel Kant said, to be necessary and universal: once grasped, its untruth is inconceivable, and it is then immediately evident that it must be true at all times and in all places.[1]

Now it is perfectly evident that we know a great many *synthetic* truths *a posteriori*. No one—not even the most enthusiastic of rationalists—denies this, and it is a caricature of the rationalist's position to say that he does.

It is equally evident that all *analytic* truths are known *a priori*. No one—not even the most incorrigible of empiricists—denies this, and it is a caricature of the empiricist's position to say that he does.

The question is, however (and this is where the rationalist and the empiricist part company), do we or do we not have any *a priori* knowledge of *synthetic* truths? The rationalist says we do, the empiricist says we do not. That is the issue.

There is much, therefore, about which the rationalist and the empiricist are in agreement. This should not be overlooked. But there is one major issue upon which they are in disagreement, and that is whether we do or do not have any *a priori* knowledge of

---

[1] Immanuel Kant, *Critique of Pure Reason*, Introduction, Sect. II, Norman Kemp Smith, trans. (New York: St. Martin's Press, 1965), pp. 43-44.

synthetic truths. It is upon this one issue that we must focus our whole attention in the chapters that follow. The controversy might be represented as follows:

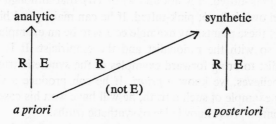

It should be apparent that what we now have before us is a statement in rather more precise terms of the problem posed earlier in a somewhat different way. We talked earlier about "knowledge of the real world," and we asked whether we can have any such knowledge in a way that is in any degree independent of experience. Now we are asking whether we can have any *a priori* knowledge of "synthetic truths." But to know a synthetic truth *is* to know something about the real world, and to know something in a way that is in any degree independent of experience *is* to know it *a priori*. We have before us, therefore, a non-technical and a technical formulation of the same problem. But the technical formulation, as we shall see, permits us to talk about it with greater precision than the other.

How the Argument Must Proceed

If we have understood the issue upon which the rationalist and the empiricist are at such loggerheads, we shall not have any difficulty in seeing how they will have to go about supporting their respective positions.

Consider a simple analogy. Suppose that I am of the opinion that there are some pink-tufted owls in captivity, and my opponent is of the opinion that there are none. How can we proceed with our dispute? Quite obviously, in order to support my position I must produce some examples. Indeed, if I can produce just one example of a pink-tufted owl, I shall have won my case. And my opponent, what must he do? Clearly, he must attempt to show that any example that I bring forth is not really an example of a pink-tufted owl. This he may do in either of two ways. He may show (a) that although the bird I am offering as an example of a pink-tufted owl is indeed pink-tufted, it is not an owl or (b) that although it appears to be an owl, it is not pink-tufted. If he can make good his claim to either of these points, my example ceases to be an example.

Just so with the rationalist and the empiricist. It is up to the rationalist to bring forward examples of the synthetic truths which, as he believes, we know *a priori*. If he can produce a single convincing example of such a truth, he will have won his case: we then have some *a priori* knowledge of synthetic truths.

The empiricist, on the other hand, must attempt to show that the examples which the rationalist offers are not, after all, examples of synthetic truths which are known *a priori*. This he may do in either of two ways. He may, concerning a particular example that is brought forward, attempt to show that although it is a synthetic truth, it is not known *a priori* at all: it is, he may say, an *a posteriori synthetic* truth. Or, alternatively, he may attempt to show that what is offered as an example of an *a priori* synthetic truth is not synthetic at all: it is, he may say, an *a priori analytic* truth. For the empiricist is convinced of two things: that all statements which are known *a priori* are analytic, and that all statements which are synthetic are known *a posteriori*. Empiricists may disagree among themselves as to which of these two categories a given statement belongs in, but they are agreed that every statement whose truth is knowable by us belongs in one or the other.

The empiricist, it should be noted, cannot fairly be expected to produce an independent argument to prove his contention that all synthetic truths (all truths about the real world) are known *a posteriori*. In the very nature of the case, this is not possible. The burden of proof lies, as in a formal debate, with the affirmative— with the one who says "there are some so-and-sos." In the present instance, therefore, the burden of proof rests with the rationalist. All that we have a right to expect of the empiricist is that he present a convincing refutation of anything that the rationalist may offer as an example of a synthetic truth that is known *a priori*.

In attempting to enter into the discussion of this issue, therefore, we must reflect very carefully on the examples which are offered by the rationalist. Concerning each example that is given, we must ask ourselves two simple questions: Is this a synthetic truth, and is it known *a priori?* If with respect to any example that is given we answer both questions in the affirmative, then we are agreeing with the rationalist. If we find no example which, after due reflection, seems to be both synthetic and *a priori,* then we are agreeing with the empiricist.

Study Questions

1. Are you satisfied with the analysis of "knowing" suggested in this chapter? Can you think of any instance that fails to meet the criteria here suggested that you would be inclined to call an instance of knowing? or an instance that satisfies these criteria that you would not be inclined to call an instance of knowing?

2. Make a list of the several ways in which the problem of *a priori* knowledge is stated in this chapter. Then check your understanding of the problem by re-stating the problem in your own words.

3. Are you convinced that rationalism and empiricism are the only possible positions to take with respect to this question? Is it true that "you cannot be both and you cannot avoid being one or the other"? Explain.

4. What is the difference in meaning between "analytic" and *"a priori"?* between "synthetic" and *"a posteriori"?* As you understand these terms, is it correct usage to speak of a statement as being *a priori* or *a posteriori?* Is it correct to speak of a statement being known analytically or synthetically?

5. Why must the argument between rationalists and empiricists proceed by way of considering examples brought forward by the rationalist? Why is it impossible for the empiricist to construct an independent "proof" of his position?

Chapter 10

THE RATIONALIST THESIS

THE GENTLEMAN WHO penned the previous chapter has presented an excellent statement of the problem about which my empiricist friends and I are in such complete disagreement. It is now my turn to enter the discussion and to present what I consider to be the correct answer to the problem there stated, that is, the rationalist answer. I believe that we do have some *a priori* knowledge of synthetic truths, and I propose shortly to offer a number of examples which I should like to think will prove convincing to any fair and open-minded reader.

Before I do that, however, there is one point in connection with my position which I should like to make clearer than it has been made thus far. The point is, I admit, somewhat subtle, but an understanding of it is absolutely essential to an understanding of my position.

The Two Roles of Experience

Let me state unequivocally, then, that I am not maintaining that we have any knowledge of any kind (of either analytic or synthetic truths) in a way that is *totally* independent of experience. It seems obvious that if we now know something, there must have been some time at which we learned it, and that the occasion on which we learned it was for us an experience. I am not a proponent of a theory of "innate knowledge," as if there were some bits of knowl-

92

edge that we were all born with and which we all, therefore, have prior to all experience. There have been philosophers who have maintained this, but it is not the position which I hold nor which I propose to defend.

What I wish to maintain, rather, is that experience does not always play the same role in learning. For much of our knowledge, experience is the whole *source* of what we come to know: this is knowledge *a posteriori*. But sometimes experience functions in another way: it is only the occasion for our coming to know, and what we come to know on that occasion vastly transcends the particular situation in which that learning occurs. We consider some statement about the world, we ponder it, and then we "see"—directly, immediately—that it is, and indeed *must be,* true. It is when we come to know something in this way—when experience is only, so to speak, a window through which we look—that we have a case of *a priori* knowledge.

Perhaps the difference can be clarified by the use of a pair of contrasting examples.

Let us first consider an example of something that is known *a posteriori*. A teacher is talking to her class about various kinds of birds and particularly the subject of crows. "What color are crows?" she asks; and the little boy in the fourth row who always likes to be the first to answer a question pipes up, "They're black." Little Suzie is not quite convinced, so she asks, "Is that right, Miss Twaddle? Are all crows black?" And Miss Twaddle says, "That's right, Suzie. All crows are black." But Suzie still is not convinced, so she presses a little further. "Miss Twaddle," she says, "how do you know that? How do you know for sure that some place, some time, there may not have been a white crow? How do you know that *all* crows are black?"

How could our poor hard-pressed teacher go about answering Suzie's question? One way, of course, would be to play a little verbal trick on Suzie. She could say, "Suzie, if you come across a bird that is just like a crow except that it's white instead of black, it isn't a crow—you'll have to invent some other name for it." But if Miss Twaddle wants to deal fairly with Suzie, she will have to proceed in a rather different way. She might ask, for example, whether anyone in class had ever seen a crow that was not black. She might report that she herself had seen thousands of crows in her lifetime and that as far as she could recall each and every one of those thousands of crows was black. She might send the class to the library to see whether they could find any reports of non-black crows. She might consult a bird expert and report to the class that as far as he knew there had never been an authenticated case of a non-black crow.

What would be the point of all of this? The point is that the statement, "All crows are black," is only as secure as the factual evidence on which it rests. The statement is a summary of the experience of many people, and if it is called in question, the only way that it can be supported is to point to that evidence. Suzie, if she is wise, will not be completely convinced. It is still possible, she may point out, that somewhere, sometime, a non-black crow—perhaps an albino—will hatch from the egg of a normal crow. And in this, of course, Suzie would be right.

But now let us consider a second example. Our class has gotten a few years older and has graduated from a study of birds to a study of geometry. A Mr. Twiddle is their instructor. "Class," he begins, "let us briefly review yesterday's lesson. What is a triangle?" And the young man in the fourth row, who still likes to be the first to answer any question, replies, "A triangle is a closed plane figure having three straight sides." "All triangles?" asks Mr. Twiddle. "All *Euclidean* triangles," our hero replies. "How big must the angles be?" asks Mr. Twiddle. "They can be any size you like," comes the reply, "provided only that you have a closed plane figure with just three straight sides. That, and that alone, is enough to make it a triangle—no matter how big it is or how big the angles are or anything else."

"Very well," says Mr. Twiddle, "but today I want to show you something else about triangles." Whereupon he demonstrates the theorem that the interior angles of a Euclidean triangle total 180 degrees. The class struggles briefly with the theorem. They watch Mr. Twiddle as he constructs a proof of the theorem. One by one they "catch on," and by the time the hour is half over they have all apparently gotten the point, and are able without difficulty to "prove" the theorem for themselves.

But Suzie is still with us, and she still wants to make sure that she is getting the straight information. So she asks, "Mr. Twiddle, how do you know that *all* Euclidean triangles have interior angles that total 180 degrees?" In this instance it would be utterly pointless for Mr. Twiddle to round up evidence to show that of all the Euclidean triangles that he or anybody else had ever seen, none had ever been found to have interior angles that totaled either more or less than 180 degrees. He can only return to the proof of the theorem and try to help Suzie see that the very nature of triangularity is such that anything that is a Euclidean triangle *must* have interior angles totaling 180 degrees. Furthermore, once Suzie really "sees" this, once she really has hold of this truth about triangles, nothing in the world could ever dissuade her from assenting to it. To know something *a priori* is to know it with a directness, and with a certainty, that experience alone can never give us.

Immanuel Kant once put the matter this way.[1] All knowledge, he said, clearly *begins* with experience—both knowledge *a priori* and knowledge *a posteriori*. But not all knowledge *arises out of* experience. It is only *a posteriori* knowledge (as in the case of the example about crows) that arises out of experience, and it is accordingly to experience alone that one can turn if a statement that is affirmed on that basis is called in question. But there is also an *a priori* knowledge of the world (as in the example about triangles); and it is characteristic of such knowledge that if a statement whose truth is known in this way is called in question one must turn not to empirical evidence for support, but rather to an inspection of the nature of the thing about which the statement is made. You may parade before my eyes as many black crows as you like: I shall still retain some doubt about whether in fact all crows are black. But I know beyond the shadow of a doubt that if anything is a Euclidean triangle, its interior angles total 180 degrees. What is the difference? The difference is that in the one case we are dealing with *a posteriori* knowledge and in the other with *a priori* knowledge. In the one case the knowledge arises out of experience; in the other experience is only the occasion for my coming to know.

---

[1] Immanuel Kant, *Critique of Pure Reason*, Introduction, Sect. II, Norman Kemp Smith, trans. (New York: St. Martin's Press, 1965), p. 41.

Examples of A Priori *Truths*

It is hoped that these few remarks have clarified what rationalists mean when they talk about knowledge that is acquired in a way that is in some degree independent of experience. The point is so important to a fair appraisal of my position, and so easily and so often misunderstood, that I want to urge my readers to ponder it very carefully—so that they are absolutely sure they see the point of it—before considering the rest of the discussion.

The remainder is relatively simple. I want to offer a few examples of synthetic truths which, I believe, we know *a priori*. This is not difficult, for there are countless examples at hand—truths about the world which all of us know, truths that we know not *a posteriori* but *a priori*.

One large class of truths which we know in this way are *arithmetical* truths. Any true arithmetical statement will do. Let us consider the statement, "7 + 5 = 12." This, of course, is simply a brief and convenient way of saying what could be said in ordinary language: seven things added to five things give you a combined total of twelve things.

The first thing to notice about this statement is that it is *synthetic:* it is a statement about the real world. It is, of course, a very general statement about the world: it applies to apples and oranges and pennies and kittens and anything else that we might have occasion to count and add together.

Consider what would have to be the case, however, if this statement were analytic. We would then have to say that simply by analyzing the subject ("seven things added to five things") we could find the predicate ("twelve things") already present. But we cannot do this. What we find, when we analyze the subject, is this: (a) the concept seven, (b) the concept five, and (c) a direction to perform the intellectual operation involved in combining seven and five into a single total ("added to"). In order to get our predicate we have to perform the prescribed intellectual operation. To do this we must leave off analysis and consider the natures of the numbers involved. Only when we do this—only when we consider the nature of "seven" in conjunction with "five" and perform the intellectual act of combining them—can we get our predicate; in order to do this, we must add to our subject the quite different concept "twelve" in the synthetic statement, "seven things plus five things are twelve things." Arithmetical statements are one and all synthetic.

The second factor to notice about this statement is that its truth is not known *a posteriori.* It is not like the example of the crows: we are not more or less confident that seven things added to five things equal twelve things, depending on how many times we may have added seven and five. We *know*—absolutely, certainly, without the slightest doubt—that any time, any place, if seven things are added to five things the total will be twelve things. There is a necessity, a universality, a self-evidence, a certainty about this statement that no statement whose truth depends upon the facts of experience can ever have. It may be exhibited in experience, but experience can never contradict it. Its truth is known *a priori:* we learned it, indeed, through experience, but not by way of summarizing the facts of experience.

Here, then, are as many examples of synthetic truths that are known *a priori* as anyone could ever ask for. What is true of $7 + 5$ is equally true of $8 + 9$ and $4 - 2$ and 6×7 and every arithmetical statement that ever has been or will be made. Each of them, it will be seen, is a synthetic truth whose truth, if it is to be known at all, must be known *a priori.*

A second large class of synthetic truths that are known *a priori* consists of the truths of geometry. We have already had an illustration about the triangle. Let us consider that example more closely.

Geometry is what we might call the science of physical space. Since any object that could ever appear to us must appear in space, we know *a priori* that it must conform to the truths of geometry. If, therefore, someone tries to tell us that one time—perhaps, say, in the jungles of Africa—he saw a Euclidean triangle whose interior angles totaled only 160 degrees, we are simply not going to believe him. We may suggest that he made an incorrect measurement, or that the sides of what he thought was a Euclidean triangle were not straight, or even that he is lying to us or trying to fool us. But we know that his report cannot be true because we know *a priori* that

Euclid's theorem is true. And because this is so, experience—wherever, whenever, and to whomever it occurs—must conform to it. Geometrical knowledge is knowledge *a priori.*

A third class of synthetic truths that are known *a priori* consists of a very large class of statements which, for lack of a better name, we shall call *logical* truths. An example of such a truth is the statement, "Anything that has shape has size." Other examples that might be considered are, "A thing cannot both have and not have the same characteristic at the same time," and "If all men are mortal, and Socrates is a man, then Socrates is mortal."

Let us confine our attention to just the first of these examples, however. It is evident that this is a synthetic statement, a statement about the real world. It asserts a fact about the world—it may or may not be an important fact, but it is a fact, and one that we know to be true—namely, that in each and every instance in which there is an object that has shape there is also an object that has size. Now shape and size are not the same thing: I can know that something is round, for example, without having the slightest idea how big it is. Shape and size are, therefore, diverse characteristics which an object may have. But—and this is the point of the statement—the nature of shape is such and the nature of size is such that whenever one characteristic is present, the other must be also. There is, we might say, a necessary connection between the character which we designate by the term "shape" and the character which we designate by the term "size," and it is this connection that we are affirming when we say that anything that has shape has size.

But it is equally clear that the truth of this statement is known *a priori.* We directly "see" the necessary connection to which we have just referred, and seeing this, we know without the slightest doubt that the statement is necessarily and universally true. We know, with a certainty that empirical evidence could never give us, that there never has been and never will be an instance of shape without size, or of size without shape. In knowing this, we know a logical truth, and experience simply must conform to it. Logical truths are known *a priori.*

The fourth class of synthetic truths that are known *a priori* which I should like to mention is *ethical* truths. Once again numerous examples come to mind, but let us confine our attention to the statement, "The infliction of needless pain is evil."

There can be no question, it seems to me, that this statement is synthetic. The notion involved in the infliction of needless pain is undoubtedly highly complex, but this much at least is clear: you can analyze that notion as thoroughly as you please, and you will not discover that the idea of being evil is a part of it. What we mean by "the infliction of needless pain" is such things as a boy's torturing an animal "just for the fun of it," or mauling a younger or weaker person in order "to show how tough he is." And what we are saying about such instances is that in addition to being instances of animal or human suffering willfully caused by some responsible agent, they have the additional character of being evil. In so saying we are adding to the concept of the subject something not a part of that concept which is connected to it in our synthetic judgment, "The infliction of needless pain is evil."

What sort of evidence could possibly be adduced in support of such a statement? Evidence could, of course, heighten our awareness of how painful such an act could be, or how absurd and pointless it is, but that is beside the point. What we are affirming is that the infliction of needless pain is not only needless and painful (that *is* analytically true), but that it is also something else, namely evil, reprehensible, morally blameworthy. Not all the evidence in the world could either confirm or disconfirm our judgment; if its truth is known at all, it is known *a priori.*

And its truth *is known,* is it not? We are not moral ignoramuses —though we may not always act in accordance with the moral truths we do perceive. We know, even if we ourselves should be the agent who inflicts needless pain, that what we do is evil. We see directly, with an immediacy and a certainty that empirical evidence could never give us, that this act has the moral quality of being evil. And so it is with all ethical truths.

Let me conclude by presenting one small but important disclaimer. In arguing as I have for the possibility and the reality of an *a priori* knowledge of synthetic truths, I have not meant to disparage in any way the importance of *a posteriori* knowledge. There are things that can only be known *a posteriori* and due credit should be given to the many scientists, historians and others who, by dint of careful observation and experimentation, have contributed so greatly to the sum of human knowledge. The point of my remarks can be summed up thusly: however great the quantity of knowledge gained in this way is or may become, it does not constitute the whole of our knowledge of reality. We have, in at least the four areas mentioned, countless instances of truths about the real world that are known *a priori*. It may or it may not be important for us to be aware of this—that is another matter. But important or not, it is the case, and that is all that I have tried to show. Perhaps at some later time we shall have an opportunity to consider whether or not some fairly important consequences may not hinge on the way we answer this question.

Study Questions

1. What difference or differences do you see between the theory of "innate knowledge" and the theory which Rationalist attempts to defend in this chapter?
2. Is there a difference between the role that experience plays in our knowledge about crows and that which it plays in our knowledge of geometrical truths? Has Rationalist succeeded in identifying a real difference here—however one might wish to account for it?
3. List the four classes of truths which Rationalist offers as examples of synthetic truths that are known *a priori*. What evidence does he offer, in each case, that the truths to which he has reference are synthetic truths? that they are known *a priori*?
4. Can you think of any examples in addition to those offered by Rationalist that might plausibly be considered as examples of synthetic truths that are known *a priori*? Which of Rationalist's own examples do you find most convincing? which least?

Chapter 11

AN EMPIRICIST RETORT

THERE IS SOME danger, I think, that readers of Rationalist's account may have gotten a somewhat mistaken view of empiricists, namely, that they are a group of rather stubborn and close-minded individuals who are so enamored of empirical methods of acquiring knowledge that they simply refuse to recognize the knowledge acquired in another way. Rationalists, it may appear, are more open and broad-minded. They allow that there is a great deal of knowledge that is acquired by way of observation and experimentation (*a posteriori* knowledge), but they do not limit man's knowledge to this: they go on to assert that the human mind is capable of a direct apprehension of some empirical truths and that in fact we know many things about the world in this direct, *a priori,* way.

This impression of empiricists is, however, quite mistaken, and I shall begin my defense of empiricism by attempting to dispel it. Let me state plainly that I am an empiricist for one reason only—and that is that I have never encountered a single example of an alleged *a priori* synthetic truth which did not prove upon closer inspection to be either analytic (and hence not a truth about the real world at all) or else *a posteriori.* I am, however, willing to be shown, and if I ever do encounter an example of such a truth, I will concede immediately to the rationalists. Until then I must honestly state that every synthetic truth known to me is known *a posteriori,* and every statement that I have ever seen that could with any degree of certainty be said to be known *a priori* is clearly analytic. Pending evidence to the contrary, I must, therefore, continue to maintain that as far as I can make out all of our knowledge of the real world is *a posteriori*.

This much, however, I will concede to the rationalists: I think it would be very nice if it were possible to acquire knowledge of the world in an *a priori* manner. The method of careful observation and experimentation—of observing, and measuring, and trying one hypothesis and then another—is painfully slow and laborious. It would be most pleasant if it were possible just to think and by mere thinking to "see" truths about the world in the way that Rationalist seems to think we can. But we have no right to demand that things be the way we want them to be: we have to take things the way they are. Unfortunately, they are not the way Rationalist says they are, as I shall now attempt to show.

Arithmetical Truths

Let us begin by reconsidering Rationalist's account of arithmetical truths. Such truths have long been the favorite examples to which rationalists have had recourse whenever challenged to defend their position; so, if we are successful in refuting these examples, we may be reasonably confident that those remaining will prove no more difficult. If it can be shown that arithmetical truths are not *a priori* synthetic, then the chief citadel of rationalism will have been destroyed.

It is my belief—and this view is shared by some but not all empiricists—that arithmetical truths are synthetic truths that are known *a posteriori*. I am, therefore, in agreement with Rationalist in affirming that the truths of arithmetic are synthetic truths, but I am disputing his claim that they are known *a priori*.

My reasons for holding that the truths of arithmetic are synthetic truths are substantially the same as those of Rationalist. It seems evident that when we know some arithmetical truth—for example, that $7 + 5 = 12$, or $4 - 2 = 2$, or $6 \times 7 = 42$—we know something about the real world: we know that whenever you add seven things to five things, you will get a combined total of twelve things; that whenever you subtract two things from a group of four things, you will have a remainder of two things; that whenever you combine six groups of seven things each (or seven groups of six things each), you will have a total of forty-two things. It also seems evident to me that, as Rationalist maintains, the notion "twelve" cannot be found by analyzing the subject term, "7 + 5." If I know that $7 + 5 = 12$, as I do, then what I know is a synthetic truth.

The crucial question, then, is *how* do I know this? My answer is that I know it by experience. I did not know this when I was born. I did not learn it in some ecstatic moment of insight, when the eternal truth of this statement suddenly flashed into my mind. I learned it in the way I have learned everything else that I know about the world: by experience, and nothing else. First I learned to count. In so doing, of course, I was simply learning the meanings of the words "one," "two," "three," and so on. Then I began to notice certain relationships—for example, that I had five fingers on each hand, and that five fingers plus five fingers made ten fingers; that I had five toes on each foot, and that five toes plus five toes made ten toes; that if I had one penny, and my father gave me another one, I had two pennies, and so on. Every way I turned, no matter what objects I had to deal with (fingers, toes, pennies, playmates, apples, kittens, everything) certain numerical relationships impressed themselves upon me. My experience, your experience, every man's experience has been thoroughly pervaded by numerical facts since the moment we first began to be aware of the world around us. It is this experience that has given us our knowledge of arithmetical truths.

What makes some people think that there must be something unique and wonderful about arithmetical truths is, I suppose, the remarkable certainty which such truths seem to have. We are, as Rationalist says, sure about these truths in a way that we are not sure about the statement, "All crows are black"—no matter how many crows we may have seen. So much is this the case, that "mathematical certainty" is for most people, as it was for the philosopher Descartes, a model of the highest degree of certainty that it is possible for us to have. How are we to account for this certainty?

The answer, I believe, is very simple: we are supremely sure of the truth of arithmetical truths because of the overwhelming amount of evidence which we have observed in support of these truths. Every day of our lives, in thousands and thousands of different ways, experience has crowded in upon us exhibiting the truths which we express in our arithmetical equations. With all of this evidence, and never a scrap of evidence to the contrary, we at length became convinced: we *know* that $7 + 5 = 12$ (and $4 - 2 = 2$, etc.), and our certainty reflects the unbroken uniformity of our experience.

Why, then, are we less certain about crows—even if we have never seen a crow that was not black? There are, I think, two reasons. The first is that the quantity of experience upon which this inference is based is infinitesimal in comparison with that upon which our inferences regarding the truths of arithmetic are based. Practically everything that we experience exhibits arithmetical truths, whereas it is only on relatively rare occasions that we happen to see crows. Furthermore, experience has taught us that in many species of living things color is a variable characteristic. Perhaps we have seen a black sheep in a flock of white sheep, or an albino mouse, and so we find it easy to conjecture that there might be an exception with respect to color among crows as well. Hence, it is not surprising that we are less than certain that the statement "all crows are black" will stand the test of further experience.

There are other empirical truths, it may be noted, which everyone agrees are known *a posteriori* about which we are much more certain than we are about the color of crows. We know with a high degree of certainty, for example, that at sea-level barometric pressure pure water freezes at a temperature of 32°F. We know this by experience. Many individuals, in many different parts of the world and at many different times, have had an opportunity to observe this phenomenon, and never has a case been reported in which these conditions failed to bring about the stated result. With all of this evidence in support of the statement, and no evidence to the contrary, we make the statement with a high degree of confidence that our experience in the future will conform to what we have observed to be the case in the past.

If we imagine an example in which we have even more supporting evidence than we have regarding the freezing of water, it is not difficult to see that the result would be a kind of knowledge that is so certain that it would be natural to call it an instance of "absolute certainty." This is the case with arithmetical knowledge. The evidence in the case of freezing water is so great that it is virtually inconceivable to us that there should ever occur an exception to it. But the evidence in support of arithmetical truths is greater yet—so great, indeed, that for most of us an exception to one of these truths is totally inconceivable. It is this inconceivability of an exception that we are expressing when we say that we know these truths with absolute certainty.

Geometrical Truths

The account which I should be inclined to give of geometrical truths is identical to that which I have given of arithmetical truths. They are, as Rationalist says, synthetic truths; but like the truths of arithmetic they are known *a posteriori,* not *a priori.*

Consider, for example, the statement, "two straight lines cannot enclose a space." This, presumably, would qualify as one of the truths which Rationalist says we know *a priori.* I shall argue, on the contrary, that we know it *a posteriori.*

In the first place (and I think Rationalist would agree with me) it is clear that we learn the meanings of the words of which this statement is composed by experience. We learned the meaning of the phrase "straight line" in the same way that we learned the meanings of words like "table" and "chair": by hearing the words applied to certain kinds of objects. We learned that matches were "straight," but barrel staves were not; that knitting needles were "straight," but the edge of a dish was not; that a pencil, or the edge of a ruler, was "straight," but a dog's nose, or a cat's ear, was not. This, surely, is how we learn the meaning of words. If we did not have any experience of this kind to tell us the meanings of certain words, those words would be nothing to us but meaningless sounds.

The question, then, is this: once we know the meanings of the words of which the statement in question is composed, how do we come to know that the statement is true? The answer to that question, I am arguing, is that we learn this by experience.

What kind of experience is it, then, that teaches us that two straight lines cannot enclose a space? The question need not puzzle us long: our experience is replete with evidence to support this general truth. We may have seen the roofs of houses, and noticed that the two lines that intersect to form the peak of the roof never (by themselves) enclose a space. We have observed the parallel sides of a road, the parallel tracks of a railroad, the intersecting lines of a leg and rung of a chair, and so on. And never—not once —have we seen an instance when two straight lines have by themselves enclosed a space. We do not, perhaps, consciously formulate the *statement* at first, but the statement is, nonetheless, a true generalization about our experience. When, therefore, we study geometry and we come upon this axiom (as it is called), it may strike us as being "obviously" or "self-evidently" true. Indeed, we may be so impressed with the obviousness of it that we are tempted to say with Plato that it is not really a case of learning at all: it is, rather, a case of "recollecting" an "eternal truth" which has been present within our soul ever since its creation. But is it really surprising, after all, that a truth that has been lavishly exhibited in our experience every day of our life should seem obvious when we see it formally stated for the first time? It does not seem so to me.

What is true of this particular example is equally true of all other geometrical truths—with one proviso. Many of the more complex and unobvious theorems of geometry are not directly exhibited in our experience, but they are deducible from those that are. What I mean is this. If proposition *A* is learned from experience, and proposition *B* is learned from experience, and proposition *C* can be validly deduced from propositions *A* and *B,* then proposition *C* has *ipso facto* been learned from experience as well. The science of geometry is a science wherein the more remote and complex truths of geometry are deduced from those that are simpler and closer at hand; and these latter, as I hope I have now made clear, are gathered from the vast data of our everyday experience.

The certainty of geometrical truths, as of arithmetical truths, rests upon the vast quantity of evidence upon which the foundational truths of the science of geometry are based. It is not necessary, therefore, to repeat what has already been said on this point in connection with arithmetical truths.

Logical Truths

If I have succeeded in showing that the truths of arithmetic and of geometry are *a posteriori* synthetic truths, my readers should have no difficulty in seeing that the truths of logic are of the same sort. Rationalist's example—the statement that anything that has shape has size—is a perfect example of a fact about the world that has been exhibited in our experience so many times that it is now inconceivable that there could ever occur an exception to it. With all this experience upon which to base our statement, what need have we for a special theory about a remarkable human capacity whereby we are supposedly able to "immediately apprehend" this homely, everyday truth?

The sort of logical truth that a man might pardonably suppose to be *a priori* would be one which states some set of circumstances in which a conclusion of some particular sort may be drawn from certain sorts of premises—the statement, for example, that if all *A*'s are *B*'s, and all *B*'s are *C*'s, then all *A*'s are *C*'s. There is, admittedly, a certain self-evidence about such a statement. We certainly cannot imagine the possibility of going wrong in asserting the conclusion if we are granted the premises—no matter what may be the value of *A, B* and *C*.

The explanation of this certainty is, nonetheless, the same as in the previous two cases. When Aristotle set about the task of formulating and systematizing the rules of logic, he did not just sit down and think—or, rather, wait for "direct apprehensions" to occur. Rather, he paid attention to the actual arguments that people used, and he noted the conditions under which arguments succeeded in establishing their conclusions and the conditions under which they did not. The conditions under which they did succeed he called "rules of inference"; the conditions under which they did not succeed he called "logical fallacies." But the data from which he began—and the data on the basis of which other logicians have modified and augmented his work—are the actual arguments, successful or unsuccessful, which people employ. The truths of logic are derived from the data of experience. The certainty of these truths is due to the quantity of the evidence upon which they are based.

Ethical Truths

There remain to be considered, then, only ethical truths, of which the statement "The infliction of needless pain is evil" is offered as an example. How are we, in a way that is consistent with our empiricism, to construe such statements?

There is, I admit, something very odd about ethical statements, and it is, therefore, understandable why Rationalist would appeal to this class of statements in support of his position. I am not sure that I understand just what it is about ethical statements that makes them seem odd, but I am quite sure that it is not the fact that they are, as Rationalist claims, synthetic truths that are known *a priori*.

It is worth noting that we rarely, if ever, know "ethical truths" with the kind of certainty that is supposedly characteristic of *a priori* knowledge. To affirm an ethical statement is, at best, to affirm a belief, a conviction. It is as if one were saying, "I don't know for sure what is right or wrong in this matter (perhaps no one does) but I will take my stand on this, that the infliction of needless pain is evil." What is affirmed as an ethical statement is not something that we know: it is something that we believe, something that we venture. And if it is not known at all, it is obviously not known *a priori*.

There are, it seems to me, two features of ethical statements that might explain their appearance of being so odd. The first is that they are typically affirmed in this venturing, convictional way. An ethical statement is not a report: it is rather a statement recording our intention to act in certain ways and encouraging others to do the same. The second is that such statements, unlike all of the others we have been considering, speak not of what *is* the case but of what *ought to be* the case. It may be this connotation of "oughtness" that makes ethical statements seem so very different from all other statements.

There are, as a matter of fact, numerous ways in which an empiricist can construe ethical utterances without compromising his empiricism. The subject is a very complex one, however, and cannot be discussed in detail at this time (see Part V). For the present, then, we may be content to leave the status of ethical statements an open question. What is fairly clear is that they are not synthetic truths that are known *a priori;* and this, so far as the refutation of rationalism is concerned, is the point of importance.

Study Questions

1. Empiricist has argued that our knowledge of arithmetical truths, like our knowledge about crows, is *a posteriori*. How does he explain the fact that we are much more certain about the one sort of truths than we are about the other? Are you satisfied with his explanation?

2. What evidence does Empiricist offer in support of his claim that geometrical truths are known *a posteriori?* Do you think he is right on this point?

3. Suppose that it is true that Aristotle worked out the "rules of logical inference" in the way that Empiricist says. Is this sufficient to establish that they are truths known *a posteriori?* Could Rationalist allow this account and still claim that they are truths known *a priori?*

4. Is there something odd, or different, about ethical statements, as Empiricist says there is? Does it seem plausible to you that this oddness (if so there be) is due to the fact that ethical truths are synthetic truths known *a priori?* Do you find Empiricist's explanation of this alleged oddness more or less persuasive than Rationalist's?

Chapter 12

ANOTHER ALTERNATIVE
FOR EMPIRICISTS

I HOPE THAT my disagreement
with the colleague who penned the last chapter does not obscure
the fact that on the main issue of the present controversy he and I
are in perfect agreement: all our knowledge of synthetic truths, we
are convinced, arises out of experience. We are, therefore, at one in
our opposition to rationalism, since we cannot allow the claim that
there are some synthetic truths—some truths about the real world
—that are known *a priori*. Whatever we know about the real world,
we have learned from experience—our own and that of others.
And whatever is known apart from experience (*a priori*) is not a
truth about the real world at all but merely an analytic truth.

Granting this common ground of all empiricists, however, and
granting also our common opposition to rationalism, there remains
some disagreement among empiricists as to whether certain classes
of statements are to be construed as analytic *a priori* or as synthetic
a posteriori. My colleague has argued that arithmetical, geometrical, and logical truths are all synthetic *a posteriori*. In my opinion
he is mistaken about this, and I shall attempt to show that, except
for logical truths, they are actually analytic *a priori* truths. I shall
also have something further to say about ethical truths, though not
so much in disagreement with as in addition to what was said at the
conclusion of the last chapter.

Arithmetical Truths

Statements about the real world, or synthetic statements, have one distinguishing feature in common: it is always possible to specify some state of affairs which, if it were the case, would render the statement in question false. The statement, "All crows are black," is rendered false by the supposition that there exists a white crow; hence, it is evident that in this case we have a synthetic statement. This test, carefully applied, should enable us to distinguish without difficulty between synthetic and analytic statements.

Our test, it should be noted, is not an arbitrary one: it is implicit in the very definition of a synthetic statement as a statement about the real world. A synthetic statement asserts that the world is so-and-so: it asserts that something really is the case. Consequently, it must be possible to specify a state of affairs in which this would not be the case—in which, accordingly, our statement would be falsified.

Let us now apply our test to an arithmetical statement. What would have to be the case for the statement "7 + 5 = 12" to be false?

Let us suppose that I put what I believe to be seven objects (oranges, say) into a bag, and then I put in what I believe to be five more. I bring them to the grocery clerk to be priced. He counts them and finds—to my surprise—that the bag contains only eleven oranges. I count them again, he counts them again, and finally I am convinced: there are only eleven oranges in the bag.

Does this state of affairs falsify the statement, "7 + 5 = 12"? Obviously not. We might adopt any one of several explanations of what happened: perhaps I miscounted the first time, or perhaps one of the oranges that I counted did not get into the bag, or perhaps some child removed one of the oranges after I had put it in the bag. But note: we would not think of adopting the explanation that this was a remarkable exception to the statement, "7 + 5 = 12." The state of affairs just described does not falsify our arithmetical statement.

What state of affairs would falsify our statement? None. The only way the statement "7 + 5 = 12" could be rendered false would be to change the meaning of one or more of the symbols of which the statement is composed. If the symbol "7" were defined to mean what is ordinarily meant by the symbol "8," then the statement would, of course, become false. But then you are no longer describing a state of affairs in the real world to which the statement in question refers: you are rather altering the meaning of the statement itself.

The truth about arithmetical statements is this: they are, one and all, analytic truths. What tends to mislead us is the fact that a number has meaning only in the context of the whole number system. The meaning of a number consists, partly, in its relation to every other number in the system. Part of the meaning of the number "7," for example, is that it is one more than "6," and one less than "8," that it is two more than "5" and two less than "9," and so on. Hence, it is a part of the meaning of "7" that it is five less than "12." Consequently, when we affirm that "7 + 5 = 12," we are only stating explicitly some of the meaning relations that obtain in the number system between the numbers 7, 5, and 12. Were this not the case, mathematical reasoning would not have the certainty which it has.

If we look, now, at the reasons which the previous two writers have given for holding that arithmetical truths are synthetic, it is not difficult to see where and why they have gone wrong.

First, they have failed to note that the concept of a number is exceedingly complex, that it involves the relations of that number to every other number in the number system. If one thinks of 7 and 5 as simple concepts—visualizing seven dots and five dots, or some such thing—then it seems very natural to conclude that you cannot get the predicate 12 by analyzing the complex symbol 7 + 5, but only by "performing the prescribed intellectual operation." But as soon as one realizes the complexity of the concept of a number—as soon as one realizes that its meaning includes its relations to the other numbers in the number system—the error becomes apparent.

Second, these writers have been misled by what I shall call the "quasi-empirical" character of arithmetical truths—a character which they share with many analytic truths.

Most analytic truths look, at first glance, as if they were "about the real world"; that is why one cannot decide on the status of a given statement simply on the basis of whether or not it "seems" to be about the real world. The statement, "All bachelors are unmarried," for example, seems to be a statement about real bachelors. It is only when one applies the test—when one tries to specify a state of affairs which, if it were the case, would falsify the statement—that it becomes evident that the statement is not really about bachelors at all, but only about the meaning of the word "bachelor."

So it is with arithmetical truths. They seem, admittedly, to be about the real world—about "apples and oranges and pennies and kittens and anything else that we might have occasion to count and add together," as Rationalist says. But this appearance is deceptive, as we have already shown. When the crucial test of *falsifiability by empirical facts* is applied, it becomes evident that arithmetical statements are purely analytic. No state of affairs can be imagined which, if it were the case, would render an arithmetical truth untrue, for the very good reason that an arithmetical truth is not a statement about the world at all: it is a statement about certain relations that obtain between certain numbers in a number system.

Arithmetical truths are, therefore, analytic, and like all analytic truths their truth is known *a priori* to anyone who understands the meanings of the symbols and is able to grasp the relations among the meanings which the statement in question is affirming. The certainty of such truths is, as Rationalist asserts, due to the fact that they are known *a priori;* but because they are analytic truths our knowledge of them does not constitute an *a priori* knowledge of the real world.

Geometrical Truths

It is not surprising that many philosophers should have believed that the truths of geometry are synthetic truths that are known *a priori*. It seems plausible to hold, as Rationalist does, that geometry is "the science of physical space" and that a geometrical statement, therefore, is a statement about the real world. And if we hold this, and then reflect on the peculiar certainty with which we are able to "demonstrate" the theorems of geometry, it is natural to conclude that geometry consists of a remarkable collection of *a priori* truths about the real world.

It must be said, however, that today there is less reason to draw this conclusion than there was in the time of Plato, or of Descartes, or of Kant. Today we know, as was not known even in Kant's day, that Euclidean geometry is not the only possible geometry and that what can be "demonstrated" in any geometry depends on the definitions with which you begin. You may or may not be able to use a given geometry (Euclidean or any other) to reason about the real world: that is an empirical question that can be decided only by trial and error. What is known, therefore, when one has demonstrated a geometrical theorem, is not anything about the real world at all but only some consequence or other of the definitions from which you began.

Geometrical truths, like arithmetical truths, are analytic *a priori*. Like arithmetical truths, they seem to be about the real world, and like arithmetical truths they can sometimes be used to reason about the real world. But in and of themselves they are not about the real world at all: they are only parts of an arbitrary system of analytic truths, and the whole system is implicit in the definitions with which that geometry begins.

One reason, perhaps, why so many people have been persuaded that the truths of geometry are synthetic rather than analytic is that in studying geometry one has the impression that as each new theorem is demonstrated one is discovering (or "grasping") a new truth. One learns, for example, that a triangle is a closed plane figure having three straight sides, and subsequently one "discovers" a truth that does not seem to be contained in this definition (for example, that its interior angles total 180 degrees). But the truth is that this latter theorem is implicit in the definition of a triangle together with the other definitions (some of which are called axioms) of Euclid's system: if this were not the case, it would not be possible to construct a valid proof of the theorem. Were it not for the fact that our intellect is limited, we would never have the sense of discovery which we sometimes have when we first succeed in proving a complex geometrical theorem: we would immediately see all of the logical consequences of our definitions and would have no need for a formal demonstration. But this human limitation should not be allowed to obscure the fact that geometrical reasoning always begins with definitions gratuitously assumed and concludes with theorems having the same gratuitous character. Geometrical truths, without exception, are analytic.

Logical Truths

I am uncertain as to how much Rationalist intends to include in the class of what he calls "logical truths." It may be that some of the truths he has in mind would require one explanation while others would require somewhat different ones. I shall do my best with the few examples before me, however, and shall add a few remarks (about what *I* should be inclined to call logical truths) that I hope will eliminate any possible misunderstanding on this point.

The example which Rationalist discusses in some detail under this heading (though I would not call it a "logical truth") is the statement, "Anything that has shape has size." To me this is rather obviously an analytic statement. The concept of a "thing"—or of an "object," as Rationalist says later—includes both the idea of having some shape and having some size. Shape and size are, indeed, diverse characteristics, but both are implicit in the idea of a spatial object—which is what Rationalist has in mind. Fully stated, Rationalist's statement should read, "Anything that occupies space has both shape and size." Rationalist has been misled by the elliptical character of his own statement.

There are, however, two sub-classes of statements which I should be inclined to call "logical truths," the status of which is very puzzling, and which I suspect that Rationalist also has in mind. These are (a) the so-called laws of thought and (b) rules of inference. Examples of the former are the Principle of Identity (if p, then p), the Principle of the Excluded Middle (p or not p), and the Principle of Noncontradiction (not both p and not p). Examples of the latter are: "If all A is B, and all B is C, then all A is C," and "If p implies q, and q is not the case, then p is not the case." I think that Rationalist would have been on more persuasive ground if he had drawn his examples of logical truths from these two classes. Regardless, it is these two sorts of logical truths that I find most threatening to empiricism, and I want to show what sort of an account an empiricist might give of these very troublesome statements.

The laws of thought are what I should be inclined to call linguistic conventions: they play the same role in language that rules play in a game. One of the rules of any language game is that every simple proposition is either true or false. Another rule is that if a proposition is true, then it is not false; and if it is false, then it is not true. Still another rule is that if a proposition is true, then it is true. These, it will be recognized, are respectively the aforementioned Principle of the Excluded Middle, the Principle of Noncontradiction, and the Principle of Identity. As linguistic conventions they are neither analytic nor synthetic, since they are not statements at all: they are rather rules that one must follow if one is to use language intelligibly.

Much the same kind of account should be given of rules of inference. It has been argued that rules of inference are empirical generalizations based upon analyses of the actual arguments, successful or unsuccessful, which people employ in the attempt to establish their conclusions on the basis of certain sorts of premises. This position contains some truth, but on the fundamental question of the logical status of the rules of inference I think it is incorrect. It rightly asserts that these rules were determined by Aristotle and others through a process of inductive reasoning. But what Aristotle discovered in this way was not truths about the real world (in any significant meaning of that phrase), but rather the rules by which, in our language, one can reason successfully from premises to conclusions. Aristotle might be compared to a man who, never having read or heard anything about the rules of baseball, figured out the rules for himself by watching how the game was actually played. Such an observer would, quite obviously, employ inductive reasoning; but what he would discover in this way would not be a group of synthetic truths, but rather a system of rules prescribing what players may and may not do in the game of baseball. Just so with the rules of inference. They are not synthetic truths, since they are not truths at all: they are rules governing logical inferences in our language. To know these rules is not to know some truths about the real world: it is to know how to speak intelligibly within the context of the remarkable game that is human discourse.

Ethical Truths

I have already indicated that I am quite in agreement with the remarks about ethical truths made by my colleague at the end of the last chapter, and I have no wish to discuss at this time the many ways in which an empiricist might handle such utterances. I would like, however, to make just one suggestion as a kind of footnote to those remarks, and then I shall conclude.

We found, in the case of what are commonly called "logical truths," that properly speaking they are not "truths" at all, but simply rules, linguistic conventions, governing the use of language. Once this was recognized, the question as to whether they are synthetic or analytic disappeared: since they are not truths at all, they are neither synthetic nor analytic. Perhaps an analogous account could also be given of ethical truths. Perhaps they are not "truths" at all, and hence neither analytic nor synthetic. What, then, are they? I shall mention three possibilities. They could be (a) statements of intention, or (b) veiled commands, or (c) expressions of feeling. The question as to the logical status of so-called "ethical truths" is still a very controversial one, and I do not wish to commit myself to any one of these options or to attempt a defense of it. I do wish to suggest, however, that it is possible that "ethical truths" are not truths at all, but rather linguistic expressions of a quite different logical type. In view of this it seems extremely hazardous to rest any part of the case for rationalism on an appeal to examples drawn from this source.

Study Questions

1. At what point or points does the author of this chapter (Empiricist *B*) claim to be in agreement with the author of the previous chapter (Empiricist *A*), and at what point or points does he claim to be in disagreement? Would it be inconsistent for someone to agree with Empiricist *A*'s account of some of Rationalist's examples and Empiricist *B*'s account of others?
2. What is the "falsifiability test" which Empiricist *B* proposes as a

method for distinguishing between analytic and synthetic truths? Does this seem to you to be a valid test? What use does Empiricist *B* make of this test in his subsequent discussion?

3. What account does Empiricist *B* give of the "laws of thought" and the "rules of inference"? Do you think he is right? In your judgment, would it be plausible for Rationalist to argue that these are examples of synthetic truths that are known *a priori?*

4. What do you think of the suggestion that what Rationalist calls "ethical truths" are not "truths" at all? Is Empiricist *B* right in saying that if this is the case, it is not proper to ask whether they are analytic or synthetic? Why?

Chapter 13

A RATIONALIST REPLY

I SUPPOSE IT WOULD be excessively unkind to whisper the suggestion that our two empiricist friends, in their respective efforts to defend an embattled empiricism, have rather effectively canceled each other out. Empiricist *A* has allowed that most of what I have offered as examples of synthetic *a priori* truths (all except ethical truths) are indeed synthetic, and he has attempted to show that the certainty with which we hold these truths to be true is due to the vast amount of experience upon which they are based. Empiricist *B* has recognized that this attempt is a failure, and he has tried the other alternative of interpreting these statements as analytic *a priori*. I cannot resist the temptation to play the role of peacemaker in the present dispute. I think each of our empiricist friends is half right: Empiricist *A* is right in holding that the truths in question are synthetic and Empiricist *B* is right in holding that they are *a priori*. It is scarcely necessary to point out that this also means that each is also half wrong.

There would be little point in rehashing all of the arguments in support of the view that arithmetical, geometrical, logical, and ethical truths are all synthetic *a priori*. I have already stated what I consider to be the most convincing reasons for so regarding them, and I have little to add by way of augmenting what I consider to be a strong positive case. Our empiricist friends have raised a number of interesting points, however, and since I have been given the last word, I should like to use the opportunity to defend my position against the criticisms which have been stated.

The Status of the Argument

Perhaps we should begin by stating once again, however, the status of the argument. There is always some danger, when arguments become numerous, that the main point at issue will become obscured, and should this happen, the whole point of the discussion would be lost.

The question at issue, then, is: Do we or do we not have any *a priori* knowledge of synthetic truths? I have argued that we do and have offered four classes of examples in support of my view. Our two empiricists have argued that we do not and have attempted to show that my several examples can all be interpreted in some other way.

Some readers may have come to the conclusion that my account of ethical truths, for example, is not correct. What effect would this have on the argument? Simply this: it would remove one group of examples of synthetic *a priori* truths, leaving the others intact. But note: it would still be the case, then, that we have some *a priori* knowledge of synthetic truths, and my basic position would remain unscathed. *Only if every plausible example of synthetic truths that are known* a priori *has been shown to have some other status, has rationalism been shown to be mistaken.*

I do not mean, in what I have just said, to withdraw my claim that ethical truths are in fact synthetic truths that are known *a priori*. I will stand by all the examples which I offered earlier. My point is simply that if someone were to disagree with me about the correct interpretation of some of my examples, while agreeing with me with respect to others, he would still be on my side insofar as the fundamental issue in the rationalist-empiricist controversy is concerned. Rationalists have some differences, too—but it only takes a single example of an *a priori* synthetic truth to clinch the case for rationalism.

I turn now to a consideration of some of the points raised by my opponents.

Necessary Truths and Empirical Generalizations

Empiricist *A* has argued that arithmetical, geometrical, and logical truths are synthetic *a posteriori,* and he has attempted to account for the certainty with which we hold these truths to be true by saying that they are based on a very large quantity of experiential data. I think he is mistaken on this point, and I want to present one final argument in support of this opinion.

An empirical generalization is only as strong as the evidence on which it rests. If a generalization is based on scanty evidence, we are very uncertain about its truth. If it is based on quite a bit of evidence, we are more certain of its truth. And when the evidence from which our generalization is drawn is extremely voluminous, so that we have good reason to believe that if there were ever an exception to the statement it would in all likelihood have been observed, our confidence in the truth of the generalization may reach a very high degree of certainty. When we are dealing with empirical generalizations, there is a perfect parallel between (a) the quantity of evidence upon which the generalization is based and (b) the degree of certainty with which it is held to be true.

But surely it is evident that the certainty with which we hold arithmetical, geometrical, and logical truths to be true is out of all proportion to the quantity of "evidence" upon which, if they were empirical generalizations, they would have to be based. There are, admittedly, some simple truths of this sort—such as simple combinations of numbers up to ten or so, and simple geometrical axioms such as the one about the impossibility of two straight lines enclosing a space—that are frequently exhibited in our experience, and of which we may therefore be presented with confirming evidence almost every day of our lives. But consider for a moment some more complex examples. How many times in your life have you multiplied 762 by 316? Perhaps never. Yet you know, *with absolute certainty,* once you work the problem, what the answer is. How many triangles have you measured to find the sum of the interior angles? How many triangles have you inscribed in a semi-circle? Yet you know, once you have understood the proof of the relevant theorems, that the interior angles of a Euclidean triangle (i. e., any figure that fits Euclid's definition of a triangle) total 180 degrees, and that any triangle inscribed within a semi-circle must be a right triangle.

There are, on the other hand, many truths that are really empirical generalizations, and for which there is a great deal of supporting evidence, to which we can readily conceive exceptions—though we may never in fact encounter an exception. I can readily imagine, for example, that on some occasion pure water at sea-level barometric pressure might fail to crystallize at 32°F. as the law says it will. I am highly confident that this will not happen, but I do not have the absolute certainty that I have about *a priori* truths: the most that I can have with even the best-documented empirical generalization is a very high degree of probability. If, then, I encounter a truth which I see to be necessarily true, and which I therefore know to be true with absolute certainty, I know that what I have before me is an *a priori* truth. And if, in addition, this truth is a truth about the real world, so that in knowing it I know not just the meanings of certain terms but something about reality, then I know that I have to do with a synthetic *a priori* truth. Let anyone who remains in doubt on this point compare any one of the examples I have given with the best-documented empirical generalization that he can think of, and I am confident that he will not fail to see the difference. There is much, very much, that we know by observation and experimentation; but what we know in this way we do not know with the absolute certainty that is the hallmark of *a priori* knowledge.

The Falsifiability Test

Empiricist *B* has recognized that the truths of which we have been speaking cannot be accounted for in the way that Empiricist *A* attempts to account for them, and he accordingly tries to account for them in yet another way. Contrary to what may seem to be the case, he argues, arithmetical and geometrical truths are not synthetic truths at all: they are analytic. And the proof of this, he goes on to say, is that it is not possible to describe a state of affairs which, if it were the case, would render one of these statements false. This "falsifiability test," as he calls it, is the big weapon in his attack on synthetic *a priori* truths, and we will do well to inspect it closely to see just how lethal it really is.

Although I would not go so far as to deny that the falsifiability test may be of some occasional value in helping us decide whether a given statement is analytic or synthetic, it is not the infallible test that Empiricist *B* thinks it is. The reason is that a *logically impossible* state of affairs cannot be consistently described. If, therefore, we find ourselves unable in some instance or other to describe a state of affairs which, if it were the case, would falsify the statement in question, there are two possibilities: the statement may be, as Empiricist *B* says it must be, an analytic statement, or it may be a synthetic truth to which there are no logically possible alternatives.

Consider once again, for example, the statement "Anything that has shape has size." I freely grant that neither I nor anyone else can imagine or describe a state of affairs which, if it were the case, would falsify this statement. (I can, of course, construct a sentence that appears to contradict the statement. I can say "Some things that have shape do not have size"—but Empiricist *B* and I both know that in saying this I would not be describing a possible state of affairs.) The reason that I cannot describe a state of affairs which, if true, would falsify the statement in question is not that my statement is analytic, but rather that there is no logically possible alternative to the synthetic truth which it expresses. We can see that although size and shape are different characteristics of spatial objects, they are, nonetheless, related in such a way that where one is present the other must be also.

Even if the falsifiability test were taken at face value, however, it would not do the job that Empiricist *B* wants it to do. I noted with great interest that he himself, as a matter of fact, did not make use of the test in his discussion of geometrical truths. And with good reason: even by this measure geometrical truths turn out to be synthetic truths. For it is not at all difficult to describe a state of affairs which, if true, would falsify almost any geometrical theorem one can think of. It is perfectly conceivable that the interior angles of a Euclidean triangle, for example, might have totaled 160 or 190 degrees instead of 180, or that a triangle inscribed on the base of a semi-circle might always have had one obtuse angle instead of one

90-degree angle. It just happens to be the case that Euclid's theorems with respect to these matters are true, and if we have studied a little geometry we know that they are true. But to know that they are true is not, in this case, to render the alternatives inconceivable.

Thirdly, even the one application that Empiricist *B* does make of the falsifiability test—namely, to arithmetical truths—is not very convincing. Certainly we would not, in the example of the oranges, adopt the explanation that the reason we only had eleven oranges in the bag was that we had here a remarkable exception to the general rule that $7 + 5 = 12$. But surely the reason we would not adopt this explanation is that we know *a priori* that $7 + 5 = 12$. Because we know this, and know it with absolute certainty, we quite naturally seek some other explanation for the fact that the bag does not contain as many oranges as we expected it to; for to know something *a priori* is to know also that experience must conform to what is thus known.

Let us suppose, however, that (in spite of his unfortunate reliance on what has turned out to be a faulty weapon) Empiricist *B* were right in his interpretation of mathematical truths. What would be the consequences?

In the first place, it would remain a gigantic puzzle that we are able to use arithmetical and geometrical reasoning to draw conclusions about the world at all. It is a remarkable fact that we are able to calculate all sorts of things—budget deficits and satellite orbits and a million other things—by applying the appropriate mathematical formulae to the data with which we begin. But remarkable though this is, it is, nonetheless, a fact. On Empiricist *B*'s account, however, this fact is not only remarkable: it is inexplicable. For on his account mathematical truths are not truths about the world at all: they are purely vacuous statements that do nothing more than to make explicit some of the meaning relations which have, apparently quite arbitrarily, been assigned to the various symbols in our number system. It is difficult to take seriously a theory which forces one to the conclusion that the applicability of mathematical reasoning to the real world is nothing but a happy coincidence.

In the second place, if the applicability of mathematical reasoning to the real world were, as Empiricist *B* holds, a matter of simply "trying it out to see if it works," then we ought to be in doubt about whether it will work when it is applied to phenomena with which we have had no previous experience. We should then entertain some doubt, for example, whether the arithmetical and geometrical truths with which we are familiar on earth will hold on the moon or on Mars. But we do not in fact entertain any such doubts, and the reason we do not is that we know that the truths that we express in our equations are necessarily and universally true.

Logical Truths

I am delighted that Empiricist *B* has seen fit to bring up the matter of the status of the so-called laws of thought and rules of inference because they do indeed constitute, as he suggests, some of the most convincing examples in support of my position.

I do hold, as my opponent correctly supposes, that both the laws of thought and the rules of inference are synthetic *a priori* truths. My second and third examples of logical truths were, as a matter of fact, slightly different versions of, respectively, the principle of non-contradiction and one of the rules of inference.

It seems to me that whatever plausibility my opponent's account of these truths has depends on the unargued assumption that speaking a language is very much like playing a game, and that the rules governing the use of language are, like the rules a game, altogether a matter of convention. This is hardly the place to enter into a full-length discussion of the question concerning the relation of language to reality (see Part I), but we should be aware of the fact that the account of logical truths with which we are now dealing presupposes a view regarding the status of language which is extremely implausible.

My own view—and I only have space to state it and hope that my readers will be able to see for themselves that it is correct—is that language has evolved out of the encounter of the human mind with reality and that it therefore incorporates a certain logical structure that corresponds to the structure of reality. Persons familiar with the problem will recognize this as a very brief summary of what is sometimes called the "modified essentialist" theory of language. The laws of thought and rules of inference, in this view, are not at all a matter of convention: they are grounded in the very structure of reality—are, in fact, universal and synthetic truths about reality—and they may be ignored not simply at the cost of speaking unintelligibly, but of speaking falsely. If I or someone else should attempt to ignore the principle of non-contradiction— should say, that is, that some simple propositions are both true and false—we would not be guilty of breaking one of the rules that people happen to have adopted in order to play the language game: we would be guilty of uttering a statement that is not true. A proposition cannot be both true and false at the same time, and the reason for this is that a given state of affairs cannot both be the case and not be the case at one and the same time. It is reality, not merely conventional rules, that determines the truth or falsity of what we say; a so-called language that did not mirror the structure of reality in its own logical structure would be no language at all.

A Word About Ethics

Perhaps it was unwise to bring ethical truths into the present discussion since it might have been anticipated that it would only lead to confusion. So much has been written of late on the status of these truths, and so many theories have been propounded, that one hesitates even to mention the matter for fear that one will be compelled to defend one's position against a vast number of opposing theories and so be diverted from the task at hand.

It is interesting to note, however, that this question did not become a matter of serious controversy until early in the present century when British and American philosophers began to rally in large numbers around the banner of empiricism. This strongly suggests a fact that is evident to anyone who is acquainted with the recent literature on this matter: the question of what to do with ethical truths is and remains one of the thorniest problems for an empiricist to handle. If there are, as Empiricist *A* has said, "a number of ways in which an empiricist can construe ethical utterances without compromising his empiricism," it is not because these various ways are all so plausible, but rather because no one of them is sufficiently plausible to win a majority of adherents. But this is a matter that is to be discussed more fully later on (see Part V), and we must, therefore, leave it for now.

My position, in any case, remains unchanged and, for that matter, virtually unchallenged by the few remarks which my opponents have made on the subject of ethical truths. If anyone is absolutely determined to be an empiricist, I have no doubt that he will be able to find among the many empiricist accounts of ethical truths one that is to his liking. If, however, I have succeeded in persuading some of my readers that we do in fact have some *a priori* knowledge of synthetic truths, I think they will have little difficulty in agreeing that ethical truths are among those which are known in this way.

Study Questions

1. Is Rationalist right in saying that "it only takes a single example of an *a priori* synthetic truth to clinch the case for Rationalism?" Explain.
2. Is Rationalist right in saying that (a) our certainty of the truth of an empirical generalization varies according to the amount of evidence on which it rests and (b) the certainty with which we hold arithmetical, geometrical, and logical truths to be true is out of all proportion to the quantity of "evidence" upon which, if they were empirical generalizations, they would be based? If so, how does this affect Empiricist *A*'s position? Empiricist *B*'s?
3. What considerations does Rationalist bring forward in his attempt to show that the falsifiability test is not capable of doing the job that Empiricist *B* wants it to do? How might Empiricist *B* answer Rationalist on this point?
4. State briefly Rationalist's attempted *reductio ad absurdum* of Empiricist *B*'s account of mathematical truths. Does it succeed? Explain.
5. Which of the following statements would you be inclined to defend:
   a. Rationalism presupposes a modified essentialist theory of language.
   b. Rationalism is more plausible on an essentialist theory of language than it is on the conventionalist theory.
   c. The rationalist-empiricist controversy has nothing to do with the essentialist-conventionalist controversy.

   Give reasons in support of your answer.

FOR FURTHER READING

Blanshard, Brand, *The Nature of Thought*. New York: Humanities Press, 1939. Vol. 1, Chapters 28-30.

——, *Reason and Analysis*. La Salle, Ill.: Open Court, 1962. Chapters 6 and 10.

Cassirer, Ernst, *The Problem of Knowledge*, trans. W. H. Woglom and C. W. Hendel. New Haven, Conn.: Yale University Press, 1950. Chapters 1-4.

Kant, Immanuel, *Critique of Pure Reason*, trans. Norman Kemp Smith. New York: St. Martin's Press, 1965 (paperbound). Introduction, Sections 1-5.

Leibniz, G. W., *New Essays Concerning Human Understanding*. Many editions. See especially Book I and Book IV, Chapters 1-9.

Lewis, C. I., *An Analysis of Knowledge and Valuation*. La Salle, Ill.: Open Court, 1947. Chapters 1-6.

——, *Mind and the World Order*. New York: Charles Scribner's Sons, 1929. Chapters 7-9.

Locke, John, *An Essay Concerning Human Understanding*. Many editions. See especially Book I and Book IV, Chapters 1-9.

Pap, Arthur, "Are All Necessary Propositions Analytic?" *The Philosophical Review*, Vol. 58 (1949), 299-320.

Plato, *Meno*. Many editions.

Quine, W. van Orman, *From a Logical Point of View*, 2nd. ed., rev. New York: Harper & Row, 1961 (paperbound). See especially "Two Dogmas of Empiricism."

Reichenbach, Hans, *The Rise of Scientific Philosophy*. Berkeley and Los Angeles, Calif.: University of California Press, 1958 (paperbound).

Russell, Bertrand, *Introduction to Mathematical Philosophy*. New York: Humanities Press, 1960. Chapters 1, 2, 13, and 14.

Ryle, G., K. Popper, and C. Lewy, "Why are the Calculuses of Logic and Mathematics Applicable to Reality?" *Proceedings of the Aristotelian Society*, Supplementary Vol. 20 (1946), 20-60.

PART III

The Problem of Induction

Chapter 14

THE LEGACY OF HUME

FORTUNATELY, IT IS not necessary to commit oneself once and for all on the question upon which rationalists and empiricists are at such loggerheads before moving on to a consideration of other problems. Philosophical problems are interrelated, but the interrelationship is such that one can begin with a consideration of almost any problem one chooses without being unduly concerned about whether or not it is the correct starting point. However, there are some valid pedagogical reasons for first considering certain problems connected with language and knowledge—what might be called meta-linguistic and epistemological problems—since, as will shortly become evident, the consideration of so many other philosophical problems again and again forces a reconsideration of these. But it is no sin to suspend judgment as long as one is unconvinced, and the student who finds himself half persuaded by both the rationalist and the empiricist positions will find himself just as well prepared for what follows as the student who is already prepared to declare himself a convinced advocate of one or the other.

Rationalists and empiricists agree, as we have seen, that there is a great deal of *a posteriori* knowledge of synthetic truths. It is obvious to everyone concerned that it is in this way, for example, that we know a great many particular facts—such as the color of the house in which we live, and the name of the street on which our house is located, and so on. (Note that these are particular facts, not general truths: I know the color of my house and you know the color of your house, but neither of us knows from this anything about the color of houses in general. A particular fact has to do with some particular state of affairs that obtains in some particular place at some particular time. Such particular states of affairs, we are saying, are known *a posteriori*.) It is evidently in this way that we also come to know a great many general empirical truths. Some of these are common everyday truths that any normal person assents to without question—for example, that fire burns, water wets, and ice is cold. Others, like the generalizations at which scientists arrive after conducting elaborate experiments, are much more abstruse and unordinary.

The process by which we proceed in our thinking from the particular facts of our experience to the general truths which seem to be exhibited in experience is called *induction*. How did we come to know the general truth that fire is hot? Presumably, somewhat like this: we tried putting our hand near a fire and discovered to our pain that it was hot. We then knew the particular truth that *that* fire was hot. Then, on some other occasion, we again tried putting our hand near another fire and discovered that it, too, was hot. How many experiments it took to persuade us of the general truth that all fire is hot depended, one supposes, on how clever (or otherwise) we were and, perhaps, on how hot the fires were upon which we conducted our experiments. But we did, in any case, come to know this general truth; and the process by which we concluded from the painful facts of our experience to the general conclusion is what is called induction. A general truth that is arrived at in this way is called an *empirical generalization.* This seems simple enough, and for a long time it never occurred to anyone that the phenomenon of inductive reasoning presented any special problems of a philosophical nature. Then came David Hume.

Hume's Question

The question which Hume raised concerning induction was: "What is the nature of that evidence which assures us of any real existence and matter of fact beyond the present testimony of our senses or the records of our memory?" [1] What, in other words, is our warrant for affirming a general empirical truth on the basis of our knowledge of some few particular facts? By what logical right do we claim to know that some empirical generalizations are true?

It is evident, Hume argued, that we do not know *a priori* what properties belong to this or that object which comes within the range of our experience:

> Adam, though his rational faculties be supposed, at the very first, entirely perfect, could not have inferred from the fluidity and transparency of water that it would suffocate him, or from the light and warmth of fire that it would consume him. No object ever discovers, by the qualities which appear to the senses, either the causes which produced it or the effects which will arise from it; nor can our reason, unassisted by experience, ever draw any inference concerning real existence and matter of fact. [2]

It must be, then, by experience that we know these things. But what, asked Hume, are we warranted in asserting on the basis of experience? Only that *in the past,* or *in all cases thus far observed,* such and such has been the case. Hume asserted:

> These two propositions are far from being the same: *I have found that such an object has always been attended with such an effect,* and *I foresee that other objects which are in appearance similar will be attended with similar effects.* I shall allow, if you please, that the one proposition may justly be inferred. But if you insist that the inference is made by a chain of reasoning, I desire you to produce that reasoning. [3]

Hume was convinced that no acceptable answer to his question was possible. He accordingly adopted the position that induction is not logically warranted, for every inductive generalization presupposes a proposition that can never be proved—namely that the fu-

---

[1] David Hume, *An Inquiry Concerning Human Understanding,* Charles W. Hendel, ed. (New York: Liberal Arts Press, 1955), p. 41.

[2] *Ibid.,* p. 42.

[3] *Ibid.,* p. 48.

ture will resemble the past and that "similar powers will be conjoined with similar sensible qualities." "If there be any suspicion that the course of nature may change," he concluded, "and that the past may be no rule for the future, all experience becomes useless and can give rise to no inference or conclusion." [4] No doubt we cannot avoid, as a matter of habit, drawing inferences of this kind and planning our affairs as if these inferences were trustworthy; but such inferences, Hume was convinced, have no satisfactory logical warrant.

A Restatement of Hume's Question

In the light of the subsequent discussion of the problem which Hume so effectively raised, it is desirable to restate that problem in a somewhat different form. It is evident that two separate but closely related questions are involved. The first question might be stated thus: Is induction a valid logical procedure? Have we any logical right to draw general conclusions on the basis of our limited observation of some particular facts? And the second question is: If induction is a valid logical procedure, does its validity rest on any *a priori* principles? Thus amplified, our question becomes: *Is induction a valid logical procedure, and if so, does it involve any a priori principles?*

Before turning to a preliminary characterization of the alternative positions which it is possible to take with respect to this question, let us look briefly at two "common-sense" reactions to Hume's puzzle. Both of these, it will be seen, reveal a failure to grasp the point of Hume's question.

A common reaction of people who encounter the problem for the first time goes something like this: Everybody knows that inductive reasoning is warranted, and this is evident from the fact that everybody does it—including philosophers who ask sophistical questions. As a matter of fact, it would not be possible to perform any of the normal activities of life if we could not assume that the empirical generalizations drawn from our past experiences are well founded and, indeed, true. It is only in this way that we know such

---

[4] *Ibid.*, p. 51.

essential everyday truths as that bread nourishes, water quenches thirst, and so on. If we could not depend on these, all activity and all life would have to cease.

This objection, which is a very natural one, misses the point of Hume's question. As a practical matter, Hume was well aware that we all do and indeed must make inductive inferences. "As an agent," Hume said explicitly, "I am quite satisfied in the point; but as a philosopher who has some share of curiosity, I will not say skepticism, I want to learn the *foundation* of this inference." [5] After it has been acknowledged that all men do in fact employ inductive reasoning, and live their lives on the assumption that the empirical generalizations thus established are well founded, the question still remains: By what logical right, if any, do we make such inferences? It was his inability to find an answer to this question that drove Hume to the conclusion that inductive reasoning has no logical warrant at all.

It is also suggested that Hume's problem disappears if one bears in mind that all one has a right to ask of an empirical generalization is that it be more or less *probable*. Hume's error, it is sometimes said, consists in his failure to recognize the difference between deductive and inductive reasoning. Deductive reasoning leads to conclusions that are as certain as the premises: in a valid deductive argument, if the premises are true the conclusion must be true. But with inductive arguments, this is not the case. However many instances of a given phenomenon are observed, it is only more or less probable that the uniformities that one has observed hold for all phenomena of that type. Once this is recognized, it is suggested, Hume's problem disappears.

Unfortunately, Hume's problem cannot be wished away in this facile manner. Hume was well aware of the fact that empirical generalizations are not certain, since, as he pointed out, "the contrary of every matter of fact is still possible." [6] Hume's point was not the truism that inductive reasoning does not establish its conclusions with the certainty and the necessity that deductive reasoning does. His point is the far more radical one that *what we call inductive reasoning is not reasoning at all*, that we have no logical right to

---

[5] *Ibid.*, p. 52.
[6] *Ibid.*, p. 40.

affirm on the basis of our past experience that it is even *probable* that such-and-such will be the case in the future. No doubt the most that anyone could ask would be that inductive reasoning be allowed to establish its conclusions with varying degrees of probability. The effect of Hume's question is to raise serious doubt as to whether even this much can be allowed.

Alternatives to Skepticism

Hume's own position with respect to this question is commonly referred to as *inductive skepticism*. It consists in affirming that induction is not a valid logical procedure—that, as Hume said, "even after we have experience of the operations of cause and effect, our conclusions from that experience are *not* founded on reasoning or any process of the understanding." [7] Our propensity to believe that the future will be more or less like the past, and that what has been observed to be the case in the past is therefore a reliable guide to the future, is nothing more than an interesting psychological fact about ourselves. Induction itself—as a logical procedure, as a species of reasoning—remains unwarranted and unjustified.

Many philosophers, though they have acknowledged the legitimacy and the importance of Hume's question, have been unwilling to accept Hume's negative and skeptical answer to that question. They have held, on the contrary, that induction is a valid logical procedure, and they have attempted in various ways to show how inductive inferences are warranted. Most of these attempts may be divided into two general classes, which we shall call *constructive empiricism* and *rationalism*.

Constructive empiricism consists in the assertion that (a) induction is a valid logical procedure and (b) its validity does not depend on an appeal to any *a priori* truths. The first proposition distinguishes this position from that of the inductive skeptic; the second distinguishes it from that of the rationalist. Any empiricist who wishes to maintain the logical validity of inductive reasoning must be prepared to defend both. Chapter 15 represents one such attempt to answer Hume's question along these lines.

---

[7] *Ibid.*, p. 47.

The rationalist's solution to the problem, as has already been intimated, consists in affirming that (a) induction is a valid logical procedure but (b) its validity depends on an appeal to some truth that is known *a priori*. The embarrassment of empiricism with respect to the problem of induction, in the view of many rationalists, is only one more proof of the inadequacy of the empiricist epistemology. If even general empirical truths cannot be established in a way that is consistent with empiricism, they argue, then it is quite clear that empiricism leaves much to be desired. This view is developed in some detail in Chapter 16.

It should be noted that it is not absolutely incumbent on a rationalist to adopt the "rationalist" solution to the problem of induction. A man might be a skeptic with respect to the problem of induction, therefore, and still be a rationalist by virtue of the fact that he held that there are some other synthetic truths that we know *a priori*. Thus one could conceivably be a rationalist without accepting the "rationalist" position on this point; but if one does accept the rationalist position on this point, one is *eo ipso* a rationalist, no matter what other views one might hold.

If we take Hume's problem at face value, these three positions—inductive skepticism, constructive empiricism, and rationalism—are the only positions that one can take with respect to it. A number of philosophers, however, have found themselves unconvinced by the attempts of both rationalists and empiricists to solve Hume's problem on its own terms, and yet they have been unwilling to draw Hume's skeptical conclusion with respect to our supposed knowledge of general empirical truths. Various attempts have been made, therefore, to discover in the problem as Hume stated it, and as it has been discussed since, some incorrect assumption in the absence of which it would be evident that the problem is not as serious as it appears to be. These attempts to solve the problem by dissolving it have taken a variety of forms. Two such attempts will be discussed in the chapters that follow.

One attempt, which for historical reasons has commended itself to a number of American philosophers, is represented by pragmatism. What is wrong with the traditional problem, according to the pragmatist, is the view concerning the nature of truth which it presupposes. How the pragmatist theory of truth is supposed to be of assistance in solving the problem of induction is explained in Chapter 17.

Another way of attempting to lay this old problem to rest has long been advocated by the distinguished contemporary philosopher, Karl Popper. Popper's position, as we shall see, involves two main parts: (a) an acceptance of Hume's refutation of induction, together with (b) a denial that this has any serious consequence so far as our knowledge of empirical truths is concerned. This position is advocated in Chapter 18 from the point of view of one who holds, with Popper, that once the status of scientific knowledge is understood the traditional problem of induction will no longer be felt to be a problem.

A student who is considering the problem of induction for the first time would be well advised, however, to approach it with the supposition that it is a genuine and important problem to which skepticism, rationalism, and constructive empiricism are the only available solutions. In this way he will be in a position to judge whether the other two attempts which are to be discussed are as successful as they claim to be in solving the problem by, so to speak, circumventing it.

Study Questions

1. What, precisely, is the difference between a particular empirical fact and a general empirical truth? Give several examples of each.
2. What exactly is the problem of induction? Test your understanding of it by attempting to restate the problem in several different ways.
3. How do the two "common-sense" reactions mentioned in this chapter miss the point of Hume's question? Do they attribute to Hume some assumption which he did not make, or do they address themselves to some question other than the one Hume was asking?
4. Give two or three examples of inductive arguments which you yourself have used, or have heard used by someone else. Does it seem to you that the premises (in your examples) provide some warrant for affirming the conclusion? If so, how? Are you or are you not making some *a priori* assumption?

Chapter 15

EMPIRICISM AND THE PROBLEM
OF INDUCTION

HUME DID NO great favor to science, empiricism, or common sense in raising the problem of induction. For both science and common sense are outraged at the thought that the generalizations affirmed on the basis of observation should have, as Hume said, no logical foundation; and it *is* a problem that is not congenial to empiricism. Yet it is unthinkable that we should resort to *ad hoc* theories of *a priori* knowledge in order to account for such a homely thing as the belief that the sun will rise tomorrow. Hence, we may be sure that if the matter is considered in the proper perspective, it will become clear that the problem of induction is not the stumbling stone for empiricism that it is sometimes believed to be.

I think we should be aware, particularly in view of the suggestions that have been made from time to time, that this is no mere pseudo-problem, and that a number of disastrous consequences would follow if it should be concluded that induction is not, after all, a valid logical procedure. It would be profitable to begin our consideration of the problem, therefore, by considering some of the consequences that we would be compelled to accept if, with Hume, we were to come to a skeptical conclusion.

Consequences of Inductive Skepticism

It should be apparent, in the first place, that our knowledge of many everyday empirical truths rests on a basis of inductive inference. We know, for example, that unsupported bodies fall toward the earth, that air-breathing animals cannot long survive under water, that bread nourishes, and water quenches thirst, and so on. If inductive reasoning is not well founded, we have no logical basis, no rational foundation, for believing these things. Then, so far as the logic of the matter is concerned, we might with as much justification hold the contrary—that unsupported bodies (evidence to the contrary notwithstanding) sometimes fly upward, that some air-breathing animals may flourish under water, that bread and water may injure rather than nourish a hungry and thirsty man. To conclude thusly, it seems clear, is repugnant to our sense of what is reasonable.

In the same way many of our particular expectations with respect to the immediate future would turn out to be rationally indefensible if induction is overthrown, for these are but particular instances of, or particular deductions from, those general truths. I believe that the dinner I shall eat tonight will nourish my body, not poison it. Why? Because I believe in the truth of the general proposition that food nourishes. I believe that if I were to leave my third-floor office by way of the window rather than by way of the elevator or the stairs I would be, at the very least, severely injured. Why? Because I believe in the truth of such general propositions as these, that unsupported bodies fall toward the earth at an accelerating rate of speed and a fall of three stories is extremely likely to be seriously injurious to the human body. Yet, if induction is not a valid logical procedure, I should have no rational basis for these expectations.

What is even more incredible, however, is that the whole enterprise that we call natural science would be without a logical foundation if induction is not defended. All of the reasoning of the scientists, then, from Galileo and Newton and Kepler to Einstein and Heisenberg and Bohr would have to be regarded as no *reasoning* at all, but simply as so many exercises of the "inference-drawing propensity" of the human psyche. This, I submit, is simply absurd. And a view of induction which compels us to draw such a conclusion is similarly absurd.

A sober consideration of what is at stake in the controversy over induction makes it evident, therefore, that Humean skepticism cannot be the last word on this matter. Simply to list the consequences of the skeptical position is at the same time to construct a powerful *reductio ad absurdum* of that position. Somehow, we feel sure, it must be possible to establish the logical validity of induction; and if we are empiricists, we will seek a way to do this consistent with our empiricism. Such a way we shall now examine.

Induction and the Principle of the Uniformity of Nature

It is hardly necessary to give an elaborate description of what we are doing when we "draw an inductive inference," since every one of us is familiar with it from personal experience. We observe some phenomenon—the sun rising in the east, for example—and then we observe another instance of that same phenomenon, and then another, and another, and at length we draw our inference—that the sun always rises in the east, or whatever the inference might be. We proceed, that is, to affirm *universal* regularity on the basis of *observed* regularity. And, in the case of a true inference, our general conclusion is constantly confirmed by our subsequent experience.

It is quite evident that in reasoning in this manner we are tacitly assuming what is sometimes called the Principle of the Uniformity of Nature. This principle may be stated in a variety of ways of which the following may be taken as representave. *P1:* The universe is so constructed that everything that occurs may be viewed as an instance of some general law or laws. *P2:* The universe is not a chaos of random events; some uniformities, or laws, are exhibited in phenomena widely separated in space and time. *P3:* Nature operates according to some uniform laws; what has occurred in the past, therefore, is a reliable guide for the future.

I do not wish to discuss in detail the differences that are evident in these three versions of the principle of uniformity. *P2* and *P3* are, I think, virtually identical, the only significant difference being that the latter specifically mentions the reliability of the past as a guide for the future. *P1* differs from the other two in that it appears to affirm universal determinism; and since we do in fact employ inductive reasoning even though we may have serious doubts about whether or not determinism is true, it is evident that we do not necessarily assume the principle in the form in which it is stated in *P1* when we are reasoning inductively. I think one can say that *if* we had some way of knowing that *P2* is true, we would have no difficulty in understanding the logical foundation of inductive reasoning.

A brief explanation of the logical structure of inductive reasoning, *if we assume the principle of the general uniformity of nature* (*P2*), might prove helpful at this point.

A typical instance of inductive reasoning would be the familiar one in which we infer, from the fact that all the crows we have observed are black, that all crows are black. The reasoning by which we arrive at this general conclusion is as follows:

Major premise: What is true of Crow 1, Crow 2, Crow 3, etc., is true of all crows.

Minor premise: Crow 1, Crow 2, Crow 3, etc., are black.

Conclusion: All crows are black.

Upon what basis, then, do we affirm the major premise? This, it seems clear, is the general conclusion of a higher-level argument, the structure of which is as follows:

Major premise: The universe is not a chaos of random events; some uniformities are exhibited in phenomena widely separated in space and time.

Minor premise: Crows are among those phenomena which exhibit such uniformities.

Conclusion: What is true of Crow 1, Crow 2, Crow 3, etc., is true of all crows.

It is important to note that the conclusion of our argument—that all crows are black—is only more or less probable and that this is exactly what we should expect if the logical structure of the argument is as I have said. The premises from which the conclusion is drawn are known with something less than absolute certainty, and the uncertainty—or, as I should prefer to say, the *varying probability*—that attaches to the premises is accordingly passed on to the conclusion.

But how do we know with any degree of certainty that the universe exhibits some uniformities? How does this ultimate major premise of all inductive reasoning get established? This is the question which now has to be answered.

Two Kinds of Induction

We may make a beginning toward unraveling this puzzle if we make a distinction between what I shall call *informal* induction and *rigorous,* or *scientific,* induction. The former must have been practiced by man since the very emergence of the human species upon earth, and even man's pre-human ancestors must have employed something analogous to it; the latter has been practiced only within the last few hundred years.

Informal induction may very well be, as Hume said it was, nothing more than the habit of generalizing from our experience. Every human being, including the most primitive people on earth, believes a vast number of general truths on this basis. The general truths that an Eskimo knows in this way, it is evident, will be on the whole quite different from those known by, say, a tribe that lives in equatorial Africa or a family of Australian aborigines. The Eskimo will know, for example, that snow is cold, that seals are good for food, that seal oil may be used for such-and-such purposes, and so on. A member of an African tribe will know that the mid-day sun is to be avoided, that certain sorts of animals are to be feared, that such-and-such berries are poison, and the like. And still other general truths will presumably be known by the aboriginal inhabitants of Australia.

Some of the things which people believe they "know" in this way may turn out to be false. Many generations of Africans must have believed, for example, that all men are black, and the Eskimos of the far north may have believed that all men live in houses made of snow. Informal induction, therefore, is not an entirely reliable procedure; but it is the starting point from which better things may come.

Let us suppose, now, a civilization in which a reasonably high level of culture has been achieved and in which there is, for some members of the society at least, sufficient leisure to cultivate intellectual pursuits. What materials would the thinkers of this culture have to work with? According to our account, they would have (a) a stock of general truths, or at any rate general beliefs, arrived at in the informal way described above and (b) as a strict correlate of this, a belief that nature exhibits some uniformities—i. e., the uniformities expressed in the particular set of beliefs that summarize the common experience of the people of that society.

In such a situation, it is not at all unthinkable that the question should be asked: May there not be other, less obvious, uniformities in nature which no one has yet taken the trouble to observe? We know that nature exhibits some uniformities: let us see if we cannot find others.

It is when this step is taken that we pass from the primitive to the scientific attitude toward the world, and therewith also from informal to scientific inductive reasoning. To look for uniformity is quite a different thing from simply noting the uniformity that is staring one in the face. In the case of informal induction, one is scarcely (if at all) aware of the fact that one is drawing an inference: one simply acts *as if* certain uniformities obtain, almost without consciously entertaining the general truth that is therein implied. With scientific induction, however, the situation is different. Here one deliberately, carefully, painstakingly *attempts* to find some general truth that will tie together the apparently diverse data of experience.

Scientific induction differs from informal induction in at least four ways.

First, in every instance of scientific induction the person who performs that induction is quite consciously taking a risk. He is not simply summarizing what he has observed: he is deliberately going beyond what he has observed and is affirming as a general truth a proposition that may, for all he knows, be erroneous.

Second, in the case of scientific induction one actively tries to disprove the generalization that is the conclusion of one's inductive reasoning. One who engages in scientific inductive reasoning is not simply "reading off" the obvious general truths that are exhibited in the world around him: he is engaged in a serious attempt to discover uniformities that are not obvious to everyone, and he is not content until he discovers uniformities that hold without exception. Informal induction reveals nothing that is parallel to this.

Third, in the case of scientific induction one continues to maintain a critical, not-quite-convinced attitude toward even those uniformities which survive one's best efforts to disprove them. The conclusion of a scientific induction, however impressive the evidence upon which it rests, is always subject to modification. With informal induction this is not the case.

Fourth, scientific induction, unlike informal induction, proceeds according to fixed rules. These rules, which were first given formal expression by John Stuart Mill (whose nomenclature, by the way, is still in common use), specify the ways in which inductive reasoning can proceed with the minimum possibility of error. Mill's Methods, as they are called—the Method of Agreement, the Method of Difference, the Joint Method of Agreement and Difference, etc.—represent scientific induction fully conscious of its own procedures. It is these methods, implicit in the procedure of rigorous thinkers of every age and explicit in the work of Mill, that have produced the impressive results that make the modern era the age of science *par excellence.*

The situation, therefore, seems to be this. The principle of the general uniformity of nature appears to be the product of informal inductions which are themselves nothing more than the "reading off" of certain rather obvious uniformities exhibited in the everyday experience of man. The principle of the uniformity of nature must, therefore, be allowed to be a product of what Hume called our "habit" or "propensity" of looking for regularity amongst the diverse data of our experience.

Once the principle of uniformity becomes known in this rather informal way, however, it may serve as the major premise in the rigorous forms of inductive reasoning. Not only so, but the principle itself comes to be subjected to the same critical spirit to which all of the conclusions of inductive reasoning are exposed, and so it becomes more and more firmly established with each successful induction. Thus, the principle itself, and the informal inductions upon which it was originally based, are justified and rendered secure by the rigorous methods to which they have given rise.

It might appear that if, as we have argued, the major premise of all scientific inductive reasoning itself rests on merely informal inductions, then the reasonings which proceed from that premise must themselves share in the insecurity of that foundation. This objection, which it is natural to raise at this point, has however been effectively answered by Mill himself, who stated:

> The precariousness of the method of simple enumeration is in an inverse ratio to the largeness of the generalization. The process is delusive and insufficient, exactly in proportion as the subject-matter of the observation is special and limited in extent. As the sphere widens, this unscientific method becomes less and less liable to mislead; and the most universal class of truths, the law of causation for instance, and the principles of number and of geometry, are duly and satisfactorily proved by that method alone. . . .[1]

The principle of the uniformity of nature, therefore, in spite of the fact that it rests on no nobler a foundation than the informal inductions of pre-scientific man, is saved from insecurity by two factors: (1) the extreme breadth of the principle itself and (2) the fact that it has subsequently been tested and confirmed according to the critical spirit of the scientific mind. Thus it is able to function as a secure foundation for all subsequent inductive reasoning.

Hume's error, it appears to me, consists in the fact that he failed to analyze carefully enough the logical structure of inductive reasoning, and to make the all-important distinction between informal and scientific induction. Hume saw, correctly enough, that inductions of the scientific type presuppose the principle of uniformity, and from this he concluded that the principle itself must simply be gratuitously assumed. It required a century or more after Hume to bring to light the distinction which Hume did not see and with which, as I hope I have made clear, the problem of induction is solved.

---

[1] John Stuart Mill, *A System of Logic*, 8th ed. (New York and London: Longmans, Green and Co., 1956), Book III, Chap. XXI.

Study Questions

1. What "disastrous consequences" does Empiricist say would follow if we were to accept Hume's skeptical conclusions regarding induction? Do you think he is right? If so, does this constitute a *reductio ad absurdum* of inductive skepticism, as Empiricist says it does?
2. What is the principle of uniformity? Is Empiricist right in saying that this principle constitutes "the ultimate major premise of all inductive reasoning"? Is it true that we would have a logical warrant for making inductive inferences if we could somehow establish the truth of this principle?
3. What exactly is the distinction that Empiricist makes between "informal" induction and "scientific" induction? What use does he make of this distinction in his subsequent argument?
4. How does Empiricist attempt to answer the objection that if the principle of uniformity is established by the relatively insecure method of "informal" induction, then all of the reasoning based upon this principle must be equally insecure? Are you convinced by his answer? Can you present a better one?

Chapter 16

THE RATIONALIST'S WAY OUT

IT IS A continuous source of interest to observe the various ways in which empiricists twist and squirm in their vain attempts to find an acceptable alternative to the inductive skepticism of Hume. Hume's question has been, as Empiricist has hinted, a distinct embarrassment to empiricists—so much so that I suspect more converts to rationalism may have been won on this single point than on any other point to which rationalists commonly appeal in support of their position.

The empiricist is in a serious predicament. On the one hand, he is aware that inductive skepticism does lead to disastrous and, indeed, unacceptable consequences with respect to the status of a good deal of our knowledge of the world. On the other hand, he is committed to the proposition that empiricism is true—and Hume appears to have shown that on empiricist premises his skeptical conclusions cannot be avoided. But on empiricist ground, Hume still has the final word; two centuries of effort have not produced a single convincing defense of inductive reasoning that does not violate the central tenet of empiricism. On the problem of induction, the only viable alternatives are skepticism and rationalism.

Critique of Constructive Empiricism

It should be apparent to everyone who is not blinded by empiricist dogmatism that the argument set forth in the preceding chapter does not succeed in its attempt to show that induction is a valid logical procedure. It is inadequate, as a matter of fact, in several different ways.

In the first place, it fails to grasp the true purport, the really radical character, of Hume's argument. Hume did not say, as Empiricist implies in the latter part of his essay, that it was only the reasoning of *scientists* that was placed in jeopardy by his critical questioning of the validity of induction. *All* inductive reasoning, he argued, proceeds on the assumption that nature is uniform, that the future will be like the past. This means, therefore, that anyone who would answer Hume must do one of two things: he must (a) show that Hume was mistaken in his claim that all inductive reasoning presupposes the principle of the uniformity of nature or he must (b) show that the principle of the uniformity of nature is not itself a product of inductive reasoning. Since Empiricist has done neither of these, it is apparent that he has not really understood the radical character of Hume's question.

From this it is also clear, in the second place, that Empiricist's argument turns on a distinction that is more apparent than real. Inductive reasoning, like almost anything else that one might do, may be done either carelessly or carefully, and there is no harm in calling attention to this difference by calling the one "informal" and the other "rigorous" or "scientific" induction. But as soon as one recognizes that this is all the distinction amounts to, it becomes apparent that one cannot make the use of it which Empiricist has attempted to make. Even "informal" induction, according to Hume's analysis, presupposes the principle of uniformity; unless Empiricist can exhibit the logical structure of "informal" induction in a way that escapes Hume's criticism, it will not be of any help to him as a foundation for "scientific" induction.

It is fair to say, therefore, that in the last analysis Empiricist's argument is circular. The very principle which he hopes to establish by means of "informal" induction—the principle of the uniformity of nature—must be presupposed before the first such inductive generalization can be made.

Empiricist seems, in a way, to have realized that his argument leaves something to be desired, and near the end of his essay he tries to patch it up as best he can. This he does by (a) a vague reference to the subsequent "purification" of the principle of uniformity once it has given birth to "scientific" induction and (b) gratuitously assuming the general principle that "the wider the generalization the more certain it is."

I do not rightly know how to distinguish between a "purified" and an "unpurified" principle, but I think I know what Empiricist has in mind. The principle of the uniformity of nature, according to his account, still carries the taint of its unscientific past: it is not, in its natural state, a suitable principle for "scientific" use. It needs, therefore, to be "purified"—or, to put it more prosaically, to be re-established by scientific induction. But this, quite obviously, cannot be done, since on Empiricist's own account "scientific" induction presupposes the unbaptized principle. It is no wonder that the reference to "purification" was rather vague.

Nor is Empiricist's case rendered any more convincing by the introduction of Mill's suggestion that the broader the generalization is, the more certain it is. This does not even appear to be true: it rather seems to be the case that the more cautious one is about one's generalizations—the closer one stays to what one has actually observed—the more confident one may be about the correctness of those generalizations. But let us assume, for the moment, that Mill is right in this: How does he claim to know that it is true? Is it *a priori?* Obviously, no empiricist can allow this. Is it, then, the product of inductive reasoning? Then the validity of induction must already be assumed, and no principle that is established thereby can be called in to enhance its validity.

The Logical Premise of Inductive Reasoning

There are, I have suggested, only two possible ways to counter Hume's attack on inductive reasoning. One is to show that the principle of the uniformity of nature is not itself the product of inductive reasoning. The other is to show that Hume was mistaken in his belief that all inductive reasoning presupposes the principle of the uniformity of nature.

Some rationalists have attempted the first of these two alternatives as a way of re-establishing the validity of inductive reasoning, but not successfully in my opinion.

It seems evident, in the first place, that we do not know *a priori* that the principle of the uniformity of nature in its "strong," or deterministic, form (*P1*, see p. 141) is true. I myself have grave doubts about the truth of the principle when it is stated in this way; hence, I cannot justly be said to "know" it either *a priori* or *a posteriori*. A defense of inductive reasoning that depends on an appeal to *a priori* knowledge at this point seems, therefore, to be very weak.

On the other hand, we do know that the principle in its weaker form (*P2* or *P3*) is true, but it is quite obvious that the principle in this form is itself an inductive generalization—is, in other words, known *a posteriori*. Our knowledge of the principle in this form, therefore, presupposes the validity of inductive reasoning, and the ground of that validity must be sought in some other place.

A clue to the correct solution of this problem may be found in the way by which we are able to proceed from premises to a conclusion in deductive reasoning. Our ability so to do depends, as has been pointed out in another place (see Chapters 10 and 13), on certain rules of inference which we know *a priori*. May it not be, then, that in inductive reasoning it is some *logical principle* that enables us to make our inferences? Let us re-examime the logical structure of an inductive argument to see whether this is not in fact the case.

We may take as our example the well-worn one about the crows. We start, in this case, with what we shall call the observational premise—that *N* crows have been observed, and all of them have been black. From this we feel justified in inferring the probable but not certain conclusion that all crows are black. The argument, thus, appears to be this:

Observational premise: *N* crows have been observed, and all of them have been black.

. . . .

Inductive conclusion: It is more or less probable that all crows are black.

If we are on the right track, we ought then to seek for some logical principle—some rule of inductive inference—that will enable us to draw the general conclusion. The principle should be such as to (a) provide a warrant for our drawing the inference and (b) account for the fact that the inference is only probable, never absolutely certain.

The principle for which we are seeking might be stated thusly: "The more often two things have been observed to be conjoined in nature, the more probable it is that they are always so conjoined." Putting this principle—which I shall call the logical premise—in the place of the elliptical dots in our argument, we get the following:

Observational premise: N crows have been observed, and all of them have been black.

Logical premise: The more often two things have been observed to be conjoined in nature, the more probable it is that they are always so conjoined.

Inductive conclusion: It is more or less probable that all crows are black.

There are three observations that I should like to make regarding this principle.

First, it should be noted that when this premise is supplied, it is no longer a mystery how we are able to draw our inductive conclusion. The reasoning that is involved is, in fact, deductive: the conclusion is validly inferred from the premises, as in any sound deductive argument.

Second, the principle does account for the fact that inductive generalizations are made with varying degrees of certainty. The conclusion—that it is more or less probable that all crows are black—follows rigorously from the premises and is known with the same certainty that the premises are known; but the proposition that all crows are black is itself only more or less probable (as is the case with any empirical generalization), and this probability is explicitly stated in the conclusion.

Third, the argument, thus stated, exhibits the fact that the probability of the empirical generalization that appears in the conclusion varies directly with the quantity of evidence upon which it is based. If I have seen one crow, my generalization has a very low degree of probability. If I have seen a hundred, the probability increases. And if I have seen thousands, and have checked the reports of others who have seen thousands more, the probability becomes very high. The principle as stated does, therefore, correspond to our intuitive conviction that the greater the quantity of evidence upon which a generalization is based, the greater the probability that it is true without exception.

I spoke just now about "our intuitive conviction that the greater the quantity of evidence upon which a generalization is based, the greater the probability that it is true without exception." It seems clear to me that we do in fact have such a conviction—and, indeed, that we *know* that this is the case. But note: What we have called the logical premise of all inductive reasoning is nothing more nor less than a statement in slightly different terms of this very truth. To say that something is known intuitively is to say that it is known *a priori*. In identifying this logical premise, therefore, we may plausibly claim to have discovered the *a priori* ground of the validity of inductive reasoning.

Hume's chief error, if this analysis is correct, consists in his assertion that inductive reasoning always involves an appeal to the principle of the uniformity of nature. This principle, he correctly observed, is itself a product of inductive reasoning, and he accordingly drew the conclusion that all inductive reasoning is circular— is, in fact, no reasoning at all. Empiricist accepted Hume's analysis of the structure of inductive reasoning, and he attempted unsuccessfully to show that the principle of the uniformity of nature could be established without appealing in the process to that very principle. It is only when this initial assumption as to the structure of inductive reasoning is rejected that the correct solution to the problem becomes apparent.

I do not suppose, however, that the solution I have proposed will be any comfort to empiricists, because it carries with it the rather surprising conclusion that there is an *a priori* element even in most *a posteriori* knowledge—in all, that is, that goes beyond the particular data of direct observation. This includes, obviously, all of the general findings of the natural sciences as well as the everyday truths which we all take for granted every day of our lives. To an empiricist, however, this conclusion is not only surprising: it is totally unacceptable, for to accept it is to concede that empiricism is a misguided epistemological theory.

It seems fair to say in conclusion, therefore, that properly understood the *reductio ad absurdum* argument which Empiricist has directed against inductive skepticism is an equally effective demonstration of the absurdity of empiricism itself. The real merit of Hume's argument is to have shown precisely that skepticism with respect to inductive reasoning is an inevitable consequence of empiricism. It follows, therefore, that anyone who wishes to maintain the empiricist position must be prepared to accept the consequences of inductive skepticism, and that if those consequences are indeed absurd—as Empiricist and I both believe they are—then empiricism itself is an absurd and untenable position. When this is clearly understood, the correctness of the solution here proposed may become even more apparent.

Study Questions

1. Rationalist suggests that anyone who would answer Hume on the problem of induction "must do one of two things." What are they? Are these the only ways of answering Hume? Is it true that Empiricist has done neither?
2. Is Rationalist right in saying that the difference between "informal" and "scientific" induction is nothing more than the difference between careless and careful reasoning? Is the *logical structure* the same in both instances? If so, does this seriously damage Empiricist's argument?
3. What "clue" to the solution of the problem of induction does Rationalist claim to find in "the way by which we are able to proceed from premises to a conclusion in deductive reasoning"? Does this strike you as a promising way to approach this problem? Do any of the conclusions you have drawn in your study of earlier problems prevent you from pursuing this approach?
4. Which of the "two things" that Rationalist says one must do to answer Hume does Rationalist himself attempt to do? Does he succeed? How would you expect Hume to reply to Rationalist's argument?

Chapter 17

THE PROPOSAL OF PRAGMATISM

WHENEVER THE DISCUSSION of a philosophical question reaches a complete impasse, as the discussion of the problem of induction appears to have done, it is a good idea to ask whether there is not something wrong with the question itself—whether, for example, some incorrect assumption is not being made or some impossible requirement being set up for any answer that is to be regarded as acceptable. Should this prove to be the case with regard to some particular dispute, it is not surprising that all of the parties to the dispute should end up by proving nothing at all, and that their attacks and counterattacks should serve no other purpose then to convince saner men that the disputants simply do not understand the business that they are attempting to prosecute with such ostentatious vigor.

That the three-way discussion of the problem of induction has indeed reached an impasse cannot be seriously doubted by any impartial observer. The absurdity of inductive skepticism and the inadequacy of what is quaintly called "constructive empiricism" have already been sufficiently demonstrated, and if Rationalist appears for the moment to have the upper hand in the argument, it is only because for the time being he has had the opportunity to speak last. It is an easy matter to show, however, that his position is as untenable as the other two, and by way of clearing our minds for a fresh and more promising way of looking at this old problem, we shall begin by pointing out what is wrong with the rationalist position.

Critique of Rationalism

We may begin by observing that the principle that "the more often two things have been observed to be conjoined in nature, the more probable it is that they are always so conjoined" is hardly a very promising candidate for an *a priori* truth, even according to the criteria which rationalists themselves commonly employ in identifying such truths. Most rationalists are in the habit of following Kant at this point, and the two criteria of *a priori* knowledge to which they customarily point are what Kant called the "necessity" and the "universality" of such truths. "If we have a proposition which in being thought is thought as necessary," Kant said, "it is an *a priori* judgment," and "[if] a judgment is thought with *strict universality,* that is, in such manner that no exception is allowed as possible, it is not derived from experience, but is valid absolutely *a priori.*" [1]

It may be argued with some plausibility that Rationalist's "rule of inductive inference" has the requisite universality, though one could raise a question as to whether it really does exhibit the "strict" universality of which Kant spoke. It does not seem that an exception to this principle is inconceivable in the way that an exception to an arithmetical truth is inconceivable; but I shall not press this point. What is clear, however, is that this principle does not exhibit the necessity that is alleged to be the hallmark of truths that are known *a priori.* There is nothing self-evidently true about this principle, as there is, for example, about the axioms of geometry. If we are reasonably sure that the principle is sound the reason is, surely, because we have found that it *works.* And this has certain implications for our whole understanding of this problem which we shall have to develop shortly. For the present, however, we may be content to have shown that even on Rationalist's own terms it cannot be plausibly maintained that what has been offered as the principle of all inductive reasoning is known *a priori.*

In addition, I do not think that Rationalist has succeeded in disengaging inductive reasoning from the assumption that nature is uniform, for the logical principle is, after all, only as secure as our

---

[1] Immanuel Kant, *Critique of Pure Reason,* Introduction, Sect. II, Norman Kemp Smith, trans. (New York: St. Martin's Press, 1965), pp. 43-44.

belief that nature does not behave in a way that is wholly capricious—as secure, in short, as the principle of the uniformity of nature. Hume's objection is equally as devastating in its effect on Rationalist's position as Rationalist has perceived it to be on constructive empiricism: "If there be any suspicion that the course of nature may change, and that the past may be no rule for the future, all experience becomes useless and can give rise to no inference or conclusion." [2] To doubt the principle of the general uniformity of nature is at the same time to doubt the validity of the proposed rule of inductive inference. Thus, Rationalist's solution to the problem is no better than that of Constructive Empiricist whom he so roundly criticizes.

We are left, therefore, with three positions—inductive skepticism, constructive empiricism, and rationalism—all of which are seen to be untenable. Yet these are the only positions that it is possible to take with respect to the question that has been stated. Something, evidently, has gone wrong. There is something artificial, something incorrect about the assumptions upon which the whole argument thus far has been proceeding. Let us try to locate the error and in so doing raise the discussion to a new and more fruitful level.

Truth

There is one assumption which all three previous writers on this question share in common, and that is that a statement is true if and only if what it asserts to be the case really is the case. They have all assumed the *correspondence* theory of truth. Proceeding on this assumption, they have asked: How can we possibly know that reality corresponds to the assertions that we make when we utter an empirical generalization? We know, indeed, that reality corresponds to the simple observational statements with which we begin; but how can we know that it corresponds to the statement with which we conclude—a statement that leaps far beyond what we have observed and purports to describe phenomena which we have not observed, and perhaps never shall observe?

[2] David Hume, *An Inquiry Concerning Human Understanding*, Charles W. Hendel, ed. (New York: Liberal Arts Press, 1955), p. 51.

To ask this question is, I submit, to ask a question that cannot be answered—and that is why none of the illustrious philosophers who have tried to do so have been able to answer it. To show why this is an unanswerable question is our task in the remainder of this essay.

William James, who seems to provide the key with which we may hope to unlock this old puzzle, once said:

> There can *be* no difference anywhere that doesn't *make* a difference elsewhere—no difference in abstract truth that doesn't express itself in a difference in concrete fact and in conduct consequent upon that fact, imposed on somebody, sometime, and somewhere. . . . Ideas . . . become true just in so far as they help us to get into satisfactory relation with other parts of our experience, to summarize them and get about among them by conceptual short-cuts instead of following the interminable succession of particular phenomena.[3]

Let us examine these ideas and see how they can be of help to us in coming to some satisfactory view with respect to the problem of induction.

"There can be no difference that doesn't make a difference." This means that the meaning of any idea *consists* precisely in the consequences which it is supposed to have for either our own experience or that of someone else. The meaning of the idea that there are tigers in India, for example, consists simply in—to quote James again—the "procession of mental associates and motor consequences that follow on the thought, and that would lead harmoniously, if followed out, into some ideal or real context, or even into the immediate presence, of the tigers."[4] The notion that there could be two different ideas that have identical practical consequences is simply meaningless.

Another way to put this is to say that ideas are "plans for action." We never desire to know just for the sake of knowing. We

---

[3] William James, *Pragmatism* (New York and London: Longmans, Green and Co., 1959), pp. 49-50, 58. Cf. also pp. 197-234.

[4] William James, *The Meaning of Truth* (New York and London: Longmans, Green, and Co., 1910), pp. 44-45.

desire to know in order that we shall be able to get about in the world of our experience, in order that we shall be able to pursue our purposes in the world (no matter what those purposes might be). It is only in this way that we are able to choose, from among the infinite things that we might conceivably attempt to understand, those things that we do in fact seek to understand; it is *our interests, our purposes,* that determine the selection.

To say, then, that an idea is true is not to say that it is an exact "copy" of reality. It is to say, rather, that it works, that it enables us to move about in the world of our experience. "True ideas are those that we can assimilate, validate, corroborate and verify. False ideas are those that we can not." [5] This is the only sense of truth and falsehood that has any relation to the purposes for which we wish to distinguish the two—the only meaning, therefore, that this distinction can possibly have for us.

Truth, therefore, is always truth for someone. What was true for medieval man—i. e., the ideas that were adequate to enable him to get around in the world of his experience—is not necessarily true for us. Experience, as James so aptly put it, has ways of "boiling over," thus compelling each generation to modify what was received from the previous generation as the truth—to make its own truth, so to speak. But the idea of a purely objective truth, a truth that has no practical consequences for human experience, is an empty and meaningless concept. The reasons that lead us to call an idea true are precisely the reasons that make it true.

The idea of an "absolute truth," therefore, can be nothing other than the idea of a truth that would be adequate to all possible experience, a truth that no experience could ever require us to modify or reject. Such truth may be the ideal goal toward which all of our attempts to know the truth are aiming, but it is not the quality of those provisional and temporary truths that constitute the truth-for-us. The truth-for-us is simply the truth that works, the truth that enables us to get about in the "booming, buzzing confusion" that is the world of our experience. It is, as James said, "the expedient in the way of our thinking."

Let us now return to the problem of induction and see how the

---

5 James, *Pragmatism,* p. 201.

ideas we have just been considering can aid us in achieving its correct solution.

The Problem of Induction Revisited

Suppose a man speaks to us as follows: "In all of my experience thus far, I have observed nothing but black crows. It seems to be true, therefore, that all crows are black. But how can I be sure that this is true absolutely? How can I be sure that the future will be like the past, that all 'future' crows will be black just as all 'past' crows have been? How can I infer from the observed to the unobserved?"

If we have understood the ideas set forth in the preceding pages, we shall have no difficulty in responding to such a query. We shall have to say, obviously, that our puzzled friend cannot be sure that the generalization that summarizes his past experience will hold in the future, but that, until experience itself contradicts him, he would, nonetheless, be well advised to regard his generalization as true. And what we would mean by this is, quite simply, that so long as no *facts* arise to compel him to alter his generalization it will serve to enable him to get around within a certain segment of his experience (to tie together, for example, what he sees in the forest, what he reads in books, and what he hears in the conversation of others). If something occurs within the field of his experience that gives the lie to his belief, then and only then will it cease to be true; and then, too, he will be compelled to seek for a new generalization which is sufficient to encompass this new experience as well as the old.

All parties to the dispute about the validity of inductive inferences have been obsessed with the idea of "absolute truth." It is this idea of truth that they have in mind when they ask, "How can we know that the generalizations that are the products of our inductive inferences are true?" They have sought, accordingly, to find a logical method that would somehow guarantee their truth. Hume, at least, saw that this was not possible and drew the skeptical consequences with which we are all familiar. Those who came after him continued the search for a method, with the inconclusive results that have made this problem the scandal of philosophy.

It is interesting to note that both rationalists and empiricists who have addressed themselves to this problem have attempted to validate induction by exhibiting it as, after all, a concealed form of *deductive* reasoning. The assumption has been, apparently, that deductive reasoning somehow "guarantees" the truth of its conclusions and that if induction could be shown to be deduction, then somehow the "absolute truth" of its conclusions could be conclusively established.

The truth of the matter is, however, that the mere form of one's reasoning can never guarantee the truth of one's conclusion. The conclusion of a valid deductive argument must, of course, be true if the premises are true, since the conclusion does nothing more than to assert explicitly what has already been asserted implicitly in the premises. But the form of the argument tells nothing at all about the truth of the premises. To determine that, you must go to experience; and to go to experience is, in the last analysis, to invoke the pragmatic criterion of truth.

The way of wisdom in this matter, therefore, is to refuse to answer Hume's question on its own terms. For the question, "Is induction a valid logical procedure?" presupposes that it is the validity or invalidity of the procedure that must decide whether or not we are warranted in believing that our empirical generalizations are true and that the truth of our generalizations consists in their being exact "copies" of reality. Both of these assumptions, we have argued, are mistaken. The truth of our generalizations consists in the fact that they work (in the sense already described), and our warrant for believing them is also simply the fact that they work. To see this is not, obviously, to answer Hume's question; it is, on the contrary, to see that no answer is required.

I am under no illusions as to the likelihood that the solution here proposed will quickly win wide acceptance among philosophers who have busied themselves with this problem. The lust for the absolute truth is a fault that has long infected the mind of sophisticated men, and it is an infection that is not easily rooted out. Philosophers, moreover, have a way of falling in love with their own problems; they cannot tolerate the thought that one of their conundrums should really have been solved and are not disposed to pass out prizes to those who claim to have done so. We are content to forego the prize, however, satisfied that the solution here proposed is indeed the answer to Hume for which so many philosophers have been seeking. For the best answer to this question, as indeed to many philosophical questions, is the one that satisfies us in such a way that we are no longer inclined to bother ourselves about it.

Study Questions

1. What criticisms does Pragmatist direct against Rationalist's attempted solution of the problem of induction? Can you think of any way that Rationalist might defend himself against these criticisms?

2. Are you inclined to agree with Pragmatist that the discussion of the problem thus far has reached an impasse and that the reason for this may be that all of the parties to the dispute have been making some incorrect assumption? Are you equally persuaded that the assumption in question is the one Pragmatist says it is? Explain.

3. What is the theory of truth which Pragmatist offers as an alternative to the "correspondence" theory? Does this strike you as a correct description of what we ordinarily mean by "truth"? Or is Pragmatist not suggesting that this is what we *do* ordinarily mean, but rather what we *ought* to mean?

4. How, according to Pragmatist, does the pragmatic theory of truth aid in the solution of the problem of induction? How do you think a Humean skeptic might respond to Pragmatist's proposal?

Chapter 18

A FOOTNOTE TO HUME

ALTHOUGH I FIND myself in general agreement with the sentiments expressed in the opening paragraphs of the last chapter, I am not at all convinced that Pragmatist has succeeded in putting his finger on whatever it is that makes the problem of induction, as he says, "artificial." Pragmatist writes with the enthusiasm and the disdain of a man who has just taken in hand a new and, to him, exciting principle, by means of which he proposes to lay low all sorts of problems that have troubled able minds for centuries. The precise connection between the pragmatist theory of truth, however—even if one accepts that theory—and the problem of induction is, to say the least, somewhat difficult to discern; and it is far from having been proven that that theory itself is one which it would be wise or prudent for us to accept.

Rather than attempting to assess the strengths and weaknesses of Pragmatist's argument, however, I propose that we return to the original problem as stated by Hume. Hume, as I shall hope to show, was not right in everything that he said about this problem, but his analysis is still more perceptive than any of the subsequent attempts that have been made to find a satisfactory answer to him. If we find that we are able to answer Hume without adopting the questionable theory of truth that is advocated in the previous chapter, then I think we may safely ignore what is there proposed.

I spoke just now about finding an "answer" to Hume. Strictly speaking, however, I do not intend to propose an answer to Hume but to show, on the contrary, that his question ought not to trouble us in the way that it is usually supposed to do. I shall, as a matter of fact, agree with a great deal that Hume has said. My comments, therefore, should not be construed as an attempt to refute Hume; they are, rather, only a footnote to Hume's own penetrating remarks on induction which appear in Section IV of the *Inquiry*.

Where Hume Was Right

Hume argued, it will be recalled, that there is no possible way of showing that induction is a valid logical procedure. Induction depends, said Hume, on the assumption that nature is uniform and that what has been observed to be the case in the past is, therefore, a safe guide as to what may be expected to occur in the future. This assumption, as Hume correctly perceived, can in no way be established. It is evidently not known *a priori,* nor can it be established inductively (since we could not reason inductively without assuming the very principle that is to be proven). We must conclude, therefore, said Hume, that induction is not a valid logical procedure, and that our propensity to draw inductive inferences is nothing but a habit that is itself a product of the repeated observation of "constant conjunction."

It seems to me that after two full centuries of more or less vigorous discussion of this problem, Hume remains triumphant on each of the following points:

1. *Inductive reasoning does presuppose the principle of the uniformity of nature.* Constructive empiricism, as we saw, does not even attempt to deny this; what it attempts to do, with notorious lack of success, is to establish the principle by a kind of "pre-inductive inference" in order that induction proper can get under way. Rationalist's attempt at a defense of induction does indeed pretend to deny the necessity of this assumption, but it has already been sufficiently shown that the "logical principle" which Rationalist attempts to put in its place derives whatever plausibility it has from this very assumption. On this point, therefore, Hume must be judged to have been correct.

2. *The principle of the uniformity of nature cannot itself be established by inductive reasoning.* Hume wrote:

We have said that all arguments concerning existence are founded on the relation of cause and effect, that our knowledge of that relation is derived entirely from experience, and that all our experimental conclusions proceed upon the supposition that the future will be conformable to the past. To endeavor, therefore, the proof of this last supposition by probable arguments, or arguments regarding existence, must be evidently going in a circle and taking that for granted which is the very point in question.[1]

Constructive Empiricist's essay, with its obvious circularity, is the best possible demonstration that on this point also Hume was right.

3. *The principle of the uniformity of nature is not known* a priori. This is a point that is not susceptible of direct proof, since the statement that something is or is not known *a priori* can never be either proved or disproved. It is significant, however, that even many rationalists are far from convinced that this principle is known *a priori,* and they have directed their efforts toward finding some other principle upon which to ground the validity of induction. If anyone is disposed to hold, therefore, that the principle of the uniformity of nature is known *a priori,* I can think of no argument that might change his mind; but the majority of philosophers who have struggled with this question, rationalists and empiricists alike, are united in their judgment that in so saying he would be simply mistaken. On this point, too, the decision must be in favor of Hume.

The conclusion appears inescapable, therefore, that induction is based on a principle that is known neither *a priori* nor *a posteriori;* consequently, it is not known at all. Induction must, therefore, be judged to be incurably irrational. This was Hume's conclusion, and since it follows from the three propositions which we have just considered, we must also agree with Hume on this. *Induction is not a valid logical procedure.*

---

[1] David Hume, *An Inquiry Concerning Human Understanding,* Charles W. Hendel, ed. (New York: Liberal Arts Press, 1955), pp. 49-50.

Where Hume Was Wrong

It seems to me, however, that there are two points on which Hume was clearly mistaken, and it is the failure of most of Hume's critics to see these mistakes that makes his attack on induction appear to have such devastating consequences.

First, Hume was mistaken in his view that our propensity to believe that nature operates according to certain invariable laws is nothing but a habit which, like other habits, is a product of repetition—repetition, in this case, of the repeated observation of what Hume called "constant conjunction." "From causes which appear similar," he said, "we expect similar effects." [2] Induction has no logical foundation, but it has a psychological foundation in the phenomenon that we call "habit."

The reduction of the process of induction to habit does not agree completely with what we know about the way that habits become established. What typically occurs when a habit is getting established is that things which at first have to be done quite consciously and deliberately come at length to be done effortlessly and, as we say, almost automatically. In learning to drive, for example—or to type, or to ski—one begins by applying certain rules, certain "laws" if you will; but when the operations in question have become a matter of habit, one is scarcely aware of applying rules: one simply does what one has learned to do. Nothing comparable to this appears to occur in the case of induction. We do not at first "induct" with effort and deliberately, and then perform with less and less conscious effort as we become better at doing it. It seems highly unlikely, therefore, that our propensity to draw inductive inferences is, as Hume said, a habit established by repetition.

Even if Hume's account of our induction-propensity as a habit established by repetition were psychologically sound, it is inadequate in yet another respect. This may be brought out in the following way. There is no such thing as "repetition" pure and simple: repetition must be repetition *for someone,* there must be someone who interprets some event as a repetition of some earlier event. This means, however, that there must be some point of view, some sys-

---

[2] *Ibid.,* p. 50.

tem of expectations or interests that leads one to note certain similarities between what is happening now and what happened at some earlier time. It is one's point of view, the interests and the expectations which one brings to an event, that determine what is to count as a repetition of some earlier event or events. It is evident, therefore, that these expectations are *prior to,* and not *products of,* repetition. Hume's attempt to explain our expectation that the future will resemble the past as a product of repetition must, therefore, be regarded as a failure.

This brings us to Hume's second error: his uncritical and mistaken assumption that it is by induction that we arrive at interesting general conclusions regarding the laws that govern empirical phenomena. Hume assumed that the everyday general truths which we all take for granted in ordering our lives, as well as the more subtle generalizations that we claim to establish in the natural sciences, are one and all "inductive inferences"; and having shown that induction is not logically valid, he concluded that we have no rational basis for believing these generalizations to be true. It is because these truths appear threatened, and because we cannot tolerate the thought that so much of our supposed knowledge should turn out to be no knowledge at all, that we are so upset at the thought that induction is not a valid logical procedure. It is the rationality of our belief in these truths, not the logical credentials of induction itself, that we feel obliged to defend. If, therefore, we can succeed in showing that our knowledge of general empirical truths is indeed obtained by a non-inductive procedure, we should have no difficulty in accepting with equanimity Hume's negative conclusions regarding the rationality of induction.

How General Empirical Truths Are Known

It is my contention that the correct account of the origin and status of our knowledge of empirical truths is as follows:

1. Our aim, in seeking empirical knowledge, is to achieve a true description of the world. The ideal goal of all science is to achieve a description that is so accurate and so complete that everything that occurs can be understood as an instance of some

general law or laws. (It will be noted that in saying this I am disagreeing with the so-called "pragmatic" or "instrumentalist" theory of truth set forth in the preceding chapter.)

2. We can never be sure that the description of the world which at any time we suppose to be true really is true, though we can sometimes be reasonably sure that in some respects it is false.

3. The method by which we replace inadequate descriptions of the world with more adequate ones is not the method of induction, but the method of *conjecture and refutation*. All our knowledge of general empirical truths is at best hypothetical, and to say that some empirical generalization is true is only to say that despite our best efforts to do so we have not been able to discover any counter-examples.

To hold a certain hypothesis about the world, to believe that certain phenomena are governed by such-and-such laws, is to have a certain set of expectations about what will happen under such-and-such conditions. In science we express this by saying that on the basis of this or that law we can "make predictions," and our predictions are descriptions before the fact of what we expect to occur whenever a given set of conditions is fulfilled. Contrary to what is sometimes said, it is not the case that an empirical hypothesis is only as secure as the evidence on which it is based; a hypothesis is secure in direct proportion to the amount of effort that has been expended in the attempt to disprove it. Any number of hypotheses may be invented to account for almost any set of empirical facts; it is not the hypothesis that is supported by the greatest number of favorable examples, but the one that survives our best efforts to find counter-examples, that wins the right to be admitted to the fund of human knowledge.

Our knowledge of empirical truths, therefore, is nothing but the set of beliefs about the world which we have adopted in order to account for the expectations with respect to the world which we have come to have. There is nothing infallible, nothing final, nothing definitive about such knowledge. A hypothesis that seems adequate for a time may at length have to be revised, as phenomena are discovered which do not conform to the expectations (predictions) which we were led to have (make) on the basis of our supposition that the hypothesis was true. Then we must seek to devise a new hypothesis, one that will account for the new phenomena as well as the old—and the search for counter-examples to the new hypothesis must be launched.

Advances in our knowledge of general empirical truths, accordingly, always come about by way of revising our earlier hypotheses, of replacing less adequate hypotheses with more adequate ones. Every hypothesis that we propose will, of course, have been preceded by observations—those observations, namely, which it was invented to explain. But those observations, in turn, must have been made within the context of an earlier hypothesis or set of hypotheses: it was precisely because the earlier hypotheses did not explain the observations in question that the new hypothesis had to be devised.

Where, then, does the whole process begin? The answer must be: with the inborn expectations with which one enters the world. A newborn child expects the world to serve his needs—to feed him when he is hungry, warm him when he is cold, and so on. His initial hypothesis, one might say, is that the world is always just as he wants it to be. This is not a very adequate hypothesis, but it (or something like it) must be the starting point for every human being. And from that point to the affirmation of the most subtle and sophisticated theory in nuclear physics the process must lead through countless revisions and refinements of hypotheses successively advanced and discarded. Every instance of learning is a modification of what was previously known.

Among the expectations with which every child enters the world is, apparently, the expectation that he will find some uniformity among the diverse phenomena that occur in the world of his experience. The experience of finding regularity does not create the habit of expecting it, as Hume said: on the contrary, the expectation that we shall find regularity gives rise to the habit of looking for it, of demanding it, of searching for it even when it is not obviously present. This is a most fortunate habit, for without it scientific inquiry could never flourish—but that is another matter.

It is time to conclude. Hume argued, as we have seen, that induction is not a valid logical procedure. In this, according to our view, he was right. Hume also believed, however, that in demonstrating the invalidity of inductive reasoning he was demonstrating the irrationality of our supposed knowledge of general empirical truths. In this, if our account is correct, Hume was mistaken. Our footnote to Hume, therefore, comes in the last analysis simply to this: It really doesn't matter.

Study Questions

1. The author of this chapter mentions three specific points on which, in his judgment, Hume was right. Do you agree? What is the view of each of the previous writers with respect to each of these points?

2. What objections does the author of this chapter raise with respect to Hume's account of induction as a "habit"? Are his objections sound? (Consider, for example, poor study habits. Do they get established in the way described? How about driving habits? eating habits? shaving habits?)

3. What, exactly, does the author of this chapter propose as an alternative to induction? Is he right in saying that this method, rather than induction, is the method by which advances are made in our knowledge of general empirical truths? Does this account really avoid the difficulties raised by Hume?

4. Would you classify the author of this chapter as a rationalist or an empiricist? On what basis?

5. Which of the views set forth in this chapter are you inclined to agree with? Which do you disagree with? About which, if any, are you still in doubt?

6. If you had now to take some position with respect to the problem of induction, what would that position be? What seem to you to be the strongest reasons in favor of this position? What do you regard as the most serious objections that might be raised against it?

For Further Reading

Black, Max, *Problems of Analysis*. Ithaca, N.Y.: Cornell University Press, 1954. Chapters 10-12.

Feigl, Herbert, "The Logical Character of the Principle of Induction," in *Readings in Philosophical Analysis*, ed. H. Feigl and W. Sellars. New York: Appleton-Century-Crofts, 1949.

Hume, David, *An Inquiry Concerning Human Understanding*. Many editions. Sections IV and V.

James, William, *Pragmatism and Other Essays*. Cleveland, Ohio: World Publishing Co., 1965. Lecture VI, "Pragmatism's Conception of Truth."

Mill, John Stuart, *A System of Logic*. Toronto, Ont.: University of Toronto Press, 1966. See especially Book III, Chapters 1-5.

Nagel, Ernest, *Logic Without Metaphysics*. New York: Free Press of Glencoe, 1956. Part II, Chapter 7, "The Ground of Induction."

Popper, Karl, *Conjectures and Refutations*. New York: Basic Books, 1963. See especially pages 33-59.

Russell, Bertrand, *Human Knowledge*. New York: Simon and Schuster, 1962 (paperbound). Part VI, "Postulates of Scientific Inference."

Strawson, P. F., *Introduction to Logical Theory*. New York: John Wiley & Sons, 1952. Chapter 9.

Wright, Georg Henrik von, *Treatise on Induction and Probability*. Paterson, N.J.: Littlefield, Adams & Co., 1960 (paperbound).

PART IV

The Ontological Status of the Physical World

Chapter 19

COMMON-SENSE REALISM AND
ITS CRITICS

"ONTOLOGICAL STATUS" IS a
phrase that is not used in ordinary conversation. It is, rather, a part
of the technical vocabulary of philosophers. Let us begin our discussion of the problem of the ontological status of the physical
world by trying to make clear what philosophers are talking about
when they use this rather forbidding-sounding combination of
words.

To talk about the ontological status of something is to talk about
the kind of being that it has. To say that the ontological status of so-
and-so is this or that is to say something about its *mode of existence:* it is to say in precisely what sense it is true to say that there
are so-and-so's. Let us consider a few examples.

It makes sense to say, for example, that there are such things as
dreams. The word "dream" does not denote a non-entity: it denotes something real, some real occurrences. But what sort of occurrences? What really are dreams? What is their ontological
status? Someone might reply, "A dream is an experience which one
has in one's astral body while one's physical body is asleep." Most
of us would probably say, "A dream is a series of occurrences which
take place in our imagination while we are asleep." To reply in
either of these ways is to say something about the *kind* of reality
that a dream has. The disagreement that is apparent in these two
answers is a disagreement about the ontological status of dreams, a
disagreement about what sort of thing the item in question is.

Or consider the case of angels. What really are angels? Someone might say, "Angels are rational, sexless, winged creatures that exist in heaven, and serve God in a variety of ways." Someone else might say, "Nonsense! Angels are mythical beings which people once imagined to exist in an imaginary place which they called 'heaven.' Angels have no more existence in reality than the elves and fairies in the familiar children's tales." The disagreement, once again, is a disagreement over the ontological status of angels; to affirm either position is to hold a particular view as to the kind of being, the mode of existence, of whatever it is that is denoted by the term "angels."

Let us consider yet a third example. Someone remarks, "I was at the theatre last night, and I saw Othello kill Desdemona. What a bloody sight it was!" A bystander exclaims (not in jest), "Goodness, how terrible! Did they catch the rascal? Is he in jail now? Will you have to be a witness at his trial?" The bystander, in this example, has mistaken the ontological status of the event in question. He has interpreted a scene in a play, a fictitious murder, as if it were an actual murder; he has treated Othello and Desdemona as if they were real people instead of fictitious characters in a dramatic production.

Three observations may be made at this point.

The first observation is that what one is prepared to regard as "live options," with respect to questions of ontological status, depends in part on what kind of a *weltbild,* what kind of a picture of reality, one has. The "astral body" theory of dreams is not a live option unless one's picture of reality includes a theory about "astral bodies" that are able to leave their physical counterparts on occasion, participate in various adventures with other people who are also wandering about in their astral bodies, and so on. The same is true of the theory that angels are real inhabitants in a real heaven. Some disputes about ontological status, therefore, resolve themselves in the last analysis into disputes about the credibility or incredibility of this or that *weltbild.*

The second observation is that within any given *weltbild* there can still be genuine disagreement as to the ontological status of this or that particular class of phenomena. By and large, it is only insofar as people share a relatively common *weltbild* that they can fruitfully discuss questions of ontological status, since otherwise some of the parties to the dispute will be proposing answers that are not considered by the others to be live options.

The third observation is that the number of ontological categories available within the context of any given *weltbild* is fairly large, and it is not capable of exhaustive enumeration. There are—to take some fairly non-controversial examples—bodies, and properties of bodies; minds, and their ideas; living creatures, and their behavior; and so on. To "place" something ontologically is to assign it to its proper place in a *weltbild,* to interpret it as belonging to such-and-such a kind of being. To ask about the ontological status of something is to ask what is its proper "place."

Ontological Dependence

Some things could not exist without other things upon which they may accordingly be said to be "dependent" for their existence. Dreams, for example, could not exist without dreamers: it is ridiculous to talk of dreams as if they were the sort of thing that could wander about on their own looking for someone to "have" them. (This is precisely the point of the joke about the poor driver who is described as "an accident looking around for some place to happen": accidents just are not the sort of thing that can "exist" in this way.)

To say that something *A* is dependent on something else *B* for its existence is to affirm a relation of *ontological dependence:* it is to say that *A* is ontologically dependent on *B*. Thoughts, in this sense, are ontologically dependent on thinkers, dreams on dreamers, actions on actors, and so on. If the ontological status of *B* is assumed to be known, the question as to the ontological status of *A* may be satisfactorily answered by pointing out its ontological dependence on *B*. If the ontological status of *B* is itself in question, then the ontological status of everything held to be ontologically dependent on it is *eo ipso* also in question.

The Physical World

The question considered in this section concerns the ontological status of a very large class of objects which we shall designate by the collective phrase, "the physical world." It includes all those things that we perceive by means of our five senses: the totality of vari-colored, vari-shaped, vari-sounding objects that we see, hear, taste, touch, or smell.

There is no serious disagreement, either among philosophers or among non-philosophers, about how the world appears to us, about how we perceive it to be. It appears to consist of a vast number of individual objects—trees, stones, birds, animals, men, etc.—that exhibit a wide variety of colors, shapes, sounds, smells, tempera-tures, tastes, textures, and so on. Were anyone to deny that this is how the physical world appears to him, we would be inclined to think that either he is not being honest with us or else he is lacking some of the normal facilities for sense perception (as in the case of a person who is deaf or blind.)

But is the physical world really the way we perceive it to be? Is the physical world *as we perceive it* an exact copy of the physical world *as it really is,* or is the reality "out there" different in some ways from our perception of it? To ask such questions is not yet to ask about the ontological status of the physical world; it is only to call in question the trustworthiness of our perceptions. But it is a very short step from this to the ontological question.

The specific question that we shall be considering is: Is the phys-ical world in any degree dependent on a perceiver for its existence? Does this vari-colored, vari-shaped, vari-sounding reality that we perceive exist even when we (or someone else) are not perceiving it, or is it in some sense constituted by, and therefore dependent on, perception? The point of the question may be made clearer by a brief preliminary survey of the answers that may be given.

Four Alternatives

The common-sense answer to this question, and certainly the view held by most people prior to any sophisticated reflection on it, goes something like this: There is a real physical world that causes us to have the perceptions that we have, and our perceptions are more or less exact copies of the qualities that are really present in those objects. An object that appears to be brown, therefore, really is brown; one that is perceived to be hard or cold or smooth really is hard or cold or smooth; and so on. The physical world, in short, *exists* quite independently of our perception of it, and it is in no way dependent on our perception for its existence. If all perceivers were annihilated, the vari-colored, vari-shaped, vari-sounding world that we now perceive would still be there—though there would not, of course, be anyone around to perceive that it was there.

The view which we have just stated is usually called "naive realism" by philosophers who address themselves to this problem. The name seems a somewhat unfortunate one, however, since the term "naive" has connotations which suggest that any position so named is obviously not worthy of serious consideration. In the discussion that follows, therefore, we shall refer to this position as *common-sense realism* and to one who holds this position as a *common-sense realist*.

A second position that may be taken with respect to this question is the view known as *subjective idealism, or phenomenalism.* The former title is rather closely associated with the name of George Berkeley, an early eighteenth-century Irish philosopher, and is not in general use at the present time. It is essentially Berkeley's position which today goes by the name of phenomenalism, although the grounds upon which the position is commonly held today are somewhat different from those upon which Berkeley first maintained it.

Phenomenalism stands at the opposite extreme from common-sense realism in the scale of possible answers that may be given to the question we have asked concerning the ontological status of the physical world. It explicitly rejects the "copy" theory of perception and asserts that the being of a physical object consists in its being perceived, and that the physical world is accordingly completely dependent on the perceptions of a perceiver for its existence. Berkeley's classical formula for this view was: *Esse est percipi:* to be (a physical object) is to be perceived. Strange as this position may appear when encountered for the first time, it can be supported by very powerful arguments, and it is widely held by philosophers in England and America today.

In addition to common-sense realism and phenomenalism there remains only one other way in which it is possible to answer this question, and that is to say that the physical world is partly dependent on a perceiver for its existence and partly independent of a perceiver. What is perceived is in some ways like, and in some ways unlike, what is really "out there." There is, therefore, both similarity and dissimilarity between the world as we perceive it and the world as it really is. This view is called *critical realism.*

Critical realists may, however, exhibit significant differences among themselves, depending upon whether the view they advocate emphasizes the similarity between our perceptions and the real world (thus staying fairly close to the realist end of the scale) or the dissimilarity between the two (thus coming closer to the phenomenalist view). We shall, in the discussion that follows, make a semantic distinction between these two forms of critical realism, calling the more mild form *critical realism* and the more radical form *hyper-critical realism.* The difference between them, it must be remembered, is only one of degree.

There is one term that occurs rather frequently in philosophical writings on this problem. The term is *sense-datum* (plural, *sense-data*). Sense-data are what we immediately perceive whenever we are ordinarily said to be perceiving something. Thus, a person who is hallucinating, for example, and who in this state "sees" a pink elephant, has the same sense-data as people who are not hallucinating normally have when they see a real pink elephant. And a person who sees a mirage may be said to be having the same sense-data as one who sees a real oasis—i. e., one that does not disappear as you approach it.

With this term in hand, one can distinguish the four positions defined above in the following way. Common-sense realism is the view that the sense-data that normal people have when their senses are not impaired are accurate copies of the real characteristics of the physical world and that the physical world is accordingly not constituted by our sense-data in any way whatsoever. Phenomenalism is the view that what we call the physical world is simply the inferred totality of our actual and possible sense-data, and apart from these sense-data the physical world accordingly does not exist at all. Critical realism (in any form) is the view that the sense-data which we directly have when we are perceiving the physical world are in some respects similar to the characteristics objectively present in the physical world, and in other respects dissimilar thereto. (Hyper-critical realism is simply a variant of this view which places the greater emphasis on the dissimilarity between the two.)

There is a special form of phenomenalism—some philosophers would say it is a logical implication of phenomenalism—known as *solipsism*. The view is difficult to state with precision, but a fair approximation is the following: it is the view that *I* alone exist in the primary or fundamental sense of "exist" and that everything else that exists does so only in the secondary sense of being my perception or thought. Just as my dreams do not exist unless I am dreaming them, so, according to this view, nothing exists unless *I* am having the perceptions or thoughts that constitute its existence. This view, though difficult to refute, is universally regarded as being highly implausible, and to the best of my knowledge it has not been seriously advocated by any major philosopher in the whole history of Western philosophy. It stands, however, as a fantastic limit to which skepticism regarding the inferences that may be made from the data of sense experience may be carried, and it does come up occasionally in discussions of the problem of the ontological status of the physical world.

It is possible to discuss many of the matters in this section in terms of a slightly different question, that is, Can our senses be trusted to give us accurate information about what the world is really like? Many philosophers prefer to discuss these matters in relation to this question, partly, at least, because discussions of ontological status are more or less out of style at the present time. The classical discussions of perception, however—those of Locke, Berkeley, Hume, Kant, and others—were quite openly directed toward a determination of the ontological status of the physical world; moreover, it seems evident that any view one might adopt with respect to the veracity of our perceptions would have important implications for one's view of the ontological status of the physical world. For these reasons, therefore, we have elected to focus our discussion on the ontological question.

The chapters that follow may be viewed as three successive critiques of common-sense realism, each one rejecting more than the preceding one of what common-sense realism affirms concerning the ontological status of the physical world. We begin, therefore, with a consideration of what may be said in support of a mild form of critical realism, a view that stays fairly close to the common-sense theory. Anyone who is unwilling to follow what has been called "the slippery road that leads to solipsism" all the way to that rather unhappy terminus should be prepared to take his stand at or near one of these stopping points.

Study Questions

1. What ontological status would you be inclined to assign to each of the following: a hunch, a plan, redness, temperature, weight, Huckleberry Finn, Abraham Lincoln, a headache?
2. What, precisely, is the main question posed for consideration in this chapter? Restate it in at least three different ways (without changing the point of the question!).
3. What, in brief summary, are the answers to this question offered by the "four alternatives" defined in this chapter? As you understand the problem, do these four alternatives exhaust the logical possibilities?
4. Do you find anything odd about the following statement? "The arguments in favor of solipsism are so convincing that I find myself compelled to adopt the position; I am surprised that more people do not come to the same conclusion."

Chapter 20

CRITICAL REALISM

IT CANNOT BE denied that most people trust their sense perceptions and that they accordingly believe that the world is really very much as they perceive it to be. They would grant, I suppose, that they sometimes err in their *judgment:* they sometimes judge, for example, that the object that they see some distance away is a dog; upon approaching it, they discover that it is a stone. But they do not, on this account, mistrust their senses; they rather chastise themselves for judging too hastily, and perhaps they make a resolution to suspend judgment on some similar future occasion until they will have had an opportunity to make a closer inspection. Once they have identified the object in question as a stone, however, they do not doubt that the stone really is hard, and rough, and heavy, and porous, and gray, as it appears to be. And if one were to ask them how they *know* that the stone really has these characteristics, they would reply with some indignation: "Because I have seen it with my own eyes, and felt it with my own hands!"

This view, however—that the world really is as we perceive it to be, that it really has all of the characteristics which we perceive it to have—is one that cannot survive critical reflection. However accustomed we may be to thinking of the world in this way, it is, nonetheless, a view that cannot be seriously maintained, as will be evident from the following considerations.

Critique of Common-sense Realism

That common-sense realism is not a defensible position is evident, in the first place, from the fact that we sometimes have illusory perceptions. A straight stick immersed in water, for example, looks like it is bent: there is no point of view which one can adopt that makes it look any other way. It is only because (a) such a stick does not feel bent and (b) when it is removed from the water, it again looks straight, that we have learned not to rely on our visual sense-data in this kind of situation. Or consider a mirage. A traveler in the desert who sees a mirage sees it just as surely as one can see real water and real trees; it is only because it recedes or disappears as he approaches it—only because he can never reach it, drink its water, and be cooled by the shade of its trees—that he calls it a mirage. The "phantom pains" of persons who have suffered the loss of a limb may also be mentioned as a case in point.

There is no reason to conclude from this, of course, that since our senses sometimes deceive us, perhaps they deceive us all the time. It is only on the assumption that they do not deceive us all the time, as a matter of fact, that we can identify our perceptions of the bent stick, the mirage, and the phantom pains as illusory. But we must conclude from this that one cannot reasonably maintain that the physical world *exactly corresponds* to our perception of it. The most that could be maintained, in view of these examples of illusory perception, is that the world is like the majority of our perceptions.

The same conclusion may be re-enforced by a second consideration, namely, that alterations in a perceiver result in changes in the perceptions which that person has. Suppose, for example, that a quantity of water is kept at a constant temperature. On one occasion I come from a hot bath, immerse my hand in the water, and pronounce it cold. On another occasion I come from having handled ice, immerse my hand in the water, and pronounce it warm. The water was not really cold in the first instance and warm in the second, but of the same temperature. It was my perception that varied, not the water itself.

A particularly interesting example of this phenomenon may be considered in connection with what we call color-blindness. Two observers, *A* and *B*, look at some patches of color. *A* perceives some patches to be red and others to be green; *B* perceives them to be all the same color. *B*, accordingly, is said to be color-blind. But note: it is only because persons able, like *A*, to make the distinction are in the overwhelming majority that the few unable to do so are said to be color-blind; were the statistics reversed, persons who perceive a distinction would perhaps be regarded by the majority to be subject to a strange illusion. Whose perception is to be regarded as an accurate copy of the real world? One cannot say, "those who are normal," since normalcy is here defined in terms of the perceptions of the majority. It is not reasonable to decide a question of this sort by means of a referendum.

Anyone who has understood the point we are now attempting to make should have no great difficulty in finding additional examples of his own. The central clue is this: certain changes in a perceiver produce changes in the way the world looks to that perceiver. When one wears colored glasses—pink, or brown, or green—the world appears more pink, more brown, more green than it otherwise does. How can we be sure that the wearing of colored glasses does not enable us to see more clearly what the world is really like? Persons under the influence of some drugs are said to perceive the world in a way different from that in which they perceive it when they are not under its influence. Which perceptions are correct? Which set of perceptions provides an accurate copy of the real world?

One could, of course, save some vestiges of the common-sense view by making a number of arbitrary decisions at this point. One could say, for example, that it is the majority of the perceptions of people who have normal perception—people who have suffered no accident or injury affecting perception, who are not color-blind, who are not wearing colored glasses, who have been for some time in a room whose temperature is exactly 68 degrees Fahrenheit, etc.— it is the majority of the perceptions of such persons that tell us what the world is really like. But it is apparent that such decisions are purely arbitrary, and with each new difficulty that appears a new requirement must be introduced. To realize this is to realize that something other than common-sense realism must be adopted.

How far must we go, then, in our departure from the common-sense view? The answer, as I conceive it, is: Not very far. Let us see upon what basis such an answer might be both rendered precise and supported.

The Case for Critical Realism

The principle that should guide us in this matter, I think, is the one enunciated by John Locke: such qualities as are utterly inseparable from a physical object, such that a particle of matter however small could not be conceived to exist without it, are real qualities of that object; everything else that we perceive, though it indeed may appear to us to be a real quality in the object, is in truth nothing but a modification of our faculty of perception.[1] We shall, following Locke, call these respectively *primary qualities* and *secondary qualities*. We shall say, accordingly, that primary qualities are indeed really in the object; and in respect to these, the object is as we perceive it to be. Secondary qualities, however, are not in the object at all, but are only modifications of our faculty of perception caused by the object through its primary qualities. Let us see what account of the physical world can be given on the basis of this distinction.

Every object that we perceive appears to us to have the following qualities: color, shape, size, temperature, degree of hardness (texture), and either rest or motion; some objects, but not all, have also some odor, some taste, and some sound. These are the qualities that our various senses perceive to be present in the objects that come before us.

Which of these qualities, then, really are present in the object? Applying our rule, we get the following: shape, size, temperature, texture, solidity, and either rest or motion. Take any object you please, and divide it up into as many and as tiny parts as you will: each part will still have some shape, some size, some temperature, some degree of solidity, and some texture, and it will be either in motion or at rest. These, therefore, are the primary qualities of an object.

---

[1] See John Locke, *An Essay Concerning Human Understanding* (New York: Dover Publications, 1959), Book II, Chap. XXIII, pp. 390-423.

What remain to be accounted the secondary qualities of an object are, therefore, its color, its odor, its taste, its sound, its warmth or coldness. These, it is apparent, depend on the sense apparatus of the percipient, and consist in nothing more than a modification of that apparatus by the object. Were the senses associated with our eyes, our ears, and our nose capable of being affected differently, things would appear to have different colors, different sounds, different odors than they now appear to us to have; and were our body temperature higher or lower than it is, things would not be perceived to be warm or cold in the proportions that they now are.

The qualities that are objectively present in an object are, therefore, according to our view, shape, size, temperature, texture, solidity, and either rest or motion. These cause, via the mechanism of our sense apparatus, (a) impressions that are like the qualities themselves, which we call impressions of primary qualities, and (b) impressions unlike the qualities, which we call impressions of secondary qualities.

There is one further point that should be made in order to make our account complete. It is impossible to conceive of an object as being made up simply of its several qualities randomly thrown together. An object has a certain unity, a certain coherence, for which our account thus far has made no provision. We must add, therefore, the admittedly vague idea of a *substratum:* an underlying something which we do not directly perceive, but which we must, nonetheless, posit as the ground of the unity of an object. The diagram on p. 188 may be of some help in clarifying what we are here proposing. (The "substratum," it will be noted, has been placed within a dotted line in the diagram to indicate that its status is different from that of both primary and secondary qualities: it is not an object of perception, but something that the mind is, nonetheless, constrained to posit in its attempt to round out and complete its concept of a physical object.)

Our answer to the question, "Is the physical world in any degree dependent on a perceiver for its existence?" is "Yes, in some degree." Color, sound, taste, smell, warmness and coldness—those things that constitute what we have called the secondary qualities of objects—are dependent on a perceiver; they are, in fact, nothing but modifications that occur within the perceiver. If there were no perceivers capable of being modified in this way, there would be no color, or sound, or taste, or odor, or warmness or coldness in the world. But the primary qualities are in no way dependent on a perceiver. They would continue to exist even on the supposition that all perceivers were to be annihilated.

The object has:		*The perceiver has impressions of:*	
		(a)	(b)
S		S	
U		U	
B	Shape	B	Shape
S	Size	S	Size	Color
T	Temperature	T	Temperature	Warmness or Coldness
R	Texture	R	Texture	Taste
A	Solidity	A	Solidity	Smell
T	Rest or Motion	T	Rest or Motion	Sound
U		U	
M		M	

The chief reason for adopting the view which I have been expounding is that it enables us to solve all of those puzzles about perception that originally caused us to question the common-sense view that the world is just exactly as we perceive it to be. We can make appropriate allowances for what we have called illusory perceptions. We can say, for example, that a perception that is not consistent with the majority of our perceptions—such as the bent stick, the mirage, hallucinations, "phantom pains," and the like— is not revelatory of the nature of the real world. The common-sense view, with its implicit confidence in the deliverances of the senses, cannot do this.

More significantly, however, our view enables us to explain without difficulty the fact that alterations in a perceiver result in certain changes in that person's perception. It is no longer a puzzle that what is perceived to be cold at one time may, without any change in the object, be perceived by the same person to be warm at another time (or even simultaneously, if one hand be warm and one cold), since the impressions of warmness and coldness are seen to be dependent on certain conditions in the perceiver. Similarly, the puzzles that arise in connection with our perception of color are easily solved: things appear to be colored differently to persons who are color-blind, under the influence of certain drugs, or wearing colored glasses, because these things alter our visual sense apparatus and because color is nothing but a modification of the appropriate sense organ.

There are other puzzles in connection with perception that can also be solved easily in the context of the view that we are advocating. For example: some people are able to hear high-pitched signals that are completely inaudible to others. From the point of view of the common-sense theory, is a signal that is inaudible to all but a few people really a sound or is it not? For us, this phenomenon causes no difficulty. Sound, we say, is nothing but a modification of the audial apparatus of some perceiver. Some people are capable of being affected by air vibrations of a higher frequency than others— hence, the difference. Any such modification is a sound, and so the difficulty disappears. Individual differences with respect to taste and smell can be accounted for in the same manner.

Some Remarks About Perception

It is evident, then, that we must reject the common-sense view regarding the ontological status of the physical world and with it must go also the "copy" theory of perception. The real world is not exactly as it appears to be; if our sense impressions are a "copy" of the real world, they are a very poor copy indeed.

What shall we say of the status of our sense impressions? How are sense-data related to the objects in the real world that are their causes?

The answer implied in the position we are propounding is that the sense-data *represent* the real objects before our minds. We directly perceive the sense-data, and we make certain inferences about the objects that they represent. What we see, hear, taste, touch, and smell we really do see, hear, taste, touch, and smell: here there is no error. But what we infer about the objects that are represented to us by these various kinds of sense-data may be in error. Common-sense realism is thus seen to consist in the view that for every sense-datum that appears in our perceptual field there is something *just like it* in the physical world. And this view, as we have seen, is one that is not consistent with the facts.

We must take care, however, lest we depart further from the common-sense view than the facts in the case either require or warrant us to do. The facts that lead us to reject the common-sense view do not, insofar as I can see, require us to reject any more of that view than we have here suggested. There are, I am aware, certain considerations that seem to favor the phenomenalist view on this matter, and these obviously are worthy of being considered on their own merits. That view, however, involves certain difficulties which I do not think can be resolved without returning to something like the view here proposed. It seems to me, moreover, that every argument that tends to support the phenomenalist position is equally valid, if it is valid at all, as an argument in support of solipsism—a view so patently absurd that the arguments in support thereof must be regarded as highly suspect. That we must depart as far from the common-sense theory as we have proposed seems obvious; but it seems equally obvious that to depart any farther would be neither wise nor prudent.

Study Questions

1. What considerations does Critical Realist bring forward to support the view that "common-sense realism" is not a defensible position? Can you think of any way to defend common-sense realism against this critique?
2. What is the criterion by which Critical Realist proposes to distinguish between "primary" and "secondary" qualities? Does he apply it consistently in drawing up his two lists? Is the criterion itself a valid one, in your opinion?
3. What, according to Critical Realist's account, are the "primary" and "secondary" qualities, respectively, of each of the following: a red brick? a book? a bowling ball? a siren? a mirage?
4. What reasons does Critical Realist give for adopting his theory regarding the status of the physical world? Do you find his reasons convincing? Can you think of any way that his case might be strengthened?

Chapter 21

HYPER-CRITICAL REALISM

I THINK MY READERS should know
that the name "hyper-critical realism" that has been tacked on to
my position is not one that they are apt to find in any philosophical
writings prior to the early 1960's. The name was originally coined
by Professor Herbert Feigl, and I think it is quite obvious that he
used it only in jest. However, it is remarkably suggestive of what I
hold concerning the relation of our percepts (i. e., what we perceive) to the physical world, and I would not object if it were to
come into general use as a descriptive title for the position that I
represent.

Anyone who is at all familiar with the advances that have been
made in the science of physics during the past few decades will
recognize immediately, I think, that we cannot stay as close to
common-sense realism as Critical Realist has urged us to do. This
rough-and-ready description of the world in terms of primary and
secondary qualities—not to mention the utterly opaque notion of a
material substratum in which the primary qualities are said to inhere—may have deserved some credence a century or two ago, but
it deserves no such credence today. We have learned a good deal
since the days of John Locke, and one of the things we have
learned is that the particles of which material objects are composed
are not little nuggets of matter, each of which retains the "primary
qualities" of which Critical Realist speaks—shape, size, motion,
and all the rest. We know, or at least we think we know, that every-

thing in the physical world is a compound of some few basic elements, that every compound is reducible to molecules, every molecule to atoms, every atom to protons, neutrons, electrons, and many other even smaller particles. To try to understand the relation of our percepts to the world thus conceived in terms of Critical Realist's theory is like trying to do fine etching with a pick axe: the tool is simply not adequate for the job to be done.

We need not plunge into the complexities of modern physics, however, in order to see that we cannot be satisfied with so minimal a departure from the common-sense theory as Critical Realist has proposed. A number of far less recondite facts which our friend appears to have overlooked are as evidently fatal to his theory as the facts he does mention are to the common-sense theory. Let us consider in some detail the "damaging" facts which Critical Realist has overlooked.

Some Paradoxes of Perception

Critical Realist has called attention to a number of rather unusual perceptual phenomena—the refraction of light as it passes through a transparent liquid (the example of the bent stick), mirages, "phantom pains," and the like—and has rested the case for his view on the claim that he is able thereby to account for these phenomena. A number of paradoxes arise, however, in connection with some far less spectacular and unusual perceptual phenomena which cannot be easily accounted for in the context of his theory.

The first group of paradoxes to which I should like to call attention arises in connection with what I shall call the "perspectification" that accompanies all visual perception.

Consider, first, the quality of an object that we call its shape. The shape that an object appears to have depends entirely on the point of view from which one is viewing it. A sheet of typing paper, for example, appears to be a rectangle if you view it from a point directly above its center; each of its four corners, accordingly, appears to be a 90-degree angle or very nearly so. Turn it at a slight angle, however, and step away from it a few feet, and two of the corners will appear to be acute angles and two obtuse. The same phenomenon occurs in all cases of visual perception: the apparent shape varies depending on the point of view of the observer, and is constantly changing as the observer moves in relation to the object being viewed (or vice versa). A lake that looks round when viewed from the air (directly above its center) looks like a wide oval when viewed from the top of a nearby mountain, and like a very long and thin oval when viewed from any point along its shore. A penny looks round from one point of view, oval from another, and rectangular from yet another, and so on.

Which of these many shapes that every object appears to have is supposed to be really present in the object? Why should the "top-side" view of a printed page, or the "air" view of a lake, or the "front and center" view of a penny be granted a privileged status? To do so is rather obviously to make an arbitrary choice. To say that something is "round," for example, is only to say that it will appear to be round if you look at it from such-and-such a point of view. No reason can be given, however, for saying that this point of view rather than some other is the one from which we can see what shape the object "really" has. In the case of three-dimensional objects there is in fact no point of view from which an object appears to have the shape that it is usually said to "really" have.

Consequently, if we wish to maintain Critical Realist's position, we must be prepared to do one of two things. Either we must say that an object has many shapes and that the one you see depends on the point of view from which you happen to observe it; or, quite arbitrarily, that this or that point of view puts us in a position to see its "real" shape. If we are not willing to accept one or the other of these alternatives—and I for one am not—then we must give up the view that objects have a "real" shape that corresponds to our perception of their shape.

The same perplexities arise in connection with size. As a boy, I used to be very puzzled when my father told me that airplanes are bigger than automobiles: every airplane I had ever seen appeared to be no bigger than a large bird, and it seemed incredible to me that grown people could actually get inside so tiny an enclosure. It was not until I had an opportunity to visit an airport and see an airplane "close up" that I began to be convinced that my father was right. So it is with all visual perception: the size that an object appears to have depends on how close you are to it when you are looking at it. I have yet to meet a person to whom the moon does not *appear* to be about the size of a basketball.

Which of the apparent sizes of an object is to be accounted its "real" size? Is it the close-up view? How close? We are faced, evidently, with alternatives comparable to those that we had to contend with in connection with shape: either we must hold that an object really has many sizes, and that the one you perceive depends on how far you are away from it; or we must claim to know that there is some precise distance from which we are able to perceive its "real" size. Or we must give up the view that objects have a "real" size to which some perception of ours exactly corresponds.

What, then, can be retained of Critical Realist's account? Is temperature a real quality in objects? Perhaps. But we do not perceive temperature, we merely infer it from what we see on a thermometer. What we perceive is only impressions of warmness and coldness, and these even Critical Realist admits to be modifications in the perceiver. Can texture be retained as a real quality in objects? Here, too, difficulties arise. What feels smooth to the touch looks rough when viewed under a microscope: hills and valleys then appear on a surface we thought to be perfectly smooth. Which is it "really," rough or smooth? Or is it both? We are back in our old dilemma.

It is scarcely even necessary to discuss the paradoxes that arise if one tries to regard rest and motion as real qualities objectively present in objects. We are all sufficiently familiar with the fact that motion is relative to realize that whether a thing is to be regarded as being in motion or at rest depends entirely on what you assume to be at rest in making your judgment. If the earth is assumed to be at rest, then a boulder lying on a mountainside is also at rest; if you assume the sun to be at rest, then the earth and everything on it, including the boulder, is in motion. To an observer on earth, the earth appears to be at rest, and the sun, the moon, and the stars appear to revolve around it. To an observer on the moon, or on Mars, the surface on which he stood would be judged to be at rest, and everything else would appear to be in motion in relation to himself. Whether a thing is perceived to be in motion or at rest depends on the point of view of the observer. Our alternatives are, therefore, (a) to say that every object in the universe really has many motions, the one you see depending on your point of view, (b) to say that only one of these is its "real" motion, and give some reason for so saying, or (c) to concede that rest and motion are not real qualities of objects at all, but only part of the way in which objects appear to an observer.

There remains of Critical Realist's list of primary qualities, then, only solidity, and by this time I suspect we are prepared to concede that this, too, is unlikely to stand up under close scrutiny. It seems evident, in the first place, that "solidity" can only mean the tendency that an object has to resist another object and that this must vary depending on the size and strength of the invading object. To a fly a piece of balsa wood must appear quite solid; to a man it does not. To a small child a piece of stiff paper appears quite solid; to an adult it appears soft and malleable. Which is it "really?" Any answer that one might give would be completely arbitrary.

In point of fact, we know that nothing in the whole world is "really" solid. This desk upon which I am writing, that appears to be so solid, to have such-and-such a shape, such-and-such a size, such-and-such a color and texture, and to stand absolutely motionless here in the center of my office, in reality has none of these qualities. All of these qualities are relative to my faculty of perception, the particular senses with which I happen to be equipped and the particular point of view from which I happen to observe it. What is really "out there" is quite different, radically different, from what I perceive to be out there. What, then, are we justified in believing about the real qualities of physical objects?

Appearance and Reality

In order to solve the paradoxes about which we have been speaking, we must, I would suggest, make a clear distinction between the world of our percepts and the world as it really is—or, to use a terminology that is very old in the history of philosophy, between appearance and reality.

The world appears to us to consist of a multiplicity of objects of various sizes, shapes, colors, textures, temperatures, and so on. On the basis of these appearances, common sense constructs a theory of a real three-dimensional space in which all of these objects are believed to exist and ascribes to them the various characteristics which they appear to have. It is this whole common-sense theory about the world that, as we have seen, collapses when it is subjected to close scrutiny.

What is really "out there," however—the physical world as it really is—is being discovered with greater and greater accuracy by the natural sciences, especially by the science of physics. This is hardly the place to begin to summarize all that we now know about the constitution of the universe, but a brief sketch may be made by way of indicating how we ought to think about an object if we would conform our thought in at least some degree to what physics tells us it is really like. We shall take as our example the above-mentioned desk.

According to modern physics, the desk on which I am writing is not, as it appears to be, a solid block of "matter" that occupies some particular position or series of positions in a fixed three-dimensional space. It consists, rather, of several series of events occurring in a four-dimensional manifold which physicists call "space-time," these several series being interrelated in a vast variety of ways. What I call my desk is, in short, something that happens; it is, in fact, a vast conglomeration of happenings that occur in the particular region of space-time which it occupies. None of the particles involved in the events constituting my desk—the protons, neutrons, electrons, etc.—is solid, or colored, or warm, or cold, or anything else that we perceive when we perceive the desk. The language that is appropriate to the desk as I perceive it is absolutely inappropriate for a description of the atomic events of which it is really composed.

It is logically possible, of course, that the atomic events of which my desk is composed should be occurring without my being aware of them in any way—just as radio waves are constantly passing through the region of space-time that I occupy without my being aware of them in any way. It happens to be the case, however, that as a result of the atomic events that constitute my desk, and as a result of certain other atomic events that are related in various ways to the atomic events that constitute my desk, certain radiations are emitted which, when I am properly situated, cause a series of occurrences in my brain which I call "perceiving the desk."

Consider, for example, the perception of solidity. I perform the activity that I call "pressing my hand against the desk" and pronounce that it is "hard" or "solid." In reality, however, no particle that is involved in the events of which my hand is composed come in contact with the particles involved in the events of which the desk is composed. What really happens is that an electrical force is created by the nearness of the former to the latter, and this force—through a complicated process involving my nerves and my brain—causes the event that I call perceiving the "hardness" or "solidity" of the desk.

Or consider color. My desk looks brown; according to the common-sense view it really is brown. Physics, however, tells us otherwise. What is really happening when I am "perceiving brown" is this: electro-magnetic waves of various frequencies are being emitted from the sun, and (after a journey requiring roughly eight minutes) they are streaming through my window and striking my desk. Some of these waves enter the desk, causing certain changes in it which we describe as an increase in its temperature. Others are scattered by the particles that constitute the surface of the desk, and by way of my eyes, optic nerve, and brain they create the event in me that I call "perceiving brown." And so on for all sensible qualities.

Our general answer to the question concerning the ontological status of the physical world, therefore, is this. The physical world is dependent on a perceiver for the existence of all of what we may call its common-sense qualities: color, sound, taste, odor, shape, size, solidity, and all the rest. It is only by virtue of the constitution of our faculty of sensation—the particular modifications of which it happens to be capable—that the world appears to us to have these qualities; and if we, or beings having a faculty of sensation like ours, were to be annihilated, all such qualities would accordingly disappear. What would not disappear, however, is the atomic and sub-atomic events which constitute the physical world and cause us to have the particular perceptions we do have. To that extent, the physical world has a real existence of its own and is in no way dependent on a perceiver for its existence.

Perception

I find myself, therefore, in agreement with old-fashioned critical realism on two important points: (a) there is something "out there" that constitutes the real world and (b) it is what is "out there" that causes us to have the perceptions we have.

We must, therefore, allow, it seems to me, that the older view was right in affirming a representative theory of perception. Perceptions do represent realities in the external world, but they do not represent them as they really are. To infer that the physical world is just like, or somewhat like, the world as it appears to us is to ignore most of what science has taught us, and moreover to involve oneself in endless paradoxes. The way to solve these paradoxes is to make the distinction we have made between appearance and reality and to allow that the perceptions that represent physical realities to us are in no way like the realities they represent.

In conclusion I should like to state that I am well aware that it is not easy for any of us to relinquish the idea that the physical world really is as we perceive it to be. As I look now at the desk that I have recently been so busy dissolving into atomic and sub-atomic events, I am as powerfully tempted as the most unconvinced common-sense realist to think that it really has the solidity, the color, the smoothness, etc., that I perceive it to have. It is only when I attend carefully to the arguments, only when I consider the difficulties involved in saying this, that I know it cannot be so. As a *theory,* common-sense realism or anything very close to it simply will not do; but as a way of looking at the world, as an attitude that governs our everyday commerce with the world, none of us is able to divest ourselves of it. For the world that we must take account of in most of our affairs is the world of appearance, not the world of reality.

Study Questions

1. What "paradoxes" does Hyper-critical Realist mention which, according to him, cannot be explained in the context of a mild form of critical realism? Can you think of any way that Critical Realist might be able to defend his position against this attack?
2. What is Hyper-critical Realist's general answer to the question posed

in this section? What, if anything, makes his position a form of "realism"?
3. What, according to this theory, is the ontological status of color? of sound? of temperature? of electrons? of atoms? of molecules?
4. What criterion does Hyper-critical Realist use in distinguishing between "appearance" and "reality"? Is it, in your opinion, a sounder criterion than that employed by Critical Realist?

Chapter 22

PHENOMENALISM

PHENOMENALISM, AS HAS already been explained, is the view that the existence of a physical object is dependent upon its being perceived by some percipient, that a physical object is nothing but a construct made up of the percepts that are the immediate objects of perception. It follows directly from this that the physical world is completely dependent on some perceiver(s) for its existence and that if all perceivers were to be annihilated, the physical world would accordingly cease to exist. It is this view which it is now my task to expound and defend.

This task is rendered easier than it might otherwise be by the fact that much of what I ordinarily would have to say in order to build my case has already been said by the two gentlemen who have preceded me in this discussion. The last writer has, indeed, brought us to the very borders of phenomenalism. I propose to show that the very considerations which have brought the argument to this point require us to take a further step that leads to the phenomenalist position.

The Inconsistency of Hyper-critical Realism

Hyper-critical Realist has argued, quite rightly, that we cannot validly infer from the fact that the world appears to us as a multiplicity of objects of various colors, shapes, sizes, textures, etc., that it really is so. If we try to say this a host of puzzles arise, and we cannot solve these puzzles without departing rather far from the common-sense view. Next, he goes on to suggest that we know, nonetheless, that there is something "out there" that causes us to have these sensations and that what this something is can be learned by studying physics. He then proceeds to give us a short course in atomic physics and supposes thereby that he has persuaded us that so much at least can be retained of the realist view.

But surely it is fair to ask, How do we know that the atomic events that we do not see are objectively real, when we evidently do not know that the size, shape, color, etc., that we do see are objectively real? How have the physicists come by this esoteric knowledge—this knowledge of what the world that is supposed to lie behind the appearances is really like?

We know the answer, of course: they have inferred it from certain phenomena which they have observed. Common-sense realism is the consequence of an unsophisticated inference from some more or less obvious facts of observation; scientific realism (which is what I prefer to call Hyper-critical Realist's theory) is the consequence of a sophisticated inference from some less obvious facts of observation. But if the inference is not justified in the first instance, neither is it justified in the second. There is no more reason to say that the latest theory of the physicists is an accurate description of something real "behind the appearances" than there is to say that the description of a common-sense realist is accurate. The two differ considerably in their respective degrees of sophistication, but insofar as validity is concerned, they are on the same ground. Realism is equally naive, whether it be maintained in a common-sense or in a scientific version.

It is worthy of note that the scientists themselves do not make the mistake that Hyper-critical Realist has made of regarding scientific theories as descriptions of anything at all. What Andreas Osiander said in his preface to Copernicus' treatise *On the Revolutions of the Heavenly Bodies* may be said of all scientific theories: "There is no need for these hypotheses to be true, or even to be at all like the truth; one thing is sufficient for them—that they should yield a calculus that agrees with the observations." Scientific hypotheses are, in short, nothing more than instruments that are useful for purposes of calculation. Their function is not to tell us what the world is really like, but to aid us in controlling the world as it appears to us.

It seems clear, therefore, that the very arguments that have been used in the preceding chapters to establish some form of critical realism really tend to support instead the phenomenalist view. We have no basis upon which to infer a universe of signaling stations beyond or behind the perceptual signals that we constantly receive: the only world of which we have or can have any knowledge is the world of our perception. But this is precisely what we mean by the phrase, "the physical world"; hence, it is clear that the physical world is altogether dependent on perceivers for its existence.

A Common-sense Argument for Phenomenalism

Let us return again to the example of the desk. If I want to teach a child the meaning of the word "desk," what I have to do is obvious: I have to show one to him, to let him see it and touch it—in short, I have to put him in a position to receive certain sense-data, and I have to pronounce the word "desk" so that he will associate it with those sense-data. If he then learns the meaning of this word, what can he possibly understand it to mean but the impressions of hardness, brownness, flatness, etc., which he was taught to associate with the word "desk"? It is in this way, surely, that all of us have learned the names of such familiar objects as desks, chairs, tables, stones, trees, and so on.

What does it mean, then, to say that something—a desk, let us say—exists? It means, and can only mean: if you go to such-and-such a place (where the desk is said to exist), you will have percepts of the sort that you have learned to associate with the word "desk." If the statement "there is a desk in my office" is true, then you will have desk-like percepts if you go into my office; if it is false, you will not. A statement affirming the existence of something is always a statement about percepts.

Suppose, now, that someone says, "But surely things continue to exist even when nobody is perceiving them, don't they?" We reply: "Yes, but to say that something exists when nobody is perceiving it is still to say something about percepts, namely, that if someone were to go to such-and-such a place (where the thing is said to exist), he would have such-and-such sorts of percepts." Every statement to the effect that something exists is a statement about actual or possible percepts. Any meaning that we try to ascribe to the word "existence" in addition to this is simply unintelligible.

If, then, someone says that there is something behind the percepts that exists, and that this is the cause of our having such-and-such percepts, he evidently is saying something that has no meaning. It makes sense to say that there are real actors in a real studio that cause us to have the particular percepts that we have when we look at our television set, because we know what it would be like to have the percepts that constitute the set of events that we call "actors in a studio." Here we can "go behind the scenes," so to speak, without forsaking the realm of percepts. But to talk about a reality behind the appearances, a non-perceptual something that causes us to have percepts, is to talk nonsense. The appearance *is* the reality. If there is anything beyond the world as it appears to us (whatever that might mean), we must remain forever in ignorance of what it is.

The physical world, therefore, exists only in our percepts. If there were no perceivers there would be no percepts, and hence no physical world. George Berkeley was right: to be a physical object is to be perceived.

Objections and Replies

I do not think that the phenomenalist view of the ontological status of the physical world is really very vulnerable to attack by opposing views. The various forms of critical realism that have been proposed are, I am convinced, nothing more than temporary stopping places for "backsliding realists": philosophers who have failed to follow all the way along the route that leads to phenomenalism have done so more by default than by acute philosophical argument. There are, however, some common-sense objections which one sometimes hears raised against the phenomenalist view. To demonstrate just how strong the case for phenomenalism really is, I should like to state these objections and show how easily they can be met.

It is sometimes objected, for example, that it is silly to say things like, "I had some corn-flakish percepts for breakfast this morning," or "Help! Someone has stolen my new-car-ish percepts," but that according to the phenomenalist view this ought to be a perfectly proper way of speaking. The answer is, however, that the phenomenalist theory does not commit one who holds it to the view that talk of this sort is proper. Indeed, it is never proper to mix ordinary language and technical theory in this way. It would be equally absurd to say, "I had a bowl of corn-flakish protons, neutrons and electrons for breakfast," or, "Someone stole my new-car-ish atoms." What constitutes proper usage for purposes of ordinary discourse cannot decide questions of physical or philosophical theory. The objection, therefore, is quite beside the point.

A second objection that is sometimes raised is this. Phenomenalism, it is said, provides no basis upon which to distinguish between valid and illusory percepts: if to be is to be perceived, then mirages and other things which even common sense regards as illusions must be as real as anything else, for a mirage is obviously something that is perceived. But we can distinguish between illusory and non-illusory perceptions, the argument continues; therefore, phenomenalism must be in error.

In answer to this objection it is only necessary to point out that the difference between illusory and non-illusory perceptions is a difference among perceptions. The reason that we call some perceptions illusory is that they lead us to have certain expectations that are not fulfilled. We regard a mirage, for example, as illusory precisely because it leads us to expect certain other perceptions—those constituting what we call "drinking water" and "resting in the shade of a tree"—that are not forthcoming. To say that something is real and not illusory is not to posit an unperceived metaphysical reality "behind" our percepts: it is to say that the expectations which our percepts create in us can be fulfilled—that we shall not be disappointed if under such-and-such conditions we count on having such-and-such additional percepts. Try as we will, I do not think we shall find any further reason for making the distinction. If the water-and-shade percepts that we anticipate when we see a mirage were forthcoming we would not call it a mirage: it would then be identical with what we call an oasis.

It is sometimes argued that according to the phenomenalist account physical objects—trees, stones, freight trains, skyscrapers and other such apparently solid and substantial things—are constantly popping in and out of existence: when someone is perceiving them, they exist, and when nobody is perceiving them, they cease to exist. And this, it is said, is absurd. Berkeley himself, it may be pointed out, found this idea so preposterous that he advanced the idea that things exist continually in the perception of God (who neither slumbers nor sleeps); and this, to say the least, seems a bit farfetched. What if God should blink?

It seems, however, that we have already answered this objection without embracing Berkeley's rather questionable *ad hoc* theology. To say that something continues to exist even when it is not being perceived is simply to say that if someone fulfilled such-and-such conditions, he would have such-and-such perceptions. Physical objects, as John Stuart Mill once said, are "permanent possibilities of sensation." A physical object consists of percepts, actual and possible; the intervals of time during which the object is not actually being perceived are filled in by the continuing "possibilities of sensation" that remain.

Even after hearing this explanation, however, one may still be inclined to ask: How is it, then, that common sense comes to take it for granted that objects continue to exist when they are not perceived, in exactly the same way that they do when they are perceived? Where does the common-sense idea of an objectively real, ontologically independent physical world come from? The answer, I think, is that certain features of our perceptual experience induce us to posit such a world. The most important of these features are (a) the resemblance between the various percepts that we call percepts of the "same thing," (b) the occurrence of these similar groups of percepts in the context of a relatively stable perceptual environment, (c) the fact that we can, within certain limits, predict what sorts of percepts we shall have under such-and-such conditions, and (d) the fact that the perceptions that we have can be varied in a more or less systematic way depending on our own movements. The idea of an independently existing world of physical objects, which objects appear to us in the vast variety of ways evident in our actual perceptions, is an ingenious hypothesis that common sense has erected to account for these features of our perceptual experience; but it is, as we have seen, a hypothesis that does not stand up under close scrutiny.

How, then, it may be asked, are we to account for the consistency and the order that obtain among our percepts, if there is no independent physical world that is the cause of them all? The answer is that we cannot—nor can the realist theory. The realist theory only pushes the problem one step further back: it accounts for order among our percepts by positing an ordered world, and it takes the order of the world for granted or leaves it unexplained. We say that the order which evidently obtains among our percepts *is* the order in the world because the only world of which we have any knowledge is the world of our percepts. If there is some explanation of why there is order in the world, then that is why there is order among our percepts; if there is no explanation, then, of course, we have none either. The discussion about order, in any case, in no way favors the realist view.

It is not to the point, therefore, to argue that the phenomenalist view is refuted by the fact that people in the same general vicinity have more or less the same sense-data. Of course they do; if they did not, they would not be able to speak and act as if they lived in a common world. But that our percepts are more or less alike, and moreover systematically related in a wide variety of ways, is simply an ultimate fact that has to be taken for granted. To try to "explain" it by positing an ordered world "behind" the percepts is like trying to explain the sleep-producing effect of some drugs by saying they have in them a "soporific power." Such a statement is not only an inadequate explanation: it is not even a meaningful combination of words.

The final objection against phenomenalism with which I should like to deal concerns our knowledge of the existence of other minds. If phenomenalism were true, it is sometimes said, then we could never know that other minds exist. For to say that something exists is to say that we are having, or could have, such-and-such percepts; but no actual or possible percepts warrant our saying that another mind exists. Therefore, it is concluded, phenomenalism must lead to skepticism regarding the existence of any mind other than our own, and in the end to solipsism.

The question concerning our knowledge of the existence of other minds has always been a difficult one for empiricists, and I shall not pretend that I am able to give a definitive answer to it. I may say, however, that neither I nor any other phenomenalist known to me is a solipsist; therefore it is evident that being a phenomenalist does not commit one to accepting the solipsist position. But it is not easy to say how it is that we know of the existence of other minds.

A great part of the difficulty consists, I think, in the obscurity of the very notion of a "mind." In some senses that have been given to that word, I do not think we know of the existence of any minds, including our own. What we really want to know, however, when we ask, "Do other minds exist?" is: "Do other beings that are, like me, conscious and sentient exist?" It seems to me that the phenomenalist can answer as follows: (a) our own existence as conscious and sentient beings is immediately evident to us (our existence consists, as Berkeley said, in perceiving, not in being perceived); (b) we perceive beings that look, talk, and act in ways very similar to ourselves; and (c) by analogy we infer that they, too, are conscious and sentient beings just as we are. Common sense, in my opinion, can do no better.

Phenomenalism and Empiricism

In conclusion I want to state briefly what I conceive to be the relation of the view I am advocating to some of the epistemological questions that were discussed earlier. The point I should like to insist on is that anyone who intends to be absolutely consistent in his adherence to empiricism must in the end adopt the phenomenalist view with respect to the ontological status of the physical world. If we are serious about the view that all we know is what comes to us in experience, then it is clear that all we know is our percepts. To posit an unseen world "behind" the world of our percepts is evidently to claim that by means of experience we can go beyond experience; and this is just what an absolutely consistent empiricism will not permit us to do. The point, briefly put, is this: phenomenalism is the ontology of empiricism. Let phenomenalism be overthrown, and rationalism will have won the day.

Study Questions

1. What argument does Phenomenalist use to enforce his conclusion that "scientific realism" (as he calls it) is no more tenable than common-sense realism? Is his argument sound? Can you think of any way to defend Hyper-critical Realist's view against this argument?

2. How does Phenomenalist attempt to establish his position? Is this a sound argument in your opinion?

3. Summarize the "common-sense objections" to his position which Phenomenalist mentions, and his reply to each. Are you satisfied with his replies? Can you think of any other difficulties with this theory that Phenomenalist may have neglected to mention?

4. Phenomenalist says, "Neither I nor any other phenomenalist known to me is a solipsist; therefore, it is evident that being a phenomenalist does not commit one to accepting the solipsist position." Is this a good argument?

FOR FURTHER READING

Adams, E. M., "The Nature of the Sense-Datum Theory," *Mind,* Vol. LXVII (1958), 216-226.

Armstrong, D. M., *Perception and the Physical World.* New York: The Humanities Press, 1961.

Austin, J. L., *Sense and Sensibilia.* London: Oxford University Press, 1962 (paperbound).

Ayer, A. J., *The Foundations of Empirical Knowledge.* New York: St. Martin's Press, 1958 (paperbound). Chapters I, II, and V.

——, *The Problem of Knowledge.* New York: St. Martin's Press, 1956. Chapter III.

Barnes, W. H. F., "The Myth of Sense-Data," *Proceedings of the Aristotelian Society,* Vol. 45 (1944-1945), 89-117.

Bergmann, Gustav, *Logic and Reality.* Madison, Wis.: University of Wisconsin Press, 1964. Chapter 14.

Chisholm, R. M., "The Problem of Empiricism," *The Journal of Philosophy,* Vol. 45 (1948), 512-517.

Dewey, John, *Essays in Experimental Logic.* New York: Dover Publications, 1960 (paperbound). Pages 1-74 and 250-302.

Eddington, A. S., *The Nature of the Physical World.* Ann Arbor, Mich.: University of Michigan Press, 1958 (paperbound).

Ewing, A. C., *The Fundamental Questions of Philosophy.* New York: The Macmillan Company, 1951. Chapter 4.

Lewis, C. I., *An Analysis of Knowledge and Valuation.* LaSalle, Ill.: Open Court, 1947 (paperbound). Chapter VII.

Price, H. H., "The Argument from Illusion," in *Contemporary British Philosophy,* Third Series, ed. H. D. Lewis. New York: The Macmillan Company, 1956. Pages 391-400.

——, *Perception,* 2d ed. New York: Dover Publications, 1950.

Russell, Bertrand, *Human Knowledge.* New York: Simon and Schuster, 1962 (paperbound). Part Three, "Science and Perception."

——, *The Problems of Philosophy.* New York: Oxford University Press, 1959 (paperbound). Chapters 1-4.

Chapter 23

FIRST RETROSPECT

THE STUDENT WHO has made his way through the forest of arguments which have been offered in the course of the discussion of the problems considered thus far will, no doubt, have gathered a number of impressions of philosophy en route. Perhaps he will, by now, have disassociated himself from most of the impressions with which he began—or, possibly, he may only have confirmed them. But at the very least it is to be hoped that he has also acquired some new insights into the nature of the philosophical enterprise; and it seems, therefore, that we should pause briefly to survey the path over which we have come and to attempt to crystallize the results obtained thus far.

We have considered four philosophical problems: (1) the problem of the relation of language to reality, (2) the problem of *a priori* knowledge, (3) the problem of induction, and (4) the problem of the ontological status of the physical world. In the course of our discussion we have become acquainted with a fairly large number of technical and semi-technical terms and have learned to use them with comparative ease in the discussion of the relevant problems. We have also come to realize, perhaps, how important precise terminology is in philosophical discussion and have thus learned to be more careful about the exact meaning of the language we are using.

One of the things that may be surprising is the degree to which we found ourselves persuaded from time to time by views that are far removed from the common-sense views with which we began. Who would have supposed that we could have been led to doubt the validity of inductive reasoning? Or who could have guessed that we—hard-headed, common-sense realists—should ever have been tempted to believe that the physical world is constituted by our impressions of it and that apart from the perceptions of some perceiver it has no existence whatsoever? These, surely, are views that but a short time ago we would never have seriously entertained. Yet, they are capable of a fairly persuasive defense. Whether or not we have adopted them, we have at least entertained them. And to realize this may be somewhat of a surprise.

If we have done this, however—or, to speak more precisely, if this has happened to us—it is at least one indication that we have succeeded in some degree in entering into the peculiar kind of inquiry that is philosophy; for philosophy, as we said earlier, tends to be critical of the status quo. Philosophers are puzzled about certain problems that arise if common-sense views are taken at face value, and in their efforts to solve these puzzles they frequently propose alternatives to the common-sense views that are distinctly *un*common. If we find ourselves similarly puzzled, it is not surprising that we should also find ourselves persuaded to some extent by the solutions that they propose. And if we find ourselves puzzled by their puzzles, but unable to accept their solutions, then we have no alternative but to propose some solution of our own. Such is the route by which students of philosophy become philosophers.

I want to make at this point an observation that students in general, and students of philosophy in particular, are sometimes reluctant to accept. The point is this: *all significant learning consists in the modification or confirmation of one's previous beliefs.* One never approaches a learning situation empty-handed (or should we say empty-headed): one always brings to it prior beliefs, and one does not really learn anything unless those beliefs are either reenforced or in some way altered by the experience. It is imperative, therefore—if learning is to occur—that we be careful to determine exactly what our beliefs are; for not to do so is to fail to subject them to close scrutiny and evaluation, and thus to fail to allow them to be either confirmed or changed.

For the study of philosophy, this observation has at least one important practical implication. It means that a student who wishes to make of this study a significant learning experience must be prepared to state *where he stands* on the various matters that come up for discussion and he must be prepared to defend his position against the arguments that may be brought against his stand. In order to learn, one has to "stick one's neck out," and "sticking one's neck out" means, in this case, stating—however tentatively— what one thinks about the matter under discussion. We might say, paraphrasing Socrates, that "the unexamined belief is not worth having"—nor, as Socrates also said, can such a belief ever be secure. By subjecting our beliefs to honest scrutiny, and only in this way, we either re-enforce them or exchange them for better ones. In either case, we learn.

How Philosophical Problems Are Interrelated

The student may have surmised, as he turned his attention first upon one problem, then upon another, that these problems are not as isolated and independent as the separate discussion of each may have made them appear to be. He will have noted, of course, the very close relationship between the problem of *a priori* knowledge and the problem of induction, and he may have felt that there were other interrelationships too. He may have sensed, for example, that a conventionalist theory of language somehow "goes with" empiricism, and that an essentialist theory of language is much more congenial to the rationalist position, and so on. The theories we have considered can be grouped as follows:

Problem	Group I	Group II
Theory of Language	Conventionalism	Essentialism
A Priori Knowledge	Empiricism	Rationalism
Induction	Skepticism or Constructive Empiricism	Rationalism
Ontological Status of the Physical World	Phenomenalism	Realism

We can all recognize that there is a certain "family resemblance" among the various members of each of these groups. In what, then, does this resemblance consist? Why would one who is persuaded by the arguments in support of some one of these "isms" tend to favor also the other members in the same group?

If we reflect on this matter with some care we shall discover that the various members of each group are interrelated in a variety of ways. They are, indeed, interdependent. It is not a psychological propensity in favor of "tender-minded" or "tough-minded" theories (as William James once suggested [1]), but a desire for consistency in our views, that leads us to favor all of the members of one group insofar as we are persuaded by any one. Let us spell out in some detail how this is so.

Let us suppose, for example, that I am persuaded that all of our knowlege of synthetic truths arises out of experience—in short, that empiricism is true. It is immediately evident, of course, that I cannot in a way consistent with this view adopt the rationalist's solution to the problem of induction. I must, therefore, for the sake of consistency, adopt either the skeptic or the constructive-empiricist position on this problem (or else I must show that the problem does not really exist). It may not be so immediately evident, however, that consistency also requires that I hold a conventionalist theory of language; for in order to establish an essential link between language and reality, it is necessary to assume that something—the essential natures of things, or the rational structure of language and reality, or something—is known *a priori,* and this, if I am an empiricist, I cannot allow. So also with respect to the question concerning the ontological status of the physical world. If all I know about reality is what I learn from experience, then I do not know that there is an independently existing reality "behind the appearances." No such reality can be validly inferred from the sense-data that I actually perceive: if I know that there is such a reality it must be directly, *a priori;* and this, if I am an empiricist, I cannot accept. *Ergo,* I must be a phenomenalist.

Suppose, on the contrary, that I am persuaded that there is an essential link between language and reality. If I am so persuaded, it must be because I see, or claim to see, some *a priori* connection between the two—in, for example, the rational structure that gov-

---

[1] William James, *Pragmatism* (New York and London: Longmans, Green and Co., 1959), p. 12.

erns both. In so saying, therefore, I am already assenting to the central thesis of rationalism. Moreover, if language has this essential relation to reality, it is not nearly so surprising that simply by thinking about certain statements I should be able to see directly, *a priori,* that the propositions they express are true. On the question of the validity of inductive reasoning I have, of course, some leeway: I may accept the rationalist solution here, or I may not. It is, however, a possible position for me to take, which it is not for the empiricist. With respect to the ontological question, I can say, as the empiricist cannot, that we just know—*a priori*—that there is a reality out there behind the appearances, and it is this reality that is known via the appearances. It is possible for me, in short, to be a realist.

Take your stand at any point among the various views that we have discussed, and certain implications will follow with respect to the others. Adopt the rationalist solution to the problem of induction, and you must in consistency adopt the rationalist position on the question of *a priori* knowledge and the essentialist theory of language. Adopt the conventionalist theory of language, and you must in consistency reject both the rationalist epistemology and a realist ontology. And so for each of the others. Every position that one adopts on any particular question implies certain positions and excludes certain positions on countless other questions. This is what we meant when we spoke in one of the introductory chapters about the systematic character of all philosophical thinking and the multi-dimensional relevance of all philosophical questions (see Chapter 3).

Combining what we have just said with our earlier remarks about the nature of significant learning, we may say that the serious study of philosophy consists in the systematic clarification of the system that is implicit in one's whole way of looking at the world (one's "world-view," as we called it earlier) and the systematic testing of this system by means of a rigorous evaluation of certain of its elements. There *is* more at stake in the answer which one gives to this or that philosophical problem than the resolution of that particular problem. Indeed, as we remarked in an earlier chapter, every philosophical problem is a kind of test case for an entire world-view. This is why the serious study of philosophy requires great intellectual courage; it is also the reason why many people regard the study of philosophy as peculiarly dangerous.

Philosophy, Critical and Constructive

Now, perhaps, we are also in a position to "internalize" what was said earlier about the critical and the constructive sides of the philosophical task (see Chapter 2).

The critical philosophical task that really counts, so far as each of us individually is concerned, is the critical evaluation of our own views, which comes ultimately to the critical testing of the adequacy of our whole world-view. Obviously, we do not all hold exactly the same world-view, since the beliefs that each of us hold derive in large measure from the various influences that have shaped our thinking and these are never identical for any two people. Allowing for such differences in detail, however, it is also true that in many respects the world-views that we hold are very similar—much more similar, for example, than the world-view of any one of us would be to that of a person raised in an African or Far Eastern culture.

In subjecting these views to the critical questioning that constitutes one important side of the philosophical task, we are, therefore, engaging in an experiment that is both very personal and at the same time "vicarious." We are not only taking the personal risk of having our views exposed as inadequate, but, since most of our views are also those of the vast majority of the rest of the people in our culture, it is the intellectual outlook of our whole culture that is here being put to the test. If we should suffer the collapse of some of our cherished beliefs (and the loss of a cherished belief does involve a very painful sort of suffering), then it is not only for ourselves that we suffer, but for those many others in our culture who share those beliefs. It is only through such suffering, however, that human thought progresses.

But human thought *does* progress, and this is what makes the enterprise worthwhile. Many people must have suffered the kind of intellectual agony of which we have been speaking, during the long interval of time that separates us from our primitive ancestors; but there can be little doubt that our way of looking at the world—our world-view—is closer to the truth than the superstitious, animistic, magical views that they are known to have held. If our view is not the whole truth—and it would surely be presumptuous to say that it is—then let us press on toward that elusive goal as best we can. It is the lure of beliefs that are closer to the truth that beckons us on and leaves us dissatisfied with beliefs that are obviously short of that goal. It is the pursuit of this goal that constitutes what we have called the constructive side of the philosophical task.

One can readily imagine that what has just been said might be objected to in two different ways.

Some people would object to what we have just said about the nature of the philosophical quest on the ground that what we have described represents a prideful and arrogant overconfidence in the power of human reason to discover the truth. The wisdom of our forebears, it may be said, is to be preferred to our own latest conjectures; better to take that and be content and for the rest confess our ignorance.

The answer to this objection is that we have no choice in the matter: we know beyond any reasonable doubt that the world is not the way our distant forebears thought it was, and there is little reason to suppose that our more recent forebears have completely closed the gap between those ancient errors and the truth. Human reason undoubtedly has its limitations, and we should therefore beware of claiming more for our beliefs—old or new—than we have a right to claim; but to demand that we forsake the quest for truth altogether is to demand something that we cannot do.

A second objection that might be raised at this point is of a rather different nature. All this talk about "intellectual suffering," it may be said, is an interesting and perhaps suggestive homily, but it has nothing to do with the philosophical task as that task is now conceived by professional philosophers. Professional philosophers, it may be said, are not interested either in questioning received beliefs about the world or in trying to establish new ones; their task is rather to analyze the logic of our language and to dispel the confusions that result from a failure to understand this logic.

In reply to this it should be acknowledged that some professors of philosophy do conceive their task in this way, but it should be added that insofar as they conceive this task as an end in itself—

apart, that is, from what we have called the critical and the constructive sides of the philosophical enterprise—they have simply abandoned the traditional philosophical quest. The result of clearing up confusions that result from mistakes concerning the logic of our language is not, after all, simply to tidy up our language, but also and more importantly to correct our thinking. But "correcting our thinking" has no meaning unless it means "helping us to think more correctly"—that is, in a way that is closer to the truth. To "cut philosophy loose" from the quest for truth is to divest it of all that makes it important and worthwhile; to see it in the context of that quest is to see it as involving the "intellectual suffering" of which we spoke.

A Glance Ahead

The problems with which we have been concerned thus far might be grouped under the rather loose heading, "Language, Knowledge, and the Physical World." The four problems that we have discussed directly, as well as the many related problems discussed along the way, have all been concerned with matters that fall under this general heading; and they are, as we have seen, closely interrelated.

The problems that we shall consider next are by no means unrelated to these, but they do require us to turn our attention in a somewhat different direction. A collective heading for the next three problems to be considered might be, simply, "Man." And concerning man we shall ask three very perplexing questions: (1) How are we using language when we say of something that it is right or wrong, good or evil? (2) How are we to understand the relationship between mind and body? (3) How are we to understand the alleged freedom of man in a world that looks more and more as if it is completely subject to causal laws? Let us hope that in the course of our discussion we shall be able to give these questions greater precision—and that in attempting to answer them we shall find ourselves somewhere in the vicinity of the truth.

Study Questions

1. Do you agree that "all significant learning consists in the modification or confirmation of one's previous beliefs"? If not, what do you consider to be exceptions to this principle? If so, what practical implications do you see for the study of philosophy?
2. Think back over the four problems that we have studied thus far. If you had to make up your mind right now, which position would you be inclined to adopt on each of these problems? What seem to be the most important considerations in favor of the position(s) you tend to favor?
3. Are the positions that you tend to favor on these problems consistent with each other? Are you aware of any tensions, or possible inconsistencies, between these several views? If so, what are the possible ways of resolving them?
4. Do the positions that you now favor with respect to these four problems tend on the whole to re-enforce the beliefs you brought with you to this study, or do they compel you to substantially modify those beliefs? Be as specific as you can.

PART V

The Language of Morals

Chapter 24

THE CENTRAL PROBLEM
OF META-ETHICS

THE PROBLEM TO which we now turn is one that has attracted a great deal of discussion among philosophers during recent years. It was first formulated with clarity by Professor G. E. Moore in his celebrated book, *Principia Ethica*,[1] and every philosopher since that time who has ventured to write on ethical matters has felt obliged to address himself to the problem so effectively raised by Professor Moore. The number of alternative answers that have been proposed to Moore's problem is, unfortunately, extremely large, and we shall therefore have to proceed carefully in our study if we are to avoid confusion as to what the problem is all about.

Let us begin by making a few distinctions that may help us to find our way about in the somewhat rare atmosphere of what is called "meta-ethics." We shall then be in a position to understand the problem formulated by Professor Moore and to see some of the alternative ways in which it can be answered.

Morality, Ethics, and Meta-ethics

There is a sphere of human life and activity that it seems natural and proper to call the "moral" sphere. It is not easily defined or circumscribed; yet everyone is aware that certain thoughts, inten-

[1] G. E. Moore, *Principia Ethica* (Cambridge: Cambridge University Press, 1903).

tions, and acts are commonly regarded as being subject to moral appraisal, and certain others are not. Certain *feelings* seem to be associated with this sphere—for example, obligation, guilt, remorse. Also, certain *beliefs* seem to be associated with it: the belief that murder is wrong, that keeping a promise is good, and so on. Certain sorts of *acts,* too, clearly seem to fall within this sphere: helping another person who is in need, for example, or causing needless pain to another human being or other sentient creature. And, finally, certain sorts of *discourse* seem to be related to this sphere: utterances employing such terms as "good," "bad," "right," "wrong," "virtue," "vice," and the like.

All of these various things appear to cluster, however, about certain kinds of behavior—acts, in other words—about which we have the above-mentioned feelings and beliefs and concerning which we employ the above-mentioned sort of discourse. What, then, are the marks of that peculiar kind of behavior or activity that we regard as being appropriately subject to moral appraisal? There are, it appears, three such marks. First, it is only *human* behavior that we appraise in this way. Second, it is only human behavior in a situation involving *choice,* i. e., one in which there are alternatives; we neither praise nor blame a person for doing something if, under the circumstances, it was the only thing he could do. And third, we always suppose that some *moral rule* is relevant to the act in question—that there is something which a human being in that situation ought or ought not to do, simply by virtue of the fact that he is a human being in such-and-such circumstances. Anyone who will take the trouble to compare a number of situations in which we would and would not be inclined to apply the categories of moral appraisal will discover that this is a fairly accurate phenomenological description of the moral sphere.

There are, obviously, a number of ways in which the phenomena associated with this sphere can be made the objects of disciplined inquiry. The psychologist, for example, can study the conditions under which what we may call the "moral feelings" characteristically occur, and in so doing he can enhance our understanding of those feelings. The sociologist can inquire into the environmental conditions under which people tend to hold certain kinds of beliefs about right and wrong, and in so doing he can enhance our understanding of the causes and cures of crime and immorality. But the beliefs themselves that are thought to be relevant to this sphere—the moral principles, or rules—can also be made the object of disciplined inquiry; and when certain sorts of questions are asked about these beliefs, the result is positive, or normative, *ethics*.

The question asked by the ethicist is, "What sorts of things really are right and wrong, and why?" His aim is to introduce order and consistency into our ethical beliefs and to relate them, if possible, to some universal principle or principles from which they supposedly derive their validity as rules for the guidance of our behavior. If I ought to help old Mrs. Jones cross a busy intersection when I see her standing there, it must be because there is some rule which —not only *de facto* but *de jure*—governs my behavior and in terms of which I am appropriately praised or blamed for what I do or fail to do. And if I also ought to attempt to rescue a child who is drowning, the same reasoning applies. The ethicist asks, "What is it that these two cases, and hundreds of others that might be mentioned, have in common? Is there not some general principle that governs these and all other cases of moral obligation?" To ask, and attempt to answer, such questions is to engage in the peculiar sort of inquiry called *normative ethics;* and to exhibit a set of ethical beliefs as a coherent system deducible from one or more general principles is to construct an *ethical system*.

It is possible, however, to make ethical beliefs, and more particularly the language in which they are expressed, the object of a different sort of inquiry. It is possible to ask *logical* questions about moral discourse (the moral appraisals that men make in actual concrete situations) and ethical discourse (the general principles of right and wrong, good and evil, etc., which are formulated in normative ethics); and when one asks, and attempts to answer, such questions one is engaging in what has come to be called *meta-ethics*. In meta-ethics one does not ask questions of the sort, "Is it always one's moral duty to keep a promise?" (that is a question for normative ethics), but rather of the sort, "Does the statement 'Promise-keeping is good' logically entail that it is always one's duty to keep a promise?" "Does the statement 'X is my duty' logically entail that I ought to do X?" The meta-ethicist, in other words, is a logician who is inquiring into the logical structure of moral and ethical discourse; the questions he asks, and the answers he gives, are directed toward an elucidation of that logical structure.

The distinction between morality, ethics, and meta-ethics might be likened to the distinction between physical phenomena, natural science, and philosophy of science, or religion, theology, and philosophy of religion. In each instance we have (a) a sphere of actual processes or occurrences (physical, moral, religious), (b) a system of beliefs relevant thereto (science, ethics, theology), and (c) an inquiry concerning the logical status of those beliefs and the character of the reasoning by which they are supposedly established (philosophy of science, meta-ethics, and philosophy of religion). We shall, throughout this section, be operating at this "third level," and the object of our interest will be the statements that people make either at the level of concrete "lived" morality or at the level of systematic normative ethics.

The Problem About Moral Predicates

It is evident, then, that at the level of actual everyday experience we frequently say, and hear said, things like "He ought not to have done that," "That was a terrible thing to do," "She is an awfully good person," and the like. It is also evident that at the more reflective level of normative ethics we say, and hear said, things like "One ought to promote human happiness as much as one can," "The infliction of needless pain is evil," and "One ought always to do unto others as one would have them do unto you." Let us call sentences of this type "moral sentences"; and let us call the appraisal words that occur in such sentences—good, bad, right, wrong, praiseworthy, blameworthy, etc.—"moral predicates." (It should be noted that not all moral sentences are of the simple subject-predicate type. Such things as advice, commands, and even expressions of feeling ("How I wish you wouldn't do that!") may, under certain circumstances, be properly classified as moral sentences. But these distinctions need not concern us here.)

The meta-ethical problem with which we shall be concerned, then, may be stated as follows: How are we using language when we say of something *in a moral sense* that it is good or bad, right or wrong? Or, what is the logical status of sentences employing moral predicates? Or, what is the meaning of a moral predicate, and how do such predicates function in sentences expressing moral appraisal? Let us, in order to understand more clearly the point of the question, look at some of the ways in which it might be—and has been—answered. The options are distressingly numerous.

The Options

In our earlier discussion of the functions of language (Chapter 5) we suggested that all language appears to serve one or more of four functions: to request information (the interrogative function), to convey information (the informative function), to direct behavior (the directive function), and to express feeling (the expressive, or emotive, function). If this is correct, then it is evident that the language of morals must also be reducible to one or more of these functions, or "types" of discourse.

It seems evident that moral discourse does not serve an interrogative function; consequently, we may dismiss this at once.

Perhaps, then, moral discourse is a species of informative language. Many meta-ethicists are agreed that it is. But informative of what? Here opinions vary, and among philosophers who hold that moral discourse is a species of informative language we may distinguish at least four different answers to our question.

There are some who hold, first, that to apply a moral predicate to the appraisal of something is to assert the presence or the absence of a certain empirical quality, or certain empirical qualities, in the thing being appraised. It may be said, for example, that to call an act "praiseworthy" or "good" is to say that it is productive of pleasure, and the question whether or not an act is productive of pleasure is obviously an empirical question. Or it may be said that to call a certain form of conduct "good" is to say that it is characteristic of those beings who have proceeded the farthest or the highest along the evolutionary path; and this latter, if spelled out in some detail, is capable of being determined empirically. This view, which is developed in Chapter 25, we shall call *naturalistic objectivism*—"naturalistic" because it affirms that moral predicates denote the presence or absence of some natural (empirically ascertainable) qualities, "objectivism" because such qualities are, in this view, asserted to be in, or absent from, the object being judged.

There are others who hold, however, that moral discourse is informative in the sense that it asserts the presence or absence of some *non*-natural quality or qualities in the thing being appraised. This was the view of G. E. Moore. He said:

> If I am asked, What is good? my answer is that good is good, and that is the end of the matter. Or if I am asked, How is good to be defined? my answer is that it cannot be defined, and that is all I have to say about it. . . . My point is that "good" is a simple notion, just as "yellow" is a simple notion; that, just as you cannot, by any manner of means, explain to anyone who does not already know it, what yellow is, so you cannot explain what good is.[2]

This position, which is developed in Chapter 26, is variously called *non-naturalistic objectivism* or, more commonly, *intuitionism*. The reasons for calling it the former are evident when one compares it with its "naturalistic" counterpart. The reason for calling it "intuitionism" is that since the qualities in question are, according to the theory, non-natural, they are not subject to empirical determination and must, accordingly, be "intuited," i. e., rationally discerned. (The term "intuition," as used by philosophers, does not mean what it means in the everyday expression, "a woman's intuition." It means, rather, direct apprehension, or rational discernment: it denotes the act by which, according to rationalists, we directly grasp some *a priori* synthetic truths.)

It may be, however, that moral discourse is informative in a different way. It may be that "moral judgments," as they are sometimes called (misleadingly, in the view of some philosophers, since to call something a judgment is to imply that it is informative), convey information not about the object or the act being judged, but about the likes or dislikes of (a) the person making the judgment or (b) some group of people for whom he speaks. Such views are called *subjectivist* views, and depending on whether it is (a) the speaker's likes or dislikes or (b) the likes or dislikes of some group for which he speaks, you have, respectively, *private subjectivism* (Chapter 27) and *societal subjectivism* (Chapter 28). A statement

---

[2] *Ibid.*, pp. 6 and 7.

such as "Honesty is good," according to these views, means either "I am in favor of honesty" (private subjectivism) or "We are in favor of honesty" (societal subjectivism). Moral sentences, according to these views, say nothing at all about what appears to be the "object" of the judgment: they say something, rather, about the likes or dislikes of some subject or subjects.

It may be, however, that moral sentences are not informative at all. Perhaps, instead, they are a species of *directive* language— "veiled commands," as they are sometimes called. Perhaps every moral utterance, even the most general moral principle that one can imagine, is an elliptical expression the real purpose of which is to say, "Act in such and such a way." This view, which is favored by a number of philosophers at the present time, is called *imperativism*.

Or, lastly, it may be that the function of ethical sentences is neither to convey information nor to direct behavior, but to express feeling, and so we have the view known as *emotivism*. This view, it will be seen, is similar to private subjectivism; it is, nonetheless, not the same. According to the private subjectivist view, "Honesty is good" means "I approve of honesty": it is an informative statement about the feelings of the speaker. According to the emotivist view, "Honesty is good" is interpreted to mean, roughly, "Hurray for honesty": it is not a report about the feelings of the speaker, but rather it is an *expression of* those feelings.

There is no certainty whatsoever that the six views just distinguished constitute all of the possible ways of answering this question. First, it is not possible to state with certainty that the four "functions" of language from which our analysis began are the only such functions which a careful study of language might reveal; and should some other function be identified, it is possible that a case could be made for the view that ethical discourse is a species of that function of language. Second, one could maintain that ethical discourse serves several functions simultaneously; hence, it is not correctly accounted for by any one of these positions (see Chapter 31). And then the possibilities would be endless: with so many variables, dozens of possibilities would have to be considered in attempting to analyze a single sentence—and different combinations might be supposed to apply to other sentences.

The diagram below may be helpful in distinguishing the six views which we have just defined. The sentences that appear in parentheses indicate the "translations" that would be proposed by each view to exhibit the supposed real meaning of the sentence "Honesty is good."

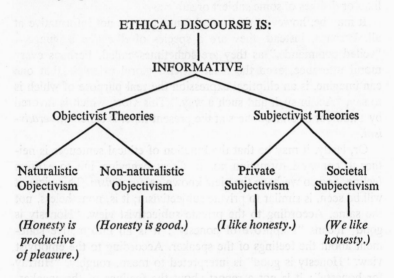

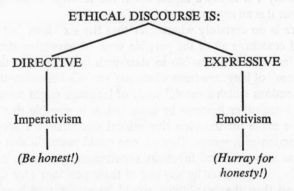

Even though the alternatives listed are not mutually exclusive, it does seem worth the effort to see what kind of case can be made for each; since, if we are to construe moral and ethical discourse as involving some combination or combinations of these functions, it is first necessary that we clearly understand the "pure types." And while we cannot claim to be absolutely sure that the four functions of language which we have distinguished constitute an exhaustive list, we may be reasonably confident that it is; and we may, accordingly, be reasonably confident that moral sentences are correctly construed either in one of the six ways defined or in some combination or combinations of these ways.

We may observe, finally, that this problem (although the discussion of it along the lines we have just attempted to describe has been confined largely to professional philosophers) is by no means a purely technical problem in which only philosophers have an interest. One sometimes hears it said, for example, that moral principles are "just a matter of opinion," and this seems clearly to be a meta-ethical view. Bull-session discussions about the "objectivity" or the "subjectivity" of moral principles are also discussions of this problem. To say that minority groups have a "valid claim" to equal civil rights and that laws preventing them from obtaining such rights are "unjust" is to make certain assumptions about the status of moral principles and about the logic of the sentences in which they are expressed. Any decision we make on this matter will, therefore, inevitably affect the way we think about the ethical issues over which our society is so deeply exercised at the present time. In this sense, the problem we are now discussing, though it may seem at times to be far removed from the concrete realities of life, is an intensely practical philosophical problem.

Study Questions

1. Define "morality," "normative ethics," and "meta-ethics." To which of these does each of the following belong?
   a. The opinion that racial segregation is wrong.
   b. The lynching of a suspected rapist.
   c. The theory that moral goodness consists in the tendency to enhance human happiness.
   d. If your enemy hungers, feed him.
   e. He governs best who governs least.
   f. To say that something is good is to say nothing more than that you like it.

   g. Nothing is good or bad but thinking makes it so.

   h. The cardinal rule of all ethics is this: so act that you could will that the maxim according to which you act should become a universal law.

2. Can you think of any act that you would regard as being appropriately subject to moral appraisal to which the phenomenological description offered in this chapter does not apply? If so, how would the description have to be altered in order to make it "fit the facts"?

3. What do you understand to be "the central problem of meta-ethics"? Does this seem to you an important problem? What bearing, if any, does it have on such matters as the civil rights controversy or the struggle between East and West?

4. What do subjectivist theories regarding the meaning of moral sentences have in common with objectivist theories? What is it that distinguishes them? What is the difference between naturalistic and non-naturalistic objectivism? between private and societal subjectivism? between private subjectivism and emotivism?

5. Why is it impossible to conclude with certainty that one has surveyed all of the possible answers to the question posed in this chapter?

Chapter 25

NATURALISTIC OBJECTIVISM

ETHICAL NATURALISM, OR naturalistic objectivism, is the view that moral sentences—both those employed in everyday moral judgments and those employed by writers on normative ethics—are reports about the presence or absence of certain natural qualities in the person, act, or state of affairs that the sentence in question is about. Moral sentences, in this view, are translatable without loss of meaning into sentences that do not employ any of the so-called "moral predicates." It is this view that I shall elaborate and defend.

Since a variety of views about the correct definitions of the key moral predicates (good, right, ought, etc.) is compatible with the central features of naturalistic objectivism, let me begin by indicating what all of us hold in common and what is the point upon which some of us within this general category hold conflicting views. I shall then go on to state the particular version of naturalistic objectivism which I hold to be correct, and I shall indicate some of the reasons why, in my opinion, this view should be regarded as correct.

It may be helpful to say a word at this point about the status of naturalistic objectivism—or, for that matter, of any meta-ethical theory. I should like to make it clear that we who hold this theory are not offering an arbitrary verbal definition of key ethical terms, nor are we making a recommendation as to how people generally *ought* to use these terms. Our claim is that people *do* use these

terms, and the sentences in which they occur, in certain ways—
even if, as philosophers, they subscribe to some other meta-ethical
theory, or if, as plain men, they subscribe to no meta-ethical theory
at all. The structure of language, we hold, allows only certain ways
in which a sentence can have meaning; naturalistic objectivism is a
theory about which of these ways correctly describes the particular
kind of meaning which moral sentences have.

Naturalistic objectivists hold that to say that something is good
or bad, right or wrong, is to say that it has, or does not have,
certain empirically ascertainable qualities. This implies at least two
things about moral sentences which all naturalistic objectivists hold
in common, namely that (a) moral sentences are, like all informative sentences, true or false and (b) questions about the truth or
falsity of such sentences are resolvable by straightforward empirical means. These may also be taken, therefore, as defining characteristics of the naturalistic objectivist view; it is incumbent on anyone who holds this position to show that moral sentences do in fact
exhibit these features.

There ought not to be any disagreement as to the method by
which this matter must be resolved. Since a meta-ethical theory is a
view about what is actually meant by moral sentences, one must
have recourse at all times to the actual judgments that people
make: the theory must conform to actual usage. To ask, for example, what is the meaning of "good" (when used in a moral sense) is
to ask for a definition that is adequate to the extension of the term
as it is actually employed by plain men and ethical theorists when
they frame what we call "moral judgments." If we lose sight of this
(if we depart from actual usage), we shall not be able to avoid
getting lost in a never-never world of arbitrary definitions which
will contribute in no way whatsoever to the task at hand.

Naturalistic objectivists are agreed, as I have said, that (a)
moral sentences are informative sentences asserting the presence or
absence of certain qualities in the object being judged, (b) moral
sentences are true or false, and (c) their truth or falsity is ascertainable by straightforward empirical means. Where, then, do we
disagree among ourselves? We disagree as to *which* qualities it is
whose presence or absence is being asserted when something is
judged to be good or bad, right or wrong. I shall not take time,

however, to survey the various proposals that have been made by naturalistic objectivists on this point, but shall proceed directly to an exposition and defense of my own view. If I can succeed in presenting a convincing case for my own view, then it will follow that naturalistic objectivists who disagree with me on this point, as well as meta-ethicists who hold fundamentally different views about the logic of moral discourse, are mistaken.

The Meanings of "Good"

If any one term may be said to be pivotal, or centrally important, among the moral predicates, that term is "good" (in the moral sense). But this term, unfortunately, has so many meanings that we shall have to analyze it very carefully in order to see its central significance in ethical thinking.

The most important moral sense of "good" is the sense in which it is the antithesis of "evil." All of the other moral predicates are definable in relation to good and evil, as we shall shortly attempt to show. But first, we must distinguish some other senses of "good," in order that in what follows we shall not be confused by them.

There is a completely *non*-moral sense of "good" in which that word means the opposite of "poor." We speak, for example, about good knives and poor knives, about good novels and poor novels, about good runners and poor runners; and by "good" and "poor" in such cases we mean, apparently, "conforming to (good), or failing to conform to (poor), the criteria appropriate to the assessment of such things." A good knife is one that cuts well (etc.), a good novel is one that makes for enjoyable reading (etc.), and a good runner is one who runs swiftly; a poor knife, or novel, or runner, is one that does not meet these criteria. "Good" in *this* sense is not a moral predicate at all, and it must not be confused with "good" in its centrally important moral sense as the opposite of "evil."

There is still another sense of "good," however, in which it is the opposite of neither "poor" nor "evil," but of "bad"; and in this sense it usually is a moral predicate. (Not always, however: we talk about good and bad pitches in baseball, and good and bad shots in basketball, and we clearly do not in such cases intend to make a *moral* judgment.) I shall speak of "good" in this sense as the *secondary* sense of "good," and "good" when it stands opposed to "evil" as the *primary* sense of good. My reasons for so doing will soon become apparent. There are three sorts of things that we call good (or bad) in this secondary sense: men, certain mental acts of men (thoughts, intentions, desires, purposes), and overt acts of men. I am unable to think of anything else that we would call good or bad in this clearly moral sense except in a metaphorical way.

The relation between "good" in this secondary sense, and "good" in the primary sense, I take to be as follows: to say that something is good in the secondary sense is to say that it promotes, or tends to promote, what is good in the primary sense. "Good" as opposed to "evil" means "*intrinsically* good"; "good" as opposed to "bad" means "*instrumentally* good." This is the reason for calling the latter a secondary, or derivative, sense of good.

All of the other moral predicates can be defined in relation to "good" in the primary sense. One's "duty," for example, is to do what, all things considered, one ought to do ("duty" and "what one ought to do," that is, are synonymous expressions), and what one ought to do is that act which, among all the things one might do, will have the greatest tendency to promote what is good in the primary sense. Any act that tends to promote what is intrinsically good is to that extent *right;* any act that tends to hinder the achievement of what is intrinsically good, or to promote what is intrinsically evil, is to that extent *wrong*. An act that has no tendency to promote either good or evil is *morally indifferent*. It is evident, therefore, that "good" in the primary sense of "intrinsically good" is the key concept in our ethical thinking.

The Primary Meaning of "Good"

The crucial question that we must ask in meta-ethics, therefore, is, "What is the meaning of good in this primary sense?" To this question the correct answer, as I conceive it, is, "maximally conducive to human happiness." This, I am saying, is what we mean by calling something "good" in this primary sense; and everything else that depends on the disposition and choices of men is good or bad, right or wrong, praiseworthy or blameworthy, insofar as it tends to promote or to hinder the achievement of human happiness.

Perhaps the best way to exhibit the truth of what I am stating is to consider a hypothetical case in which two people are disagreeing as to whether or not a certain proposed course of action is "good" or "right." Let us suppose that the argument concerns the right or wrong of using tear gas to quell a riot. *A* thinks it would be wrong to use it; *B* thinks it would be wrong *not* to do so. So far, then, *A* and *B* are in disagreement about whether the proposed act is good or bad in the *secondary* sense defined above.

How, then, might either party attempt to support his view? The best way would be to indicate the probable results of the proposed action. *A* might argue, "If tear gas is used, the rioters will retaliate by using fire-arms, and the situation will be even worse than it is now. So far, all we have to worry about is a small riot; the course you are proposing could turn it into a civil war." *B* might argue, "I think you are mistaken. Tear gas has been thoroughly proven as an effective means of controlling riots, and it should be used immediately. The longer this situation is allowed to remain out of control, the greater is the danger of its turning into a civil war—the very thing you fear. I say tear gas should be used without delay."

What is worthy of note in this dispute is that both parties are agreed that the "right" course of action is the one that will have the greatest tendency to promote human happiness—or, what comes to the same thing, to prevent human suffering. If *A* were to become convinced that the result of using tear gas would be as *B* says, he would *on his own premises* have to concede that the proposed action is indeed right; and if *B* were to become convinced that the result would be as *A* described it, or similar thereto, he would have to concede to *A*. The argument of both *assumes* that what is right or wrong in the case in question can only be decided by attempting to calculate the human consequences.

The same point can be re-enforced in another way. Suppose that a third party, *C*, enters the dispute. "I agree with *B*," says *C*. "I think tear gas should be used—although I agree with *A* that it will probably lead to civil war. Nonetheless, even though it will cause suffering for many people, I think it is the right thing to do." *A* and

B, surely, would be equally astonished by such a statement. They could only ask, "What on earth does *C mean* by 'good?' " Obviously, *C* does not mean by "good" what most people mean by it; for most people, when they use this term, mean "that state of affairs, among the options available to us, in which the maximum of human happiness, and the minimum of human suffering, is achieved." If this meaning is not assumed, the whole context in which the dispute was carried on is destroyed, and the dispute itself becomes unintelligible.

Let us consider a second example. Most people would agree, I think, that the excessive drinking of alcoholic beverages is morally wrong—though if there are some who disagree, it makes no difference to the argument. In any case, those who do hold that the excessive drinking of alcoholic beverages is morally wrong do so because of certain well-known consequences: it is injurious to one's health; it can (and often does) become a causal factor in the occurrence of auto accidents; it can deprive one's family of many of the conveniences and even the necessities of life (because of its cost); it poisons human relationships by changing people who are normally pleasant and kind into people who are belligerent and cantankerous; and so on. If the excessive drinking of alcoholic beverages did not have these consequences (as the drinking of water in any quantity does not), we should not regard it as wrong, and "drunkenness" would not be a term of moral disapprobation. But it does have, or tend to have, these consequences; hence, it is widely regarded as wrong. But these consequences, it is evident, are all descriptions of some adverse effect which the act or habit in question has, or tends to have, on human happiness. Thus it seems clear that it is human happiness that is regarded as intrinsically good, and that everything else is regarded as being good or bad insofar as it tends to promote or to hinder that end.

One could continue to give examples indefinitely, but it hardly seems necessary or worth the effort. Consider any example that you wish, and you will discover that anything that people commonly assess in moral categories—people, the thoughts, dispositions or intentions of people, or the acts of people—lends itself to such appraisal solely by virtue of its assumed tendency to promote or to hinder human happiness. If we could know (a) what state of affairs would achieve the absolute maximum of human happiness and (b) what acts would have the maximum tendency to promote that state of affairs, we should have no difficulty in deciding in any particular case what is the right thing to do. The moral dilemmas that we face are due not to our ignorance of what "good" means, but of what to do in order to achieve that ideal state of affairs in which the maximum of human happiness and the minimum of human suffering are realized.

When I say that a moral judgment consists in the assertion that some empirically ascertainable qualities are or are not present in the thing being judged, I do not mean that these qualities are precisely ascertainable in the way that, say, the presence or absence of sodium chloride in a solution is precisely ascertainable. I do mean, however, that there is nothing over and above the empirical facts to which we must attend in order to decide whether the judgment in question is true or false. The problematic character of many moral judgments is due not to the supposed fact that "goodness" consists in some odd non-empirical quality, but to the fact that such judgments often involve suppositions—conjectures even, and guesses—about the probable results of this or that action which, with our present knowledge at least, cannot be made with certainty. But it is a mistake to look beyond or behind the empirical facts for some non-empirical quality to remove the uncertainty from our judgments: the uncertainty will remain and must remain until we are able to calculate much more certainly than we now can the human consequences of alternative courses of action.

The chief reason, I suspect, that the account here suggested is not as obvious to most people as one would expect it to be (in view of the fact that they handle the language of moral appraisal without difficulty almost every day of their adult lives) is that most of us are taught moral principles in a way that does not clearly exhibit their relation to human happiness. We are taught that certain sorts of things (like slapping or biting other children, or taking things that belong to them, or telling lies) are "naughty," and certain other sorts of things (like paying compliments, or helping people in need, or visiting the sick) are "nice." There is a kind of "implicit legalism" in our upbringing, and if we pause to reflect on the many rules we have learned in this way, we may be very puzzled, and we may be tempted to look for some odd quality that gives these rules their "obligatory" character. What we fail to understand if we think in this way, however, is that the rules have gotten erected precisely because they specify some of the most common ways in which human happiness can be enhanced and human unhappiness minimized. To see moral principles in this light is to rid them of the purely arbitrary character which they sometimes seem to have and to exhibit them as legitimate rules of behavior for anyone who desires to know and to do what really is right.

I said earlier that anyone who holds the naturalistic-objectivist view must be prepared to show that moral sentences are capable of being true or false and that their truth or falsity is ascertainable by empirical means. Let us now consider these features as they apply to what might be thought the most difficult sort of case for a naturalistic objectivist to account for: one in which some particular person—Joe Doakes, let us say—is said to be (in the moral sense) "a good person" or "a good man."

Is there any evidence which, if it were supposed to obtain, would count against the statement, "Joe Doakes is a good man"? Yes. If we were to learn that Joe is a heavy drinker, or that he commonly maltreats his wife and children, or that he is habitually careless in his work, or that he does not get along well with most people, we would be inclined to regard the statement as false. To say that Joe Doakes is a good man is to say that he commonly acts in certain sorts of ways, and the ways we have in mind in so saying are not compatible with the ways just described. The difference between these two kinds of behavior—what makes one type of behavior "good" and the other "bad"—is precisely the tendency of each to promote or to hinder human happiness.

But the means by which it can be determined which of these ways is descriptive of Joe's behavior are clearly empirical. We must watch him to see how he behaves and listen to what other people say about his behavior. On that basis we make up our minds. If Joe is like most of us, it is quite certain that he is neither unambiguously good nor unambiguously bad: sometimes he acts in ways that promote human happiness and sometimes in ways that decrease it. But however this may be, it is the facts about a man's actual behavior that determine whether and to what extent he is truly described as "good" or "bad"; and these facts are ascertainable only by the empirical route of watching to see how he behaves. *Ergo,* moral sentences are true or false and confirmable or disconfirmable by empirical means.

Study Questions

1. True or false: a number of mutually incompatible theories belonging to *normative ethics* could be correctly described as "naturalistic objectivist" theories. Why?
2. What does Naturalistic Objectivist say is "the method by which this matter must be resolved"? Is he right? How do you determine what method is appropriate? Is it implicit in the question that is being asked, or is it determined in some other way? Can you think of any reason why any of the other parties to the dispute might object to this method?
3. Do you think Naturalistic Objectivist is on the right track in distinguishing three meanings of "good"? Suppose that he is right: does this in any way substantiate his main thesis? Does he claim that it does?
4. Is Naturalistic Objectivist right in saying that the statement, "Joe Doakes is a good man," can be refuted by empirical facts? How does this argument affect Naturalistic Objectivist's case?
5. Summarize Naturalistic Objectivist's arguments in support of his position. Can you think of any arguments against it?

Chapter 26

NON-NATURALISTIC OBJECTIVISM

THERE ARE TWO kinds of hedonists: those who affirm that "good" just *means* "pleasurable" or "conducive to happiness" and those who maintain that whatever "good" means, pleasure (or happiness) is the only thing to which it applies. We might call these positions, respectively, "analytic hedonism" and "synthetic hedonism" since according to the one view the statement "Happiness is good" is an analytic statement, and according to the other view it is a synthetic one. Both forms of hedonism, I am convinced, are mistaken; but hedonism in its analytic form is by far the more seriously in error of the two. And Naturalistic Objectivist, unfortunately, is an analytic hedonist.

I may say at the outset that very much of what Naturalistic Objectivist has said seems to be both true and valuable. He is quite right, for example, in distinguishing three meanings of "good" (the non-moral sense and the instrumental and intrinsic senses of moral goodness), and also in his contention that most (though not all, in my view) other moral predicates can be defined in relation to the very important concept of intrinsic goodness. But the crucial question for meta-ethics, as he himself says, is: What is the meaning of "intrinsically good"? And on this question I think he is profoundly mistaken.

The *"Open-question"* Test

There is a simple test, which I shall call the "open-question" test, by which one can easily assess the accuracy of any proposed definition. Let us call a word for which some definition is being proposed the *definiendum,* and the definition that is proposed the *definiens.* If, then, we ask a question of the form, "Are all *(definiens)* really *(definiendum)*?" it is evident that if our definition is accurate we shall not be putting a significant (or open) question; and if our definition is not accurate, we shall. Suppose, for example, that I define "bachelor" as (a) an unmarried male and as (b) an unmarried adult male human being. If, now, I apply the test, it is clear that in the one case I do, and in the other case I do not, have an open question. If I say, "Are all unmarried males bachelors?" I have an open (significant) question to which the correct answer is "No"; for pre-adult human males, and non-human males of any age, are unmarried males who are not bachelors. But if I ask, "Are all unmarried adult male human beings really bachelors?", it is equally evident that I am not asking an open, or significant, question; for the briefest reflection makes it clear that the *definiens* is what I mean when I use the term "bachelor."

If, now, we apply the test to Naturalistic Objectivist's proposed definition of "intrinsically good," it is evident at once that this definition will not do. For the question, "Are all instances of human pleasure, or happiness, really good?" is an open question, to which it is highly unlikely that an affirmative answer would be correct. Consider a few examples. Is it plausible to maintain that the enjoyment which a young boy might get out of torturing a frog (or some other presumably sentient creature) is good? or the happiness that an adult sadist might get out of tormenting another human being (even if his happiness should exceed his victim's suffering)? or the perverted pleasure of a masochist who allegedly enjoys being punished? Clearly not. If, on the whole, we judge human happiness to be good, the reason is not that goodness simply *means* human happiness: the reason is that we discern that the quality which we denote by the term "good" is present in most (but not all) instances of human happiness. It is this insight that we express in our synthetic judgment, "Human happiness, by and large, is good."

There are, as Naturalistic Objectivist has pointed out, a number of rival theories of the naturalistic-objectivist type, and space obviously does not permit us to list them and apply our test to each of them in turn. It may fairly be said, however, that of the theories of this type the hedonistic version is by far the most plausible; and since it fails to pass the open-question test, we may be reasonably confident that any other theory of this type will also fail.

Refutation of Hedonism

The inadequacy of hedonism can, however, be demonstrated apart from the open-question test. The test, it is to be noted, only shows the incorrectness of analytic hedonism; the arguments that I shall now put forward demonstrate the inadequacy of hedonism in both its analytic and its synthetic forms. Although our discussion will require a brief venture into the domain of normative ethics, the digression is necessary in order to more clearly present what I consider to be the correct meta-ethical theory.

The incorrectness of hedonism is evident, first, from the fact that there are a number of things other than pleasurable states of mind which we regard as being intrinsically good. Professor W. D. Ross has shown, for example,[1] that (a) virtuous disposition and action, (b) the apportionment of pleasure and pain to the virtuous and vicious respectively, and (c) knowledge and right opinion are *intrinsic goods,* and that they cannot be reduced to pleasurable states of mind or to acts tending to increase the sum of human happiness. A universe in which these things obtain—quite apart from any consideration of the balance of human happiness which it may or may not produce—is intrinsically better than a universe in which these things do not obtain. One has only to contemplate the two states of affairs, assuming the quantity of human happiness to be equal in the two cases, to see that this is so.

The same conclusion may, however, be established in another way. There are some instances of human pleasure which, if we suppose them to occur, reduce the total quantity of goodness in the universe. Suppose, for example, that a person, *A,* suffers great mis-

---

[1] W. D. Ross, *The Right and the Good* (Oxford: Clarendon Press, 1930), Chap. V.

fortune; and suppose that another person, *B,* who has long been jealous of *A* because of *A*'s earlier good fortune, contemplates *A*'s misfortune *with pleasure.* There can be no doubt in this case that the quantity of pleasure in the universe is greater than it would be if *B* did not react in this way to *A*'s misfortune; but it is equally clear that *B*'s responding in this way is not a good, but an evil. Indeed, it would be better if there were *less* pleasure in the universe: there would be more good in the universe if *B* were sorrowful instead of happy. It seems obvious, therefore, that goodness is not simply identical with pleasure and that not all instances of human pleasure are good.

The inadequacy of hedonism can also be exhibited by the following *reductio ad absurdum* argument. If human happiness were the only thing that is intrinsically good, and if the amount of good in the universe depended entirely on the amount of human happiness, then a universe in which there is but one individual who is moderately happy *forever* would be intrinsically better than one in which a finite number of individuals is happy in whatever degree for any finite length of time. But we obviously do not think this to be the case. Even if we were persuaded that some one person could be rendered moderately happy forever (thus producing an infinite quantity of happiness and, therefore, goodness in the universe), we would not, in order to achieve this, countenance the annihilation of all other human beings—though, according to our hypothesis, their happiness is a merely finite quantity, and therefore inferior to that of our hypothetical eternal individual. And since, according to the hedonistic theory, we ought to draw this conclusion, it is evident that the hedonistic theory is false.

The Indefinability of "Good"

We have been speaking—without any misgivings about the meaningfulness of what we have been saying—about a variety of things (states of mind, acts, states of affairs in the universe, etc.) which we would or would not call good. We have said that, contrary to the claim of ethical hedonists, we do not mean "pleasure" or "human happiness" when we call something good (analytic hedonism), nor is it only pleasure or human happiness that we regard as being good (synthetic hedonism). What, then, do we mean when we call something good? The correct answer to this question is, I think, the one given by Professor Moore: We mean good, and nothing else. "Everything is what it is, and not another thing." [2] We can, indeed, find other *words* to denote the quality that we commonly denote by the word "good": we can use the German word *gut,* or the French *bon,* or even the English phrase "worthy of being valued in and of itself"; but *that which* we denote in these various ways is a simple, indefinable, non-natural quality whose presence in a person, act, or state of affairs is what makes us call it good.

"Good" is indefinable because it is a simple concept. In order to define a concept, it is necessary that that concept be complex, that it be composed of simpler concepts. One can define "daffodil," for example, as "a yellow flower of the genus narcissus" because these various elements—being yellow, being a flower, and being of the genus narcissus—are all constituent parts of the complex concept of a daffodil. Of these constituent elements, "flower" and "genus narcissus" can also be defined. But, as Moore also pointed out, "yellow" cannot be defined (except, of course, ostensively); and the reason it cannot be defined is that it is a simple concept. All definitions must ultimately be built up out of such concepts, for the process of defining concepts by pointing to the elements of which they are composed cannot go on indefinitely: at length one must come to those elements which, like "good" and "yellow," are simple, and therefore indefinable.

"Good," then, like "yellow," is a simple and, therefore, indefinable concept. But the quality that it denotes, unlike the quality denoted by the term "yellow," is not a natural quality. By this I mean, simply, that the goodness of a person, act, or state of affairs is not something that can be perceived by the senses; it must be *rationally discerned,* or *intuited,* if it is to be apprehended at all. That this is, in fact, how we apprehend the goodness of things will become evident if we reflect on a few examples.

Let us consider again the illustration of the man who contemplates with pleasure the misfortune of another human being. There

---

[2] Bishop Butler, quoted by G. E. Moore on the title page of *Principia Ethica* (Cambridge: Cambridge University Press, 1959).

is no question here of the probable effects of *B*'s malice: we can very well imagine that *A* is already dead, or that *B* expires shortly after entertaining his unkind thoughts about *A*'s misfortune, and still we would judge that *B*'s malice was evil. But how do we know this? Certainly it is in virtue of the supposed facts that we render our judgment; but our judgment that "*B*'s pleasure in *A*'s misfortune is evil" is not simply a confused way of reporting that *B* did, in contemplating *A*'s misfortune, entertain feelings of pleasure: it is a judgment about the *moral significance* of those facts. And this judgment rests not on the perception of some additional natural qualities or some supposed tendency of *B*'s act (of contemplation), but on our direct intuition of the evilness of the act itself.

Consider a second example. A person, *X*, has borrowed a sum of money from a wealthy friend, *Y*, and has promised to repay him on a certain date. The date arrives and *X*, being a man who keeps his word, repays the loan. This, although hardly an instance of moral heroism, is, I presume, an act on which we should without hesitation pronounce a favorable judgment. Since it is an instance of promise-keeping, and promise-keeping is something which under normal circumstances we regard as a moral duty, the act in question is judged to be good. But note: no calculation of the probable consequences of alternative possible courses of action is involved in this judgment. Indeed, it is highly likely that the same sum of money given to a poor family would produce more human happiness than it would if returned to the bank account of *Y*. But the calculation of consequences is not relevant in this case: *X* has contracted a duty in making a promise to *Y*, and that duty takes precedence over all but the most unusual of circumstances. We judge, therefore, that *X*'s act of returning the money on the date promised is good.

What are we saying, then, when we say, "this act is good," and on what basis? Clearly we are not saying that *X*'s act is the one which, of all the alternatives available to him, has the greatest tendency to increase the sum of human happiness. Indeed, we can be quite sure this is not the case. We are saying, simply, that *X*'s act, as an instance of promise-keeping, is good, and that is all we are saying. Our basis for saying this is not that we perceive some empirical facts in addition to those which make us call this act an instance of promise-keeping but simply that we apprehend such an act as being good.

There is, I realize, a widespread tendency among philosophers today to reject intuition, or direct rational insight, as a mode of acquiring knowledge, and to insist that the only knowledge available to us must come by empirical means. This bias against rational insight explains, I think, the great flurry of activity that has recently been in evidence in the empiricist camp to find some way to account for our knowledge of ethical truths and our ability to make valid moral judgments, without admitting these as instances of rational, or non-empirical, insight. But the effort is doomed to failure. Even our judgment that human happiness is, on the whole, good, is a synthetic judgment which we could not make apart from our direct apprehension that the quality of goodness is in fact present in most (but not all) instances of human happiness. It is this apprehension, and this alone, that allows us to distinguish between those many instances of human happiness that are good and those few that are not; and what is apprehended, in such cases, is "not another thing" but *goodness itself*.

If this view is correct, any attempt to define "good" in terms of some natural quality or combination of natural qualities is mistaken: it consists in the mistake of confusing the non-natural quality designated by the term "good" with something else that it is not. I propose, following Professor Moore, to call this particular kind of mistake the "naturalistic fallacy"; it is a fallacy because it is a logical error (an error in logic), and it is naturalistic because it is the specific error of confusing a natural and a non-natural quality. It is this fallacy, regardless of what set of natural qualities may be proposed as a definition of "good," that is effectively exposed by the open-question test; many writers on ethics, as Moore has shown, have been guilty of it.

A Word About Moral Duty

Earlier I stated that I am not in complete agreement with Naturalistic Objectivist's suggestion that all of the other moral predicates can be defined in relation to the centrally important concept "good." I want, in conclusion, to indicate why I am inclined to disagree with him on this point.

My chief misgivings on this score concern the concept of "moral duty." I do not think it is correct to say, as Naturalistic Objectivist does, that one's moral duty is always to do that act which, of all the alternatives available to one, will produce the greatest total increase of good in the world. Some acts, I think, have an obligatory character quite apart from their supposed consequences; but before we go into that, I want to make a preliminary observation about "moral duty" that may be of some help in clearing up this rather elusive concept.

It is important to distinguish between (a) one's objective duty and (b) one's apparent duty. This distinction is necessary in order to make intelligible the very commonplace fact that it is possible for a person to be mistaken about what is his moral duty in a certain situation. "I believe it is my duty to do thus and so" is an intelligible statement, and its intelligibility rests on the assumption that what one *believes* to be one's duty may be different from what really *is* one's duty.

It is certainly evident that we cannot possibly know which of the many things that we might do at any moment will in fact produce the greatest increase of good in the world; so if this is what Naturalistic Objectivist means, his view would entail that we never know what our duty is. And this, I think, is absurd. We must, then, interpret him to mean that we ought always do that act which *we believe* will produce the greatest increase of good in the world—in other words, we must construe his remark as applying not to our objective duty, but to our apparent duty. Even if we construe his remark in this way, however, his view does not stand up; for what I believe to be my duty on many occasions is not at all the act which I believe, all things considered, will likely produce the greatest increase of good in the world. Neither objective duty nor apparent duty, therefore, seems to be definable in relation to "good."

The "obligatory" or "dutiful" character of certain sorts of acts is a quality of those acts that must be rationally discerned in the same way that the goodness of certain states of affairs must be rationally discerned. Just as good things are good in virtue of their possessing certain other characteristics, however, so duties are such, and are apprehended as being such, in virtue of their possessing certain characteristic features. There are, as Ross has pointed out,[3] various kinds of duties—duties of fidelity (telling the truth, keeping one's promise), duties of reparation (making amends for a wrongful act done in the past), duties of gratitude (expressing thanks for favors done by others), duties of justice (assisting the needy), duties of beneficence (relieving suffering), and so on. No doubt we sometimes err in thinking something to be our duty when it is not, just as we sometimes err in judging some state of affairs to be good when it is not; for our knowledge of moral truths is not infallible. But our knowledge of moral truths, insofar as we have such knowledge, is non-empirical; and the reason is that the qualities which we judge when we make a moral judgment—both the goodness of good things and the obligatoriness of acts that are our duty—are non-empirical, or non-natural, qualities.

Study Questions

1. What is the "open-question" test? Can you think of any examples in which the test fails to prove what Non-naturalistic Objectivist says it proves?
2. What distinction does Non-naturalistic Objectivist make between "analytic hedonism" and "synthetic hedonism"? What is the relationship between hedonism of these two types and naturalistic objectivism? How does Non-naturalistic Objectivist attempt to refute hedonism of both types?
3. Would it be logically consistent for a person to be both (a) a non-naturalistic objectivist and (b) a synthetic hedonist? Explain.
4. Consider very carefully Non-naturalistic Objectivist's examples of moral judgments. Does he convince you that they *cannot* be construed in the way that Naturalistic Objectivist would have us construe them? Does he convince you that they should be construed in the way he proposes? Try his proposal with a few examples of your own.
5. Would it be logically possible for Non-naturalistic Objectivist to agree with Naturalistic Objectivist's analysis of "moral duty"? How does Non-naturalistic Objectivist analyze "moral duty"?

---

[3] W. D. Ross, *op. cit.,* Chap. II.

Chapter 27

PRIVATE SUBJECTIVISM

IF ONE HAD to choose between the
two theories concerning the logic of moral discourse presented in
the two preceding chapters, one would, I think, have an exceedingly difficult time making up his mind. Each of them, it seems to
me, presents a theory that explains some of the facts about the
language of morals, and each leaves certain facts unexplained. Let
us try to separate the truth from the error in each of the foregoing
accounts and go on from there to develop a theory about the logic
of moral discourse that is adequate to all the relevant facts.

Naturalistic Objectivist has argued that (a) "good" has three
distinguishable meanings, namely a primary moral meaning (good-
evil), a secondary moral meaning (good-bad), and a non-moral
meaning (good-poor); (b) the most important concept for understanding the logic of moral discourse is "good" in its primary moral
sense; (c) all other moral predicates are definable in terms of this
concept; (d) the meaning of "good" in this primary sense is "providing a maximum of human happiness"; (e) moral judgments are,
therefore, true or false; and (f) their truth or falsity is ascertainable by straightforward empirical means. Of these six propositions,
Non-naturalistic Objectivist has agreed, either explicitly or by implication, with propositions *a, b,* and *e* and has disagreed with the
other three. He has argued, on the contrary, that (g) "duty," at
least, is not definable in terms of "good" in the primary sense, (h)
"good" in the primary sense is indefinable since it denotes a simple

non-natural quality, and (i) the truth or falsity of moral sentences is ascertainable not by empirical, but by extra-empirical, means (intuition).

Of these nine propositions I think we can, without further ado, simply accept propositions *a, b, e,* and *f.* My reasons for holding propositions *e* and *f* to be true are, however, quite different from those given by Naturalistic Objectivist, as will shortly be apparent. I do think, though, that moral sentences consist in the assertion, in a rather misleading way, of some very commonplace facts. I am, therefore, bound to hold that the two propositions in question are true. I have no wish to enter into the side argument between Naturalistic Objectivist and Non-naturalistic Objectivist as to whether or not "duty" is definable in terms of "good" in the primary sense; so I shall refrain from expressing myself on propositions *c* and *g.* I am inclined to doubt whether our moral concepts are as neatly organized into a coherent system as Naturalistic Objectivist has suggested; but I am even more certain that what we know when we know that something is our duty is not what Non-naturalistic Objectivist says we know, nor do we know it in the way he says we do (proposition *f*). But this is, in any case, a trifling side issue, and I do not wish to commit myself to a definite position on it.

There are, then, three propositions among the nine that have been enunciated by my two predecessors—propositions *d, h,* and *i*—with which I definitely disagree. I propose to indicate briefly my reasons for rejecting each of them.

Let us consider first proposition *i*—the claim, put forward by Non-naturalistic Objectivist, that the truth or falsity of moral sentences is ascertainable by non-empirical means. I disagree with this claim for two reasons. First, I hold that all of our knowledge of synthetic truths arises out of experience: I am, in short, an empiricist. If there were some other convincing examples of synthetic truths that are known *a priori*—"intuited," as Non-naturalistic Objectivist says—then we might, of course, entertain the possibility that the truth of moral sentences is also known in this way. But it has been amply shown (See Chapters 11 and 12) that the most plausible examples of such truths can be easily accounted for in a way that is consistent with empiricism. Since this is the case, it seems unlikely that moral truths are an exception to the rule. Second, even if the correctness of the general thesis of empiricism be disallowed, it cannot be plausibly argued that moral truths are examples of synthetic truths that are known *a priori*. These truths do not exhibit the qualities of necessity and universality—or of self-evidence—that are alleged to be the hallmarks of *a priori* knowledge. There is, admittedly, a certain oddness about moral sentences; but this oddness, as we shall see, is due to something quite different from the alleged fact that they are synthetic truths that are known *a priori*.

As for proposition *h*, it is sufficient to point out that if proposition *i* is rejected, proposition *h* must be rejected as well—or else one must draw the conclusion that we are in complete ignorance with respect to moral truths. I think that in most cases we do know that what we are asserting, when we say that something is "good" or "right," is the case—though we are seldom explicitly aware of exactly what it is that we are asserting when we express ourselves in this way. I, therefore, conclude that the theory that "good" denotes a simple non-natural quality is incorrect.

Naturalistic Objectivist's thesis—the thesis that "good" means "providing for a maximum of human happiness"—is inadequate in a number of ways. Non-naturalistic Objectivist has pointed out, for example, that our judgment that a state of affairs is good, or that an act is right, does not vary exactly with the quantity of human happiness supposed to be present; and I think that in this he is right. But the inadequacy of the theory can also be shown in another way. There is no valid argument by which one can, from premises containing no moral predicates, deduce a sentence that does contain a moral predicate. If Naturalistic Objectivist's thesis were correct, we ought to be able to argue as follows:

State *X* is a state of the universe in which there would be substantially more human happiness than there is at present.

Act *W* is, of all the things I might do, the act which would be maximally conducive to the achievement of state *X*.

I *ought* to do act *W*.

Now it is apparent, I am saying, that we cannot validly argue in this way. The "ought" that appears in the conclusion is not deducible from the merely descriptive statements that constitute the premises of the argument, whereas according to Naturalistic Objectivist's thesis it should be. Moreover, insofar as we do feel that the conclusion is somehow appropriate to (even though not deducible from) those premises, it is because of another unexpressed premise—that one ought, on the whole, to do things that are conducive to human happiness.

It seems to me, therefore, that the attempts of both Naturalistic and Non-naturalistic Objectivists to describe the peculiar logical structure of moral discourse must be regarded as failures. Moral predicates do not refer to either observable or unobservable qualities in the objects of which they seem to be descriptive. Hence, the conclusion is inescapable that moral predicates are not property-referring words at all, and moral sentences are not informative in the sense of conveying some information about the object that is said to be good or bad, right or wrong. It remains to be seen, however, whether such sentences are not informative in another sense.

The Case for Subjectivism

An important fact about moral utterances, for which objectivist theories give no account whatsoever, is that they are always expressive of some attitude, either positive or negative, on the part of the person making the judgment. Some moral predicates, like "good," "right," "praiseworthy," and "virtuous," are expressive of what we may call a "pro-attitude"; others, like "evil," "bad," "wrong," "blameworthy," and "vicious," are expressive of an "anti-attitude." This fact about moral predicates, and the sentences in which they are employed, is a valuable clue to the logical structure of the language of morals, for it suggests that what we are saying when we call something good or bad, right or wrong, is that we have, or tend to have, a favorable or unfavorable attitude toward it. The real meaning of the statement, "The infliction of needless pain is evil," is: "I disapprove of the infliction of needless pain." Moral sentences, in short, are not informative of the qualities of the apparent object of the judgment: they are informative of the attitude of the person rendering the judgment.

My point may be illustrated by considering the somewhat parallel case of food preferences. *A* says, "Rutabagas are good." *B* says, "I disagree: rutabagas are not good at all." On the surface of it, it looks as if *A* and *B* are engaged in a disagreement about rutabagas: do they, or do they not, possess the quality of "tasting good"? (And whether they do or not, is "good taste" a natural, or a non-natural, quality?) It is evident upon reflection, however, that *A* and *B* are not really disagreeing about any empirical or non-empirical qualities of rutabagas at all. What *A* means by "Rutabagas are good" is "I, *A,* like rutabagas," and what *B* means by "Rutabagas are not good" is "I, *B,* do not like rutabagas." *A* and *B* have, then, different *attitudes* toward the taste of rutabagas, and their respective statements about the goodness or non-goodness of rutabagas are simply misleading ways of reporting their private tastes.

Moral sentences, I am suggesting, are misleading in exactly this way. Like statements about tastes, they look as if they are informative statements about the object that is said to be good or bad, right or wrong; but they are in fact informative only of the feelings, or attitudes, of the person making the statement. "Helping someone in need is praiseworthy" is like "Rutabagas are good," not like "Daffodils are yellow"; but the misleading character of moral sentences is less obvious than is that of sentences about food tastes.

There is one common, and at first sight quite plausible, objection to this view with which it will be convenient to deal at this point. The objection is this: it is apparent that people do argue about ethical matters, whereas on the theory here proposed it would seem that there is nothing to argue about. If you like rutabagas and I do not, there is no point in discussing the matter: the most we can do is recognize that our tastes differ at this point, and that is the end of it. But people do argue about ethical matters, and they even cite empirical evidence in support of their views. How, then, can this be accounted for in the subjectivist theory?

The answer, I think, is that (a) by and large people do tend to approve and disapprove of the same "ends" and (b) they disagree, when they do, about the most effective means of achieving those ends. Naturalistic Objectivist's example about the two men who disagreed about whether it would be right or wrong to use tear gas in a certain situation is a case in point. The two men, it will be recalled, did not disagree in what we may call their basic moral attitude: they both favored a restoration of order and regarded with disfavor the occurrence of a civil war. Their disagreement was only about the likely results of using the tear gas; because they held different opinions on this point, they held different attitudes toward the proposed action. Since empirical evidence is relevant to assessing the probable consequences of this or that course of action, the citing of evidence is appropriate in such circumstances.

As a general rule, significant disagreement on ethical matters is possible only if, and insofar as, the disputants tend to hold the same basic attitudes toward the same actual or imagined states of affairs. If they reach agreement about the facts but still persist in holding conflicting attitudes, there remains nothing that can be settled by rational argument: all that either can do, if he is not content to leave the other's attitude as it is, is to resort to name-calling or some other form of non-rational persuasion.

"But surely," it may be said, "people do disagree in their basic moral attitudes, and they do try to persuade other people to agree with them." Indeed they do. People seem to feel more strongly about their moral attitudes than they do about their food preferences (we do not talk, for example, about our "culinary convictions"), and few people appear willing simply to accept differences at this point and let it go at that. But the methods by which anyone can persuade anyone else to change his basic moral attitudes, as I have said, are not those of rational argument but only the methods of non-rational persuasion: name-calling, intimidation, threats, and so on. This is probably why our language has words like "prude," "moral ignoramus," and the like.

Does not this view lead to pessimistic conclusions about the possibility of achieving enough ethical agreement among men to make harmonious life on our planet possible? Not at all. To so conclude would be equivalent to a restaurateur's concluding that, since people's tastes differ, he might as well give up trying to develop a menu that will win the general approval of his customers. Fortunately, people by and large tend to approve and disapprove of the same sorts of things: that is why one seldom finds anyone who will disagree with statements like "The infliction of needless pain is evil," or "It is good to help others who are in need." It is not the alleged objectivity of moral judgments, but the substantial similarity of our basic moral attitudes, that renders possible a reasonably harmonious society.

The Truth and Falsity of Ethical Statements

I have already stated that I agree with Naturalistic Objectivist's assertions that ethical statements are capable of being true or false and that their truth or falsity is ascertainable by empirical means. I want now to indicate why and in what sense I hold these assertions to be true.

Since ethical statements are assertions that one has, or tends to have, a favorable or an unfavorable attitude toward the object in question, such statements are always either true or false: they are true if the speaker really has the attitude which he claims to have and false if he does not. Moreover, the means by which one determines whether a person has the attitude he claims to have are straightforwardly empirical: introspection in the case of oneself and observation in the case of others.

It seems to be possible, incidentally, for a person to be mistaken about his own attitudes and thus to make false ethical statements without any intent to deceive. The reason for this is, I think, that one sometimes affirms general principles which one has learned earlier in life, and which may have been truly descriptive of one's attitudes at that time, without realizing that one's present attitude (as judged by one's behavior) is no longer what it formerly was. A person who has been taught that all drinking of alcoholic beverages is wrong, for example, may continue to say this on occasion even if he engages in moderate drinking himself and has no objection to others doing the same. There is, so far as I can see, no logical inconsistency in this; it is just that the general principle learned earlier in life is no longer truly descriptive of this person's present attitude.

Moral Attitudes and Objectively Descriptive Inferences

There is a sense, however, in which moral utterances are implicitly descriptive of the objects that are asserted to be good or bad, right or wrong. It is true, as Naturalistic Objectivist says, that if someone is said to be "a good man," we should be very surprised to learn that he is a poor husband and father, difficult to get along with, careless in his work, and so on; and this gives some credence to the view that the statement "Joe Doakes is a good man" is an assertion to the effect that Joe Doakes has certain qualities and does not have others.

That the assertion "Joe Doakes is a good man" is not as straight-forwardly descriptive as this example makes it appear to be, how-ever, is apparent from the fact that what we would regard as its "objective descriptive content" would vary considerably depending on whether we understood the statement to have been uttered by (a) the president of the local temperance union, (b) a fundamen-talist minister, (c) oneself, or (d) the head of the Mafia. There are some "objective descriptive implications" in each case, but their precise character varies depending on the speaker. How can this be?

The correct solution to the puzzle, I would suggest, is as follows. What is sometimes called the descriptive content of a moral utter-ance is a result of an inference that we make from (a) what we know or suppose about the basic moral attitudes of the speaker in conjunction with (b) the particular statement that he makes to the effect that so-and-so is good. We know, for example, that Mr. X, the head of the Mafia, generally approves of men who can rob a bank without getting caught, who always share their loot with the rest of the mob, and so on. If, then, Mr. X says "Joe Doakes is a good man," we infer that Joe Doakes is not a psalm-singing philan-thropist but a man who exhibits the sorts of qualities that Mr. X is in the habit of commending. If we knew nothing about the attitudes of the speaker, we should be very much in doubt about what kind of a man Joe Doakes is even though he is said to be a "good" man.

If, when we hear someone described as a "good" or "virtuous" person, we are not usually in doubt about what sort of person he is, it is not because "good" or "virtuous" directly mean such-and-such a combination of qualities, but because people by and large tend to favor certain sorts of qualities and behavior in their fellow men. It is this fact that lends whatever plausibility there is to the naturalistic-objectivist theory, and it leads us, mistakenly, to conclude that the primary meaning of moral utterances is their objective descriptive meaning. The variability of this descriptive meaning depending on the basic moral attitudes of the speaker makes it evident, however, that this descriptive content is inferential rather than direct, and it is precisely the subjective theory of the primary meaning of moral utterances that enables us to account for this undeniable variation. I take this, therefore, as a most powerful confirmation of the correctness of the view here proposed.

Study Questions

1. What are the "three propositions" enunciated by one or the other of the two preceding writers with which Private Subjectivist feels obliged to take issue? With whom are you inclined to agree on each of these points? Why?

2. Is Private Subjectivist right in saying, "There is no valid argument by which one can, from premises containing no moral predicates, deduce a conclusion that does contain a moral predicate"? If he is right, is this fact damaging to naturalistic objectivism? Explain.

3. What, exactly, is Private Subjectivist's own view about the meaning of moral sentences? Do the examples he gives especially lend themselves to this kind of interpretation? Can you think of any examples that he might find it difficult to interpret in this way?

4. In what sense does Private Subjectivist maintain that ethical statements are capable of being true or false? How, according to this view, can the statement, "The infliction of needless pain is evil" be contradicted?

5. What does Private Subjectivist mean by the statement that the "descriptive content" of ethical statements is inferential rather than direct? Do you think he is right?

Chapter 28

SOCIETAL SUBJECTIVISM

THERE CAN BE little doubt that the view of the status of moral judgments presented in the preceding chapter represents a decided advance over the two objectivist theories introduced earlier. It seems clear that "pro-attitudes" and "anti-attitudes" are involved in an important way in the meaning of moral judgments, and any theory that fails to take account of this fact must, therefore, be regarded as inadequate.

Some things about Private Subjectivist's proposal, however, strike me as being very strange. I shall point out what I consider to be certain oddities in this theory—features which, in my opinion, demonstrate beyond a reasonable doubt that it is not the whole and correct answer to our problem. I shall then suggest a slight emendation by means of which the difficulties inherent in the private-subjectivist view can be overcome.

Some Oddities of Private Subjectivism

If we were to adopt the private-subjectivist theory, we should have to conclude that moral judgments are never false except in the very unusual instance in which the person making the judgment has made some mistake in assessing his own attitude; and this seems very strange. Let us suppose that two people, A and B, are discussing the rightness or wrongness of r. A says, "r is right," B says "r is wrong." It would hardly be appropriate for A to say in this situation, "But *B*, you don't really disapprove of *r:* you do it all the time!" Even if *A* confronted *B* with evidence in support of the fact that he regularly had a "pro-attitude" toward *r,* this still would not make *B* withdraw his statement. One could imagine him replying, "I didn't say I *disapproved* of *r;* I said that *r* is *wrong*—notwithstanding the fact that I, reprobate that I am, approve of it." And in speaking thus, *B* would not be talking nonsense.

This brings me to my second point. According to the theory we are now considering, it would be nonsensical (because self-contradictory) to say, "I approve of some things that are wrong," or "I disapprove of some things that are right." The self-contradiction, in the private-subjectivist theory, is plain: "I approve of some things that are wrong" means, according to this theory, "I approve of some things that I do not approve of"; and that, clearly, is a self-contradictory assertion. But certainly it is not self-contradictory to speak in this way; a theory that requires us to banish such statements to the realm of nonsense is somehow mistaken.

There is another type of statement that has a perfectly legitimate use in ordinary discourse which becomes nonsensical according to the private-subjectivist view. Consider the statement, "One ought never do anything that one believes to be wrong, even if one wants to." This, surely, is a statement that it would be very natural to make in certain sorts of contexts—in a treatise on normative ethics, for example—and we should have no difficulty in understanding it or, probably, assenting to it. But according to the private-subjectivist view this is a nonsensical statement: it means "I disapprove of people doing things that they disapprove of, even when they approve of them." Now the purpose of a meta-ethical theory is not to reform moral discourse, but to explain it; and since we do have a use for statements such as this, and private subjectivism does not allow that use, the theory surely needs some improvement.

Further, if the private-subjectivist theory is correct, then it follows that treatises on normative ethics tell us nothing except the private likes and dislikes of their authors; and this, to say the least, would be a very strange opinion to hold. No doubt the great ethicists of our culture—Aristotle, St. Thomas, Kant, and many more—did have their private likes and dislikes on moral questions, just as they presumably had their own peculiar tastes in food; but surely it is not because of a purely biographical interest that we read Aristotle's *Nicomachean Ethics,* St. Thomas' *Summa Theologica,* or Kant's *Critique of Practical Reason.* We read them because we expect these men to help us understand, among other things, what we *ought* to approve of or what *really is* right or wrong, good or evil; and we should not be interested in such questions, or even be able to ask them, if these terms expressed nothing but the speaker's private likes and dislikes. On this score also, the private-subjectivist theory appears to be inadequate.

Finally, it seems that part of the persuasiveness of Private Subjectivist's account results from a confusion of which he evidently is not aware and of which many of his readers may also not be aware. I suspect that the most persuasive feature of private subjectivism for many people is its apparent capacity to account for shifts in the "objective-descriptive content" of ethical statements depending on who it is that makes the statement: one infers certain things about the apparent object of the judgment, says Private Subjectivist, on the basis of what one knows about the general likes and dislikes of the person making the judgment. What Private Subjectivist fails to note, however, is that when the statement "Joe Doakes is a good man" is made by, say, the head of the Mafia, it is no longer a *moral* judgment: it is a judgment employing "good" in a *non*-moral sense such as we find in the sentence, "A Buick is a good automobile." When the head of the Mafia says that Joe Doakes is a "good man," he certainly does not mean that Joe is a paragon of virtue: he means that Joe is a good gangster—i. e., one who does well the things that he (the speaker) expects a gangster to do. How, then, do we distinguish between the moral and the non-moral uses of good? We *do* distinguish. Indeed, we do so without difficulty: we recognize immediately, once our attention is called to it, that the judgment of the number-one man in the Mafia that Joe Doakes is a "good man" is not a moral judgment, whereas one's own judgment, for example, normally would be. Private subjectivism fails to recognize this difference and is unable to account for it. Hence, we must look further for a meta-ethical theory that is adequate to all the relevant facts.

An Alternative to Private Subjectivism

The theory which I should like to offer as an alternative to the one just weighed and found wanting is a theory known as *societal subjectivism*. Moral judgments, according to this view, are (as they are according to the private-subjectivist theory) reports about "pro-attitudes" and "anti-attitudes"; but the attitudes that they purport to describe are not necessarily or exclusively those of the person making the judgment, but those of some group with which he identifies. Basic moral attitudes, in short, are never simply the private attitudes of this or that individual: they are always the common attitudes of some community of which the individual is a part. Indeed, it is precisely the generality of such attitudes—their *non-private* character, in other words—that gives them the force of moral principles. Let us see how, if we construe moral sentences in this way, the features of moral discourse that have proved to be so perplexing for the private-subjectivist theory can be understood.

What sort of meaning can be allowed for the statements "I approve of some things that are wrong" and "I disapprove of some things that are right"? Both of these, as we have seen, are meaningless if we interpret them to mean what Private Subjectivist contends they mean. According to our view, however, they are perfectly intelligible statements. "I approve of some things that are wrong" means "I approve of some things that are not generally approved of by people whose opinions I ordinarily respect"; and "I disapprove of some things that are right" means "I disapprove of some things that are generally approved of by people whose opinions I ordinarily respect." As soon as one recognizes that the approval or disapproval which is expressed in a moral judgment is not necessarily or exclusively that of the speaker, but of some "community" with which he identifies, the apparent self-contradiction of such statements disappears.

There is a certain deliberate vagueness in the expression "generally approved of by people whose opinions I ordinarily respect," and it is in order to discuss it at this point. There is considerable variation from one individual to another with respect to the "community" with which he identifies and consequently with respect to whose opinion it is that each must take into account in making his moral judgments. In every culture—and especially, one suspects, in a self-consciously pluralistic culture such as our own—there are various "sub-cultures" that in many cases are the "communities" of which their members feel themselves to be a part. No one is *just* an American, or a Russian, or a Swede. A given American, for example, may be at one and the same time (a) an American, (b) a Catholic, (c) a Democrat, (d) a college professor, and (e) a member of the Society for the Prevention of Cruelty to Animals; and each of these "communities" may, on different occasions, be the one to which he has reference when he calls something right or wrong, good or evil. Which community is relevant in a given case depends on what sorts of basic attitudes are typical of each. For our hypothetical American it would vary depending on whether the topic under discussion were, say, (a) the freedom of the press, (b) birth control, (c) the proper role of the federal government, (d) plagiarism, or (e) slaughterhouse procedures. It is to allow for this varying reference of moral judgments that we have used the phrase "generally approved of by people whose opinions I ordinarily respect," it being understood that *whose* opinions a man respects varies greatly from one individual to another, and even from one occasion to another for the same individual (depending on what it is that is being considered). "Morally neutral," then, would mean "not an object of either pro-attitudes or anti-attitudes in any of the communities whose opinions I tend to respect."

All of the moral predicates are, I think, correctly construed as purported descriptions of the basic attitudes—positive or negative —of whatever community or communities the speaker has reference to in making his judgments. "Ought," however, is not a predicate, and it is not definable in terms of them. It too is descriptive, however—not of the attitudes but of the *expectations* of the community with respect to its members. To say "I ought to do so-and-so" is to say "It is expected of me by those whose good will I cherish, that I do so-and-so." The meaning of the sentence "One ought never to do what one believes to be wrong, even if one wants to" is, therefore, rather complex: it means, according to the explanations here proposed, "It is expected of a person, by those whose good will he cherishes, that he refrain from doing those things which they generally disapprove of, even if his personal inclination is to do them." And this interpretation expresses exactly what we would understand a person to mean if he were to make the statement in question.

It also becomes clear, in our theory, how a person can make a false moral judgment apart from the rather unusual circumstance in which he might be mistaken about his own attitude toward the thing in question. His own attitude is scarcely relevant to the truth or falsity of the moral judgment. According to our view, a moral judgment is true if the people in the community to which the speaker has reference have the attitude which he is attributing to them, false if they do not. It is not at all unusual or puzzling that a person should occasionally be mistaken about the "pro-" and "anti-" attitudes of the members of his community with respect to some matter which he may never have had an opportunity to discuss with them—especially when one remembers that most people are simultaneously members of several communities. Thus, at this point too our theory appears to solve a puzzle that the private-subjectivist theory left unsolved.

What shall we say, then, is the content of treatises on normative ethics, which according to the other subjectivist theory appeared to be nothing more than expressions of the private likes and dislikes of the author? The answer is: an ethical treatise is an attempt by one member of a community to assist the other members of that community to clarify their moral attitudes, to eliminate any inconsistencies that may be present (to render them "coherent"), and to adopt certain additional attitudes which may be shown to be consistent with the attitudes already held. Indeed, a very daring and original ethical thinker may do even more: he may recommend adopting attitudes different from those currently held—in which case he will be regarded by the community either as a great teacher or as an eccentric, depending on whether or not his recommendations are accepted by the community. The difference between a prophet and a "crackpot" is not altogether a matter of what a man says.

This brings us to the final difficulty which we noted in connection with the private-subjectivist theory: the fact that no basis could be given for the difference which we instinctively sense between moral and non-moral meanings of "good." The question is, how do we know that the statement, "Joe Doakes is a good man," when spoken by the head of the Mafia, is not a moral judgment, whereas the same statement when spoken by someone else may be? The answer, I think, is as follows. The sub-culture to which the head of the Mafia has reference in calling Joe Doakes "a good man" is not a "community" in any meaningful sense of that word. It is only a group of men whose common bond is a parasitic relation to a community. If the head of the Mafia were to call Joe a good man in the *moral* sense of "good," therefore, he would have to have reference to the basic attitudes of the community—i. e., law-abiding society—to which the Mafia stands in this parasitic relation; and this, of course, would be tantamount to saying that Joe is quite unfit for further service in the Mafia. Were he to call Joe a good man in this sense of "good," therefore, we could only construe it as an expression of his disapproval of Joe. ("Buy off Joe Doakes? Forget it. He's a *good* man—unfortunately.") If, then, he says "Joe Doakes is a good man" in an approving way ("You need somebody to help you on that Jones job? Take Joe. He's a good man."), we know immediately that what he is expressing is not a moral judgment at all, but simply what we may call "goodness of function." (Compare: "You need another car for the Jones job? Take mine. It's a good car.")

Concluding Unphilosophical Postscript

It should be apparent that the view presented here not only solves the difficulties noted in the private-subjectivist view, but also retains everything that is most persuasive in that view. For example, the variability of the objective-descriptive content of a moral judgment depending on who happens to utter it—a fact that is absolutely fatal to any objectivist theory—is easily explicable in terms of the different communities to which a given speaker may have reference (or, as we said before, the same speaker on different occasions or with respect to different topics). No doubt the approval- and disapproval-habits of people tend on the whole to coincide with those of the communities with which they identify. Therefore, we can often infer directly from our knowledge of a person's general attitudes to the descriptive statements implied in his judgment that something is good or bad (in the moral sense, of course). But the fact remains that we can distinguish between a person's private attitudes and his moral convictions, and our theory provides a basis for this distinction whereas the private-subjectivist theory does not.

There is one further feature of moral judgments which none of the previous writers has mentioned, but which is rather important. The discussion of it will require us to venture briefly into the realm of social psychology, however, and here I can only offer my comments as a layman's surmise—a "concluding unphilosophical postscript" to what I have already said.

The feature of moral judgments to which I refer is what might be called their "constraining" or "obligatory" character. Moral principles sincerely held seem to make a claim, to demand (but not force) obedience. Discussion of moral issues, accordingly, always seems to be a matter of unique importance: one is concerned about them "in the center of one's being," so to speak.

The explanation of this fact, I would suggest, is that as social beings our acceptance by the communities with which we identify is deeply important to us and, consequently, our conformity to the expectations of the community, and our identity with the community by way of sharing its basic moral attitudes, are also very important to us. As John Donne, the English poet, has put it, "No man is an island." We do not exist as isolated individuals, but as men in community with other men. The attitudes and expectations of the community thus *impinge* upon us, *constrain* us, *make demands* on us: it is this that gives us our sense of duty and obligation and our attitudes concerning right and wrong, good and evil, virtue and vice. Morality is a social phenomenon, and we are social beings; therefore, moral questions, and problems, and principles, strike us as being among the most important matters with which we can be concerned.

Study Questions

1. List the objections which Societal Subjectivist raises with respect to private subjectivism. Are these serious difficulties for the private-subjectivist view? Can you think of any way to defend private subjectivism against these objections?

2. What does Societal Subjectivist offer as an alternative to private subjectivism? To what extent does this involve disagreement with Private Subjectivist's position?

3. What analysis does Societal Subjectivist offer of the sentences which he earlier cited as being "nonsensical" if interpreted according to the private-subjectivist theory? Are you satisfied with this analysis? Can you think of any moral sentences that Societal Subjectivist might have difficulty in construing in a way consistent with his theory?

4. *Do* we know that the statement, "Joe Doakes is a good man," spoken (in an approving way) by the head of the Mafia, is not a moral judgment? How? (If you are not satisfied with Societal Subjectivist's account, devise one of your own.)

Chapter 29

EMOTIVISM

THE NUMBER OF meta-ethical theories to which we have been introduced is already so large that one almost feels compelled to apologize for offering yet another alternative. Surely, we are inclined to think, there must be something very odd about moral sentences if they are capable of being construed, with at least some degree of plausibility in each case, in so many different ways. Have any of the theories thus far discussed succeeded in pinpointing the precise character of this oddness—have they succeeded, in other words, in explaining the unique character of moral sentences? I do not think that they have. The unique feature of moral sentences—what gives them their unique "flavor"—is something that has been ignored completely by the first three writers and only briefly hinted at by the fourth. Let us try to isolate this feature and attempt to grasp the unique character of moral sentences by reference to it.

In order to isolate this feature, however, it is first necessary to notice some of the *non*-ethical language forms which commonly or even regularly accompany ethical language. Once these have been accounted for, we have then to ask: what is the character, or meaning, of what remains? It will then be this remainder, or residue of meaning, that constitutes the unique feature of ethical language.

The Non-ethical Elements of Ethical Language

It cannot be denied that moral sentences are often obliquely descriptive of the object or act or state of affairs that is the apparent object of the "judgment." If a man states, "You ought to stop drinking so much," or "It is wrong for you to drink as much as you do," it is apparent that part of what he is saying is "You are currently drinking to excess." The latter constitutes a straightforward empirical assertion that might be either true or false. This is evident from the fact that one to whom such a statement was made might defend himself by saying, "What do you mean? I haven't had a drink for six months!" The moral judgment, then, obliquely asserts that something is the case, that some state of affairs obtains; but it is not this empirical content that gives to moral utterances their unique character.

Further, moral utterances frequently contain not only oblique assertions of some alleged matters of fact, but also oblique predictions that a certain act or course of events will lead to such-and-such consequences. The man who says to his son, "Tom, you ought not to drive so fast," is not only asserting that Tom does in fact drive at excessive speeds: he is also predicting, in a rather vague and imprecise way, that if Tom continues to drive this way, he may become involved in an accident and thus be the cause of serious injury (or worse) either to himself or to others. This is why it is at least to the point, if not altogether convincing, for Tom to reply, "Don't worry, Dad; I may be a fast driver, but I'm always careful. Nobody is going to get hurt."

Because of these two characteristics of ethical language, ethical disagreements can be discussed—that is, up to a certain point. Two people who express varying "judgments" of right and wrong may disagree about some matters of fact (as in our first example), or they may disagree about the probable consequences of a certain act or pattern of behavior (as in our second example); and these, obviously, are empirical questions that can only be settled (if at all) by trying to find out what the facts are and what are the probable consequences of the act or pattern in question. Questions of the latter sort, in particular, are difficult to settle; but the loosely "predictive" element in ethical sentences explains the appropriateness of, for example, bringing into a discussion of the rightness or wrongness of speeding information about the number of accidents caused each year by speeding, the number of people injured or killed in such accidents, and so on.

Moral sentences, however, do not consist only, or even primarily, in factual assertions and loose predictions. The statement, "You ought not to drive so fast" is not reducible to the conjunction of the two sentences, "You commonly drive at speeds that are excessive" and "If you continue to do so, you are apt to become involved in an accident." There is something more involved in the moral sentence, "You ought not to drive so fast"—something expressed in the moral word "ought." What, then, is this additional element?

Another Look at Subjectivism

The most plausible suggestions that have been made thus far as to what it is that constitutes this additional element are those made by the two subjectivist writers. According to Private Subjectivist, affirmative moral "judgments" are statements to the effect that one has feelings of approval toward the person, act, or state of affairs in question and negative moral "judgments" are statements to the effect that one has feelings of disapproval. Quite apart from the difficulties that Societal Subjectivist has noted in this theory, however, it is obvious that this is not correct. Consider, once again, the sentence "You ought not to drive so fast." If we now add the private-subjectivist account of "ought" to our earlier analysis of this sentence, we get the following: "You commonly drive at speeds that are excessive, and if you continue to do so you are apt to become involved in an accident; moreover, I have feelings of disapproval toward your so doing." And this, quite obviously, is not what we mean when we say "You ought not to drive so fast." On this ground alone, therefore, the private-subjectivist theory is shown to be inadequate.

Societal subjectivism fares no better. According to this view, the meaning of the above sentence is "You commonly drive at speeds that are excessive, and if you continue to do so you are apt to become involved in an accident; moreover, your mother and I, and many others whose opinions you normally respect, have feelings of disapproval (or an "anti-attitude") toward your so doing." This, I am saying, does not express what we mean by the moral sentence, "You ought not to drive so fast."

It seems, therefore, that we must seek further for this elusive element that gives to moral sentences their unique character, or "flavor." It evidently has something to do with "pro-attitudes" and "anti-attitudes," but it most certainly cannot be construed as a report that the speaker, or some group to which he has reference, has the attitude in question. Let us then try another alternative.

The Case for Emotivism

The proposal I should like to make is this: the specifically moral character of moral sentences consists not in the assertion that the speaker, or some group to which he has reference, has certain feelings, but in a non-descriptive expression of those feelings. Moral words, insofar as they have a distinctively moral flavor, are not descriptive either of the object being "judged" or of anybody's feelings: they are not descriptive at all. Grammatically, they have the status of an interjection. "You ought not to drive so fast" means, roughly, "You commonly drive at excessive speeds: For Shame!!"

Not all moral sentences, however, can be reduced to (a) a factual assertion ("You commonly drive at excessive speeds") plus (b) an expression of approval or disapproval ("For Shame!!"). A sentence like "Driving at excessive speeds is wrong," for example, has no factual meaning; its only meaning, therefore, is emotive. It is as if one said "driving at excessive speeds!" in a "raised-eyebrows" tone of voice, thus indicating one's disapproval of the behavior in question. General moral sentences, therefore, are neither true nor false. One who says "Driving at excessive speeds is wrong" cannot be contradicted because he is making no assertion; anyone who appeared to be disagreeing with him would only be expressing a contrary attitude.

It has already been pointed out that our moral words can, without exception, be classified according to whether the attitude that they express is positive (pro-) or negative (anti-). Within these two general categories, however, the moral words that appear in each can be loosely arranged on a scale according to the degree of feeling which they commonly are used to express. To say that something is "reprehensible," for example, is to express a far stronger negative feeling toward it than if one were to say that it is "not very nice," and to say that something is one's "moral duty" is to express stronger positive feelings toward it than if one were simply to say that it is "good." The point can be illustrated by the following diagram (where the direction of the arrow indicates decreasing feeling):

Pro-attitudes	*Anti-attitudes*
moral duty	reprehensible
ought to be done	ought not to be done
ought to be desired	evil
virtuous (virtue)	vicious (vice)
good	bad
worthy	naughty
nice	not nice

Many people have great difficulty in understanding the difference between this view and the private-subjectivist view. The difference can be stated as follows: according to the private-subjectivist theory, moral sentences are informative sentences; according to my view, they are not. Or the difference could be expressed in this way: according to the private-subjectivist view, moral sentences are always either true or false; according to my view, they are not. According to the private-subjectivist view, the statement "Driving at excessive speeds is wrong" can be contradicted by the statement "You do not really disapprove of fast driving." According to my view the statement cannot be contradicted because it makes no assertion.

The difference between private-subjectivism and emotivism is not over the point whether a person who utters a moral sentence has the feelings in question or not: both views assert that he normally does. The question is: does the meaning of a moral sentence consist in an assertion by the speaker that he has such-and-such feelings, or is a moral sentence a non-reportive expression of those feelings? Private Subjectivist says the former; I say the latter. The difference is subtle, but important.

All of the facts about moral discourse to which the previous writers have called attention are easily explicable in terms of this theory—and any meta-ethical theory must, of course, finally be judged primarily on the basis of its explanatory power. There are, however, three additional considerations that particularly favor the emotivist theory.

First, the theory is consistent with what we know about how people learn to use the language of morals. Children learn the meanings of moral words by hearing them in certain contexts. "Bad," "wicked," "naughty," etc., they learn to associate with frowns, spankings, cross voices and other non-verbal expressions of disapproval; "good," "nice," and "worthy" they learn to associate with smiles, rewards, and other non-verbal expressions of approval. If, then, when they come to use these words themselves, they use them as a verbal expression of the attitudes which they have learned to associate with them, this is just precisely what one would expect. What else, one might ask, could they be supposed to mean by words learned in this way?

Second, the emotive theory is consistent with the purpose for which we normally utter moral sentences. That purpose is to influence other people's behavior—to create in them an inclination to act in certain ways and not to act in certain other ways. There can be little doubt that moral utterances do tend to influence us in just this way. The utterance, "So-and-so is morally wrong," made by someone whose opinions we normally respect, has a tendency to evince a negative attitude toward "so-and-so" corresponding to that of the speaker. Thus it seems very plausible to say: the meaning of a moral sentence is the feeling that it expresses, and because it has this meaning it is suitable for the purpose for which people normally utter such sentences. This is exactly what the emotive theory affirms.

Third, the emotive theory provides a convincing account of the nature of ethical disagreement. One can conceive of two sorts of ethical disagreement: that in which the disputants share a broad range of common attitudes but have conflicting attitudes toward some particular act or state of affairs, and that in which the disputants have fundamentally conflicting attitudes toward a very large proportion of those things in which they both have an interest. It will be convenient to deal separately with these two types of cases.

Naturalistic Objectivist's example of the two men who disagreed as to whether it would be right or wrong to use tear gas to deal with a certain situation would be an example of the first type. Note how the discussion of the issue proceeds. Each of the disputants cites such evidence and advances such considerations as he thinks will be effective in *changing the attitude* of the other. One may talk about the probability of igniting a civil war, and of the death and destruction that would ensue, and so on; the other may talk about the danger to life and property of the rioting itself and of the importance of putting an end to it by whatever means are available. But note well: the argument would be over as soon as one or the other of the disputants changed his attitude toward the action in question, *whether or not they had reached agreement on all of the facts*. This shows that it is conflict in attitude—not disagreement about the facts—that is central in a dispute of this kind. The reason it is worthwhile to talk about facts at all is that since the disputants share a common pattern of basic attitudes, it is reasonable to expect that if they were in agreement about the facts, they would (or probably would) adopt the same attitude toward those facts.

If, however, the disputants in a case of ethical disagreement are people whose basic moral attitudes are fundamentally different, the situation is radically altered. In such a case, specific moral issues are hardly worth discussing; if there is to be any discussion at all, it must be directed toward finding some common basic attitudes and trying to enlarge this common ground as much as possible. Failing this, discussion of particular issues is futile (witness the Geneva disarmanent talks of the 1960's). However much the disputants may agree regarding the empirical facts, they remain in unresolvable ethical disagreement so long as they hold conflicting basic attitudes; and agreement on particular moral questions under such circumstances is all but impossible to obtain.

To summarize: conflict in attitude is fundamental to ethical disagreement in two ways. First, it determines what empirical evidence is relevant to the dispute—that which it is presumed will have some tendency to alter the attitude of one or the other of the disputants. Second, it is fundamental in the sense that it is only when agreement in attitude has been reached that the dispute is settled—regardless of whether or not the disputants have reached agreement regarding the facts. The emotive theory of the meaning of moral discourse, therefore, enables us to understand, in a way that we otherwise could not, the nature of ethical disagreement; and this, I am suggesting, provides additional confirmation of the correctness of the theory.

Normative Ethics

One consequence of this theory which some people will undoubtedly think strange is that there can be no such thing as scientific normative ethics; for if our theory is correct, the questions with which writers on normative ethics have traditionally been concerned—questions of the sort, "What things really are right and wrong, and why?"—are not meaningful questions.

A man who writes a treatise on normative ethics may, of course, do many things that are interesting and valuable. He may, for example, do the work of a historian and in so doing provide us with interesting information about the moral attitudes of some of the well-known theorists of the past (Plato, Aristotle, Kant, etc.). Or he may do the work of a psychologist and help us to understand why we tend to feel approval or disapproval toward certain sorts of things. Or he may do the work of a meta-ethical theorist and in so doing help us to understand some of the peculiarities of the logical behavior of our moral terms. But insofar as he addresses himself to the questions with which writers on normative ethics have traditionally been concerned, his remarks can only be construed as personal exhortations designed to induce us to adopt certain attitudes which, for whatever reasons, he wishes his readers to adopt. His recommendations, however noble, have no objective validity whatsoever, for a sentence affirming that something is good or bad, right or wrong, praiseworthy or blameworthy, is not an assertion at all. It is a verbal expression of the attitude of the speaker, the purpose of which is to encourage us to adopt a similar attitude.

There seems no doubt, therefore, that normative ethics as it has been traditionally conceived is based on a mistake—the mistake of assuming that moral sentences are descriptive sentences that are capable of being true or false, and that reasons could be given to support the view that certain of them are true and certain others false. The truth of the matter is, to paraphrase Shakespeare, that "nothing is right or wrong but *feeling* makes it so." The job of explaining *why* we feel positively toward some things and negatively toward others is one that is best left to the psychologist.

Study Questions

1. What "non-ethical" elements does Emotivist claim to find in ethical language? Is he right in asserting that these elements are frequently present? What justification is there for calling them "non-ethical" elements?
2. What, exactly, is Emotivist's proposal regarding the meaning of moral sentences? How does it differ from the private-subjectivist view? (Review Societal Subjectivist's objections to private subjectivism. Do they apply with equal force to Emotivism, or do they not?)
3. Emotivist claims that "all of the facts about moral discourse to which the previous writers have called attention are easily explicable in terms of [the emotivist theory]." Is this the case? Can you recall any facts to which earlier writers have called attention that might prove difficult for Emotivist to explain?
4. What additional considerations does Emotivist offer in support of his theory? Do you find them convincing? Do they lend equal support to any of the other theories?

Chapter 30

IMPERATIVISM

A TENDENCY EXISTS, both among plain men and among philosophers, to depreciate any uses of language other than the informative. This is most unfortunate, for it creates a desire to translate any sort of discourse that one values highly into informative language—to exhibit it, that is, as a species of the sort of discourse that one values most. It is difficult to believe that this tendency has not been at work in at least some of the discussion on the present problem.

One fact about ethical discourse seems to be very important, although none of the previous writers has made mention of it, and that is that we all know how to *use* this type of discourse without too much difficulty. This fact should give us pause. If the status of ethical discourse is as mystifying as all this discussion would seem to indicate, how is it that all of us, even children, can use it with such apparent ease? It seems likely that if we look carefully at the way in which children learn to use this kind of discourse, and the purposes for which they and we employ it (ridding our minds of any bias in favor of informative discourse), we would discover that moral talk is not nearly so mystifying as we have thus far been led to believe.

Before we do that, however, we shall have to consider emotivism. My quarrel with emotivism, as may have been surmised, is not that it fails to exhibit moral talk as a species of informative discourse, but rather that it interprets it in a way that is inconsistent

with the general purpose for which we commonly employ such discourse. That moral utterances are frequently delivered with feeling no one will deny; but that the primary function of those utterances is simply to give vent to those feelings ought to be denied by
anyone who knows how to use this sort of discourse.

Defects of Emotivism

I do not wish to dwell at great length on the defects of the emotivist theory. The theory has been widely and soundly criticized
since it was first put forward some thirty years ago, and many of its
early supporters have abandoned it in recent years. I do want, however, to mention just three or four of the most serious objections
that have been raised against the theory.

The theory does not do justice to the seriousness with which
moral sentences are commonly uttered. Questions calling for moral
appraisal and decision are frequently matters of great moment: the
fates of men and nations are sometimes at stake. To say that the
sentence "War is evil" means "Boo for war" or that the sentence
"Bravery is good" means "Hurray for bravery" is absurd. No
doubt we human beings not infrequently take ourselves too seriously, but we surely are not guilty of this when we say that our
moral appraisals of war, or of bravery, or of thousands of other
things that we appraise in this way, are serious and important matters. The "boo-hurray" theory offends us because it makes light of
serious matters. For this reason alone it deserves to be rejected.

Moreover, a number of odd and distressing consequences follow
if one assumes this theory to be true. It would follow, for example,
that one could never be in error in making a moral "judgment,"
and from this it would follow, in turn, that neither blame nor remorse is ever appropriate. Moreover, according to this theory,
there could never be a rational basis for an ethical appraisal or
decision. And most distressing of all, it would follow that ethical
disputes cannot be resolved by rational means: if men or nations
cannot agree on some matter of importance to both of them, there
is nothing to do but to fight it out until the strongest one—man or
nation—wins.

The issue resolves itself, really, to: are moral utterances rational, or are they not? The unanimous answer of our whole Western ethical tradition, from Plato and Aristotle to Kant, Mill, Moore, and Ross, is that they are; the reply of the emotivists is that they are not. This is no trifling matter. If ethics can be rational, then moral progress—the gradual improvement of one's moral principles by reflection and criticism—is possible; if not, such progress is not possible. Indeed, the very notion of "progress" becomes, in this theory, incomprehensible. Anyone concerned about the future of civilization would do well to ponder these consequences.

The best answer to emotivism, however, is not destructive criticism but a better theory—that of imperativism.

Some Features of Directive Language

Rational beings employ language for a variety of purposes, only one of which is to convey information. Because so much of our use of language does consist in this informative function, however, conventional logic has dwelt almost entirely on the logical behavior of language so employed. But the directive function of language— the use of language to guide behavior—is an equally rational function.

The difference between these two kinds of language might be understood in terms of the different kinds of questions to which each type might appropriately be conceived as an answer. One uses language informatively (to convey information) only in instances where one presupposes a question of the form, "What are the facts?" or "What is the case?" One uses language in its directive function only in instances where one presupposes a question of the form, "What shall I do?" To a question of the latter form, any statement of fact would be inappropriate; to a question of the former type, a moral appraisal would be equally inappropriate. (We all know this in practice; it is only when we come to theorizing about our practice that some of us become a little confused.)

There are many different instances in which the function of the language used is quite evidently "directive." Consider the following list: a typical verbal communication from a sergeant to his platoon; a recipe; assembly instructions for a child's toy that is delivered unassembled; instructions from ground control to a team of astronauts; a teacher's remarks in preparation for an examination; a parent's word to a small child who is dallying after bedtime. All of these, and dozens of others, are instances of language being used directively—to guide behavior.

Language used directively, just like language used informatively, envisages a fairly specific state of affairs. "Johnny, go to bed" (directive), like "Johnny is going to bed" (informative), envisages Johnny's going to bed in the very near future. Both utterances are about Johnny's going to bed, but what is said about Johnny's going to bed is different in the two cases. The directive sentence is addressed to Johnny, and it might be translated, "Johnny's going to bed: do it!" The informative sentence is addressed to anybody who cares to listen, and it might be translated, "Johnny's going to bed: it is occurring."

Language intended to serve a directive function is typically addressed to the person or persons whose behavior is intended thereby to be guided. Some directives are intended for some one specific individual ("Johnny, go to bed!"). Others are intended for whoever may be in a position to benefit from them ("Tear on dotted line"). Some appear to be addressed to everyone, i. e., they are intended to be universally applicable ("Do not take for yourself what belongs to another"). We shall return to this shortly.

The directive function, like the informative, is *sui generis:* neither can be reduced to, or derived from, the other. A given sentence may, of course, serve both functions ("Bring me the book that is lying on the dresser"), but the functions themselves may, nonetheless, be distinguished.

One cannot determine the intended function of a sentence simply by identifying its mood. Function depends on the intentions of the speaker, whereas mood does not. The sentence in the parentheses in the preceding paragraph, for example, is in the imperative mood, but it is bi-functional. "Johnny, go to bed" and "Johnny, it is past your bedtime" may both serve a directive function, but the two sentences differ in mood.

Ethical Discourse as a Species
of Directive Language

Let us return to ethical discourse and see how the foregoing reflections on the nature of directive language may help us to understand this very common type of talk.

The vast majority of moral sentences are in the indicative mood. This may be one of the reasons why most of the earlier efforts to ascertain the status of moral sentences proceeded on the assumption that they must be understood as some sub-variety of informative language. It is not at all inconsistent with this fact to suggest, however, that the function of moral sentences is to guide behavior —is, in short, directive.

Consider, first, the way in which children learn to use moral concepts. A typical instance would be the following: Johnny accompanies his mother to the grocery store, and seeing some tasty-looking candy within reach, he decides to help himself. Mother says, "No, Johnny, you must put that back. It is *wrong* to take something that belongs to someone else without paying for it." Three elements of this situation should be noted. (a) The moral sentence is uttered in a situation involving choice, a situation like many Johnny may be expected to encounter in the future in which he must choose among alternative ways of behaving. (b) The evident function of the moral utterance is to serve as a principle for the guidance of conduct—a rule that may help Johnny decide how to act in future situations of this type. And (c) the moral principle thus enunciated is universal in scope: it applies not only to Johnny, but to every one. It is this, chiefly, that identifies it as a moral principle rather than a merely conventional rule.

Note also the situations in which we commonly employ moral talk: the same three features, it will be found, are always present. Moral principles, we might say, play a role among men analogous to the role of instinct in the behavior of animals: they serve as rules of conduct, guiding us in the multifarious choices that we are constantly called upon to make. Because moral principles are universal in scope, it is always in a way appropriate to state them—even, for example, when there is no one around (except ourselves) to hear our utterance or to be guided by what we say. The fact that moral judgments are sometimes spoken in solitude ("How noble!" or "How reprehensible!" uttered in response to something one has read) in no way controverts the claim that the primary and normal function of such utterances is to guide behavior.

It may be thought that what I am urging as the primary function of ethical discourse is identical with Emotivist's suggestion that the purpose for which we normally utter moral sentences is "to influence other people's behavior—to create in them an inclination to act in certain ways and not to act in certain other ways." This, however, is not the case. Uttering a moral principle is a wholly rational procedure: it is an attempt to supply an answer to the question, "What shall I do in situations of such-and-such a kind?" In Emotivist's view, uttering a moral sentence is an attempt to persuade or coerce someone to do something: it is a particularly prevalent kind of propaganda. I do not think moral talk is a kind of verbal club: I think it is an appropriate form of discourse for rational beings who share a common concern about how they ought to act. Just as in informative discourse there is a difference between *informing* and *convincing,* so in directive discourse there is a difference between *directing* and *persuading.* The difference is subtle but important.

We may observe, in conclusion, that it is absolutely impossible for men to live without principles of this kind—that a human being without an ethic is an impossibility. This is true for several reasons. First, our knowledge of the probable consequences of acting in this or that way is severely limited: we need general rules of conduct, embodying the accumulated wisdom of preceding generations, to guide our behavior in those countless situations in which we do not know how to calculate the likely consequences of various alternatives. Second, however extensive our knowledge of probable consequences, we require principles that will provide reasons for preferring one set of consequences over another. This would be true even if we were omniscient, knowing in precise detail what would be the short- and long-range consequences of each alternative before us. Finally, without such principles we should not be able to accumulate practical wisdom—to profit from our experiences, so to speak —or to pass the wisdom gained on to our children. For all learning, it must be remembered, involves generalization: it is only via generalizations that we escape the irrationality of sheer individuality. Moral principles are to the practical life what general truths are to the intellectual—the generalizations that relate the particulars of experience, thus casting them in an intelligible pattern.

There is no danger, therefore, that men will cease to have ethical principles as a consequence of this or that inadequate meta-ethical theory, however widely such a theory may come to be held. There is danger, however, that widespread bewilderment about the meaning of moral utterances may lead to a weakening of their directive power, and thus to a chaotic situation in which the groping for new principles goes on without the benefit of the foundation of the old. It is necessary, and important, that these principles change, else men should not be able to adjust to the constantly changing conditions in which they live. But change, if it is to be healthy, must be orderly—a creation of the new by way of a modification of, and addition to, the old. This cannot occur if old principles are simply ignored or if they altogether lose their directive power. Hence, it is a matter of more than casual importance that their status be understood and their role duly respected.

Study Questions

1. What, exactly, do you understand to be the imperativist theory about the meaning of moral sentences?
2. Summarize Imperativist's criticisms of the emotivist theory. Do these seem to be sound criticisms? How might Emotivist defend himself against these objections?
3. Summarize the "features of directive language" discussed by Imperativist. Do these features in fact distinguish directive language from informative language, as Imperativist apparently believes?
4. What arguments does Imperativist offer in support of his central thesis regarding the meaning of moral sentences? Do you find his arguments persuasive?
5. How does Imperativist's theory differ from Emotivist's suggestion that the *purpose* for which we normally utter moral sentences is "to influence other people's behavior"?
6. For what reasons, according to Imperativist, do we need moral principles? Is it possible to agree with him on this without accepting his main thesis?

Chapter 31

MULTI-FUNCTIONALISM

THE DISCUSSION OF the status of moral judgments is in need of summation. In my estimation, what would be most helpful at this point is a summary of the main facts about moral judgments that have emerged from the foregoing discussions. Each writer has emphasized certain facts and has offered a theory tailor-made to fit just those facts. None thus far, however, has offered a theory that satisfactorily explains all of the relevant facts. The reason, I shall suggest, is that moral sentences serve a variety of functions, any one of which may predominate in a given instance. As a result, a number of "uni-functional" theories can be rendered more or less plausible since one can always find examples that tend to support whichever theory one is attempting to defend. But, as we have seen, critics of each theory can with equal ease find examples that do not favor the theory in question and, in fact, cannot be plausibly explained by it.

I shall return to an exposition and defense of a "multi-functional" theory shortly, but first, the summary.

Some Facts About Moral Judgments

A few logical and phenomenological observations have been made which are, as far as I can judge, completely neutral with respect to the competing theories. The neutral facts are: (a) Moral judgments are applicable only to *human* behavior. (b) Moral judgments are applicable to human behavior only in situations involving *choice*. (c) Some terms that often function as moral predicates (e. g., "good," "right," and "ought") also function on occasion as non-moral predicates. (d) There is a distinction to be drawn between "instrumental" and "intrinsic" moral goodness: some things are said to be good (instrumentally) because they contribute to the coming-into-being of something else that is said to be good in itself (intrinsically good). These seem to be incontrovertible and completely unexceptionable facts about moral judgments, and I should suppose that all parties to the dispute about the status of moral judgments could accept them without in any way jeopardizing their respective positions.

Next we note a group of facts about moral judgments that tend to favor objectivist theories. (e) A consideration of the probable *consequences* of an act is usually relevant to the judgment that the act in question is good or bad, right or wrong. (f) Empirical facts are frequently relevant to our judgment that a given act or state of affairs is good or bad, right or wrong. (g) A moral judgment to the effect that so-and-so is a "good" or a "bad" man, or that such-and-such an act was a "virtuous" or a "vicious" one, does ordinarily convey some information, however imprecise, about the man or act in question. These, I am saying, are facts about moral judgments, facts that any theory about the status of moral judgments must somehow take into consideration.

There are also some facts about moral judgments that tend to favor subjectivist views. (h) Moral judgments are normally associated with certain attitudes on the part of the person making the judgment—pro-attitudes with affirmative moral judgments, and anti-attitudes with negative moral judgments. (i) People tend to have rather strong feelings about matters on which they render moral judgments: these matters commonly strike them as being important, serious, matters of great moment. (j) The attitudes and expectations of the human community or communities with which one identifies are evidently related in some way to the moral judgments that one makes.

In view of what has been said, one further fact may be noted. (k) Children learn to associate the language of morals not only with certain sorts of conduct, but also with certain sorts of empirical facts and with attitudes of approval and disapproval. This being the case, it is easy to see that the defenders of various theories can appeal to the way in which children learn to use ethical discourse in support of their view, provided only that they emphasize those features of the learning process that tend to support their theory. (It is not my intention to suggest that this is done deviously, but only that the advocates of this or that theory tend to find in this learning process what they are looking for, and to overlook everything else.)

It seems evident that uni-functional theories of the objectivist type get established because of a one-sided emphasis on items *e*, *f*, and *g* in the above list and those of the subjectivist type because of an equally one-sided emphasis on items *h*, *i*, and *j*. A rationalist who focuses his attention on the objectivist-favoring facts will probably advocate an intuitionist theory; an empiricist will more likely find himself adopting the naturalistic-objectivist view. Both, however, will be guilty of overlooking, or at least of downgrading, the facts that are less favorable to objectivist theories. So also with theories of the subjectivist type (among which, for our present purposes, we may include the emotivist theory). A philosopher who fastens his attention on the feelings and/or attitudes of the individual making the moral judgment, and de-emphasizes everything else, will tend to favor either private subjectivism or emotivism; one who gives more weight to the way in which the attitudes and expectations of the community impinge on moral judgments will advocate a societal-subjectivist theory. All, however, will be guilty of forgetting, or underemphasizing, those facts to which objectivists commonly point in support of *their* theories.

Imperativism is also a uni-functional theory, one that appeals particularly to the fact that the way in which we learn moral principles makes it inevitable that we associate them with conduct. This is, of course, true—but so are many other things, which imperativism, unfortunately, leaves out of account. Thus, imperativism is unable to account, for example, for moral judgments rendered with respect to people and/or events in the past: it is not at all plausible to say that "Judas ought not to have betrayed Jesus" really means "Judas, do not do it!" Similarly, imperativism would make a command to do something wrong self-contradictory: "Murder is wrong, but you must murder Clytemnestra" would mean, in this view, "Do not murder anyone, ever—but do murder Clytemnestra" —and that, plainly, is a self-contradictory command. Thus imperativism fares no better than the other uni-functional theories as an account of the whole meaning of the language of morals.

Therefore, there appears to be only one way out of the dilemma, and that is to say that moral talk serves a *variety* of functions, any one of which may be primary at any given time. The language of morals is not a solo instrument: it is an ensemble, and at some times one instrument has the lead, and at other times another. There is, after all, no good reason to suppose that all moral talk must be reducible to sentences of some one logical type: it may well be that to attempt to do so is to impose an artificial simplicity on moral talk that is not to be found in that talk itself. The failure of the various uni-functional theories that have been proposed strongly suggests that this is so. Let us see if we cannot make a more convincing case for a multi-functional theory.

The Moral Judge and the Moral Judgment

It is important to bear in mind, when talking about the meaning of language, that the meaning of any piece of discourse depends on what the speaker intends it to mean. Moral judgments are not autonomous entities, whose meaning is independent of the intentions of the persons making those judgments: they are the attempts of men—moral judges—who in making these judgments are attempting to say something. What is it, then, that people are trying to say when they utter sentences like "Joe Doakes is a good man," or "The infliction of needless pain is evil"?

Once we put the question this way, it becomes apparent that there are many things that people might want to say when they utter such sentences, and what it is that they are primarily intending to say in any given instance can only be determined by paying very close attention to the total context in which the sentence is uttered. Among the relevant contextual factors that have to be considered in each case are such things as the general pattern of likes and dislikes of the person making the judgment, the features usually possessed by people, acts, or states of affairs that this person is in the habit of commending, the non-verbal indications of feeling (facial expressions, vocal inflections) that attend his utterance, the person or persons to whom the judgment is addressed, and so on. In actual conversation we do normally note these things, and so we usually have little difficulty in "getting the meaning" of the person making the judgment. It is only when we abstract from the concrete situation in which a judgment is made and try to theorize about the judgments themselves that we encounter difficulty.

It is surely apparent, for example, that (to use imperativist's example) a mother who says to her son, "It is wrong to take things that belong to other people without paying for them," is attempting to convey to him a rule of conduct. She is saying, in effect, "Do not ever just help yourself to other people's things"; moreover, she and her son both know perfectly well that that is what she means. She may also mean, of course, that she disapproves of what is called stealing, but that is a very subordinate part of her meaning in this instance. It is examples like this that give credence to the imperativist theory.

It is equally apparent, however, that the enunciation of a general principle of conduct would not be the primary purpose of a man who says, "Albert Schweitzer was a great and good man; his death was a great loss to good men everywhere." Such a sentence, uttered by almost anyone, would mean primarily (a) that Albert Schweitzer possessed in a high degree the qualities that we commonly commend in other men (humanity, compassion, unselfishness, etc.) and (b) that the speaker thoroughly approves of people who possess these qualities. In this case the judgment is almost completely informative in character—informative with respect to the character of Albert Schweitzer and informative of the attitude of the speaker. The directive function, insofar as it is present at all, is quite subordinate to these other kinds of meaning.

Consider a third example. A man is reading his evening newspaper and comes upon the story of a hold-up in which an aged grocery store proprietor and his wife have been mercilessly killed. "How terrible!" he exclaims. "Whoever did this should be put away for life!" In this case it is clear that the moral judgment is primarily an expression and/or assertion of feeling—feeling so strong that it seems wholly inadequate to describe it simply as an "anti-attitude." There is little or nothing in the way of "objective-descriptive content" in such an utterance, and nothing at all in the way of enunciating a rule for the guidance of future conduct. Moral judgments can (and to some extent usually do) express feeling, and in certain sorts of situations this function of moral utterances may overshadow or exclude all others.

It is quite impossible—and, fortunately, quite unnecessary—to lay down rules to determine when one function is predominating in ethical discourse and when another. One can say with a reasonable degree of assurance that when one has to do with the moral instruction of the young, it is the directive function that predominates, but even this generalization is probably subject to exceptions. I return, however, to a point made earlier: in actual practice, we usually have little difficulty in understanding what it is that people are trying to say when they employ the familiar locutions of moral talk. Were it not for the fact that the whole discussion of this problem was undertaken on the mistaken assumption that all moral sentences must serve some one single function, the diverse meanings of such sentences would not have remained for so long unrecognized.

Study Questions

1. Can you think of any "facts about moral judgments" that Multi-functionalist has omitted from his summanry? Are any of those he does list controversial—i. e., likely to be denied by advocates of certain meta-ethical theories?
2. What objections does Multi-functionalist raise against imperativism? Are they sound? Defend imperativism against these objections as best you can.
3. Is it true that "the meaning of any piece of discourse depends on what the speaker intends it to mean"? If so, what relevance does this have for the present controversy?
4. Multi-functionalist offers several examples in support of his theory regarding the status of moral sentences. Could these same examples be interpreted in a way consistent with any of the theories discussed earlier? Which? Which (if any) might have difficulty with these examples?

For Further Reading

Aiken, H. D., *Reason and Conduct: New Bearings in Moral Philosophy.* New York: Alfred A. Knopf, 1962.

Ayer, A. J., *Language, Truth and Logic,* 2d ed. New York: Dover Publications, 1946 (paperbound). Chapter VI.

Baier, Kurt, *The Moral Point of View,* abridged ed. New York: Random House, 1965 (paperbound).

Blanshard, Brand, *Reason and Goodness.* New York: The Macmillan Company, 1961.

Brandt, R. B., "The Emotive Theory of Ethics," *The Philosophical Review,* Vol. 59 (1950), 305-318.

———, *Ethical Theory.* Englewood Cliffs, N.J.: Prentice-Hall, 1959. Chapters 7-11.

———, "The Status of Empirical Assertion Theories in Ethics," *Mind,* Vol. LXI (1952), 458-479.

Edel, Abraham, *Science and the Structure of Ethics.* Chicago, Ill.: University of Chicago Press, 1961 (paperbound).

Edwards, Paul, *The Logic of Moral Discourse.* New York: Free Press of Glencoe, 1955 (paperbound). Chapters VII-IX.

Ewing, A. C., *Second Thoughts in Moral Philosophy.* New York: The Macmillan Company, 1959. Chapters I and II.

Falk, W. D., "Goading and Guiding," *Mind,* Vol. LXII (1953), 145-171.

Frankena, W. K., "Moral Philosophy at Mid-century," *The Philosophical Review,* Vol. 60 (1951), 44-55.

Gewirth, Alan, "Meanings and Criteria in Ethics," *Philosophy,* Vol. XXXVIII (1963), 329-345.

Hancock, Roger, "The Refutation of Naturalism in Moore and Hare," *The Journal of Philosophy,* Vol. 57 (1960), 326-334.

Hare, R. M., *Freedom and Reason.* New York: Oxford University Press, 1963 (paperbound).

———, *The Language of Morals.* New York: Oxford University Press, 1964 (paperbound).

Harsanyi, J. C., "Ethics in Terms of Hypothetical Imperatives," *Mind,* Vol. LXVII (1958), 305-316.

Kerner, George C., "Approvals, Reasons and Moral Argument," *Mind,* Vol. LXXI (1962), 474-486.

Mill, John Stuart, *Utilitarianism.* Indianapolis, Ind.: Liberal Arts Press, 1960 (paperbound).

Moore, G. E., *Principia Ethica.* Cambridge University Press, 1959 (paperbound). Chapters I-III.

Nowell-Smith, P. H., *Ethics.* Baltimore, Md.: Penguin Books, 1954.

Perry, R. B., *General Theory of Value.* Cambridge, Mass.: Harvard University Press, 1926.

Prichard, H. A., *Moral Obligation.* New York: Oxford University Press, 1949. Chapters 1, 2 and 5.

Prior, A. N., *Logic and the Basis of Ethics.* New York: Oxford University Press, 1949.

Raphael, D. Daiches, *Moral Judgement.* New York: Hillary House, 1955. Chapters IV, VII, and VIII.

————, *The Moral Sense.* New York: Oxford University Press, 1947.

Ross, W. D., *Foundations of Ethics.* New York: Oxford University Press, 1939. Chapters II, III and XI.

————, *The Right and the Good.* New York: Oxford University Press, 1930. Chapter II.

Sidgwick, Henry, *The Methods of Ethics,* 7th ed. rev., Constance Jones. Chicago, Ill.: University of Chicago Press, 1962. Chapters III, VIII and IX.

Singer, M. G., *Generalization in Ethics.* New York: Alfred A. Knopf, 1961.

Stevenson, C. L., *Ethics and Language.* New Haven, Conn.: Yale University Press, 1960 (paperbound). Chapters I, II, IV, V, VI.

Stroll, A., *The Emotive Theory of Ethics.* Berkeley and Los Angeles, Calif.: University of California Press, 1954.

Taylor, Paul W., *Normative Discourse.* Englewood Cliffs, N.J.: Prentice-Hall, 1961.

Toulmin, S. E., *The Place of Reason in Ethics.* Cambridge: Cambridge University Press, 1960 (paperbound).

Wellman, Carl, *The Language of Ethics.* Cambridge, Mass.: Harvard University Press, 1961.

PART VI

The Mind-body Problem

Chapter 32

THE TRADITIONAL PROBLEM OF
BODY AND MIND

THE PROBLEM OF the present section is exceedingly puzzling and therefore it is important that we begin by trying to understand exactly what that problem is. We shall take as our point of departure the apparent facts about body and mind that give rise to the problem.

Mental Events and Physical Events

We are all acquainted with a class of events which it seems natural and proper to describe as "mental" events. We know what it is like, for example, to have pleasurable and unpleasurable feelings: a cool shower after a hard day of work provides an example of the former; a dentist drilling too close to a nerve, an example of the latter. We know, moreover, what it is like to experience emotions: love, hate, affection, concern, jealousy, and so on. Certain sorts of activities also appear to be mental, or at least partly mental, such as perceiving, remembering, imagining, deliberating, inferring. Finally, volition is a mental occurrence: willing or deciding to do something in preference to something else.

Events of the kinds just mentioned appear to be different in a number of ways from "physical" events. The most obvious difference, perhaps, is that mental events, unlike physical events, do not appear to be publicly observable. If I am in pain, for example, nobody but me feels the pain. Other people may, of course, infer that

I am in pain from the way I act (I may grimace, cry out, or perhaps clutch the part of the body that has been injured), but they cannot feel the pain that I feel. Indeed, I can fool other people about pain: I can pretend to be in pain, and lead them to infer that I am in pain, by going through the motions of one who is in pain; but I cannot fool myself on this score. Either I feel pain or I do not, and it makes no sense at all to say, "I thought I felt a pain, but I was mistaken."

We need not raise at this point the question, how are we aware of such mental events? The question is worth discussing, and it will be considered incidentally in the discussion that follows; but it is not the question upon which we shall focus our attention at present. We may observe, however, that the name which philosophers use for this process by which we appear to be directly aware of our own mental states is *introspection.* One knows one's own mental states by introspection, and the mental states of others (if at all) by inference.

Another feature of mental events distinguishing them from physical events is that they cannot properly be said to be locatable in space. With respect to a physical event it is always meaningful to ask, "Where, exactly, did it occur?" But with respect to a mental event, such a question (unless it is construed to mean, "Where were you when you felt, or decided, thus-and-so") has no precise meaning. A volition, or an emotion, or a recollection, is not the sort of thing that can occur, say, "on the sidewalk in front of the White House, about six feet in front of the main gate"—though an explosion, or a collision, or a demonstration, or anything else that we would classify as a physical event, could.

Most people would not remain puzzled very long over these differences. The differences, they would say, result from the fact that the subjects of physical events are *bodies,* whereas the subjects of mental events are *minds.* Bodies occupy space and are locatable in space; hence, the events in which they participate are also locatable in space. Minds, however, do not occupy space (they are neither round, nor square, nor any other shape, nor do they come in various sizes) and are not, properly speaking, locatable in space; consequently, the events of which they are the subject are not locatable in space.

What, precisely, is this notion of "mind" (or "consciousness" or "self") that is so deeply imbedded in the common-sense view of man? It is difficult to say precisely. It involves, certainly, the idea of something that is the subject of what we have called mental events—feeling, willing, desiring, thinking, etc.—and it involves the denial that it can be described in terms of shape or size or other qualities that are said to be applicable only to bodies. It is evidently supposed to be very closely associated with the brain, but since that is locatable in space (and for other reasons), it is not considered to be identical with the brain. It probably does no injustice to the common-sense view to say that each mind "inhabits" a particular body; in any case it is clear that each mind is believed to be intimately related in some way or other to some particular body, however this is to be expressed.

We do, it is true, sometimes use "spatial" language in talking about certain mental phenomena. We say things like "I can't seem to get this idea *into my head*," or "Intentions are hard to detect because they occur *in a person's mind* where no one else can see them"; but when we do speak in this way, we are using spatial language metaphorically. We could, without altering the meaning of these statements, say instead, "I can't seem to comprehend this idea" and "Intentions are hard to detect because they are mental events and thus not publicly observable." It seems very doubtful, in any case, that the common-sense view of the nature of mind would allow that spatial categories are properly applicable to it.

There is something else about bodies and minds that is a part of the common-sense view, however, and that is that a given mind and the body with which it is associated mutually influence one another. The mental event that we call "seeing a flash of lightning," for example, seems to be related causally to a series of physical events involving an event in the sky, light waves, my optic nerve, and so on. The mental event that I call "feeling a pain" seems to be causally related to (a consequence of) certain physical events occurring in my body: the flame touching my finger, the bee stinging my ear, the dentist drilling my tooth, and so on. I cannot, indeed, always infer a physical event from the mental event of feeling a pain: some pains are "psychosomatic," by which we mean that they do not appear to be caused by the organic disturbances that normally are the causes of such pains. In very many cases, however, the mental event that we call "feeling a pain" does seem to be caused by a physical event that we might call "receiving an injury"; and this supposition—that some mental events are caused by some physical events—seems clearly to be a part of the common-sense view.

It is also commonly supposed, however, that some causal series run in the opposite direction, i. e., that some mental events cause, or at least partly cause, some physical events. At the present moment, for example, I am engaged in writing, which obviously consists of a series of physical (publicly observable) events. But it seems very natural to say that at least part of the cause of my writing now is the fact that some time ago I decided to spend this day in this way, and an act of deciding is precisely the sort of thing that we call a mental event. Our thoughts, our wishes, our decisions seem to make a difference in the way we speak and act, and speaking and acting are physical events. These, in turn, sometimes cause other physical events to occur; so it appears that at least some mental events are related to some physical events as a cause is related to its effect.

These various beliefs about body and mind may be stated in two simple propositions. (1) Bodies and minds are two distinct sorts of entities, neither of which can be adequately explained simply as a special form of the other, (2) Bodies and minds are capable, nonetheless, of acting causally with respect to each other. The first proposition states the central thesis of what is called *anthropological dualism.* The second, which presupposes the first, states what is central in the view called *interactionism*. Interactionism, then, is simply the technical name for the "plain man's" view regarding the relation of body and mind.

Some Questions Regarding the Common-sense View

Thus far we have not stated, or even attempted to state, what we have called "the traditional problem of body and mind." We have only called attention to some of the prevailing beliefs concerning "bodies" and "minds," and we have introduced some of the technical terminology that philosophers customarily employ in discussing them. What, then, is the problem, and how has it arisen?

Let us consider the second question first. The problem has arisen because of (a) the opaqueness of the notion of "mind," (b) certain difficulties in the way of knowing that any such entities exist, (c) the difficulty of understanding how there can be causal relations between physical and non-physical entities, and—more recently—(d) the belief of some philosophers that the interactionist account presupposes metaphysical views which they regard as incorrect. The effect of these problems is to raise doubts about the correctness of the common-sense (interactionist) account, and subsequently to initiate a search for a more adequate alternative.

The traditional problem of body and mind, therefore, may be stated as the question to which the common-sense view regarding body and mind is one possible answer, namely: are bodies and minds two distinct sorts of entities neither of which can be explained as a form or function of the other, and how are the apparent two-way causal relations between them to be understood? The first part of the problem calls in question the dualism that is implicit in the common-sense view. The latter part asks for some explanation of the fact that bodies and minds appear to be involved in mutual causal relations.

Historically, it was the latter part of this problem that first caught the attention of philosophers; the dualism implicit in the common-sense view was simply taken for granted. During the sixteenth and seventeenth centuries the question that philosophers debated was: How are we to understand the apparent mutual causation between bodies and minds? To this question a number of interesting (and sometimes far-fetched) answers were given.

René Descartes (1596-1650), whose reflections on the problem really launched the modern discussion, advocated the interactionist view. Body and mind, said Descartes, are radically distinct sorts of entities, two kinds of substances, neither of which is reducible to the other: body is "extended, unthinking substance," and mind is "thinking, unextended substance." Nonetheless, said Descartes, it is evident that body and mind interact; indeed, said he, it seems a reasonable conjecture that the precise point where this interaction occurs is in the pineal gland—for which, it may be said in defense of Descartes, nobody had previously been able to find any worthwhile function.

Descartes' sucessors by and large accepted his dualistic account of man, but some of them found his "pineal gland" theory rather unconvincing. A number of alternatives were therefore proposed. Gottfried Wilhelm Leibniz (1646-1716), for example, advocated a theory known as *parallelism*. Bodies and minds do not interact, said Leibniz, but they appear to do so because God has created the world in such a way that there is a perfect "pre-established harmony" between any given series of mental events and a corresponding series of physical events. Mental events, therefore, are always caused by prior mental events and physical events by prior physical events, but thanks to God's thoughtful provision for a perfect harmony between the two kinds of events the appearance of interaction results. Nicolas Malebranche (1638-1715), a contemporary of Leibniz, advocated a special form of parallelism known as *occasionalism,* which might be described as harmony on the installment plan: God, said Malebranche, did not establish perfect harmony between physical and mental events "in the beginning," but as the occasion arises (which presumably is rather frequently), he does what needs to be done to keep the two series parallel. The result is the same, except that Malebranche's theory provided for the possibility of a certain kind of freedom for minds which Leibniz's theory did not. Benedictus Spinoza (1632-1677), a predecessor of Leibniz and Malebranche, advocated what has been called a "double-aspect" theory, the details of which we shall not pause to recount. Suffice it to say that none of these proposals has commended itself to more than a few of those who have concerned themselves with the problem, and it seems safe to conclude that anyone who wishes to maintain the dualism that is inherent in the common-sense view must be prepared to maintain interactionism —mutual causation—as well. In the discussion that follows, in any case, we shall ignore all except the interactionist version of the dualistic account.

The Alternatives

If we turn our attention to the first part of the problem, we shall find that the central focus of our concern must be the question, "Are body and mind two distinct sorts of entity, neither of which can be understood as a form or function of the other, or are they not?" And to this question, three and only three answers appear to be possible.

First, it is possible to deny that they are radically distinct and to argue that mind is explicable in terms of body—that mind is, so to speak, a purely physical phenomenon that is governed by, and explicable according to, the same sorts of laws as any other physical phenomenon. Mind, in this view, is not ontologically unique: it is not a "spiritual substance," a non-physical reality, that acts apart from and independent of the laws of nature. It is a part of nature, even a product of nature, and wholly subject to its laws. The collective name for views which attempt to account for the relationship between mind and body in this way is *reductive materialism.*

Second, it is possible to take a position just opposite to that of reductive materialism—to reject the dualism implicit in the common-sense view and to argue that body is explicable in terms of mind rather than the reverse. It would be tempting, for the sake of terminological consistency, to call this view "reductive mentalism," or something of that sort, but common usage dictates otherwise. We shall, accordingly, refer to this view as *pan-psychism.*

Third, it is of course possible to hold that the common-sense view in this matter is the correct one and to maintain the interactionist position, which we have already described. It then is necessary to show that the interactionist position, with whatever problems it may involve, has at least as much to commend it as either of the other two alternatives.

All three positions have one task in common, however, and that is to give some account of the apparent inter-causal relations between mind and body. Whether one adopts the reductive materialist, the pan-psychist, or the interactionist position, the problem with which the philosophers of the sixteenth and seventeenth centuries wrestled so unsuccessfully remains a genuine problem that demands some kind of an answer.

A Word About Metaphysics

We may as well recognize at the very outset of our consideration of this problem that we cannot hope to proceed very far without venturing into the rather forbidding area of metaphysics, for none of the views we shall be considering really stands by itself: each is integral to a particular metaphysical position and can scarcely be made intelligible apart from the more inclusive view. Reductive materialism, for example, is not just one view among many that one may take with respect to the mind-body problem; it is the view of man, and especially of mind, that is implicit in _monistic materialism_—the view that the whole of reality consists of matter and its determinations. Pan-psychism, on the other hand, is the view of man, and especially of body, that is implicit in the more inclusive metaphysical view known as _monistic idealism_—the view that the whole of reality is explicable in terms of mind and its determinations. And interactionism, or at any rate the anthropological dualism which it presupposes, is the view of man that is implicit in _ontological dualism_—the view that matter and mind are ontologically distinct and that reality includes both. It is possible to carry on the discussion for a greater or shorter period of time without explicitly bringing in these wider metaphysical views, but they are always hovering in the background when the problem of mind and body is being discussed.

It has been said that the mind-body problem has given rise to more "isms" than any other problem in the history of philosophy, and this is probably true. The problem is a complex one. The more variables there are, the greater are the possibilities for a unique combination of views—each of which eventually gets christened some kind of an "ism." We have attempted in this introductory chapter to narrow the problem down somewhat in order that in what follows we may concentrate on just three theories—reductive materialism, pan-psychism, and interactionism. Any theory on the nature of body and mind, it would seem, must be reducible to one of these three types, and a comprehension of them will enable an understanding of extensions and related matters with little difficulty.

Study Questions

1. Give some examples of what are here called "mental events" and "physical events." Do you in practice have any difficulty in distinguishing the two? By what criterion do you make the distinction?
2. Summarize what you understand to be the common-sense view regarding body and mind. Is this also your view? What "puzzles," if any, seem implicit in this view?
3. What, exactly, is reductive materialism? pan-psychism? interactionism? Do these three exhaust the logically possible alternatives with respect to the mind-body problem? Explain.
4. Does it seem that anything of importance is at stake in the discussion of this problem? Do you see any possible implications for psychology? for sociology? for ethics? for religion? Be specific.

Chapter 33

REDUCTIVE MATERIALISM

PHILOSOPHERS CALL THE common-sense theory about the nature of body and mind, and of the relations between them, dualistic interactionism; and in view of its wide prevalence, it must be capable of support by fairly persuasive considerations. One could, no doubt, distinguish between the reasons that have led people to adopt the view and the additional reasons that philosophers have invented to support the view once it was called in question. No doubt for some purposes this would be an illuminating distinction. For the present, however, I propose to ignore this distinction. By way of preparing for what I hold to be the correct view on this matter, I wish to state, first, what I believe are generally regarded as the most persuasive reasons in favor of the interactionist account. I shall then offer several reasons for doubting the correctness of this account and shall conclude by attempting to present the case for a materialistic view of mind.

Reasons for Holding the Dualistic View

There are four main reasons why people generally have adopted —or perhaps unconsciously presupposed—the dualistic view.

First, the apparent irreducibility of "mental events" and "physical events" seems to imply that they occur, respectively, in "minds" and "bodies." Thinking, feeling, desiring, wishing, willing, and the like appear to be different in kind from moving, being moved, accelerating, decomposing, and so on. The most plausible explanation of this difference, it is then asserted, is that minds are the subjects of the one set of events and bodies the subjects of the other. Hence, it is concluded, minds and bodies must be regarded as two distinct sorts of entities.

Second, the fact of personal continuity seems to favor the dualistic account. Not one single particle of the matter of which my body is now composed was in my body twenty years ago. Yet, it seems, there is some sense in which I am the same "person" that I was twenty years ago. The only acceptable explanation of this fact, it is held, is that there is something that remains unaltered by these physical changes, namely my "mind" or "soul." So on this ground, too, it appears that "mind" or "soul" must be something different from body.

Third, certain facts alleged to be discoverable by introspection— for example, our awareness of acting "deliberately" or "purposively"—are sometimes said to demonstrate that conscious activity cannot be adequately described simply as physical process. In the act of "weighing alternatives," for example, it seems that I am directly aware of the fact that I am not simply observing a process that is going on, say, in my brain: I am actively doing something, and this something that I am doing, it is held, is irreducibly "mental." The point of this argument is that we are directly aware of the uniquely "mental" character of such activities in the act of performing them; hence, they are not reducible to some other kind of process different from what we allegedly know them to be.

For many people the same conclusion is strongly re-enforced, however, by a fourth and very different sort of consideration. In Western culture a widespread belief in, and hope for, life after death prevails. This evidently presupposes a "soul" capable of existing apart from the body, for it is evident that after the event that we call "death," the body decomposes and is eventually reduced to its basic elements. If, then, we are to give any meaning to the phrase "personal immortality," something must be presupposed in the constitution of man that is not subject to the process of decomposition; and this something is called the "soul," "mind," or "consciousness." The emotional fervor with which the dualistic account is sometimes maintained is largely a result of this consideration.

These, then, are what I take to be the chief grounds upon which the dualistic theory of body and mind has been erected. Some of these reasons are very persuasive since they exhibit the dualistic theory as an explanation of certain undeniable facts—facts that must obviously be accounted for in some way or other by any theory that may be proposed. Nonetheless, a number of other considerations provide strong grounds for doubting the correctness of this account, and I propose now to indicate in some detail what they are.

Reasons for Doubting the Correctness of the Dualistic View

The theory is suspect, in the first place, because it is impossible to form a clear concept of what is meant by "mind," "soul," or "consciousness." We have here a case parallel to that of the now thoroughly discredited idea of a "material substratum," which John Locke defined as "something I know not what that supports qualities." [1] Mind, apparently, is "a something we know not what that thinks, feels, decides, etc." It is the name for our ignorance concerning the true nature of mental events. To infer to minds as the causes of mental events is equivalent to inferring to "wind gods" as the causes of the blowing of the wind: the inference, in both cases, is vacuous.

In addition, whatever it is that is supposed to be meant by "mind" or "soul," there seem to be insuperable difficulties in the way of our knowing that any such entities exist. That some organisms are capable of perception and feeling seems evident: more or less definite criteria can be established to determine when such an event is or is not occurring. But there appear to be no criteria on the basis of which we could say in any given instance, "There is a mind." There is nothing that we can see, feel, taste, touch, or smell —no observational evidence, in other words—that is in any way relevant to confirming or not confirming the statement, "A mind exists." To the purely conceptual difficulty of trying to understand just what it is that is being affirmed to exist when minds are being

---

[1] John Locke, *An Essay Concerning Human Understanding* (New York: Dover Publications, 1959), Book II, Chap. XXIII.

affirmed to exist, we must, therefore, add the epistemological difficulty that there seems to be no conceivable way by which the existence of these elusive entities could ever be known.

Even if it were possible to give conceptual clarity to the notion
of "mind," and even if some evidence could be adduced to render
the existence of minds probable, there remains the further difficulty
that it is quite impossible to conceive how they could be involved in
causal relations with bodies. Let me illustrate. Given a minimal
knowledge of the laws of physiology, I can understand without too
much difficulty how the movement of an arm, say, can be caused
by the contraction of certain muscles, how the contraction of those
muscles can be caused by certain nerve impulses, and how the
nerve impulses can be caused by certain neural events—events occurring, that is, in the brain. All of these, it will be noted, are physical processes that are theoretically observable by anyone who approaches them with the proper instruments and the requisite
knowledge. But how are we to understand these neural events as
being "caused" by an allegedly non-physical event called a "volition"? Is this a sort of causation—an instance of pushing, or pull-
ing, or does it consist in the passage of an electrical current, or
what? No answer that one might give to this question would even
be intelligible; and that is what I mean when I say that it is impossible to conceive how bodies and minds can be involved in causal
relations. The same difficulty arises, of course, whether it is minds
that are alleged to act causally upon bodies (as in volition) or
bodies upon minds (as in sensation).

Moreover, what we know about the structure of the nervous system makes it extremely unlikely that the process of deliberation,
for example, and the purposive behavior that commonly follows
upon it, is different in kind from other processes that are universally admitted to be non-mental. All of the higher animals, for example, exhibit a process known as "reflex action," the detailed
workings of which are quite thoroughly understood; and it seems
very likely that purposive activity is fully explicable as a process
that differs only in complexity from reflex action. It is only because
of the lapse of time between the stimulus and the response that we
regard purposive behavior as something different in kind from a
reflex action; and since this lapse of time is readily explicable in

other ways, the similarity of such allegedly "mental" occurrences to some clearly non-mental occurrences must be regarded as a serious problem by anyone who would maintain the dualistic view.

Finally, there is a very serious objection of a purely scientific nature against the interactionist view. The interactionist account, if true, would violate the principle of the conservation of energy, but we have a great deal of evidence to show that this principle is true, and even experimental evidence in support of the view that it is not violated in the case of human activity. To the extent that we are convinced of the truth of this principle, therefore, we must with equal surety conclude that the interactionist account of mind and body is false.

A few words of explanation may be in order in connection with this last point. The principle of the conservation of energy may be stated thus: in all physical processes, the total amount of energy in the universe remains constant; its form may be altered, but never its quantity. Moreover, every instance of causation known to us involves the transference of energy from the cause to the effect. If, then, it is said that some events in bodies have effects in minds, there must be some transfer of energy from the body to the mind. Since minds are allegedly unperceived, this energy should supposedly "disappear" for a time: the measurable energy in the body should decrease. And if minds cause effects in bodies, the amount of energy in the body should then increase. This does not appear to be the case. Thus either (a) body-mind interaction does not occur or (b) body-mind interaction is an exception to the principle of the conservation of energy.

I think it must be conceded that the objections to which I have called attention constitute very substantial grounds for doubting the correctness of the dualistic theory and thus justify the search for a more adequate alternative. Such an alternative is to be found, in my opinion, in the materialistic view of mind.

A Materialistic Theory of Mind

One difficulty of a purely semantic nature stands in the way of the general acceptance of a materialistic view of mind, and I should like to do what I can to remove it. The difficulty is that the term "materialism" has strong negative connotations for many people which derive in large part from the association of that term with some rather crude theories advocated about a century ago. Let me at the very outset state, then, that I do not propose to account for mind in terms of tiny nuggets of matter that act and react upon one another according to Newton's Laws of Motion: nothing except a few fairly simple macroscopic phenomena can be accounted for in this crude way. Nor is it my intention, in this account of mind, to "dehumanize" man in any way. Man is clearly a noble and fortunate creature, whatever be the correct account of mind and body, and his capacity for intelligent behavior remains his most noble endowment, however we are to understand it.

I am not advocating either (a) that mental phenomena are reducible to physical phenomena in the sense that a feeling of pain is "nothing but" the occurrence of certain neural events or (b) that mental events are simply "epiphenomena" of physical events in the way that a flickering light is cast off by an unsteady flame. Some men who are usually classified as reductive materialists have held one or both of these views, but I do not hold them and do not propose to defend them. I agree with most dualists in holding that mind is exceedingly important in the constitution of man; but I think they are mistaken in their account of its status.

Any account of the nature of mind must begin with the fact that human beings (and, in an analogous sense, some of the higher animals) are capable of intelligent behavior. Restricting our attention exclusively to man, however, it is evident that man does not respond in an obviously mechanical way to his environment in the way that a stone or a plant does. Man is capable of sensation, feeling, memory, imagination, desire, reflective thought, and willing; stones and plants are not. It is facts such as these that have led common sense (not to mention some philosophers) to posit mind as the subject of such activities.

The thesis which I should like to establish is that mind is related adjectivally and adverbially, not substantivally, to body. *Intelligence denotes some of the ways in which human beings behave, not an unperceived non-spatial entity that is somehow "within" man.*

The dualistic account of body and mind has been aptly called "the dogma of the ghost in the machine." [2] Reductive materialism is sometimes thought to consist simply in exorcising the ghost, leaving only the machine. I am arguing, on the contrary, that man is neither a ghost nor a machine: he is a complex psycho-physical organism capable of a peculiarly complex type of behavior which we call "intelligence."

A complete exposition and defense of this view would require an extensive analysis of each of the types of events commonly called "mental" events: thinking, feeling, desiring, willing, and so on. Limitations of space make this impossible, and we must accordingly be selective. Let us select the mental process which we call "thinking." If we can show that thinking is analyzable without having recourse to a substantial theory of mind, we may justly claim to have defended our view in what must be regarded as a crucial test case; for thinking is without doubt the activity *par excellence* of which minds are supposed to be the subjects.

A typical example of what we call "thinking" would be a case in which someone—e. g., a student—is attempting to solve a problem. It makes no difference, for our purposes, what the problem may be. Let us suppose that it is the mathematical problem of finding the square root of 196. What does the student do? If he knows the procedure for finding square roots, he will simply apply that procedure, presumably with the help of pencil and paper. If he does not know that procedure, he will have to tackle the logically prior problem of finding out how to do square roots. If he is a bright student and if he has had a lot of practice solving problems of this sort, he may even be able to dispense with paper and pencil—to do it, as we say, "in his head."

What is it, then, that is going on "in his head" when he is attempting to solve this problem? The answer would seem to be that certain processes are occurring in his brain. He may, as an aid to these processes, put some numbers down on paper, but this is not absolutely essential to the process itself. What is essential to the process is only that the answer he comes up with should in fact be

---

[2] Gilbert Ryle, *The Concept of Mind* (New York· Barnes & Noble, 1949), p. 15 and elsewhere.

the square root of 196—that he should end up by "knowing" what is the square root of 196.

It is not absolutely essential to such a process that the person engaged in it should even be directly aware of what he is doing: mathematicians frequently are able to give the answer to a problem without consciously and deliberately going through the steps by which the answer is deduced. The same conclusion can be drawn from the fact that one sometimes wakes up knowing the answer to a problem which one tried unsuccessfully to solve the night before: the relevant "thinking" occurred, apparently, during sleep.

A number of further considerations may be adduced in support of the view that thinking consists in a process that occurs in one's brain. For one thing, we are able to do it better at some times than at others: when we are fatigued, for example, we do not do it nearly so well as when we are rested. Also, our ability to think can be enhanced or decreased by administering certain drugs. Drugs and fatigue do have certain effects on the body, including the brain; hence, it seems likely that the process itself is a process occurring in the brain.

"But," it may be objected, "surely one's *awareness* that one is thinking is not itself a process going on in one's brain!" Granted. But this awareness, as we have already noted, does not always accompany the process that we call "thinking"—though sometimes, admittedly, it does. To explain this we should have to analyze not "thinking" but "introspection"; and this, too, is a physiological process, as are all of the phenomena that we call "mental events."

Replies to Objections

The most serious objections that could be raised against the materialistic view of mental occurrences are precisely those considerations that led in the first place to the adoption of the dualistic theory.

The apparent irreducibility of "mental events" and "physical events" amounts, in my opinion, to little more than the irreducibility of the *language* of personal experience to the *language* of objective occurrences. We recognize that the sentence, "I am seeing a blue object," is not translatable into a sentence of the form, "Such-and-such processes are occurring in my brain," and we conclude from this that the two sentences are not about the same thing. That we have these two kinds of language to describe mental events is undeniable, but no conclusion about the status of such events follows from this fact.

The notion of personal continuity is something of a puzzle, but that it is not to be accounted for by positing a "soul" or "self" that persists throughout all bodily changes is evident when one considers that institutions, and other complex existences, are also said to exhibit continuity. Consider, for example, a university that has been in existence for two centuries or more. None of the original faculty, students, administration, or regents is now associated with the university. It is very possible that none of the original books is any longer to be found in the library and that no building now on the campus was there in the beginning. Yet, in some sense, it is said to be the "same" university. In what sense? In the sense, surely, that over relatively short spans of time at least some of the elements that constitute the university remain unchanged. Within any given year, for example, some of the elements that constitute the university are changed: some new faculty and students come, a building is razed, a new building is erected, and so on. But during that year other elements remain relatively constant: some of the same old teachers, the same old students, the same old buildings are to be found. The continuity, then, does not consist in the fact that some one element remains throughout, but that the change occurs in the context of a relatively stable structure.

It may well be that continuity in the case of persons ought to be understood in much the same way. My continuity with the self of yesterday consists in the fact that in looks, in habits, in faults, in abilities, in physical structure, etc., I am for the most part identical with that person—but only "for the most part." Changes do occur, however—witness the fact that we are sometimes shocked (and amused) to see pictures of ourselves taken ten or twenty years ago. Must some *one thing* be posited to establish the continuity of the person we now are with the person who was born on such-and-such a date and at such-and-such a place so-and-so many years ago? I think not. It is enough to establish continuity that the changes that do occur should occur within the context of a relatively stable organizational structure.

No conclusion about the status of mind can be drawn, it seems to me, from the fact that we are allegedly directly aware on occasion of acting "deliberately" or "purposively." We are apparently in a position to know our own mental states in a way that others are not (although it is to be noted that fairly precise criteria can be established for judging someone's behavior to be "deliberate" and/or "purposive"), but it can scarcely be argued that this puts us in a position to know that a mental state consists in some determination of a non-physical entity which we call our "mind." It is just as plausible to hold that this awareness is simply one of the by-products of the occurrence of a neural process of such-and-such a kind.

On the question of life after death, it can hardly be said that one's hope for such a thing constitutes a valid reason for holding that the conditions thereof do, in fact, obtain. It is indeed a consequence of the materialistic view of mind that when death occurs, mind perishes no less than body; for, in our view, it is as meaningless to talk of the continuation of mind after the deterioration of the brain as it is to talk of the continuation of running after the deterioration of one's legs. "Mind" is the collective—and misleading—name for those dimensions of human behavior that we call "intelligent"; and when the human organism dies, it ceases to behave at all, and so intelligent behavior also ceases. When running stops, "swiftly" cannot continue by itself; when behavior ceases, "mind" no longer has any meaning.

The old puzzle about how minds and bodies could "interact," or how the appearance of interaction was to be accounted for, is evidently a consequence of the mistake of separating body and mind in the first place and regarding the latter as a substantial entity that has then to be re-related to body in some odd way. What God has joined together, once separated, is very difficult to get together again! Mind is minding; it is adjectivally, adverbially, related to the body and its behavior. But body is explicable in terms of the laws governing matter, particularly matter as organized in complex living organisms; hence mind, too, is explicable in terms of those self-same laws.

Study Questions

1. What are suggested in this chapter as the main reasons why people generally have tended to favor the interactionist view of body and mind? Can you think of any additional reasons for this? How would you rank these reasons, from "strongest" to "weakest"?

2. Summarize Materialist's reasons for doubting the correctness of the dualistic view. Which list of reasons—this list or the one written in answer to the previous question—strikes you as being the most convincing?

3. What, exactly, is the view of mind which Materialist is proposing? What arguments does he use to support this view?

4. What are Materialist's answers to what he regards as the chief arguments in favor of the interactionist view? Which do you personally find more convincing—the arguments in support of the interactionist view or Materialist's replies to them?

Chapter 34

PAN-PSYCHISM

IF ONE IS to arrive at some acceptable view with respect to the relation of mind and body, it is important to distinguish carefully between (a) the considerations that might lead one to reject the dualistic-interactionist account and (b) the considerations that are sometimes offered in support of a materialistic theory of mind. It is often assumed that if the dualistic theory can be shown to be inadequate, then we shall be able to see without difficulty that the materialistic account of mind is correct; and this, I am convinced, is erroneous. There is at least one other alternative, and that is that body—or "matter"—is to be understood mentalistically. I believe that this is the correct view.

I should like to begin by re-enforcing an observation made incidentally in the introductory chapter. Although the problem of the relation between body and mind appears to be a straightforward problem about how we are to understand *man,* at root it is a metaphysical problem. It is not plausible to argue that mind is simply a particular determination of matter: no one, I think, who confined his attention to the known facts about the relevant physical and psychological phenomena would even be tempted to subscribe to such an account. The reason that some philosophers, nonetheless, attempt to account for mind in this way is that they approach the problem with a prior conviction that all phenomena are ultimately explicable in terms of matter and its laws: they approach it, in other words, with a prior commitment to the metaphysics of monistic materialism. The existence of mental phenomena, therefore, constitutes an embarrassing problem for them, and they are accordingly compelled to try to "reduce" mind to matter on pain of having their metaphysical theory discredited. This is true whether the metaphysics that inspires the attempt is overt, as in the case of the nineteenth-century materialists, or covert, as it is with some philosophers at the present time.

The materialistic account of mind is not at all convincing, and for this reason I am almost inclined to simply ignore it and proceed directly to an exposition of what I am convinced is a far more plausible alternative. However, many people today find monistic materialism very attractive. Consequently, I dare not assume that everyone who has read Materialist's account will have found it as unconvincing as I did. I shall, therefore, point out some of the most serious inadequacies of this account; and since this account is the one that anyone who wishes to maintain the metaphysics of monistic materialism must give, my critique of the materialistic theory of mind may also be construed as a *reductio ad absurdum* of that metaphysical theory.

Critique of the Materialistic Theory of Mind

The materialistic theory of mind is inadequate in at least four respects.

First, this theory does not provide a believable account of what is happening when we are thinking, feeling, perceiving, remembering, desiring, willing, and the like. Let us consider "thinking," since this is the example that Materialist has briefly discussed. It seems evident that (a) whether or not a neural process of some unique sort is occurring whenever a person is thinking of some particular thing, this certainly has never been shown to be the case, and (b) even if it should be the case that thinking of a determinate sort is always accompanied by some corresponding neural process, it does not follow that thinking simply consists in this neural process. The question of what neural processes are correlated with what mental states is, surely, an empirical question, and it can scarcely be claimed that the investigation of this matter has proceeded to the

point where one can with any assurance claim a one-to-one correspondence between the two. But even if this were to be established,
it is extremely implausible to hold that thinking is the *same thing* as
the neural process that accompanies it. A well-designed and properly programmed computer, for example, is capable of solving certain sorts of problems far more quickly and efficiently than even
the brightest of mathematicians; yet, we should not (except in metaphor) describe the process by which it does so as one of "thinking." What is the difference? The difference is that to say that
something is an instance of "thinking" is to posit a mind, a consciousness, as the subject of the thinking; nothing other than metaphysical prejudice could ever induce one to give a different answer.

Materialist has, in a way, attempted to answer this objection.
"The apparent irreducibility of 'mental events' and 'physical
events' amounts," he says, "to little more than the irreducibility of
the language of personal experience to the language of objective
occurrences." But this way out of the difficulty is not open to the
materialist; for if the materialistic account of mind is correct, then
a sentence like "I am seeing a blue object" *ought to be* logically
equivalent to the sentence, "Such-and-such processes are occurring
in my brain." The statement, "Rutabagas do not taste good," for
example, is translatable into the statement, "So-and-so does not
like rutabagas" since these statements are *about* the same thing—
the likes and dislikes of some particular person or persons. Alternative languages that are descriptive of the same state of affairs are
always translatable into one another. If, then, it is conceded that in
the present case the two languages are not mutually translatable,
the conclusion is inescapable that the two languages are not descriptive of the same state of affairs: mental states are not *equivalent to* neural processes.

The only way that Materialist could get around this difficulty
would be to recant his rejection of epiphenomenalism. Consciousness, he would then have to say, is not exactly identical with neural
processes, but it is an accidental and inconsequential by-product of
those processes—like "a flickering light (that) is cast off by an
unsteady flame." So to argue is to burden oneself with a host of
absurdities that few materialists are willing to accept—for exam-

ple, that conscious intention has absolutely nothing to do with the production of poetry, novels, philosophical treatises, or scientific hypotheses.

Materialist's account of personal continuity is also quite obviously inconsistent with what we know about this phenomenon in the one case that each of us knows best, i. e., *our own* continuity. My knowledge that I stand in a relation of continuity with a certain person born on such-and-such a date and at such-and-such a place rests, surely, on the fact that I have recollections of experiences that are related to one another in such a way that I cannot but regard them as members of a single series. I know that I am the "same person" who last evening watched a baseball game, and last year took a trip to Chicago, and some years ago attended a certain university, and before that lived in a certain city because I *remember* having the experiences that constitute these several events. It may well be that the "stuff" of which my body is now composed has been completely changed during this long span of time; but certain patterns, a certain more or less constant organization of this "stuff" and certain serially related memories have endured. It is to these that I have reference when I say that throughout this time I have been the "same person."

It seems grossly misleading, therefore, to explain personal continuity on the analogy of the continuity of a non-organic complex like a university; the analogy, if there is one, must surely be applied in the other direction. An institution has, admittedly, a kind of fictional unity that bears some analogy to the unity of a person (as does also a nation, a club, a political party, etc.), and the recorded history of an institution might be compared in some ways to the remembered experience of a human being. We can even "personify" a university and sing "her" praises in song and verse, but we know well enough that the "person" we thus posit does not really exist except in a metaphorical sense. It is not nearly so evident that Materialist is aware of the fact that he is using a metaphor, and a misleading one at that, when he attempts to "thingify" our experience of personal continuity.

One final objection. The materialistic theory of mind implies that men never act in terms of conscious purposes freely chosen by them, but only in the ways resultant from the mechanical causes operative upon them; but in our own experience, at least, we know that this is not true. Despite Materialist's disavowal of the older mechanism his view involves, in short, a mechanistic view of human behavior; and mechanism, old or new, is a bitter pill to swallow. We surely believe ourselves to act freely and purposively a good share of the time—indeed, I should say that we know ourselves to do so. Unless we are to regard this knowledge as no knowledge—as illusory, in other words—we must reject the materialistic account of mind; and if we do adopt that account, we must not hesitate to accept its mechanistic consequences.

Another Alternative

The position at which we have now arrived in our consideration of the problem of mind and body is the following: we have agreed with Materialist that the dualistic account of body and mind—the view that body and mind are two distinct kinds of entities that are involved in mutual causal relations—is untenable; and we have rejected the materialistic alternative of attempting to account for mind as a peculiar determination, or set of determinations, of matter. There appears, then, to be only one possibility remaining, and that is to regard *mind* as fundamental and body as explicable in terms of mind. What kind of a case can be made for this alternative? Since we have acknowledged that any way of resolving this problem presupposes some metaphysical theory, let us begin by noting some of the more important features of such theories.

Metaphysics consists in the attempt to elaborate a system of concepts in terms of which every phenomenon that we encounter is capable of being interpreted and understood. The requirements that a metaphysical system must meet are (a) that some phenomena shall be explicable in terms of it, (b) that no phenomena shall be inexplicable in terms of it, (c) that it shall be internally consistent, and (d) that it shall not be productive of implications that are absurd or contrary to fact. The method by which such systems are elaborated consists in (a) generalizing some concepts that are known to have application in some limited sphere and (b) attempting to apply the concepts thus developed to all phenomena—attempting, in other words, to give them a universal application.

Monistic materialism, for example, is a metaphysical system, the central concepts of which were originally adapted from the science of mechanics; our criticism of it is based on the fact that it does not provide a plausible explanation of mental, or psychological, phenomena.

Suppose, then, that we relinquish the idea that everything that occurs is explicable in terms of tiny units of lifeless matter that act and react upon one another according to certain laws. Suppose that we say instead that the ultimate constituents of which the universe is composed are to be conceived on the analogy of *mind* and see if in this way we cannot give a better account of things. Everything, then, is to be conceived as being composed of a greater or lesser number of "droplets of experience," or "atoms of consciousness," each of which is in some degree aware of the environment that constitutes its world, and each of which accordingly takes account of its environment in a way that is appropriate to its particular level of awareness. Let us, following Whitehead (1861-1947), call such a center of experience an "actual occasion." [1]

Since the idea of an actual occasion is derived from our direct awareness of our own selfhood, it is natural that we should develop the idea in terms of other concepts derived therefrom as well. We know, for example, that our own life is describable as a career in which we are constantly obliged to choose among alternative possibilities. Our past, and the constitution of the rest of the world, severely limit the possibilities open to us, but there are for each of us some possibilities—a variety of alternatives that we might choose—and we must choose among them. Let us say, then, that the life of every actual occasion is a career in which it must choose, among the possibilities available to it, what it is to become, and that its possibilities, like ours, are determined by (a) its past, (b) the constitution of the rest of the world that it has to take into account, and (c) its own level of awareness. Every actual occasion, then, will experience something—something appropriate to its own level of awareness—analogous to what in man is called perception, feeling, remembering, willing, and so on.

What is a "material object" according to this account—for ex-

---

1 See Alfred North Whitehead, *Process and Reality* (New York: Harper & Brothers, 1960), p. 113.

ample, a stone? Let us call it a "society of actual occasions"—an aggregate of actual occasions united together in a quasi-unity analogous to that of a society of persons. No doubt the level of awareness of the actual occasions that compose a stone is of a very low order—lower, for example, than that of the lowest organism—and the alternatives open to them are so severely limited that so far as we can see they do little more than perpetuate themselves virtually unchanged from moment to moment. So unvarying are their "choices," in fact, that we can observe statistical uniformities in the behavior of the society—can formulate, in other words, certain "laws" descriptive of the behavior of the aggregate. We can do the same thing, it is to be noted, with respect to a colony of ants or bees.

Our way of "taking account of" such aggregates is by way of what we call "perception"—in the case of our perceiving a stone, by means of sight and touch. Its way of taking account of us is to resist our efforts to penetrate it, to allow itself to be moved on occasion, and so on.

The level of awareness of actual occasions appears to vary greatly, and the options available to an actual occasion seem to widen as the level increases. In inorganic substances, the level appears to be at its lowest: we cannot even begin to imagine what it would be like to be a grain of sand or a particle of calcium. With the simplest organisms, we reach a higher level: the very simplest plants are able to exercise a degree of freedom that is unknown to any particle of inorganic matter. The level increases when we come to insects, still more when we come to the higher animals, and reaches its highest realization in men. So high is it in the case of the higher animals—dogs, horses, monkeys and the like—that we can almost imagine what it would be like to be such a creature; in any case, we cannot seriously doubt that they have a consciousness that is in many ways similar to our own.

How, then, ought we to conceive of man? As a society of actual occasions of varying levels of awareness. Some one of these dominates and gives unity to the society, and this we call our "mind" or "soul." In the experience that we call perception—feeling a pain, for example—the pain is experienced by the finger, say, as a pressure or a piercing, by the nerves as an electrical current, by the brain as certain brain waves that occur in it, and by the mind as the feeling of pain. The experience that we call willing is experienced by mind as deliberation and decision, by brain as a directive to enact such-and-such an alternative, by the nerves as electrical impulses of a certain kind, and by the appropriate muscles as a directive to contract in such-and-such a way. The society, when it is healthy, is a cooperative society, each member doing its part to ensure the welfare of the whole under the guidance of its dominant member. When a hostile "foreigner" enters (as in infection), or when some members of the society become uncooperative (as in cancer), the whole society suffers; and if it cannot repel the invaders, or get rid of the uncooperative members, the whole society may be destroyed.

Limitations of space have permitted only the very briefest sketch of the metaphysical scheme in terms of which, as I believe, the relation of body and mind can be correctly understood. Much more should be said by way of filling in the details, and countless additional examples of its explanatory power would have to be provided before I could hope to persuade even a few of my readers that what I am proposing is at least in the direction of the truth. Since space does not permit this, I must be content to let the plausibility of my proposal rest for the present on its ability to solve the familiar puzzles in connection with the problem of the relation between body and mind in man. These puzzles may be summarized as follows: (a) the alleged impossibility of forming a clear concept of "mind," (b) the alleged difficulty of knowing that any such entities exist, (c) the difficulty of trying to understand how unthinking bodies and unextended minds can interact, (d) the problem of how we are to conceive of personal continuity in the case of conscious organisms, and (e) the problem of how certain "mental events" are related to the so-called "physical events" with which they are associated.

My answer, in brief, to each of these puzzles follows. (a) There is no difficulty whatsoever in forming a perfectly clear concept of "mind" unless one demands that the concept be formed in spatial terms. The question, "What kind of a body is a mind?" is not a proper question, and it deserves no answer. I cannot form an "image" of a mind because a mind is not the sort of thing that occupies space, and only things that occupy space can be "imaged." But I know as clearly as I know anything what a mind is: a conscious center of feelings, perceptions, thoughts, and volitions. (b) There is also no difficulty in knowing that minds exist. In the very act of thinking, feeling, doubting, etc., I know that *I* exist, and in the intelligent behavior of other organisms, and especially in the intelligible communication which I have with other minds, I know that other minds also exist. (c) There are no unthinking bodies, and hence there is no "gap" between body and mind that has to be bridged by some half-mind—half-body "connecting link." There are only minds of varying levels of awareness; and every mind is able to take account of those that constitute its world in ways appropriate to its level of awareness. (Minds at a relatively low level of awareness, for example, take account of one another by means of what we call "mechanical causation.") (d) Personal continuity in the case of any organism—whether or not it is "conscious" in the strict, unextended, sense of that word—consists in the persistence of its structural unity and its unique relation to its past history, which past history it must "take into account" in choosing the next stage in its career. Something analogous to memory, therefore, must characterize the experience of every actual occasion. (e) There are no such things as purely physical events properly so-called. Everything that occurs is an event in the career of some actual occasion; it is only when we abstract from this and view it, so to speak, "from the outside" that we get the derivative notion of a "physical event." A given event may be perceived by a neural surgeon, for example (via certain instruments which he employs) as the occurrence of certain neural processes; the same event is perceived by the actual occasion (mind) that is dominant in the society of which that brain is a part as a feeling of pain. It all depends on the way that one takes account of the experiences of other actual occasions; and that way depends in large part on the particular ways in which one happens to be related to them.

Study Questions

1. What inadequacies does Pan-psychist claim to find in the materialistic theory of mind? Do these seem to be serious objections to the materialistic theory? How might Materialist attempt to answer them?

2. What, precisely, is pan-psychism? How well, in your opinion, does it measure up to the "requirements that a metaphysical system must meet" as itemized by Pan-psychist?
3. What theory of man does Pan-psychist propose? How is this theory supposed to provide a solution to the mind-body problem?
4. What, at this point, seem to be the strongest arguments in favor of the pan-psychist theory of body and mind? What seem to be the strongest arguments against it?
5. Write a critique of pan-psychism from the point of view of a reductive materialist, answering the objections raised by Pan-psychist against the materialist theory and raising appropriate objections to the pan-psychist theory.

Chapter 35

DUALISM RECONSIDERED

THIS IS HARDLY the place to launch a detailed critique of the metaphysical scheme that has been briefly intimated in the preceding chapter; that would obviously be premature until more of the details of the scheme have been provided, and it would hardly be germane to the immediate task at hand. However, I want to mention one small problem with the theory that is frequently glossed over by those who advocate it. The problem is: if, as the theory allows, minds do not occupy space, how does it come about that bodies, which are held to be aggregates of minds, do? Is this not very much like the shopkeeper who claims to lose money on every sale but "makes it up on the volume"? If a single actual occasion occupies no space, then a society of actual occasions—however many members it may have—must also occupy no space. But I do not wish to press this particular point. Let us consider instead the more limited question whether the panpsychist account really does succeed, as it claims to do, in solving the many puzzles that are inherent in the problem of the relation between body and mind.

On at least two points I am in very close agreement with Panpsychist. First, I think he is quite right in saying that there is no special difficulty in forming a clear concept of "mind" and that those who have felt some difficulty at this point have been looking not for a *concept* but for an *image*. No non-spatial entity can be "imaged" since "image-ing" is modeled after visual perception and

323

visual perception is always spatially determined. Any attempt to form an "image" of mind or soul—such as Plato's famous picture (in the dialogue *Phaedrus*) of the two horses and the charioteer— is clearly metaphorical in character, and it is, at best, a pale reflection of the reality itself. I find nothing obscure, however, in the concept of mind as a conscious center of feeling, perception, thought, and volition.

Second, I agree with Pan-psychist that there is no special difficulty in the way of knowing that minds exist. Descartes was essentially right, I think, in saying that our own existence as a thinking being (*res cogitans*) is the most indubitable fact that it is possible for us to know; for even if we should doubt that anything else exists, we must exist in order to do the doubting. As for the existence of other minds, no doubt we do have to do a bit of analogical reasoning: we have to infer from the outward behavior of the other person that he or she is in a mental state such as we know ourselves to be in when we behave in that way (tears when we are sad, grimaces when we are in pain, laughter when we are happy, etc.). But our inferences in such cases are as warranted, surely, as any inference can be.

I am not at all persuaded, however, by Pan-psychist's suggestion that the problem of how minds and bodies can interact, or appear to interact, is to be solved by simply disallowing that there is any such thing as body. I can understand two processes well enough— well enough, in any case, so that I do not normally feel puzzled about them. These are (a) communication between minds by means of intelligible discourse and (b) communication between bodies by means of mechanical causation. Whatever it is that goes on between minds and bodies—in perception and in volition—does not seem to be reducible to either of these. Pan-psychist, who suggests that it is to be understood as an instance of communication of the former type, therefore, seems to be talking nonsense just as surely as Materialist, who proposes to reduce it to the latter type. We must look further for our explanation of body-mind inter-causality.

Is it, indeed, even meaningful to say that the ultimate constituents of which a stone, for example, is composed are "minds with a very low level of awareness"? It makes sense, I think, to talk about animals and insects as having something like a human consciousness because something like the behavior that we know to be associated with consciousness in man is to be observed in the behavior of animals. We have, in this case, three points of reference in relation to which we can fill in the fourth: human consciousness is to certain kinds of human behavior as X is to somewhat similar animal behavior. But in the case of stones—and in the case of individual parts of the human body—we lack the "similar behavior" that would permit us to work the sum. What, then, does it mean to posit "low-level consciousness" in such things? We must conclude that it means nothing at all.

With respect to the question concerning the nature of personal continuity, I am not sure that I understand what Pan-psychist is suggesting; consequently, I am not sure whether I agree or disagree with his view. It seems clear to me, in any case, that our awareness of our own personal continuity is tied up with our awareness of having a mind that is one and the same mind from the beginning to the end of our life. In the strict sense of the word, therefore, I do not think that we should attribute personal continuity to any beings except persons—beings who have minds like ours. In an analogous sense, however, we can attribute some kind of continuity to animals on the ground that they possess a consciousness somewhat similar to our own, and we can attribute organic continuity to any organism so long as it maintains its organic structure and unity. Aggregates of inorganic matter—stones, for example—have continuity only in the sense that they have a relatively stable structure, but this is very loose: a piece of a stone is itself a stone and has as much structure as the larger one from which it came.

Finally, it appears wholly gratuitous to say, as Pan-psychist does, that there are no such things as physical events "properly so-called." In one sense of this statement, it is obviously false: there *are* lightning flashes and thunder-claps and planetary motions and things of that sort, and these are surely more properly described as "physical events" than as anything else one might be inclined to call them. But this, obviously, is not what Pan-psychist means to deny. He means to deny, rather, that we should think of such events as the consequences of the actions and reactions of bits of lifeless, unconscious matter operating according to certain invariable laws. What is really the case, he wants to say, is that everything that exists—including electrons, protons, etc.,—is composed of tiny "droplets of consciousness" and that everything that occurs—including what we call "physical events"—is, properly understood, an experience in the career of some such droplet or droplets. It is this whole account which seems to me, for reasons already given, to be altogether gratuitous, fantastic, and meaningless; it is, as someone has said, so incredible that no one but a very learned man could ever have thought of it.

Therefore, the attempt to reduce body to mind must be regarded as a failure, just as the attempt to reduce mind to body has been shown to be a failure. There appears to be no viable alternative to the dualistic view of body and mind which has seemed to so many to involve insuperable difficulties. In view of this, we should look once again at these alleged difficulties to see if they cannot be removed in a way that does not do violence to our sense of what is credible. The *prima facie* evidence certainly must be conceded to be on the side of dualism: it is only the difficulties that are supposed to attend this view that have led to the fruitless search for a monistic alternative. Let us then see whether on this matter common sense cannot, for once, be vindicated.

The Alleged Difficulties of the Dualistic View

The difficulties alleged to be inherent in the dualistic view of body and mind have been nicely summarized by Materialist as follows: (a) the conceptual difficulty of trying to understand what the term "mind" is supposed to denote; (b) the epistemological difficulty that there seems to be no way by which we could know anything about such entities, if there were any; (c) the alleged impossibility of conceiving how bodies and minds could interact; (d) the alleged impossibility of distinguishing between purposive behavior and "reflex action" behavior in view of the fact that the same nervous system is apparently involved in both; and (e) the suggestion that interaction, if it occurred, would violate the principle of the conservation of energy. We shall consider each of these difficulties in turn.

To what I have already said regarding the first two points I should like to add that it is only materialistic dogmatism that creates the first-mentioned difficulty and only empiricist dogmatism that creates the second. On the first point, enough has already been said; anyone who is able to distinguish between a concept and an image should have no difficulty forming a precise concept of mind. On the second point, one can only say, *"Of course* we cannot see, feel, taste, touch or smell minds: they are not the sort of thing that can be perceived in that way." But we have already discussed this point sufficiently in our earlier remarks.

Let us leave the interactionist puzzle for a moment and consider the two quasi-scientific arguments.

With respect to what I shall call the "nervous system argument," it is to be observed that there must be *some* difference between deliberate actions and reflex actions that leads us to make the distinction in the first place. It is not necessary to go into the laboratory in order to discover, at least at one level of analysis, what this difference is: we can readily observe it firsthand in our own behavior. What is it, then, that leads us to call some instances of behavior—blinking, sneezing, "flinching," etc.—reflex actions? The answer, surely, is that these actions occur without deliberation or decision on our part: there is a stimulus (a thrown object, a tickle in the nose, a loud noise), and the response follows immediately—"automatically," as we say. We do not have to decide to do something in such cases: we just do it. Reflex actions are, as it were, natural habits of the human organism. With deliberate actions, the situation is different. In such cases we must decide both what we shall do and when we shall do it; and the process of deliberation may be as brief or as protracted as we choose to make it.

It is not at all plausible to argue that the difference between these two kinds of behavior is due only to the relatively greater complexity of the neural processes involved in behavior of the latter kind. Even if it should be the case that the neural processes involved in deliberate action are more complex than those involved in reflex action (whatever "complexity" means in this context), it does not follow that this is the only difference. Of course, the same nervous system must be employed in the two cases: it is the only nervous system we have. But what our own experience tells us is that there is, nonetheless, a qualitative difference between the two, and the

most plausible explanation of this difference (most plausible because it accords with our actual experience) is that in the one case
mind is active and in the other case it is not; in the one case mind is
agent and in the other it is only a spectator. The "nervous system
argument," therefore, has no force whatsoever as an objection to
the dualistic view.

Nor, I think, is the "conservation of energy" argument any more
convincing. There are, actually, two different forms of this argument. It is sometimes argued (a) that the dualistic theory implies
that in man the principle of the conservation of energy is violated,
but we know that this principle is universally valid, therefore the
dualistic theory is false. At other times it is argued (b) that the
dualistic theory implies that in man the principle of the conservation of energy is violated, but we have experimental evidence to
show that this is not the case; hence, the dualistic theory must be
false. The argument, in either form, is usually put forward with a
great show of scientific learning, leaving the impression that either
the dualist or the late Albert Einstein must be mistaken—and there
is little doubt, in such a contest, who will be the winner.

Whether or not the principle of the conservation of energy is
universally valid is a question for physicists to decide, and neither
Materialist nor I have any basis for an opinion. Be that as it may,
however, the argument cannot succeed unless it can also be shown
that the interaction of body and mind, if it were to occur, must
involve the transference of energy from one to the other. This has
never been demonstrated: it has only been presupposed. It may
well be that every instance of purely physical causation involves
such a transference of energy; this, again, is a question for the
physicist, not the philosopher, to decide. But it is surely begging the
very question at issue to simply presuppose that body-mind interaction, if it occurs, must be an instance of physical causation and
must therefore conform to the laws governing such events.

Both the "nervous system argument" and the "conservation of
energy" argument are thinly veiled attempts to bring not scientific
facts but scientific *prestige* to bear against the interactionist view.
Neither argument arises because of any puzzles inherent in the dualistic view: they are arguments invented for the purpose of dis-

crediting the dualistic view after that view has already been rejected on other grounds. Those grounds, as I think Pan-psychist has amply shown, are at root metaphysical ones: the dualistic view of body and mind is distinctly uncongenial to the metaphysics of materialism. The arguments must, of course, be considered on their own merits, but it helps one to understand why such patently weak arguments should have been proposed if one is aware of the motivations behind them.

We are left, then, with only one difficulty in the way of adopting the dualistic view of body and mind, and that is the difficulty of understanding how bodies and minds can interact. What is it about this phenomenon that strikes us as being so odd?

Why Interaction Is Puzzling

Perhaps the reason why mind-body interaction appears so puzzling is that minds and bodies seem to be so dissimilar to one another: how, we want to ask, can a non-spatial and non-physical entity like a *mind* be involved in mutual causal relations with an unthinking physical entity like a *body?* But this does not really locate with precision the source of our bewilderment, for there are innumerable examples of causation between dissimilar entities where we feel no such puzzle to exist. We believe without difficulty that there is a causal relation between a mosquito bite and malaria, between the throwing of a switch and the blowing of a siren, between the pressure on the accelerator and the increasing speed of an automobile; yet the two terms in each of these examples are highly dissimilar. We must look further for the source of our bewilderment.

Perhaps, then, the reason why we are mystified about apparent instances of mind-body interaction in a way that we are not mystified by instances of intra-physical causality is that in cases of the latter kind we conceive of the cause and the effect (however dissimilar they may be) as being parts of a *single system,* governed by the *same laws.* We assume that there is some coherent set of laws— chemical, physical, biological, etc.—in terms of which the several series of events from the mosquito bite to the malaria, the throwing of the switch to the blowing of the siren, and the pressing of the accelerator to the increase in velocity of the automobile, are all explicable. If we are mystified at this level, it is because we are puzzled as to which laws are relevant to the phenomenon in question. (Compare: How do mosquitoes cause malaria? and, How do burns cause feelings of pain?) But in the case of mind-body interaction it seems that we have to deal with, so to speak, two "systems," and the laws governing the interaction of body and mind do not seem to be assimilable to either.

Let me illustrate. We can explain a burn—up to a point. We can, with the help of the relevant physical laws, relate the occurrence of the flame to the increase of temperature on the surface of a finger, this increase in temperature to the occurrence of tiny electrical impulses in certain nerves, and the occurrence of these impulses to the occurrence of a certain pattern of brain waves. But then we reach a "gap" in our explanation: we have no laws—none, that is, that are coherent with, a part of, the system of laws we have been using thus far—that will enable us to relate the occurrence of the brain waves to the feeling of pain in the consciousness of the injured person.

Once we posit the feeling of pain in that consciousness, however, we have no difficulty understanding subsequent mental events related thereto: the injured man "deliberates" between going to the doctor and treating himself; he "remembers" that his wife warned him to be careful about lighting camp stoves; he "decides" to attempt treating the burn himself; and so on. Once we get to *mind*, we can "lock in" on the other system, and everything is all right. But then there is volition, and the ensuing behavior (brain waves, nerves, muscles, etc.), and once again we encounter the "gap."

Our puzzlement about the interaction of body and mind is, therefore, an expression of our desire to reduce all phenomena to some single unitary system, with one set of laws applicable to all events. But this desire, it appears, cannot be fulfilled in the present case. The only possible way of fulfilling it would be to explain mental phenomena in terms of physical laws (reductive materialism), or physical phenomena in terms of mental laws (pan-psychism), and neither of these is adequate to the facts. We are left, therefore, with an ultimate and irreducible dualism—a dualism that may leave us puzzled and dissatisfied but must, nonetheless, be accepted.

Although we cannot understand mind-body interaction either in terms of the laws governing physical phenomena or in terms of the laws governing mental phenomena—cannot construe it, that is, either as a physical phenomenon or as a mental phenomenon—we have the best possible evidence that interaction does occur, namely, our own experience. Physical events do cause mental events: we know this from countless instances of what we call perception. Mental events do cause physical events: we know this from countless instances of willed, or deliberate, behavior. These are the facts, and they cannot be denied, however puzzled we may be about the *modus operandi* of that unique mode of causality that occurs in the mutual relations of body and mind.

To realize why we are puzzled about mind-body interaction, however, is in some degree to rid ourselves of the puzzle. We then understand why this particular sort of causality seems so odd, and we are free to look at it without being tempted to deny the obvious in order to assimilate it to some other mode of explanation; we are no longer, so to speak, "bothered" by its oddness. It is only in this sense that an informed dualism constitutes a "solution" to the mind-body problem. The odyssey that begins with common sense, and seeks a solution to its puzzles in monism of either the materialistic or the mentalistic type, reaches its culmination in a view which might be best described as common sense made sure of itself. To accept such a view is to accept the puzzle of how minds and bodies interact in preference to the even more bewildering puzzles that result if one attempts to deny the reality of either.

Study Questions

1. On what points does Dualist agree with Pan-psychist? What objections does he raise against Pan-psychist's position? Could Materialist, without abandoning his own position, join Dualist in urging these same objections?

2. Write a defense of pan-psychism against the objections raised by Dualist. Which of Dualist's arguments do you find most difficult to refute?

3. What is the "nervous system argument" against dualism, and how does Dualist attempt to answer it? Who do you think has the stronger case on this particular point?

4. What is the "conservation of energy argument" against dualism? What is Dualist's answer to this argument?

5. What is it, according to Dualist, that makes apparent mind-body interaction so puzzling? Do you think he is right about this? Are you satisfied with his final answer to the puzzle?

FOR FURTHER READING

Aune, Bruce, "Feelings, Moods, and Introspection," *Mind,* Vol. LXXII (1963), 187-207.

———, "The Problem of Other Minds," *The Philosophical Review,* Vol. 70 (1961), 320-339.

Broad, C. D., *The Mind and its Place in Nature.* Paterson, N.J.: Littlefield, Adams & Co., 1960 (paperbound). Chapters III and XIV.

Dewey, John, *Experience and Nature.* LaSalle, Ill.: Open Court Pub. Co., 1958 (paperbound).

Ducasse, C. J., *Nature, Mind and Death.* LaSalle, Ill.: Open Court, 1951.

Ewing, A. C., *The Fundamental Questions of Philosophy.* New York: The Macmillan Company, 1951. Chapter 6.

Feigl, Herbert, "The Mind-Body Problem in the Development of Logical Empiricism," in *Readings in the Philosophy of Science,* ed. H. Feigl and M. Brodbeck. New York: Appleton-Century-Crofts, 1953. Pages 612-626.

Hume, David, *A Treatise of Human Nature.* Many editions. Book I, Section VI.

Joske, W. D., "Behaviorism as a Scientific Theory," *Philosophy and Phenomenological Research,* Vol. XXII (1961), 61-68.

Krikorian, Y., "A Naturalistic View of Mind," in *Naturalism and the Human Spirit,* ed. Y. Krikorian. New York: Columbia University Press, 1944. Pages 242-269.

———, "The Publicity of Mind," *Philosophy and Phenomenological Research,* Vol. XXII (1962), 317-325.

Lachs, John, "Epiphenomenalism and the Notion of Cause," *The Journal of Philosophy,* Vol. 60 (1963), 141-146.

Laird, John, *Our Minds and their Bodies.* London: Oxford University Press, 1925.

Laslett, Peter, ed., *The Physical Basis of Mind.* Oxford: Basil Blackwell, 1951.

Malcolm, Norman, "Knowledge of Other Minds," *The Journal of Philosophy,* Vol. 55 (1958), 969-978.

Russell, Bertrand, *The Analysis of Mind.* New York: Humanities Press, 1958.

Ryle, Gilbert, *The Concept of Mind.* New York: Barnes & Noble, 1965 (paperbound).

Shaffer, Jerome, "Could Mental States be Brain Processes?" *The Journal of Philosophy,* Vol. 58 (1961), 813-822.

Skinner, B. F., *Science and Human Behavior.* New York: The Macmillan Company, 1953. "The Self," pages 283-294.

Strawson, P. F., *Individuals*. New York: Doubleday, 1959. Pages 87-116.

Wisdom, John, *Other Minds*. New York: Philosophical Library, 1952.

————, *Philosophy and Psychoanalysis*. New York: Philosophical Library, 1953.

————, *Problems of Mind and Matter*. New York: Cambridge University Press, 1963 (paperbound).

Freedom and Determinism

Chapter 36

THE PROBLEM
AND THE ALTERNATIVES

WE TURN NOW to one of the most frequently discussed—and most vexing—problems in philosophy: the problem of determinism and free will. It is a problem in which almost every one is interested—the scientist, the theologian, and the ethicist as well as the philosopher and the man in the street. It is more than likely that anyone who is reading these words has encountered the problem in some form or other many times before. Let us simply try, then, to put our thoughts in order, beginning with an attempt to understand exactly what the problem is.

The Problem

Like many philosophical problems, the free-will problem arises because of an apparent conflict between beliefs based on two different groups of facts.

On the one hand, certain facts of moral experience convince most of us that we are *morally responsible*. For example, we praise and blame one another on the basis of observed behavior. Moreover, we accept praise and blame from others (and occasionally from ourselves) for our own acts. We say things like, "I ought not to have done that," "What he did was shameful," and so on. One could summarize this by saying that we believe ourselves to be morally responsible, and we treat others as if they were morally responsible. And it seems very natural to say that if we are morally responsible, then we must be free: moral responsibility seems to presuppose moral freedom. This is one side of the picture.

But there are other facts which seem to support the view called *universal determinism,* i. e., the theory that every event in the universe is a theoretically predictable consequence of antecedent causes. It seems self-evident to many people, for example, that "Every event has a cause." Every scientific inquiry presupposes that the phenomena under investigation are governed by some laws and that these laws are capable of being discovered and stated with mathematical precision. We all act, as a matter of fact, as if the universe is orderly: we expect pure water always to freeze at 32°F. at sea-level barometric pressure; we expect the laws of aerodynamics to remain constant when we take a plane trip; and so on. Moreover, an immense and steadily growing quantity of scientific evidence bears out the hypothesis that this is an orderly universe, that every event has a cause, that everything that occurs is a theoretically predictable consequence of antecedent causes. Thus, we are also readily persuaded that the deterministic hypothesis is correct.

However, if we try to affirm both these views, we encounter a serious problem. How can we be free in the way required to render us morally responsible if every event in the universe (including, therefore, our decisions and our actions) is a theoretically predictable consequence of antecedent causes? Does this not imply that we are not the real agent of our acts, and is not our belief that we are morally responsible mistaken? Or, if we are indeed morally responsible, and free in the sense required to render us morally responsible, must not the view that every event is a theoretically predictable consequence of antecedent causes be mistaken? And does this not contradict the mass of evidence on which our belief in the orderliness and regularity of the universe is based?

It is apparent that a very important part of our thinking with respect to this question must be concerned with the nature of "moral freedom." Thus far we have spoken of moral freedom simply as that freedom (whatever be its nature) that is a condition of moral responsibility. But the really important question is: what is the nature of that freedom that is a condition of moral responsibility? Is it consistent with universal determinism or is it not? If it is, then it should be possible to show that the apparent conflict between universal determinism and moral responsibility is only apparent; thus the problem would be solved.

Precisely stated, therefore, the problem of freedom and determinism is this: Is the freedom that is a condition of moral responsibility compatible with universal determinism or not, and if not, which is the case?

Three Alternatives

This question is capable of being answered in three different ways.

First, one could reply to this question by saying that (a) the freedom that is a condition of moral responsibility is not compatible with universal determinism and (b) universal determinism is the case; therefore (c) man is not free in the sense required to render him morally responsible. This position is commonly called "hard determinism." It has been maintained by a large number of eminent thinkers and is more plausible than it appears when stated in summary form as it is here.

Or, second, one could reply by saying that (a) the freedom that is a condition of moral responsibility is not compatible with universal determinism and (b) man has this freedom; therefore (c) universal determinism is not the case. This position is commonly called "libertarianism." It also can claim a large number of eminent defenders, and it is probably the "plain man's" view—i. e., the view of most people prior to systematic reflection on the problem.

Or, third, one could hold that (a) the freedom that is a condition of moral responsibility is compatible with universal determinism and so (b) man may be morally responsible even if determinism is true. This view is commonly called "soft determinism." It has been supported by such well-known philosophers as David Hume and John Stuart Mill, and it is probably the dominant view among British and American philosophers at the present time.

It should be noted that a soft determinist is no less a determinist than a hard determinist: both hold that universal determinism is true, i.e., that every event in the universe is a theoretically predictable consequence of antecedent causes. The difference between them is only in the consequences that they draw from this view. A hard determinist, because he believes that the freedom that is a condition of moral responsibility is not compatible with universal determinism, draws the "hard" conclusion that man is not morally responsible. A soft determinist, because he sees no incompatibility between universal determinism and moral freedom, draws the "soft" conslusion that man may be morally responsible even though universal determinism is true. This is a point which people who are only casually acquainted with the freedom-determinism problem often fail to understand.

Four Crucial Terms

Before considering the grounds upon which one might adopt any one of these positions, it is advisable to clarify two pairs of terms that enter frequently into discussions of this problem.

The first pair of terms is "determinism" and "indeterminism." *Determinism* (or *universal determinism,* as we have called it above) is a theory about the universe—the theory, namely, that every event in the universe is a theoretically predictable consequence of antecedent causes. To say that every event in the universe is theoretically predictable is not, of course, the same as saying that every event is actually predictable—since it may readily be conceded that no one actually is in possession of all the data, or knows all the laws, that would permit the actual prediction of all events. What determinism does say, however, is that the universe is constituted in such a way that it is *in principle* possible (given an exhaustive knowledge of the relevant laws and data) to predict any event anywhere in the universe at any instant in the future.

Indeterminism is simply the denial of determinism. Like determinism, therefore, it is a theory about the universe—the theory, namely, that the universe is so constituted that some events that occur are not theoretically predictable. This does not mean, of course, that the universe as conceived by an indeterminist is utterly chaotic. An indeterminist readily admits that there are vast areas of the universe in which events are not only theoretically predictable, but actually predictable. His position is simply that however wide the domain of causal law may be, it is not universal: some events, he maintains, are not subject to it and are not, therefore, predictable even in principle—no matter how exhaustive a knowledge of the relevant laws and data is posited.

We may also observe at this point that either determinism or indeterminism must be true: there is no third possibility. Determinism is the theory that every event in the universe is the theoretically predictable consequence of antecedent causes and indeterminism is the denial of this. Since determinism either is or is not true, and indeterminism is identical with the view that determinism is not true, it is evident that either determinism or indeterminism must be the case. A great deal of confusion in the literature relating to this problem might have been avoided if this simple point had been clear to everyone who has written on the problem.

Two other terms which should be clearly understood at the outset of our consideration of this problem are "behaviorism" and the "free-will theory." These, unlike determinism and indeterminism, are theories about man rather than theories about the universe.

Behaviorism may be defined as the view that man is so constituted that the whole of his behavior—his every wish, thought, decision and act—is the theoretically predictable consequence of antecedent causes. Man, according to this view, is not in any degree the original cause of his own actions; his decisions and his choices are only links in a complex chain of causes whose ultimate origins lie outside himself.

The *free-will theory,* stated negatively, is simply the denial of behaviorism (just as indeterminism is simply the denial of determinism). Positively stated, the free-will theory may be defined as the view that man is so constituted that he is in some degree the original cause of his own actions. According to this theory, it is impossible in principle to predict every detail of a man's behavior since some of the causes of his future behavior are not now present to be taken into account in making the prediction. Similarly, if you try to trace the chain of causes backward from a given act, it is impossible in principle to press your inquiry to a set of antecedent conditions lying outside the agent to which the act can be reduced as to a sufficient cause. However strong the influence of antecedent conditions may be, according to this view, they are not sufficient to produce the act.

We shall have occasion in a later chapter to note in some detail the difficulties surrounding this notion of "free will." For the present, however, the student will do well to concentrate his attention on what the theory denies rather than what it affirms. He may justly expect of Libertarian (who is committed to affirming the free-will theory) that he will give a positive account of this theory in the course of stating and supporting his position.

Study Questions

1. State in two or three different ways what you understand to be the freedom-determinism problem.
2. How might this problem arise for each of the following: a physicist? a psychologist? a sociologist? a theologian? a juror?
3. Is it true that this problem is capable of being answered in just three ways? If so, explain why; if not, describe the additional alternatives.
4. Define carefully each of the following: hard determinism, soft determinism, universal determinism, indeterminism, libertarianism, behaviorism, free-will theory.
5. X says, "I do not believe in either determinism or indeterminism: I believe in *self*-determinism." Criticize this statement.

Chapter 37

THE CASE FOR HARD DETERMINISM

IT IS MY purpose in this chapter to persuade the reader that of the three alternative answers which can be given to the question posed in the preceding chapter, hard determinism is the most plausible. I shall begin by pointing out exactly what, as a hard determinist, I am obliged to defend. I shall then go on to support this position with what seem to be the strongest arguments available.

What Hard Determinism Is

Hard determinism, as was stated in the preceding chapter, is the view that (a) the freedom that is a condition of moral responsibility is not compatible with universal determinism, and (b) universal determinism is the case; therefore, (c) man is not free in the sense required to render him morally responsible. I hold, that is to say, a certain view of what would have to be the case if man were to be morally responsible; I hold that this condition of moral responsibility is not compatible with universal determinism; and I hold that universal determinism is true. I conclude, therefore, that man is not in fact morally responsible. This conclusion—i. e., the assertion that man is not in fact morally responsible—follows inevitably from my two premises.

What Constitutes Moral Freedom?

At the outset of our discussion, it is advisable to distinguish two meanings which, though different, are often conveyed by the single word "freedom."

One common meaning of the term is "the opportunity to do what one wants to do." In this sense, one has the freedom to do whatever one is not hindered from doing by external constraints or natural limitations. Thus, for example, I am "free" at this moment to write or not to write, to remain sitting at my desk or to get up and leave it, to open my office door or to leave it closed. I am not "free" to help myself to all the money in the vault of the nearest bank (because of external constraints) or to jump thirty feet into the air (because of natural limitations). Let us call this kind of freedom the "circumstantial freedom of self-realization." [1]

It is apparent that freedom in this sense varies greatly, depending on abilities and circumstances. The strong are "free" to do some things which the weak are not; the rich are "free" to do some things which the poor are not; the average citizen is "free" to do some things which the prison inmate is not "free" to do; etc. Circumstantial freedom of self-realization, the opportunity to do what one wants to do, is a matter of degree.

Some writers, however, speak of man's freedom as a power of the self to enact any one of a number of genuinely open alternatives. This is what libertarians ascribe to man when they credit him with having a "free will." Let us call freedom in this sense the "natural freedom of self-determination."

It should be noted that freedom in this sense does not admit of degrees. Either man has it, or he does not. If he has it, he has it at all times—whether he be rich or poor, strong or weak, in prison or out of prison.

I assume that everyone will allow that freedom in the first sense,

---

[1] The terminology is borrowed from Mortimer J. Adler, *et al, The Idea of Freedom* (New York: Doubleday & Company, 1958). This study constitutes the definitive analysis of the concept of freedom, and it is highly desirable that the terminological recommendations included in this study be adopted by all participants in the dispute over determinism and free will.

i. e., the circumstantial freedom of self-realization, is a necessary condition of moral responsibility. We do not hold people responsible for not doing something if we are satisfied that they wanted to do it but were not able to. This much is agreed by everyone who is a party to the freedom-determinism dispute.

It is my view, however, that while the circumstantial freedom of self-realization is indeed a *necessary* condition of moral responsibility, it is not a *sufficient* condition. If man is to be regarded as morally responsible, it is also necessary to ascribe to him the natural freedom of self-determination. The libertarians are right, therefore, in affirming that this freedom—or "free will" as they like to call it—is a necessary condition of moral responsibility; but they are wrong in affirming that man has it.

The question is a very difficult one, and we must be careful not to get lost in a forest of abstractions and arbitrary definitions. To reiterate, our question is: in what sense must man be free if he is to be regarded as morally responsible? Or, more simply, what constitutes *moral* freedom? It would be easy to arbitrarily define moral responsibility in such a way that the circumstantial freedom of self-realization would be a sufficient condition of its possibility. But we are not at liberty to define moral responsibility in any way that happens to fit our fancy: what we really mean by moral responsibility is implicit in the ways in which we ascribe praise and blame and in the ways in which we regard men as deserving reward and punishment. The "brute facts" to which we must constantly refer are facts concerning the actual ways in which we handle the categories of moral responsibility, i. e., praise and blame, reward and punishment.

In order to decide, therefore, whether or not the natural freedom of self-determination is a condition of moral responsibility, we have only to scrutinize carefully the sorts of judgments of praise and blame which we in fact make. Then we may ask ourselves: would we or would we not alter our judgment if we were persuaded that the agent of the act was not "free" in the sense of possessing the natural freedom of self-determination? I am confident that anyone who reflects carefully on a few hypothetical cases of this kind will find that we would alter our judgment in such a case, thereby demonstrating that our judgments of praise and blame do make the supposition that man is free in the sense of possessing the natural freedom of self-determination.

Let us consider a hypothetical example. Two boys—Tom and George—are apprehended attempting the armed robbery of a supermarket. Subsequent questioning reveals that the idea of robbing the supermarket was first suggested by Tom, but that the detailed planning of the robbery was done in cooperation and that the two participated equally in the attempted holdup. Therefore, both are guilty of committing a felony, and they are presumably deserving of equal punishment before the law.

If we were given no more information than this, I suppose the moral judgment which most of us would pronounce on the matter would be quite parallel to the legal judgment. Tom and George, we would say, are equally blameworthy for planning and attempting to execute this reprehensible act. Indeed, if there is any difference at all in the blame attaching to the two boys, the greater blame must be Tom's since it was he who first suggested the idea. Nonetheless, we would say, both are highly blameworthy, and they deserve the punishment that they will now presumably receive at the hands of the law.

But suppose that we acquired some additional information about the two boys. Suppose we learned that Tom was raised in a family of habitual criminals, and that from earliest childhood he had been taught that armed robbery was a feat of heroism rather than a blameworthy act. And suppose that George, on the other hand, was the product of a very different kind of home: his father was the governor, his mother a leader in civic affairs, and his elder brother a congressman. All the opportunities of a fine home and a good education were his, while Tom had none of these.

Would we not, knowing this, alter our previous moral evaluation of the acts of these two boys? I am certain that we would—and in some readily predictable ways. We would say that George, having had the advantages of his upbringing, is much more deserving of blame than Tom. We would say that Tom, owing to the untoward circumstances in which he was raised, is almost more to be pitied than to be blamed. Whatever be the status of these two before the law, we would maintain that so far as their *moral* guilt is concerned, they are not deserving of equal blame—for of him to whom much is given we expect much and of him to whom little is given we expect less.

But what is the principle according to which we thus alter our judgment of moral guilt? Why do we judge Tom less harshly than George? Clearly it is because we attribute Tom's act to causes lying outside himself—to the environment in which he was raised—whereas we attribute George's act to his own perverse choice of a mode of behavior that contradicted everything we would expect from him. In other words, *we do not hold a man responsible for any act insofar as we believe that act to be the consequence of causes lying outside himself.* Anyone who is willing to consider objectively a number of hypothetical cases of moral judgment will readily persuade himself that this is indeed an important principle on which our everyday moral judgments are formulated.

In order for a man to be morally responsible, then, he must be in some degree the original cause of his act, and he is morally responsible for his act only if, and insofar as, he is the original cause. Moral freedom—i. e., the freedom that is a condition of moral responsibility—includes the natural freedom of self-determination. Without this—without "free will," as the libertarians say—there is no moral responsibility.

The Case for Determinism

Unfortunately, however, although man would have to have the natural freedom of self-determination in order to be morally responsible, it is impossible for man to have this. It is impossible because this is a deterministic universe. And to complete my case, I shall set forth a number of arguments which, I am persuaded, make it necessary for anyone who considers the matter carefully to adopt the determinist hypothesis.

First, every instance of regularity that is discovered in nature is evidence for the hypothesis that all macroscopic phenomena are reducible to the regular operations of natural laws. The quantity of evidence now available from the many special sciences is so great as to make the contrary hypothesis exceedingly improbable.

The era of modern science began when men ceased asking for

the *purposes* of natural phenomena and asked instead for their *causes*. To the question, "What is the purpose of the revolution of the heavenly bodies (about the earth, or about the sun)?" all sorts of fanciful answers are possible, and no answer can ever be demonstrated to be the right one. But to the question, "What *uniformities* are exhibited in the motions of the heavenly bodies?" or "What are the *causes* of celestial phenomena?"—to such questions clear and mathematically precise answers can be given on the basis of data available to anyone who cares to concern himself with the question.

For a long time it was assumed that "lawlike regularity" applied only to the realm of inanimate matter and that human behavior, at least, was exempt from the reign of such laws. Severe doubt was cast on this view by the researches of Charles Darwin, however, and a short time later researches into human behavior were undertaken by Sigmund Freud and others on the supposition that these phenomena, like all others, are governed by laws which may be discovered by painstaking inquiry. This supposition has been progressively verified by the researches of Freud's successors. As B. F. Skinner says, "We cannot apply the methods of science to a subject matter that moves about capriciously." [2] Every advance in descriptive psychology, every discovery that is made with respect to the laws governing human behavior, adds to the steadily and rapidly growing accumulation of evidence in support of the view that human behavior, too, is thoroughly subject to the vast network of causes that govern all phenomena.

Should anyone be disposed to quarrel with what has just been said, let him reflect for a moment on what it would be like for a scientist to abandon the deterministic hypothesis. Given the deterministic hypothesis, a scientist asks about whatever phenomenon he has chosen to investigate, "What are its causes? What are the uniformities, the laws, exemplified in this phenomenon?" Should he abandon the deterministic hypothesis, he could not ask such questions. He would have to ask instead, "Does this phenomenon have any causes—or is this perhaps one of those things that occurs haphazardly, one of those things that does not have any regular

[2] B. F. Skinner, *Science and Human Behavior* (New York: The Macmillan Company, 1953), p. 6.

causes?" And this, I submit, is absurd. It would cut the nerve of the whole scientific enterprise, which has made its well-publicized advances on precisely the opposite supposition.

In a less rigorous but perhaps equally important way, we all make a similar supposition whenever we have occasion to predict the behavior of other human beings. We know, for example, that if we want to avoid an argument we had better stay off the subject of politics whenever Uncle George is around. How do we know this? We know it because, in a rough and ready way, we know some of the "laws," the "regularities," that govern Uncle George's behavior. Consider any person that you know reasonably well: is it not true that you could, with a high degree of accuracy, predict how he would act in a wide variety of situations? But to acknowledge this is to acknowledge that his behavior exhibits certain uniformities, uniformities which differ only in the degree in which they are known from the uniformities exhibited in the motions of bodies, the interactions of chemicals, and the migration of birds.

That human behavior is not exempt from causal laws becomes evident when one reflects on the experience of "choosing among alternatives." Here, if anywhere, one would expect the "natural freedom of self-determination" which libertarians defend to be evident. But it is not. Consider: one never chooses without a motive. Just as one's motives are determined by one's desires, so one's choice is determined by one's motive: one always chooses that alternative for which one finds the strongest motive. But what constitutes the strongest motive for any given individual depends on his personal likes and dislikes, which are, in turn, the consequences of his heredity and environment. Thus, the "chain of causes" leading to an act stretches back indefinitely: "decision" is not an original cause, but merely one link in the chain.

I have dwelt at length on this matter of human behavior because it is, so to speak, the last outpost of indeterminism. If it is conceded that human behavior is as completely subject in principle to causal explanation as are other phenomena, then so far as I can see there will remain no further objection to adopting the determinist hypothesis. Thanks to the efforts of psychologists and sociologists, we have already come far in the direction of adopting a behaviorist view: we now speak without hesitation of "the causes of crime," "the conditions that create anti-social attitudes," and the like. We have, admittedly, still very much to learn about the laws that govern human behavior. But it is not unreasonable to hope, with Skinner, that:

> Eventually a science of the nervous system based upon direct observation rather than inference will describe the neural states and events which immediately precede instances of behavior. We shall know the precise neurological conditions which immediately precede, say, the response, "No, thank you." These events in turn will be found to be preceded by other neurological events, and these in turn by others. This series will lead us back to events outside the nervous system and, eventually, outside the organism.[3]

It may be conceded that the foregoing considerations do not conclusively demonstrate the truth of the determinist hypothesis. Like any hypothesis, it does not admit of conclusive demonstration. What these considerations do suggest, however, is that it is more reasonable to affirm the determinist hypothesis than it is to affirm its only alternative, i. e., indeterminism. And this is the conclusion which I have been attempting to re-enforce.

Consequences for Ethics

The "upshot" of this so far as ethics is concerned is, I admit, quite disturbing. For since, as I have shown, (a) moral responsibility presupposes the natural freedom of self-determination (b) which is not compatible with universal determinism and (c) universal determinism appears to be the case, it seems impossible to avoid the conclusion (d) that man is not morally responsible. And this, in turn, seems to carry with it the following consequences:

1. No human act, however "noble" or "base," is ever worthy of either praise or blame. John F. Kennedy's heroism and dedication were as much a product of his heredity and environment as Lee Harvey Oswald's hatred and perversion were a product of his.

2. Punishment (or "retributive justice" as it is sometimes called)

---

[3] *Ibid.*, p. 28.

cannot be defended on the ground that a person who acts in a certain way is "guilty" and, therefore, "deserving of punishment." Thus it will make no sense to talk about a criminal "paying his debt to society"; since, like everybody else, he has acted in the only way possible for him (given his heredity and environment), and therefore he has incurred no such debt.

3. If we are to continue to praise and blame, or reward and punish, people on the basis of their behavior, it can only be on the ground that such things will tend to influence their behavior in certain desirable ways.

Study Questions

1. What, precisely, is the difference between "the circumstantial freedom of self-realization" and "the natural freedom of self-determination"? In what sense, according to Hard Determinist, must man be free if he is to be morally responsible? Do you think he is right about this?

2. What is the point of Hard Determinist's insistence that in the discussion of this question one must constantly refer to the "facts concerning the actual ways in which we handle the categories of moral responsibility"? Does this seem to be at all important?

3. Does Hard Determinist's example bear out his claim that we do not hold a person responsible for an act insofar as we believe that act to be the consequence of causes lying outside himself? Suggest three or four additional examples that either confirm or disconfirm this principle.

4. What arguments does Hard Determinist offer in support of the truth of the determinist hypothesis? Does this evidence seem to be conclusive? Can you think of any additional arguments in support of this hypothesis which Hard Determinist has failed to mention?

5. Do the "disturbing consequences" which Hard Determinist itemizes at the end of his essay really follow from his view, as he says? Are there other similar consequences which Hard Determinist has neglected to mention?

Chapter 38

THE CASE FOR SOFT DETERMINISM

IT MUST CERTAINLY be acknowledged that Hard Determinist, in the chapter just concluded, has made a very good case for his view that determinism is true and that this excludes the possibility of the freedom without which man cannot be morally responsible. His arguments in support of the determinist hypothesis are particularly cogent, and I am delighted to simply accept everything he has to say on that score as a part of the case which I propose to build in defense of a position called "soft determinism."

Before I do this, however, I should like to say that I do not particularly care for the name "soft determinism" that has come into common use as a description of my position. There are two reasons for my dislike of this title. The first is that it was invented by William James, a noted libertarian, who coined it precisely for the purpose of disparaging the position which I represent. Just listen to James' words:

Nowadays, we have a *soft* determinism which abhors harsh words, and, repudiating fatality, necessity, and even predetermination, says that its real name is freedom; for freedom is only necessity understood, and bondage to the highest is identical with true freedom.[1]

---

[1] William James, "The Dilemma of Determinism," in *The Will to Believe, Human Immortality, and Other Essays on Popular Philosophy* (New York: Dover Publications, 1956), p. 149.

James, in other words, used this title pejoratively; and if, to avoid confusion, I allow my position to be called "soft determinism," I insist that these pejorative connotations be laid aside and that my position be considered simply on its merits. If I reject Hard Determinist's conclusions with respect to ethics, it is not because I am "soft" but because I think his conclusions are unwarranted.

The second reason for my displeasure with the name "soft determinism" is that it has led to a great deal of confusion as to what my position really is. I am no less firm in my adherence to determinism than is Hard Determinist. I hold, with him, that the universe is so constituted that everything that occurs—including actions by human beings—is a theoretically predictable consequence of antecedent causes. Both Hard Determinist and I are what may be called "strict determinists." The difference between us is not that he is more consistent in his determinism than I, but that he draws certain consequences from his determinism (with respect to ethics) which, as I have said, are in my view unwarranted. I propose now to show where Hard Determinist makes his mistake and how, therefore, it is possible to maintain a consistent determinism without drawing the dire ethical consequences which he insists must be drawn.

Moral Freedom

The crucial question that must be asked about this vexing problem is, *"In what sense* must man be 'free' if he is to be morally responsible?"* Hard Determinist has argued that he must be free in a contra-causal sense, i. e., that he must possess a "natural freedom of self-determination." It is at this point that he is mistaken, and it is because of this mistake that he feels obliged to deny that man is morally responsible. My view, on the contrary, is that the "circumstantial freedom of self-realization"—i. e., the opportunity to do what one pleases—is a necessary *and sufficient* condition of moral responsibility; and I think that a careful consideration of the ways in which we actually ascribe praise and blame will demonstrate that this view is the correct one.

Let us suppose that Hard Determinist were right in his contention that man could be morally free only if this were not a deterministic universe, and that he could be morally responsible only if (*per impossibile*) any act for which he would be held responsible were not the theoretically predictable consequence of antecedent causes. What then? We would then be in the position of saying that a man is responsible for an act if and only if that act is uncaused. But to say that something is uncaused is to say that it is a "chance" event, a mere random occurrence; and apart from the difficulty of even conceiving of such a thing, it is absurd to maintain that a man could be morally responsible only if his actions, or some of his actions (those for which he would be held responsible) occurred "by chance." This is not what we have in mind when we say "So-and-so is morally responsible for doing *r*."

What, then, do we have in mind? Simply, I submit, that the agent had the opportunity—the circumstantial freedom—to do a number of things, and that he did what he did because he wanted to. We do ask, when applying appraisal concepts, whether the agent could have done otherwise had he so desired; we do not ask whether he could have desired to do otherwise. And the reason we do not ask is that this latter is simply not relevant to our judgment as to the praiseworthiness or blameworthiness of his actions.

Let us consider a hypothetical example. Johnny has been instructed always to come directly home from school, and his mother has learned (through repeated observation of Johnny's arrival time) that when he does he normally arrives home no later than 3:15 P.M. On a few occasions, however, Johnny has arrived home at a slightly later time, but on each of these occasions his mother has determined that "he could not have done otherwise": he had to stay after school, or the extreme cold made it necessary for him to stop briefly at a store to warm himself, etc. But one spring day Johnny arrives home at nearly five o'clock, and Mother naturally asks, "Johnny, where have you been?" Johnny replies, "I've been playing in the puddles." "But Johnny," Mother objects, "don't you know that you are supposed to come directly home from school?" "Yes." "Well, why didn't you?" "Well, I just didn't want to. I wanted to play in the puddles." "Well, son, you will have to be punished for this." "But Mother," Johnny cries, "you can't punish me for that. I couldn't want to do anything else."

We obviously do not, and would not, consider Johnny's objection relevant. Why? Because in holding someone responsible for something we do not ask why he wants to do so-and-so, but only whether his doing so-and-so was a result of his wanting to do it. So long as Johnny's late arrival was unavoidable—so long as his wanting to be home on time was thwarted by circumstances— Johnny was not held responsible for the late arrival; but when the late arrival was the consequence of his wanting to do something that caused him to be late, he was immediately held responsible *no matter what may have been the causes* of his wanting to play rather than obey.

Let us consider a second hypothetical case. The manager of a supermarket is apprehended in the act of removing the contents of the store safe at 2 A.M. He is accordingly suspected of attempting to commit an act of theft. Investigation discloses, however, that (a) a gunman is holding the manager's wife and children hostage and has threatened to harm them if he does not comply with orders, (b) a second gunman has forced the manager to drive to the supermarket and open the safe, and (c) the manager tried unsuccessfully to attract the attention of police (at risk of his life) by exceeding the speed limit and running through a red light en route to the market.

Knowing these facts, we would not blame the store manager— i. e., we would not hold him responsible—for the attempted theft. Why? Simply because we are satisfied on the basis of the facts that he was not doing what he wanted to do. And the reason that he was not doing what he wanted to do was that he did not have the circumstantial freedom, the opportunity, to do it.

It is significant that the only question relevant to determining moral responsibility in either of these two cases is: was the agent, in the circumstances in which he found himself, able to do what he wanted to do? That is, did he have the *circumstantial freedom* to actualize his own wishes? Johnny had this freedom; therefore, we hold him responsible for his late arrival. The manager in our second example did not have this freedom; therefore, we do not hold him responsible.

Who was responsible, then, for the attempted robbery of the supermarket? Obviously, it was the gunmen who forced the store manager to comply with their wishes. And in this we may see what is really meant by the notion of moral responsibility. *To be morally responsible is to be the person whose motives, whose desires, need to be changed if a given kind of behavior is to be encouraged or prevented.* We do not blame people for doing what, under the circumstances, was the only thing they could reasonably have been expected to do. We do blame them if a different desire on their part would have been sufficient to produce a more desirable kind of behavior.

Reasons for Confusion

The problem of freedom and determinism has been debated vociferously and inconclusively for many hundreds of years. One might well ask why this should be so if the solution is really as simple as I have suggested. Since this question may in itself constitute for some people an obstacle to accepting the position which I am advocating, I should like in conclusion to deal briefly with it.

There are two reasons why the true solution to this much-discussed problem has eluded most of those who have addressed themselves to it.

The first reason, and in my judgment the most important one, is that they have misunderstood the nature of moral judgments. To be morally responsible, as we said above, is to be the person whose motives need to be changed if a given kind of behavior is to be encouraged or prevented. This is what we mean in both of the hypothetical cases cited above, and I am confident that anyone who will take the trouble to reflect on any example whatsoever in which he would be inclined to regard a person as morally responsible will find that this is equally the case there. It is inevitable that this should be so because this is what we mean when we say that a person is morally responsible. Moreover, the function of moral judgments is precisely *to alter the motives of the person being judged and thus to influence his future behavior.* Praise and blame are simply mild forms of reward and punishment. The reason for employing either is always—in the case of blame or punishment— to discourage or prevent certain kinds of undesirable behavior or —in the case of praise or rewards—to encourage certain kinds of desirable behavior.

Let us now suppose that someone approaches the question concerning the conditions of moral responsibility without understanding the true nature of moral responsibility or of moral judgments. How would he be apt to construe them? In all likelihood he would construe moral judgments on the analogy of statements of fact, and accordingly he would interpret blameworthiness and praiseworthiness as "intrinsic qualities" of the persons or acts being judged. From this mistaken starting point it is a very short step to the view —shared by Hard Determinist and Libertarian—that some obscure power ("freedom") *within the agent* is a condition of moral responsibility.

A second reason for the mistaken views of many people regarding this question involves a series of semantic confusions with respect to the terms "law" and "freedom." Our perception of the meaning of the term "law" derives largely from its use in connection with statutes and ordinances—the sorts of things enacted by city councils, legislatures, and parliaments. It is of the very nature of this sort of "law" to prescribe behavior—indeed (by virtue of the threat of punishment) to coerce behavior. Implicit in every such law is the "or else" embodied in the system of fines or other punishments that await the offender. If we disobey, we become subject to the prescribed punishment; and because we fear the punishment, we usually obey—whether or not the prescribed behavior is what we ourselves really want to do.

But in science the term "law" is used to designate a very different sort of thing, namely, an observed uniformity. Scientific law is merely a report about what has actually been observed to be the case in such-and-such a class of phenomena. Here there is no coercion, no "or else." Pure water (at sea level) is not compelled or constrained to freeze whenever the temperature reaches 32° F. It just does. And the "law" which states this is simply a description of what in fact has been observed to occur.

Had this distinction between prescriptive and descriptive law been clearly recognized, it probably would never have occurred to anyone to insist that moral responsibility requires exemption from causal laws. Moral responsibility does indeed require exemption from coercion—but causal laws do not coerce. The opposite of causality is acausality, or indeterminism, whereas the opposite of compulsion is freedom. Hence, the failure to distinguish the two different kinds of law led to the absurd view that moral responsibility requires a contra-causal, or indeterministic, freedom.

Moral Responsibility Requires Determinism

Thus far I have only argued that moral freedom is consistent with the determinist hypothesis and that one need not, therefore, conclude with Hard Determinist that man cannot be morally responsible in a deterministic world. In arguing thus, however, it may appear that I am being purely defensive—that I am trying to "salvage" what can be salvaged of human moral responsibility in a deterministic universe. By way of countering this impression, therefore—which is of course implicit in James' unfortunate labeling of my position as "soft" determinism—I should like to conclude by taking the offensive in this argument. The thesis which I propose to support is: not only is it the case that moral responsibility is consistent with the determinist hypothesis, but *moral responsibility would not be possible in anything other than a deterministic universe.*

This is evident, in the first place, from my earlier argument concerning the absurdity of maintaining that a man could be responsible for only those of his acts which occurred "by chance." For any event whatsoever, one can conceive of only two possibilities: either it has a cause or it does not have a cause. If it has a cause, then it is explicable within the context of the deterministic hypothesis. If it does not have a cause, then it is a "chance event." To reject determinism, therefore, on the ground that it is incompatible with moral responsibility—or, alternatively, to reject moral responsibility on the ground that it is not possible in a deterministic universe—is to adopt the absurd position referred to above.

My thesis can also be supported in another way. Let us suppose that this were not a deterministic universe—i. e., that everything that occurred were not a theoretically predictable consequence of antecedent causes and that a given set of circumstances would not, therefore, always produce a predictable effect. In such a universe it would be impossible to hold a man responsible for anything because he could never know what would be the result of any act which he might perform. In such a universe the glass of water which yesterday quenched the thirst of a dying man might today poison him instead, or turn him into a giraffe, or do any one of countless other thoroughly unpredictable things. It is only insofar as we can predict what will be the effects of a given course of action that we can act responsibly; and hence it follows that we can act responsibly only in a universe where certain predictable effects follow ineluctably from certain causes. An indeterministic universe— a universe in which the orderly sequence of events is interrupted by more or less frequent "chance events"—would be a moral chaos. It is doubtful if life would even be possible in such a universe; but there is no doubt about the fact that in such a universe responsible behavior would be utterly impossible.

It seems, therefore, that the time has come to lay this old problem to rest. What is really of concern to Hard Determinist is the truth of the determinist hypothesis. It is this that he feels obliged to insist on, and in this he is right. What is really of concern to Libertarian is the truth of the conviction that man is morally responsible. This is what he feels obliged to insist on, and in this he is right. Where both Hard Determinist and Libertarian err—and this is the unargued assumption that has kept this debate alive for so many years—is in assuming that moral responsibility requires a contra-causal freedom in man. Once the absurdity of this assumption is perceived, the problem is solved.

Study Questions

1. Where, precisely, does Soft Determinist agree with Hard Determinist, and where does he disagree with him? Is there any difference between them as to the *method* by which this question must be decided?
2. Does it follow from Hard Determinist's position, as Soft Determinist says, that "a man is responsible for an act if and only if that act is uncaused"? How might Hard Determinist defend himself against this objection?
3. Do the two hypothetical examples offered by Soft Determinist support his claim that the only relevant question in deciding on a ques-

tion of moral responsibility is whether the person in question did what he did because he wanted to? Could Hard Determinist explain these examples in a way consistent with his position?

4. What does Soft Determinist say is the meaning of "moral responsibility"? Do you think he is right about this? If not, what alternative would you suggest?

5. What considerations does Soft Determinist offer in support of his claim that moral responsibility actually *requires* determinism? Do you agree or disagree with this thesis? Why?

Chapter 39

THE CASE FOR LIBERTARIANISM

AFTER THE FORMIDABLE array of arguments which Hard and Soft Determinist have presented in support of their respective positions and after the devastating cross-fire to which libertarianism has been subjected in these discussions, it may appear futile to attempt to construct an argument that could have any chance of persuading people that the truth lies with my position. Yet I am convinced that my stand is really the correct one, and I, therefore, welcome the opportunity to defend my position and to show how the various objections raised against it can be rather easily overcome.

Let me begin by stating where I agree and where I disagree with each of my opponents.

Hard Determinist has argued that determinism is true and that the freedom that is a condition of moral responsibility is not compatible with determinism. From these two premises he has drawn the unhappy conclusion that man is not morally responsible. My position vis-à-vis Hard Determinist is clear: I reject his first premise, and I affirm his second. And I, of course, do not accept his view that man is not morally responsible. I believe it can be established on independent grounds that man is morally responsible and that one must therefore accept the conclusion that determinism is not the case. I shall attempt to show in due time that the consequences of accepting this conclusion are not nearly so dire as some determinists would lead us to believe.

Soft Determinist offers a more elusive argument. Consequently, it is more difficult to state sharply just exactly where we agree and where we disagree. We disagree, of course, in our views with respect to determinism: he holds that it is the case, and I hold that it is not. We disagree, moreover, in our respective views as to what sort of freedom is required in order to render a man morally responsible. He holds that the circumstantial freedom of self-realization is a sufficient condition of moral responsibility; I hold (in agreement with Hard Determinist) that man is not morally responsible unless he possesses also the natural freedom of self-determination.

It may seem as if Soft Determinist and I agree on one point, namely, that man is morally responsible. But anyone who is acquainted with both his position and mine will immediately recognize that our agreement is only verbal. We both say that man is morally responsible—but we do not mean the same thing. When he says that so-and-so is morally responsible, he means that so-and-so is the one whose motives need to be changed if a certain kind of behavior is to be encouraged or avoided. When I say that a man is morally responsible, I mean that he is fittingly, or deservingly, subject to praise or blame, reward or punishment. So even at this point we are not in agreement—except, of course, verbally.

I propose to proceed in two stages. I am convinced that soft determinism is not a tenable position—despite the fact that it is a position that is very widely held. I shall begin, therefore, by showing why this position is untenable. This will prepare for a direct confrontation with hard determinism—a position which I respect but which I, nonetheless, consider to be mistaken. I do think that a clear-thinking person must finally choose between my position and that of Hard Determinist, and I shall do my best to show that the strongest considerations are on my side.

Refutation of Soft Determinism

I have the greatest sympathy for the kinds of considerations that have led Soft Determinist to adopt his position. The conclusions which Hard Determinist draws with respect to man's moral responsibility are "hard" conclusions indeed, and it is not surprising that some determinists should have sought a way to avoid them within the context of their deterministic beliefs.

Nonetheless, the mistake which Soft Determinist makes—the mistake which vitiates his whole position—is obvious. What Soft Determinist does is to start from the assumption that determinism is true; he then (a) arbitrarily re-defines "moral freedom" in such a way as to render it compatible with determinism, and (b) arbitrarily re-defines "moral responsibility" in such a way as to make "moral freedom" as he has defined it a sufficient condition thereof. He then announces that he has "reconciled" determinism and moral responsibility and that the traditional problem which has divided libertarians and determinists for so many years has at last been solved.

But all that has been accomplished by this little verbal sleight of hand is simply a blurring of the relevant concepts, a confusion of the issue. The question never was whether human moral responsibility *as arbitrarily re-defined* could be shown to be compatible with determinism: any two theories can be rendered compatible if you are willing to allow one of them to be freely re-defined. The question was, and still is, whether moral responsibility *as this concept is employed in our everyday judgments of praise and blame* is compatible with determinism; and Soft Determinist's argument does not show in the slightest that this is so.

To illustrate, let us consider the question, "Are all of the citizens of Flamenco absolutely loyal to their government, or do some of them occasionally commit acts of treason?" One could imagine two straightforward answers—either that all of the citizens are absolutely loyal and, therefore, there is no treason in Flamenco ("hard loyalism"); or that treasonous acts are sometimes committed and, therefore, not all of the citizens are always loyal to their government ("occasionarianism"). But it would be distinctly unhelpful to have someone say to us, "Look, I can define treason in such a way that occasional acts of treason do not contradict the view that all of the people of Flamenco are absolutely loyal to their government." It would be unhelpful because we do not want to know whether treason *as thus re-defined* can be made to square with "universal loyalism." If we must ask this question about the compatibility of the concepts, what we want to know is whether treason in its ordinary unaltered meaning is compatible with "universal loyalism"; and it is evident that it is not.

Hard Determinist has already cautioned us to remember—and his point is an important one—that if we intend to address ourselves to the real problem that is at issue in this discussion, we are not at liberty to define moral responsibility in any way that happens to suit our fancy. What we really mean by moral responsibility is implicit in the ways in which we ascribe praise and blame and in the ways in which we regard men as deserving of reward and punishment. We have, therefore, to attend carefully to our actual employment of judgments of praise and blame in order to "read off" from that employment the meaning that is implicit therein. Anyone who will do this will shortly discover, I am confident, that "being morally responsible" means more than simply "being capable of having one's behavior altered through an alteration of one's motives."

If Soft Determinist's account of moral responsibility were correct, what would follow? In the first place, it would follow that we ought to hold animals morally responsible no less than we do men —for there is every reason to suppose that reward and punishment will influence the behavior of dogs and horses just as much as they will influence the behavior of men. But it is significant that although we do indeed reward and punish animals, we do not apply judgments of moral appraisal to them; whereas on Soft Determinist's account of moral responsibility we should. Further, if moral responsibility means what Soft Determinist says it means, it would make no sense whatsoever to speak of a dead person as "responsible" for something; for on this hypothesis there is no one whose motives could be influenced in such a way as to bring about a different sort of behavior. Yet, we do blame dead persons for acts committed by them: Adolf Hitler and Stalin are examples. Again, we commonly "make allowances," in making judgments of praise and blame, for such things as a poor childhood environment: the child who grew up in the slums, whose father was a petty thief, etc., "did not have the chance" (as we say) that his more fortunate fellows did, and so we judge him less harshly. But on Soft Determinist's ground we would have no reason to judge him less harshly, since we have no reason to suppose that his behavior is either more or less subject to influence than anyone else's. Indeed, if Soft Determinist is right, we ought, if anything, to judge such a person more harshly, since there is reason to suppose that more counteracting influences are needed if his behavior is to be brought into tolerable conformity with society's norms. Thus at a number of crucial points Soft Determinist's account of moral responsibility is at variance with our actual judgments of praise and blame; and since it is in reference to such judgments that we must decide this matter, Soft Determinist's inability to account for the cases mentioned must be regarded as decisive against his position.

Soft Determinist has argued that his view—i. e., that moral freedom consists simply in having the circumstantial freedom of self-realization—is supported by the fact that in concrete cases we never inquire about anything else. "It is significant," he writes, "that the only question relevant to determining moral responsibility . . . is: was the agent, in the circumstances in which he found himself, able to do what he wanted to do? That is, did he have the *circumstantial freedom* to actualize his own wishes?" But surely the reason for this is that we assume that all men always have the natural freedom of self-determination: hence, we do not need to inquire about that in each particular case. The reason Johnny's mother (in Soft Determinist's example) does not accept his objection that he "could not want to do anything else" is not that his objection, if true, is not relevant, but rather that she does not believe him. If she were to become convinced that he had suddenly been afflicted with a "puddle-playing syndrome" that literally compelled him to want to play in the puddles, her attitude would be very different.

We may safely conclude, therefore, that the recent attempts of some determinists to affirm the moral responsibility of man without relinquishing their belief in determinism do not succeed. If man is to be regarded as morally responsible, it is necessary, as Hard Determinist has argued, that he have both the circumstantial freedom of self-realization and the natural freedom of self-determination (free will). And since, as Hard Determinist has shown, the latter is not compatible with determinism, one must finally choose between Hard Determinist's position and my own.

Replies to Objections

Hard Determinist has stated very cogently the arguments which, in his view, make it unreasonable to deny the truth of the determinist hypothesis; and since my position commits me to just such a denial, it is incumbent on me to show why I think his arguments are not convincing.

The first argument—and the one, incidentally, which people usually find most convincing—was that "every instance of regularity that is discovered in nature is evidence for the hypothesis that all macroscopic phenomena are reducible to the regular operations of natural laws" and that "the quantity of evidence now available from the many special sciences is so great as to make the contrary hypothesis exceedingly improbable."

I have no desire to belittle in any way the tremendous advances which modern science has made in its progressive discovery of nature's laws. What I wish to point out, however, is that the determinist hypothesis is not a super-hypothesis that is progressively being established by mounting evidence: it is rather a heuristic principle which is presupposed in each particular scientific inquiry. It is important to the scientific enterprise that no limits be established in advance as to the scope of natural laws—since to do so would arbitrarily prevent inquiry beyond a certain point. It is not important to the scientific enterprise to maintain, either as a dogma or as a hypothesis, that there are no such limits.

Suppose, for example, that my view that man is free in a "contra-causal" sense were correct. This would not, so far as I can see, in any way hinder the scientific study of man. My view does not deny that there are any laws governing human behavior: it only denies that human behavior is *completely* explicable in terms of such laws. Let the scientific study of man proceed as rapidly and as far as it can; let the independent variables affecting man's behavior be discovered and stated with as great precision as possible; there will still remain the "freedom factor," as a consequence of which man's behavior will not become perfectly predictable and as a consequence of which man is and will remain morally responsible. This factor may be more or less influential in determining a man's behavior than we now commonly suppose; outside influences may, as psychologists and sociologists are inclined to believe, play a much greater role in determining behavior than was once assumed. But unless and until laws have been discovered in terms of which *every detail* of man's behavior is explicable, there is no reason whatso-ever to deny the presence of this "freedom factor." Indeed, as we shall see presently, there is excellent reason to affirm it.

Hard Determinist's second argument in support of determinism (actually it is in support of behaviorism, i. e., determinism as ap-plied to human behavior) is that we can, in a rough and ready way, predict the behavior of people whom we know well. This, he con-tends, supports the hypothesis that their behavior is governed by certain "laws" or "uniformities" which, apparently, we vaguely discern in making our prediction.

I grant that we can, within certain limits, make some informed guesses as to how people that we know well will act in certain kinds of situations, but I fail to see how this in any way supports the behaviorists' thesis. It is not my position that human behavior is always erratic and irrational, but only that it is not altogether the product of causes lying outside the agent. Such uniformity as we actually observe in people of our acquaintance may be due to either (a) controlling causes such as a behaviorist believes completely dominate human behavior or (b) habits of character acquired through many years of training and experience—or both. If *a,* in the absence of evidence to support the view that the whole of a man's behavior is the product of such causes, there would seem to be nothing to prevent us from adopting the opposite hypothesis; and if *b,* it is surely plausible to hold that one's character is at least in part a product of one's own past choices freely made and that it may be further modified by choices yet to be made. Thus it appears to me that such regularity as we do observe in the behavior of individuals in no way supports the hypothesis that *all* human be-havior is the product of causes lying ultimately outside the agent.

Hard Determinist's third argument is that reflection on the expe-rience of "choosing among alternatives" makes it evident that (a) one always does that action for which one finds the strongest motive and (b) what constitutes the strongest motive for any indi-vidual depends on causes lying outside the agent. This, in one form or another, is one of the oldest and most persuasive arguments used in opposition to the libertarian position, and the refutation of it must be somewhat complex.

The apparent force of this argument lies in the tacit adoption of a mechanical model in terms of which the description of human volition and action is given. According to this model, the self is conceived as a "thing" that is pulled (or pushed) in various directions by the "motives" and that inevitably moves in the direction of the strongest pull (or push). But the model is not adequate, and to draw deterministic conclusions from it is to be misled by a faulty model. Selfhood cannot be conceived "from the outside," but only from within—in terms of what it means to *be* a self. The reality of responsible selfhood, therefore, cannot be adequately described in the para-mechanical language of motives-determining-acts; it can be expressed only in the personal-life categories of decision and choice.

Space does not permit the detailed development of an alternative to the mechanical model employed by Hard Determinist. However, we may observe that it is the moral freedom of man, not the indeterminacy of some "faculty" of man, that is here in question. As moral agents we know that (a) there are some situations in which we are "morally obliged" to act in a certain way—i. e., that there is something that we "ought" to do—and (b) very often in such situations there is something that we "want" to do that differs from what we "ought" to do—that is, there is some other thing that is our "desire" in that situation. I am willing to allow that, in any given situation, man is not free to choose what shall be his strongest "desire" in that situation: that, it seems to me, is determined by his character as thus far formed in relation to the concrete details of the situation in which he finds himself. What I would insist upon, however, is that in such a situation a man need not act in the way that is in accord with his strongest desire; he may, instead, choose a way of acting that contradicts his desire because he believes it to be his *duty* to do so. He alone decides whether his action shall correspond to duty or to desire; hence he alone is answerable for his behavior.

This is admittedly a gross oversimplification of the matter since in actual experience the conflict between duty and desire is seldom as sharp and explicit as this account suggests. It is, nonetheless, truer to our actual experience as moral agents than the mechanistic model which we are attempting to refute; and the student who desires a fuller explanation of this matter can at some later time inquire more fully into the notion of the self. For the present we must be content with the negative statement that a self is not a "thing" and that its operations, therefore, cannot be understood in terms of a mechanical model appropriate only to "things." Beyond this we can only provide at this time the merest hint as to how the self may be more adequately conceived.

The Basis for Libertarianism

If the arguments just concluded do suffice to remove the chief objections to libertarianism, does this suffice to establish the libertarian position? Obviously not. What we still require is some positive ground for affirming the libertarian thesis, and I shall conclude by indicating what that ground must be.

There is one, and only one, ground upon which libertarianism rests, and that is that we know ourselves to be morally responsible; therefore, we also know that whatever is necessary to render us morally responsible must be the case. Sometimes, indeed, we find ourselves in situations where we have only one way of action open to us, and in such situations we accept neither praise nor blame for doing what, under the circumstances, was the only thing which we could do. But more commonly life presents us with a variety of alternatives, some of which are in varying degrees attractive to us (desire) and some of which may appear to make some kind of claim upon us as moral agents (duty). In such situations we must choose among the alternatives; and in the experience of choosing— of saying yes to one of the alternatives and no to all the rest—we know directly that it is *our choice* that determines what shall be done. Our choice is not arbitrary: for any choice we can give a reason ("I wanted to," or "I felt it was my duty," etc.). But neither is it predictable, for we, and we alone, decide whether and to what extent to follow duty or desire.

Since we are, and know ourselves to be, morally responsible, the universe must be the sort of place in which moral responsibility is possible. Therefore, it cannot be strictly deterministic, for in such a universe moral freedom and responsibility could not be. But neither, obviously, can it be a chaos since in such a universe I could never know what would be the result of any act I might perform. (This, incidentally, is the answer to Soft Determinist's claim that moral responsibility *requires* determinism. He is, of course, wrong in this; but he is close since moral responsibility does require that the universe exhibit sufficient uniformity to enable one to know what will be the probable consequences of this or that act.) The universe must, therefore, be sufficiently uniform in its operations to enable us to "count on" certain actions producing certain effects and it must be sufficiently "loose" in its structure to permit men to make genuinely free and responsible decisions.

Fortunately, from my point of view, that is just how the universe appears to be. There certainly is a very large area in which perfect uniformity appears to prevail: hence, I can depend on bread to nourish and water to quench thirst, and I can give these to the hungry and the thirsty confident that my action will not produce unintended results. But the universe happily allows me to decide whether I shall feed the hungry and give drink to the thirsty; consequently, I am fittingly held responsible for what I do or fail to do. Because there is a considerable degree of uniformity, science is possible; and I for one would not want to set any *a priori* limits to the extent of that uniformity. But because there is a certain amount of "looseness" in the universe, moral freedom and responsible behavior have also found a place; and I would be equally reluctant to set any *a priori* limits to the extent of man's moral responsibility. In a strictly deterministic universe science would presumably be possible, but moral freedom and responsibility would not. In a chaotic universe neither science nor morality would be possible. But in the universe as it is, highly uniform but not strictly determined, there is ample room both for scientific knowledge and for moral freedom and responsibility. To abandon either would be to err in our understanding of man and his world.

Study Questions

1. Where, exactly, does Libertarian agree and where does he disagree with each of the two previous writers? Where, on each of these points, do your own sympathies lie at the present time?

2. How, according to Libertarian, has Soft Determinist accomplished the apparent reconciliation of determinism and moral freedom? Is this an accurate description of what Soft Determinist has done? If not, where does it go wrong?

3. Libertarian offers a *reductio ad absurdum* of Soft Determinist's account of moral responsibility. Summarize the argument. Does it succeed in your opinion?

4. What is a "heuristic principle"? How does the suggestion that the determinist hypothesis is a heuristic principle tend (if it does) to weaken Hard Determinist's case?

5. Summarize Libertarian's replies to Hard Determinist's arguments in support of determinism. Which of them (if any) do you find most convincing? Which least convincing?

6. What does Libertarian say is the "one and only one ground upon which libertarianism rests"? Do you find his argument at this point convincing? Why, or why not?

For Further Reading

Adler, Mortimer, et al., The Idea of Freedom. New York: Doubleday & Company, 1958.

Beardsley, Elizabeth L., "Determinism and Moral Perspectives," Philosophy and Phenomenological Research, Vol. XXI (1960), 1-20.

Bergson, Henri, Time and Free Will. New York: Harper & Row, 1962 (paperbound).

Campbell, C. A., "Is 'Free Will' a Pseudo-problem?" Mind, Vol. LX (1951), 441-465.

————, On Selfhood and Godhood. New York: Humanities Press, 1957.

Cranston, M., Freedom—A New Analysis. London: Longmans, Green and Co., 1953.

Eddington, A. S., The Nature of the Physical World. Ann Arbor, Mich.: University of Michigan Press, 1958 (paperbound). Chapter XIV.

Edwards, Jonathan, Inquiry Concerning the Freedom of the Will, ed. Paul Ramsey. New Haven, Conn.: Yale University Press, 1957.

Farrer, Austin, The Freedom of the Will. New York: Charles Scribner's Sons, 1960.

Halverson, W. H., "The Bogy of Chance," Mind, Vol. LXXIII (1964), 567-570.

Hook, Sidney, ed., Determinism and Freedom in the Age of Modern Science. New York: New York University Press, 1958.

Hospers, John, "Free-will and Psychoanalysis," in Readings in Ethical Theory, ed. W. Sellars and J. Hospers. New York: Appleton-Century-Crofts, 1952.

Hume, David, A Treatise of Human Nature. Many editions. Book II, Part III.

James, William, "The Dilemma of Determinism," in The Will to Believe, Human Immortality, and Other Essays on Popular Philosophy. New York: Dover Publications, 1956 (paperbound). Pages 145-183.

Laird, John, On Human Freedom. New York: Hillary House, 1947.

Lehrer, Keith, "Can We Know That We Have Free Will by Introspection?" The Journal of Philosophy, Vol. 57 (1960), 145-157.

Macmurray, John, The Self as Agent. New York: Humanities Press, 1957.

Matson, W. I., "On the Irrelevance of Free-Will to Moral Responsibility," Mind, Vol. LXV (1956), 489-497.

Pears, D. F., ed., Freedom and the Will. New York: St. Martin's Press, 1963.

Rankin, K. W., *Choice and Chance: A Libertarian Analysis.* Oxford: Basil Blackwell, 1961.

Rashdall, Hastings, *The Theory of Good and Evil.* Oxford: Oxford University Press, 1924. Book III, Chapter III.

Schlick, Moritz, *Problems of Ethics,* trans. David Rynin. New York: Prentice-Hall, 1939 (Orig. pub. in German in 1931) Chapter 7.

Sidgwick, Henry, *The Methods of Ethics,* 7th ed., rev. Constance Jones. Chicago, Ill.: University of Chicago Press, 1962.

Skinner, B. F., *Science and Human Behavior.* New York: The Macmillan Company, 1953. Chapter 1.

Smart, J. J. C., "Free Will, Praise and Blame," *Mind,* Vol. LXX (1961), 291-306.

Stebbing, L. S., *Philosophy and the Physicists.* New York: Dover Publications, 1958 (paperbound).

Stevenson, C. L., *Ethics and Language.* New Haven, Conn.: Yale University Press, 1960 (paperbound). Chapter XIV.

Wilson, John, "Freedom and Compulsion," *Mind,* Vol. LXVII (1958), 60-69.

Chapter 40

SECOND RETROSPECT

THE CONSIDERATION OF the problem of the language of morals, the mind-body problem, and the problem of freedom and determinism, has taken us into "deeper water" than did the consideration of the earlier problems. We have been forced to consider *rival metaphysical theories* in connection with these later problems, and it has become increasingly evident that a position on these matters depends very much on the kind of metaphysical theory held. The time has come, therefore, to ask, "What, precisely, is a metaphysical theory, and how are theories of this sort constructed?" The answers to these questions will illustrate the nature of the controversies involved in all the problems discussed thus far and will provide a perspective for the discussions which follow that will enable a better understanding of what is involved in them.

Metaphysics

Perhaps the best way to approach an understanding of metaphysical theory is to note some of the features of what we call "explanation." In order for a person *A* to "explain" something to person *B*, it is necessary that there be some phenomenon which *A* understands and *B* does not, that *B* have certain general concepts through which he can understand the phenomenon in question, and that *A* inform *B* which of these general concepts are applicable to the phenomenon in question—that *A* exhibit it, so to speak, as an instance of such-and-such general concepts. Suppose, for example, that a child is looking out toward the ocean as a ship is approaching, and is puzzled because at first he can see only the smoke stack of the ship, then a bit more of it, and finally all of it that is above the water line. One can "explain" this phenomenon to him by telling him that the earth is like a very big round ball and by showing him how a ship coming over the horizon becomes visible a bit at a time in the same way that an object attached to a beach ball becomes visible a bit at a time as the ball is rotated toward him—or, to keep the illustration more accurate, as the object is moved "over the top" toward him as an observer. The child already knows the meaning of "big" and "round," and he knows (or can learn very quickly) the relevant visual phenomena as they apply to the beach ball: he has only to be told that it is these concepts that he should apply to the phenomenon in question, and it will no longer puzzle him. To *explain* something to someone is to help him to *understand* it, and to understand something is to conceive it as "standing under" certain general concepts.

Most children, it may be assumed, would be satisfied with the explanation just given, and they would have no further questions about the phenomenon we have described. The idea that the earth is a "big round ball" may strike them as being very odd at first, but at length it becomes a quite familiar idea and is henceforth available to explain other phenomena (such as the daily rising and setting of the sun). But one can readily imagine that a very inquisitive child might have further questions: "What *makes* the water stay up in the middle?" *"Why* can't I see around corners—over the curvature of the earth, or over the top of a beach ball?" To explain these things to him we should have to acquaint him with the law of gravity, with some of the laws governing optical phenomena, and so on.

Each succeeding question, it is to be noted, is a demand for an explanation *at a higher level of generality* of the phenomenon that constituted the original puzzle. The "big round ball" story constitutes an adequate explanation only if the relevant optical phenomena and the curvature of the surface of the water are taken for granted—are not, that is, regarded as puzzling. If these are called in question, an explanation must be given at a higher, or more inclusive, level.

A metaphysical system is a scheme of very general concepts in terms of which *all* phenomena are held to be explicable. With respect to any explanation that is given of any phenomenon whatsoever, it is always possible to raise a further question which is, as we have said, a demand for an explanation at a higher level of generality. At length, however, one must come to a level of generality beyond which it is not possible to go—not possible because the concepts in question are held to be universally applicable. To any "Why?" that may be raised at this level one can only say, "Because that is the way things are."

Certain philosophers maintain that metaphysical theories are "meaningless" on the ground that it makes no sense to ask, "What is the explanation of everything?" Without doubt there is something odd about such a question; but it does not follow from this that metaphysical theories are meaningless, for metaphysical theories are not attempts to answer this question. They are, rather, attempts to answer the question, "What are the most general truths about reality in terms of which questions raised at the highest level of generality are to be resolved?" In a sense, of course, this means that everything is supposed to be "explained" by the theory; but only in the sense that if you persist in raising questions long enough, you must at length come to some theory at this very highest level of generality.

The question, "Are metaphysical theories intelligible?" does not lend itself to fruitful discussion *in abstracto*. We should ask, rather, "Is it meaningful to assert that all phenomena are ultimately explicable in terms of matter and the laws governing matter?" "Is it meaningful to assert that all phenomena are ultimately explicable in terms of mind and its determinations?" These questions are meaningful. A real issue does exist between Materialist and Panpsychist with respect to the proper understanding of the nature of body and mind, and the issue is precisely over which conceptual scheme constitutes an adequate "ultimate explanation" of the relevant facts. To both of these theories, metaphysical dualism is an intelligible alternative. The whole controversy over the problem of body and mind is quite unintelligible on any other supposition.

The resistance of many philosophers today to metaphysical theories—the tendency to call all such theories "meaningless" or "nonsensical"—is largely because of their rejection of *transcendentalistic* metaphysical systems of the sort that prevailed in Great Britain and America up until the beginning of the present century. But one cannot get rid of metaphysics in this way. One can only replace a metaphysical scheme with another metaphysical scheme, whether more or less adequate, for there must be *some* conception of the whole in terms of which it can be decided when explanation has reached its highest limit.

There is, however, a certain oversimplification in what we have just said. A metaphysical system is not simply a world-view (as one might be tempted to conclude from the description just given): it is a world-view expressed in terms of a coherent system of concepts and defended on the basis of its explanatory power. A given world-view is capable of being expressed in terms of a variety of conceptual schemes. St. Augustine and St. Thomas Aquinas, for example, shared a substantially common world-view, but they elaborated this world-view in terms of two quite different metaphysical systems. The same may be said of Plato and Aristotle: their world-views were very much the same, but the metaphysical systems in terms of which they attempted to *conceptualize* the world thus viewed were quite different. A world-view is more on the order of a "picture" or an "image"; a metaphysical system is a system of concepts and allegedly universal truths.

A metaphysical theory, moreover, is not simply identical with a metaphysical system: it is only a part of such a system. A metaphysical system of the mentalistic type is defined as one in which it is affirmed that all phenomena are explicable in terms of mind and its determinations; therefore, any system of this type will include this theory. But the theory may be elaborated in terms of a variety of conceptual schemes, as is evident from the many differences that obtain between the systems proposed by Leibniz, Schopenhauer, and Hegel, for example. The same generalization applies, *mutatis mutandis,* to metaphysical theories of the materialistic, or the dualistic, types.

How, then, are metaphysical systems constructed? Perhaps the answer is obvious: they are constructed by men who for one reason or another become dissatisfied with the prevailing system or systems and who attempt to develop an all-inclusive conceptual scheme that is more to their liking. Dissatisfaction may arise from one or more of several sources: the prevailing system may be internally incoherent (giving rise to "tensions" within the system); or it may fail satisfactorily to explain some phenomena; or it may seem in some respects to be superfluous. The aim, then, is to elaborate a system that is coherent, adequate to the known facts, and universally applicable. If a philosopher succeeds in "catching up" the knowledge and the concerns of the most enlightened people of his day and in elaborating a conceptual scheme that provides a context for understanding and explanation that illuminates matters which before seemed obscure, then the system which he creates may become an intellectual home for many for a greater or lesser period of time—until new tensions develop, or new and unexplainable facts appear, and the job has to be done all over again.

The elaboration of a metaphysical system is a huge and important intellectual task, and it is quite impossible to make more than a few general statements about how those who have done it best have gone about it. They appear to have been perplexed about certain problems inherent in the received views, and their starting point appears to have been some "clue" or "insight" which seemed to point the way toward a more adequate conceptual scheme in which their initial perplexities could be resolved. With Plato, for example, the initial "clue" appears to have been a suggestion which had been made by Anaxagoras, but never developed by him or applied to the problems that puzzled Plato. With Descartes, it was the exciting thought that the method of reasoning employed by mathematicians might be applied in other areas as well. Starting with his initial "clue," or "insight," the philosopher then generalizes the concepts involved and attempts thereby to complete a scheme in which the tensions with which he began can be resolved.

A Backward Glance

If, with these considerations in mind, we look back over the route that we have just traversed, it becomes evident that the mutual congeniality of certain philosophical theories is much more deeply rooted than it first appeared to be. "Group I" theories (see Chapter 23)—conventionalism, empiricism, skepticism or constructive empiricism, phenomenalism, and (we may now add) reductive materialism, determinism (hard or soft), behaviorism, and a wide variety of meta-ethical theories—tend to "go together" because they are all parts of a particular type of philosophical system. "Group II" theories—and to our earlier list we can now add dualism or pan-psychism, libertarianism, and non-naturalistic objectivism—tend to "go together" because they are parts of a philosophical system of a different type. There are, as we suggested earlier, many instances of mutual entailment among the various "positions" of each type; and the entailments, we may now add, are expressive of the internal coherence of the systems of which each group is a part.

We may go further. The theories in Group I belong, without exception, to the type of philosophical system which we have called "naturalistic." The theories in Group II belong, on the other hand, to the type of philosophical system which we have called "transcendentalistic" (see Chapter 3). If one is on the whole persuaded by the theories in the former group, then the most inclusive statement that can be made about one's philosophical position is that one is a naturalist. If on the whole one is persuaded by the theories in the latter group, then one is best described as a transcendentalist. Being a naturalist or a transcendentalist does not rigorously imply that one holds this or that position on every question: there are a few options. It does imply, though, that one cannot consistently hold certain positions which are incompatible therewith. Even philosophical laymen must obey the rule of internal consistency.

To discover that one is, or tends to be, a philosophical naturalist or transcendentalist is not by any means to discover a ready-made metaphysical system which one has only to adopt. Suppose, for example, that I discover that I am, or tend to be, a transcendentalist: I must still decide what particular *form* of transcendentalism, what particular conceptual scheme, I shall accept. Shall it be Platonism? or Thomism? or Whiteheadianism? These are some of the options—but only some. Perhaps some other conceptual scheme, as yet unknown to me, will strike me as having the greatest explanatory power—or perhaps I shall elaborate my own. So also if I am a naturalist. Must I adopt the conceptual scheme of Democritus? or Epicurus? or Huxley? or Dewey? No, indeed. I may prefer another *form* of naturalism, another way of elaborating the general scheme in terms of which I shall attempt to understand all phenomena, but it will have certain features that distinguish it from transcendentalist systems of whatever form.

But how, it may be asked, can one decide between naturalism and transcendentalism? The answer is: by considering individual philosophical problems and trying to decide where the truth lies in each individual case. There are no arguments for or against either naturalism or transcendentalism over and above the arguments relevant to particular philosophical problems. In coming to a decision on almost any philosophical problem, one *is* deciding between naturalism and transcendentalism, for—and this is no accident—there are few philosophical problems where any of the options are equally congenial to both.

A Glance Ahead

We turn now to a consideration of two final problems with which this introduction to philosophy must come to a close. The two problems are: the existence of God (Part VIII) and religious language (Part IX).

It should come as no surprise to anyone who has understood the difference between the naturalistic and the transcendentalistic types of philosophical systems that the two problems with which we shall conclude this study provide a particularly direct confrontation between the two types. For theism, obviously, is the belief that there is a reality that transcends space and time and, consequently, is not compatible with naturalism; this means, in turn, that the claim of some theists that they can prove the existence of God (Part VIII), and that religious language is in some sense descriptive of such a reality (Part IX), must be rejected by anyone who would uphold the main tenets of naturalism. The controversy over the soundness or unsoundness of the traditional arguments for the existence of God has gone on for centuries; the dispute over the meaningfulness or non-meaningfulness of religious language is of relatively recent origin. But both problems lend themselves in a very direct way to the confrontation between naturalistic and transcendentalistic philosophical systems.

Study Questions

1. What does it mean to "explain" something? Can you think of any examples of what you would call "explanation" that are not covered by the analysis suggested in this chapter?
2. What, according to the suggestions made in this chapter, is a metaphysical system? What function is such a system said to serve? Do you think it is true that metaphysics cannot be dispensed with?
3. Define as precisely as you can "world-view," "metaphysical system," "metaphysical theory."
4. According to this chapter, what is the fundamental basis for the mutual congeniality of certain philosophical theories? Does this seem to hold true for the problems you have studied thus far?
5. Do the positions you have been inclined to favor on the problems considered thus far tend to fall in the "naturalist" or the "transcendentalist" group? Which of the positions that you have tentatively adopted do you feel most certain about? About which do you have the most serious doubts?

The Existence of God

PART VIII

The Existence of God

Chapter 41

A CLUSTER OF PROBLEMS

THERE ARE A number of questions about God that philosophers, at various times in the history of Western philosophy, have been inclined to ask. Many of these have been concerned with the *nature* of God: Is God rightly described as a "person"? Is God absolutely eternal and immutable, or does He in some sense participate in change? If God does not change, how is it possible for Him to experience love, or solicitude, or compassion? These, and dozens of other questions of this kind, figure prominently in the writings of such Christian philosophers as St. Augustine, St. Anselm, St. Thomas Aquinas, and Duns Scotus. To modern ears, such questions often sound exceedingly strange, even unimportant; but to the philosophers of the Middle Ages they were questions of the first importance. One measure of the distance that modern thought has traveled from the thought of the Middle Ages is the infrequency with which such questions are discussed today.

There is another question, however, which has been of interest to at least some philosophers in every age. That is the question: Does God exist? Some philosophers—for example, St. Augustine —thought the existence of God was so self-evident that it did not even require to be proved (though St. Augustine does offer one such proof in his treatise *On the Free Will*). Others, like St. Albert the Great, St. Thomas Aquinas, and Descartes, thought the existence of God required proof, but they considered it a relatively simple matter to construct such a proof. St. Thomas, for example, offers no less than five such "proofs" in the space of just two or three pages. Most philosophers today are at least in agreement on this, that the proof of the existence of God, if it is possible at all, is no easy matter; and it is probably true to say that the majority of them regard it as impossible.

The Problem of Definition

Before we can discuss intelligently the various arguments that have been offered as proofs of the existence of God, it is necessary that we consider carefully a prior question, namely: What is the meaning of the term "God"? Let us see why, in connection with the arguments concerning the existence of God, this is such an important question.

Suppose that someone proposed for discussion the following: Do *snergs* exist? It would be obviously futile, would it not, to begin to construct arguments for or against the existence of "snergs" until some agreement had been reached as to what was *meant* by the term "snergs"? Indeed, confusion would most surely occur, for those who affirm the existence of "snergs" might have one sort of thing in mind, and those who deny their existence might have another sort of thing in mind. As a result their disagreement would be merely verbal rather than real (see Chapter 5). Unless there is agreement on this key point, and thus agreement as to what is the point of the question that is being asked, the question itself cannot be intelligently discussed.

Even philosophers, unfortunately, have not always understood clearly the crucial importance of this prior question and, consequently, a good deal of confusion has been created in the discussion of this problem. Some philosophers have supposed, for example, that the question, "Does God exist?" is equivalent to: "Does there exist, some place beyond the reach of even our most powerful telescopes, a very wise and powerful being who once upon a time brought the world into existence, who occasionally even now interferes in its orderly operations, and who will some day reward the righteous and punish the wicked?" They have supposed, that is to say, that it is God *as conceived by popular unsophisticated Christian piety* whose existence is in question; and they have relatively little difficulty in showing that none of the arguments that have been offered in an attempt to "prove the existence of God" succeed in proving the existence of such a being. They do not always realize, however, that no philosopher who has seriously proposed an argument for the existence of God has ever wanted to prove the existence of a being so conceived.

What, then, have those philosophers who have attempted to prove the existence of God meant by the term "God"? It is very difficult to answer this question with the precision that might be desired. It seems, however, that those philosophers who have entered most seriously and profoundly into the discussion of this question—philosophers such as St. Anselm, St. Thomas, Descartes, and Kant (who, by the way, are far from agreeing on the soundness of the various arguments for the existence of God) have meant by the term "God" at least the following:

> *a.* A reality that transcends space and time.
> *b.* The ground of being and value.
> *c.* A reality worthy of man's worship.

The question, "Does God exist?" means, therefore, "Is there a reality that transcends space and time, that is the ground of being and value, and that is worthy of man's worship?" To answer this question in the affirmative is to affirm that God exists. To answer it negatively is to deny that God exists. To affirm or deny the existence of any other sort of being is to miss the point of the question, "Does God exist?"

There are in this formulation of the question, however, certain terms that are frightfully unclear, notably the terms "reality" and "ground." Let us try to clarify them.

Perhaps the best way to get at the meaning of the term "reality" as used in this context is to note the reasons for using this term instead of the term "being." To speak of God as "a being" would not do justice to what philosophers who have attempted to prove the existence of God have meant by the term "God." Why? Because our notion of "a being" is the notion of a spatio-temporal something that exists alongside other spatio-temporal somethings. To speak of "a being" is to speak of something that exists in some places but not in others, at some times but not at others—and philosophers who have believed that God exists, and that His existence could be proved, have not intended to assert the existence of *a being* occupying some particular region of space-time. They have meant to assert, rather, the existence of a reality that is not subject to the categories of space and time—a reality, in other words, that transcends space and time. Hence, we must speak of God not as a being, but as a reality.

To say that God is to be conceived as a reality that transcends space and time is to say, really, that God is not to be conceived simply as a natural object, as one of the many objects that one might encounter within the realm of nature. No telescope will ever be constructed, no space journey ever undertaken, that will reveal God's habitation—not because the distance is too great, but because the question of God's existence does not concern distance at all. If we cannot attach some meaning to the phrase, "a reality that transcends space and time" (and many philosophers today insist that they cannot), then we simply cannot enter into the discussion of the question, "Does God exist?"

Next, what is meant by the term "ground" in the above formulation? Why do we not use instead the word "cause"? For the same reason cited in the previous case: the term "cause" is (in contemporary usage) too closely tied up with the notions of space and time. A "cause" is a spatio-temporal something that stands in a certain relation to something else that we call its "effect." But the notion of God, we have said, is the notion of a reality that transcends space and time: hence, we must not speak of God in such a way as to suggest "a spatio-temporal something." We want, however, to affirm something like the relation of cause and effect between God and being and value. How shall we do this? Philosophical usage has given us the term "ground" which means, roughly (in philosophical usage), "non-spatio-temporal cause." Let us say, then, that God is the "ground" of being and value.

What, finally, does it mean to say that the idea of God is the idea of a reality "worthy of man's worship"? This is in many ways the most puzzling of the three statements. Something like this must be said, however, to take account of the fact that the term "God" is in the first instance a *religious* term—so much so that one would not be too far from the truth if one were simply to define "God" as "the object of the act of worship." The supposition is, however, that the object of worship is somehow worthy of man's devotion, which in our philosophical tradition at least has meant that God is conceived to be holy, just, good, merciful, and so on. Many philosophers (St. Thomas, once again, is an excellent example) have attempted to construct proofs of a number of such "attributes" of God, but it seems clear that the very notion of God includes in embryonic form the idea that He possesses in an eminent degree those virtues which we normally admire in one another; and it is this notion that we are including in the idea of God when we say that, in the third place, God is to be conceived as "a reality that is worthy of man's worship."

The question whether God exists—whether, that is, there exists a reality that transcends space and time, that is the ground of being and value, and that is worthy of man's worship—is no trivial question. Most people would, I think, agree with the sentiments of the philosopher who said (though he himself rejected all of the arguments for the existence of God):

> If we found that any of the traditional arguments for the existence of God were sound, we should get out of our one hour this . . . afternoon something of inestimable value, such as one never got out of any hour's work in our lives before. For we should have got out of one hour's work the answer to that question about which, above all, we want to know the answer.[1]

Many philosophers who, like the one just quoted, believe that none of the traditional arguments for the existence of God is sound, believe, nonetheless, that the question of the existence of God is an exceedingly important question. In fact, some of those who have come to the conclusion that God does not exist (e. g., Friedrich Nietzsche and Jean-Paul Sartre) have recognized that this conclusion must profoundly alter one's way of understanding himself, his fellows, and his world. It is probably safe to say that anyone who does not regard the question of the existence of God as a serious

---

[1] J. J. C. Smart, "The Existence of God," a public lecture given at the University of Adelaide in 1951, and published in Antony Flew and Alasdair MacIntyre, eds., *New Essays in Philosophical Theology* (London: S. C. M. Press; and New York: Macmillan, 1955), pp. 28-46; see p. 28.

and important question has not really understood the point of the question.

A Related Question

To the question, "Does God exist?" there are, obviously, only two possible answers: Yes, and No. Philosophers, however, are not just interested in people's opinions on this matter: they are interested primarily in the reasons that might be given in support of an opinion. The philosophical discussion of the existence of God has, therefore, had a slightly different focus than we have suggested thus far.

Let us, then, approach the question of the existence of God obliquely—by asking a slightly different question: Are there any *rational grounds* for believing in the existence of God? Are there any *good reasons* for believing that the proposition "God exists" is true? Such a question may be answered in a number of ways.

One way of answering this question is to say that there are some rational grounds for believing in the existence of God—in which case one ought to be prepared to say what those grounds are. What this means in practice is that an *argument* for the existence of God is put forward and an attempt is made to show that the argument succeeds in establishing the truth of the assertion that God exists. Chapters 42-44 attempt to do this in terms of three of the traditional arguments for the existence of God.

It should be noted at this point that what is to be allowed to count as "rational grounds" in this connection depends very much on one's epistemological persuasion. If one is persuaded on other grounds of the correctness of empiricism, for example, one cannot go along with the proponent of the cosmological argument when he makes an appeal to "rational insight" (Chapter 43). If, on the other hand, one is persuaded by this author's argument, then one must be prepared to draw the epistemological consequences. Here, as with every philosophical problem, intricate and important interrelationships with other philosophical issues are evident.

A second way of answering this question is to say that none of the arguments offered in support of the existence of God is sound and to draw the conclusion that God does not exist. It is evident that philosophical naturalism cannot allow the existence of God (as defined above). It is, therefore, incumbent on a naturalist to take this position with respect to the proposed arguments. A critique of the arguments from this perspective is offered in Chapter 45.

Not all of those who deny the soundness of the traditional arguments for the existence of God are philosophical naturalists, however. A large number of recent and contemporary theologians, including both Karl Barth and Paul Tillich, deny that the existence of God can be established by rational argument; yet they obviously do not draw the conclusion that God does not exist. This position—the view that (a) there are no sound arguments by which the existence of God can be proved, but (b) God nonetheless exists, and His existence is certified in certain (presumably) non-argumentative ways—represents a third way of responding to the question posed in this section. Chapter 46 attempts to build the case for such a view.

A Preliminary Look at the Arguments

Basically there are, and indeed can be, only two kinds of arguments for the existence of God.

It is possible to argue, first, that the proposition "God exists," when properly understood, is self-evidently true. The purpose of argument, from this point of view, is not to proceed from evident premises to a less evident conclusion, but to exhibit the self-evidence of the proposition, "God exists." Such an argument (if, indeed it can properly be called an "argument" at all) is termed an *ontological* argument for the existence of God.

The other possibility is to start with some empirical or quasi-empirical fact—the existence of material objects, or of order in the universe, or of some feature of moral or religious experience—and attempt to show that this fact presupposes, implies, or points to, the existence of God. The collective name for arguments of this type is *cosmological* arguments. St. Thomas Aquinas' famous "five ways" (five arguments for the existence of God) are all versions of this type of argument; so also are the teleological argument (see Chapter 44), the "moral" argument, and the "argument from religious experience." The phrase *"the* cosmological argument" is commonly used to refer to an argument of this type that starts with the assertion that some material objects exist (as in Chapter 42), but sometimes it is used more narrowly to refer to some particular classical formulation of this argument—for example, that of Avicenna, or one of the first three of Aquinas' "five ways."

There are few areas of philosophical inquiry in which the poverty of our language is more evident than in the discussion of the arguments for the existence of God. The "five ways" of St. Thomas Aquinas, for example, are stated in the language of Aristotelian metaphysics and are quite unintelligible apart from an understanding of that metaphysical system; but Aristotelian metaphysics does not inform the conceptual vocabulary of most people today, and an intelligent appraisal of Aquinas' arguments is for most people, therefore, simply impossible. It will be evident in the essays that follow that the advocates of the various arguments for the existence of God are groping for a terminology that is both (a) adequate to express the ideas they are trying to express and (b) intelligible to modern ears.

Study Questions

1. Why is it necessary to come to some agreement about the meaning of the term "God" before engaging in a discussion of arguments purporting to prove the existence of God?
2. Does the definition of "God" here proposed agree with what you have ordinarily understood the term to mean? If not, how would the definition have to be altered in order to express what you have understood it to mean?
3. What are the reasons given for using the terms "reality" and "ground" rather than "being" and "cause" in the definition of "God?" Do these strike you as being sound reasons? What difference would it make in the discussion if the terms "being" and "cause" were substituted for "reality" and "ground"?
4. What is an "ontological" argument for the existence of God? a "cosmological" argument?

Chapter 42

THE ONTOLOGICAL ARGUMENT

THE HISTORY OF Western man's struggles with the problem of the existence of God during the past sixteen hundred years provides an interesting commentary on the development of Western thought during this period of time. At the first stage in this development—in the thought of St. Augustine— the existence of God is simply taken for granted: it is regarded as a matter so self-evident that a proof of God's existence would be simply superfluous. At the present stage of this development (I do not say the last), it is the *non*-existence of God that is commonly taken for granted: any attempt to prove the existence of God today is, in the view of many of our contemporaries, anachronistic and therefore futile. The intervening chapters in this history, marked by the explicit formulation of the ontological argument (St. Anselm), the rejection of the ontological argument in favor of the cosmological argument (St. Thomas Aquinas), and the rejection of both of these in favor of the teleological argument (Deism), indicate the course by which our culture generally has moved from an implicit belief in the existence of God to an implicit disbelief in the existence of God. An advocate of any argument for the existence of God today, therefore, and most of all an advocate of the ontological argument, has little reason to be optimistic about his prospects for winning a substantial number of adherents for his point of view.

Moreover, the task is rendered even more difficult by the incredible ignorance of many people regarding what it is that one is trying to prove. One would suppose that a reasonably well-educated person would know that philosophers—and theologians—who believe it is possible for us to know, and to demonstrate, that God exists emphatically do *not* believe in the existence of "the Old Man in the Sky" of primitive supernaturalism. Even St. Augustine, who might have been excused for holding what we would regard as "primitive" ideas, knew better. If the only alternatives before us were naturalism and supernaturalism, then it is clear that the only honest choice anyone could make would have to be naturalism; for supernaturalism, with its demons and its angels, its throne in the heavens, and its Old Man in the Sky, belongs to the childhood of our culture. These things may survive indefinitely in the symbolism of religious communities and as the picture language of simple religious faith, but they have no place in the serious discussion of the question concerning the existence of God. It would be better if the problem of the existence of God were never discussed at all than to have it discussed in such a childish and superficial way.

There is, happily, an alternative, and that is to enter seriously and passionately into a consideration of what it means to affirm that God exists, to try to grasp this great affirmation so profoundly and so intimately as to understand how some men—not simple and unlettered men, but some of the intellectual giants of our culture—could have regarded it as unthinkable that any man *who knew what he was doing* could refuse to affirm it. Let this question be our point of departure: How could intelligent and learned men—men like St. Augustine and St. Anselm—have been persuaded, as almost nobody is today, that the existence of God is self-evident? What did they see, or think, or feel, or understand that most men today apparently do not? Perhaps in this way we may begin to understand what a twentieth-century version of the ontological argument would be and why, even today, it deserves our attention and respect.

St. Anselm

St. Anselm of Canterbury (1033-1109) was one of the few truly original thinkers who appeared during the long interval of time between St. Augustine (354-430) and St. Thomas Aquinas (1225-

1274). Like St. Augustine, whom he sought to emulate, Anselm conceived his task to be that of an apologist for Christian orthodoxy. All his writings, therefore, reflect his theological and apologetic concerns; indeed, he did not really make a hard and fast distinction between theology and philosophy. In two of his writings, however—the *Monologium* and the *Proslogium*—he advanced a number of arguments for the existence of God. These are worthy of study in themselves quite apart from the apologetic context out of which they arose.

The ontological argument was the product of St. Anselm's quest for

a single argument which would require no other for its proof than itself alone; and alone would suffice to demonstrate that God truly exists, and that there is a supreme good requiring nothing else, which all other things require for their existence and well-being.[1]

The arguments which he had previously offered (in the *Monologium*) were, Anselm realized, extremely complex and, therefore, unconvincing to many readers; the argument for which he sought, and which he believed he now had found, was to be so simple that no one could fail to understand it and so cogent that no one who understood it could fail to be convinced by it.

The argument as developed by St. Anselm is, alas, far from simple, at least to modern ears. The crucial passages read as follows:

Even the fool is convinced that something exists in the understanding, at least, than which nothing greater can be conceived. For, when he hears of this, he understands it. And whatever is understood, exists in the understanding. And assuredly that, than which nothing greater can be conceived, cannot exist in the understanding alone. For, suppose it exists in the understanding alone: then it can be conceived to exist in reality; which is greater. Therefore, if that, than which nothing greater can be conceived, exists in the understanding alone, the very being, than which nothing greater can be conceived, is one,

---

[1] St. Anselm, *Proslogium*, in S. N. Deane, *Anselm*, 2nd ed. (La Salle, Ill.· Open Court, 1962), p. 1.

than which a greater can be conceived. But obviously this is impossible. Hence, there is no doubt that there exists a being, than which nothing greater can be conceived, and it exists both in the understanding and in reality. . . . There is, then, so truly a being than which nothing greater can be conceived to exist, that it cannot even be conceived not to exist.[2]

This is a far more forceful argument than most of St. Anselm's critics have realized. In order to appreciate its cogency, however, it is necessary first to understand it; and this is not easy.

The force of this remarkable argument may be seen more clearly if it is restated as follows:

Proposition 1: By the term "God" is meant a being (reality) than which none greater can be conceived (NGBC).

Proposition 2: Whether one affirms or denies the existence of God, NGBC exists in the understanding.

Proposition 3: It is possible to conceive of NGBC existing not only in the understanding, but in reality as well; and this is greater.

Proposition 4: If, therefore, NGBC exists *only* in the understanding, it is not NGBC.

Proposition 5: Therefore, NGBC exists also in reality.

I do not think that anyone would deny that if Propositions 1-4 are allowed to stand, Proposition 5 (the conclusion) would follow therefrom. Let us consider, then, what may be said in defense of Propositions 1-4.

Proposition 1 simply asserts a minimal definition of the term "God." St. Anselm is saying, in effect, that people who believe in the existence of God believe in the existence of a being (or, as I should prefer to say, a reality) than which none greater can be conceived, that the only way to deny the existence of God is to deny the existence of a being than which none greater can be conceived. Thus far, it seems to me, Anselm's opponents have no reason to object. If they do, in any case, the result could only be a quibble over terms; it is this definition that determines the substance of what St. Anselm means when he affirms that God exists.

---

[2] *Ibid.,* pp. 8-9.

Proposition 2 simply points out the obvious fact that anyone who affirms or denies the existence of God must, first, understand the meaning of the term "God." If anyone says the words, "God does not exist," but means something other than "a being than which none greater can be conceived does not exist," he is not, properly speaking, denying the existence of *God:* he is only denying the existence of something else to which he incorrectly gives the name "God." In order to really affirm or deny the existence of *God*—in order, that is, to be a party to this debate at all—one must understand what the term "God" means. And since, as St. Anselm says, "whatever is understood, exists in the understanding," Proposition 2 must be affirmed.

This brings us to Proposition 3, which is surely the crux of St. Anselm's famous argument. What is St. Anselm saying? He is saying that it is possible for us to distinguish in thought between (a) a being that exists only in our concept and (b) a being that exists in our concept and in reality; he is also stating that a being of the latter sort is greater than a being of the former sort. Let us consider this matter very carefully.

Two important questions must be asked: Can we make the distinction St. Anselm says we can make? and, Is it self-evidently true that a being existing in reality is on that ground alone greater than a being existing only in concept?

As to the first, it seems evident that in some cases, at least, we have no difficulty in making the distinction that St. Anselm asks us to make. We can distinguish without difficulty, for example, between an imaginary dog and a real dog; and the proof that we are making a distinction between the two is that we have certain expectations in connection with the one that we do not have in connection with the other. I am thinking at this moment, for example, of a particular Dalmatian. I expect to see him occasionally as I drive by the yard where he usually is kept, I expect to observe him playing with the neighborhood children, and so on. But I can also form the concept of a dog identical with him in every respect save one: this dog exists only in my concept, not in reality. This dog, I know, will never be lying in the yard as I drive by, will never play with the neighborhood children, will never chase my car—unless, of course, I provide some *imaginary* children and cars for him to frolic with. I do not have the same expectations with respect to the latter that I have with respect to the former; and the reason is that I can and do distinguish between real and merely conceptual existents. If Kant's oft-quoted statement that "existence is not a predicate" [3] means, as it is usually supposed to mean, that it is not possible for us to make this distinction, then I think we must conclude that on this point Kant was simply mistaken. We can, and do, make the distinction that St. Anselm is asking us to make.

Is it self-evidently true, then, that a being existing in reality is on that ground alone greater (more perfect) than an otherwise identical being existing only in concept? Here, it seems to me, we must choose among three alternatives: either (a) whatever order of excellence may be attributed to a thing in concept, some additional excellence accrues to that thing if, in addition, it is conceived to exist in reality; or (b) whatever order of excellence may be attributed to a thing in concept, that excellence is totally unaffected if, in addition, it is conceived to exist in reality; or (c) whatever order of excellence may be attributed to a thing in concept, that excellence is diminished if, in addition, it is conceived to exist in reality. I know of no way to *prove* that the first of these alternatives is to be preferred to the other two. For myself, however, I have no doubt that St. Anselm's assumption on this point is correct, and I should think that the burden of proof must lie with those who would adopt either of the other two alternatives.

If St. Anselm is to be contradicted at this point, therefore, it must not be on the ground that it is impossible in principle to make the sort of distinction he is asking us to make nor on the ground that real existence does not add to the excellence of whatever may be conceived, but on the ground that the distinction in question cannot be applied to one's thinking about God. It is at this point that a modern reader finds it difficult to go along with St. Anselm's reasoning. If we could make the distinction St. Anselm is asking us to make in our thinking about God, we should have little difficulty in proceeding with St. Anselm to affirm Propositions 4 and 5. But most of us have great difficulty in applying the distinction in the present case. Why?

---

[3] Immanuel Kant, *Critique of Pure Reason,* Norman Kemp Smith, trans. (New York: St. Martin's Press, 1965), pp. 500-507.

The reason, I suspect, is that we cannot, as St. Anselm (and many of his contemporaries) apparently could, attach a clear and precise meaning to the phrase, "a being than which none greater can be conceived." And the reason that we cannot do this is that we do not conduct our thinking within the context of a metaphysical system in which everything that exists is conceived to exist in some definite position in a vast and all-inclusive *hierarchy of being*. In this (Neo-Platonic and Augustinian) metaphysical system, which St. Anselm simply takes for granted, the phrase "a being than which none greater can be conceived" has a rich and reasonably clear meaning: it denotes that being that is "at the top" of the hierarchy, that being that (in contrast to everything else that exists) is in no way deficient in being, that being that possesses every conceivable excellence, that being that is everything that it is better to be than not to be. St. Anselm writes:

> What art thou, then, Lord God . . . except that which, as the highest of all beings, alone exists through itself, and creates all other things from nothing? For whatever is not this is less than a thing which can be conceived of. But this cannot be conceived of thee. What good, therefore, does the supreme Good lack, through which every good is? Therefore, thou art just, truthful, blessed, and whatever it is better to be than not to be.[4]

If we are correct in saying that the cogency of St. Anselm's argument depends upon a prior acceptance of the metaphysical system in the context of which that argument was formulated, a general truth of considerable importance emerges: an ontological argument for the existence of God, if it is to be successful, must be formulated in the context of the metaphysical system that prevails among those whom one is attempting to persuade. Implicit in any such argument is the contention that the reality of God is presupposed in the fundamental categories of all thought and experience; to deny the reality of God is to deny the validity of these categories and thus to call in question the validity of all knowledge and the structure of all experience. If the fundamental categories of all thought

---

[4] St. Anselm, *op. cit.*, pp. 10-11.

and experience (the metaphysical beliefs, in other words) that prevail in any given age cannot be shown to imply the reality of God, an ontological proof in the conceptual vocabulary of that day is not possible; if they can, it is. A crucial question facing the philosopher who is interested in the problem of the existence of God (rather than in ancient history) is: Do the fundamental categories of thought and experience that prevail in *our* day imply the reality of God? Can the task which Anselm performed so brilliantly in the eleventh century be performed *today,* in the metaphysical categories of the twentieth century? I propose to argue that it can.

The Ontological Argument: A Reformulation

The twentieth century, unlike the eleventh century, lacks an explicit "metaphysical consensus" in the context of which a philosopher who desires to articulate a modern version of the ontological argument might carry out his project with some degree of confidence. The metaphysical presuppositions that inform modern culture are implicit rather than explicit—implicit particularly, one must suppose, in the scientific method of inquiry, which is so uniquely characteristic of the modern era. A truly adequate modern version of the ontological argument must presumably await the explicit formulation of a metaphysical system which is widely recognized as descriptive of the fundamental presuppositions that inform this scientific age.

It seems clear, however, that implicit in the scientific method are at least two assumptions of considerable importance for our purposes—namely (a) there is a real world that science is attempting to describe and (b) the ideal goal of scientific inquiry is to achieve a description of this world that is objectively *true.* Taking these assertions as clues to the metaphysical presuppositions of our age, we offer the following as a first and very tentative approximation to a modern version of the ontological argument:

Proposition 1: By the term "God" is meant the ground of being and value.

Proposition 2: Whether one affirms or denies the reality of God, one presupposes that there is some reality that is capable of a true description and that either the statement "God exists" or the statement "God does not exist" is objectively true.

Proposition 3: The very denial of the reality of God, therefore, presupposes the objective reality of being and of truth, and therewith also the ground of both.

Proposition 4: Therefore, the statement, "God does not exist," is self-contradictory.

Proposition 5: Therefore, God exists.

I have little doubt that this formulation is capable of vast improvement, and that such improvement will be forthcoming if and when the metaphysical presuppositions of the modern age are identified and adequately described. Then it will become apparent to many, as it is today to very few, that to deny the reality of God is indeed to utter a self-contradictory statement. Pending such a formulation, we must make shift with poor approximations. The formulation offered here claims to be no more than that.

Study Questions

1. The author of this chapter seems to be rather pessimistic about the prospects for convincing many of his readers of the soundness of his (or any other) argument for the existence of God. Why? What factors in our culture does he cite as obstacles that an advocate of any such argument must try to overcome?
2. Does the "restatement" offered here accurately reproduce St. Anselm's argument? If not, how should it be revised in order to do so?
3. We are advised in this chapter that we ought to accept the first two premises of St. Anselm's argument without question. Do you agree? Defend your answer.
4. What difficulty does the writer of this chapter locate in the third premise of St. Anselm's argument? Do you agree with him on this? Are you satisfied with his solution of the other difficulties that he mentions in connection with this premise?
5. What "general truth of considerable importance" does our author draw from his analysis of St. Anselm's argument?
6. Evaluate the "reformulation" of the ontological argument premise by premise. Do you find it at all persuasive?

Chapter 43

THE COSMOLOGICAL ARGUMENT

ANYONE WHO HAS involved himself at all seriously in the discussion of the problem of the existence of God—or, more specifically, the problem of assessing the cogency of the several arguments for the existence of God that have been put forward—is painfully aware that the present-day advocate of any such argument must somehow try to overcome a number of serious obstacles. Chief among these are the following: (a) the apparently inescapable vagueness of the concept "God," (b) the anti-metaphysical bias of modern thought, and, as a corollary, (c) the absence of a vocabulary acceptable to the modern mind that is suitable for the construction of a proof of the existence of God. I am not sanguine about the prospects for overcoming these obstacles in what follows; but I do think the existence of God is capable of strict demonstration, and I shall do my best to state my proof in a form which will not require a modern reader to stretch his ordinary categories of thought too far.

It is not surprising that the concept of God is less precise than most of the concepts that we customarily employ; for most of our concepts are of objects that exist in space and time—objects concerning which it is appropriate to ask questions like: "Where is it?" "How big is it?" "What color is it?" and so on. If the concept of God were to be given that kind of precision, we would no longer be talking about *God* at all; for whatever we do mean by "God," it is clear that we do not mean "one object (or being) among others in the world of space and time."

The question concerning the existence of God is, therefore, a unique question. It would be silly to try to prove the existence of a spatio-temporal object. The existence of any such object is a purely contingent fact: to convince anyone of the existence of any such object you must produce not an argument but *the object itself.* Only if it presents itself in some way to some one of our senses are we willing to say that it "exists." And rightly so.

But God cannot be presented to any one of our senses in such a way that we can know of His existence in the same way that we know of the existence of spatio-temporal objects. If we are to know of the existence of God, therefore, it must—in this one, unique case—be by way of argument, or demonstration. The question we must ask is this: Is there any feature of the world of space and time that points to a reality that *transcends* space and time, a reality that is the ground of the being and value of this world and that is worthy of man's worship? To answer this question in the affirmative is to construct (or at least to affirm that it is possible to construct) a cosmological argument for the existence of God.

St. Thomas Aquinas

"The existence of God," said St. Thomas Aquinas," can be proved in five ways." [1] Thereupon, in a scant three pages, the great Angelic Doctor gave to the world five of the most famous arguments for the existence of God that have ever been formulated.

None of the "five ways" is original with St. Thomas (nor, of course, did he claim that they were), and they are not equally persuasive. The first three "ways," in particular, are very similar, and all three differ markedly from both the fourth and the fifth arguments. There are some reasons for regarding the third "way" as the fundamental, or centrally important, one of Aquinas' five arguments. The complete text of this argument reads as follows:

---

[1] St. Thomas Aquinas, *Summa Theologica,* Part 1, Question 2, Article 3, Anton C. Pegis, ed., *Basic Writings of St. Thomas Aquinas* (New York: Random House, 1945), Vol. I, p. 22.

The third way is taken from possibility and necessity, and runs thus. We find in nature things that are possible to be or not to be, since they are found to be generated, and to be corrupted, and consequently, it is possible for them to be and not to be. But it is impossible for these always to exist, for that which can not-be at some time is not. Therefore, if anything can not-be, then at one time there was nothing in existence. Now if this were true, even now there would be nothing in existence, because that which does not exist begins to exist only through something already existing. Therefore, if at one time nothing was in existence, it would have been impossible for anything to have begun to exist; and thus even now nothing would be in existence—which is absurd. Therefore, not all beings are merely possible, but there must exist something the existence of which is necessary. [But every necessary thing either has its necessity caused by another, or not. Now it is impossible to go on to infinity in necessary things which have their necessity caused by another, as has already been proved in regard to efficient causes. Therefore we cannot but admit the existence of some being having of itself its own necessity, and not receiving it from another, but rather causing in others their necessity.] This all men speak of as God.[2]

Although I hold this to be a sound argument, I do think it suffers from one serious defect. It is more complicated than it needs to be because of Aquinas' inclusion of a multiplicity of "necessary things which have their necessity caused by another." It may have been necessary to include this for polemical reasons at the time that St. Thomas was writing, but to a modern reader it appears as excess baggage that serves only to clutter up the argument. Nothing essential to the argument is lost, I think, if one simply omits this reference to a series of hypothetical "necessary beings" (everything within the brackets above), and concludes directly from the existence of "beings [that] are merely possible" to the existence of "something the existence of which is necessary . . . [which] all men speak of as God."

---

[2] *Ibid.,* pp. 22-23. The brackets will be explained in the following paragraphs.

Both defenders and critics of this argument sometimes assert that the starting point of the argument is a fairly obvious feature of the world, namely that something exists. I think that this assertion is incorrect and that it indicates a serious misunderstanding of the argument. The starting point of the argument is not that something exists (that *is* obvious) but that some *contingent beings* exist—and that is not obvious at all. It is precisely at this point that one determines whether or not one is going to go along with Aquinas' argument; either one shares his insight into *the contingency of finite beings,* or one remains unconvinced by his argument.

Two Common Criticisms

It will be convenient to deal at this point with two criticisms which are frequently made of this argument.

The words "necessary" and "contingent," it is sometimes said, are words that apply not to *things* but to *propositions.* To speak of God as a "necessary being," or "something the existence of which is necessary," must mean (if it means anything at all), "The proposition 'God exists' is a necessary proposition." But this is precisely the claim of the ontological argument. Therefore, the cosmological argument reduces ultimately to the ontological argument, and if the ontological argument is not sound, then neither, obviously, is the cosmological.

It is easy to show, however, that this is a superficial criticism. It is superficial because it starts with purely arbitrary definitions of the terms "necessary" and "contingent," and it then attempts to employ these definitions to make St. Thomas—or anyone else who advocates this form of the cosmological argument—say something he clearly and definitely did not say, and did not mean to say. Let it be granted that in logic the terms "necessary" and "contingent" apply only to propositions (i. e., not to terms or to arguments). In logic, a necessary proposition is one the negation of which involves a self-contradiction; a contingent proposition is one the negation of which does *not* involve a self-contradiction. Does this exclude the possibility that *outside* the realm of logic—in metaphysics, for example—these same terms may have a somewhat different meaning? Of course not.

The cosmological argument, in whatever form, always moves from the *ontological contingency* of finite being to the *ontological necessity* of the ground of being. St. Thomas does not, in the argument quoted above, use the term "contingent"; he speaks instead about "things that are possible to be or not to be." But that is precisely what "ontological contingency" means.

A second very common—and, in my view, mistaken—objection to Aquinas' argument concerns his claim that "It is impossible to go on to infinity," to which appeal is made in each of the first three ways. "Why can you not go on to infinity?" some critics have asked. "Mathematicians regularly employ the notion of an infinite series. Why should we regard it as self-evident that a series of 'contingent beings' or of 'causes' cannot proceed to infinity?"

This objection, like the first, rests on a misunderstanding of the cosmological argument. Aquinas' point is not that this being—a man, let us say—is dependent on his parents for his existence, and they on their parents, and they on theirs, and so on—all the way back to God. The cosmological argument has nothing to do with the relation between parents and children: it has to do with the present ontological contingency of some being and its present dependence for its existence on some non-contingent ground. The possibility of an infinite mathematical series is, therefore, totally irrelevant to the argument.

That the cosmological argument has nothing to do with this story of one generation succeeding another may also be seen in this, that the argument construed in that way could at best prove that *at some time in the past* there was a remote ancestor of this presently existing contingent being who, if you wish, you may call "God." It is not the purpose of the cosmological argument to prove the present existence of somebody's great-great-great-great . . . grandfather. Therefore, it should be evident that to construe the argument in this way is to *mis*construe it, indeed to render it altogether ludicrous.

I have dwelt briefly on these two objections to the cosmological argument for two reasons: first, because they are commonly accepted as sound objections to the argument and for that reason seem to require some answer; second, because they reveal some of the most common misunderstandings of the cosmological argument. The discussion of them, therefore, affords an opportunity to point out and attempt to remove these misunderstandings. I may, of course, be wrong in my view that the cosmological argument is a sound and convincing proof of the existence of God, but I surely cannot be wrong in insisting that any opinion with respect to this argument should be based on a serious effort to understand the argument as it is understood and intended by those who support it.

A Restatement

By way of exhibiting even more clearly the truly persuasive character of the cosmological argument, I should like to offer a restatement of the argument in what I take to be its simplest possible form. The argument can, I think, be reduced to just two premises and a conclusion. I propose to state it in this way and to indicate the grounds on which each of the premises rests; I should then hope that some of my readers might find it possible to join me in affirming the conclusion.

The cosmologial argument, reduced to its simplest possible form, may be stated as follows:

Some contingent beings exists.
Contingent beings require a non-contingent ground of being in order to exist.

A non-contingent ground of being exists.

The crucial step in this argument, as I have already indicated, is the first premise. In assessing this argument the question that must be asked is: *On what basis* is it affirmed that "some contingent beings exist"?

The answer that must be given will, I fear, be disappointing to many. The ontological contingency of finite beings must be grasped directly; it cannot be demonstrated on the basis of some other more evident truths. I know only too well that the notion of "rational insight" is distinctly out of favor at present; but if we do not have such direct insight into the ontological contingency of finite things, we cannot know it at all.

Though this truth cannot be demonstrated, it may be possible to suggest a few things that will, so to speak, help to "elicit the insight." St. Thomas does this, for example, when he calls attention to the fact that things in nature are subject to "generation and corruption"—i. e., they come into being and pass away. "My days," says the psalmist, "are like a shadow that declineth, and I am withered like grass." [3] The coming-into-being and the passing-away of individuals is, of course, a fact that can be observed. This fact can, and often does, give rise to the feeling of the transiency of all things, of the tenuous and precarious character of finite existence. From here it is but a step to the rational insight into the ontological contingency of finite being upon which the cosmological argument rests.

Or we may take a slightly different approach. At the present moment you are, of course, existing. If you are like most people, you probably take your existence for granted: you ask, concerning the future (tomorrow, for example), not "Will I *be?*" but "What will I be *doing?*" But in all seriousness, can you simply take your own existence for granted? Is not existence rather a gift received anew moment by moment? Is it not conceivable that in the next moment we, and our world, should be utterly annihilated, that we should simply cease to exist—in short, that the gift of existence should be withdrawn, and that in our place there should be . . . nothing? To ponder our own existence in this way is to feel the uncertainty, the precariousness, the gratuitousness of all finite existence, including our own. To conceptualize this feeling is to grasp the ontological contingency of finite being, the rational insight with which the cosmological argument begins.

The second premise of the argument—that contingent beings require (i. e., presuppose) a non-contingent ground of being in order to exist—is analytically true. To say that something is "contingent" is to say that it is "ontologically dependent": it is to affirm a relation and therefore implicitly to posit that to which the relation refers. If we understand what we have said when we have affirmed the contingency of finite being, there is no difficulty in affirming this second premise. Its function is simply to spell out what is implied

---

[3] Psalms, 102:11.

in the initial insight into the contingency of finite being, and this in such a way as to make it evident that this insight does indeed imply the existence of God.

The Object of Worship

Although in my discussion thus far I have had in mind chiefly those critics of the cosmological argument who think it tries to prove too much (i. e., that God exists), I am not unaware that there is another group of critics who object to the argument on the ground that it proves too little. One could well imagine a deeply religious person responding to the cosmological argument with profound indignation on the ground that the "ground of being" who appears at the conclusion of the argument—this "God of the philosophers," as Pascal said—bears little or no resemblance to the loving Heavenly Father of living religious faith. "Away with these abstractions!" is the battle cry of such well-meaning people. What is to be said in answer to such an objection?

Part of the answer—and the only answer I shall attempt to give—is that it is not the business of the philosopher to attempt to prove everything about God that is of importance for religious faith. Faith simply presupposes the reality of God and by means of a rich symbolism seeks to worship Him in a way that is worthy of Him. Faith lives in symbolism and in imagery, not primarily in concepts; this is why any *concept* of God—even those formulated by theologians—seems, from the point of view of faith, woefully inadequate.

But philosophers, *qua* philosophers, are not entitled to such a presupposition. For philosophy the question whether God exists is a legitimate and, indeed, inescapable question. I believe, as I have indicated, that we are entitled to answer this question in the affirmative. I believe, further, that the concept of God which emerges at the conclusion of the cosmological argument is capable of considerable enrichment, when the argument is applied to a wide variety of contingent existents (as St. Thomas does, for example, in the first three of his "five ways"). But the God whose existence is thus established, though surely worthy of man's worship, can never acquire by philosophical argument the rich (but profoundly anthropomorphic) connotations which religious faith ascribes to Him in poetry, prayer, and song. In comparison with the God of living faith, the God of the cosmological argument must appear highly abstract, austere, and remote. Philosophical argument cannot deal in imagery: it is limited to concepts, which it must strive to make as precise as it possibly can. Philosophical argument cannot disclose to us the richer reality that is the object of religious faith, but it can and does disclose to us the reality of God as the ground of the being of finite things. We must not expect of it more than this.

Study Questions

1. What is meant by the statement that the question concerning the existence of God is "a unique question"? Is it? What assumptions is one making if one holds that it is? if one holds that it is not?
2. Restate St. Thomas Aquinas' "third way" premise by premise, just as St. Anselm's argument was restated in the previous chapter.
3. What are the "two common criticisms" of the cosmological argument which our author attempts to refute? Does he succeed?
4. What is the difference between attempting to "prove a proposition" and attempting to "elicit an insight"? Why does the author of this chapter resort to the latter?
5. Who would be apt to criticize the cosmological argument on the ground that it proves too much? on the ground that it proves too little? What is your own opinion of the argument?

Chapter 44

THE TELEOLOGICAL ARGUMENT

LIKE THE TWO writers who are to succeed me in this discussion, I am not at all impressed with either the ontological argument or the cosmological argument for the existence of God. I have never been impressed with them in their "classical" formulations—those of St. Anselm and St. Thomas, respectively—and I am no more impressed with them in the so-called "contemporary reformulations" which the preceding two writers have offered. Both of these arguments are vulnerable to a really devastating and, I think, decisive critique, which I assume will be forthcoming in the chapters that follow. I shall be content, therefore, to simply state my rejection of these arguments, leaving the detailed criticism of them to others, and shall proceed directly to the formulation and defense of a third argument which in my estimation is far more persuasive.

The argument of which I speak is commonly called the "teleological" argument (from the Greek word *telos,* meaning "end" or "goal"). St. Thomas Aquinas' "fifth way" is a version of this argument, but the *locus classicus* of the argument is William Paley's *Evidences of the Existence and Attributes of the Deity.*[1] It is an argument that deserves to be studied with great care.

---

[1] William Paley, *Evidences of the Existence and Attributes of the Deity* (Boston, Mass.: Gould and Lincoln, 1852). Originally published in London in 1802, this work went through many editions in both England and the United States.

The Sense of Wonder

We shall be better prepared both to understand and to appreciate the teleological argument if we first consider briefly the kind of human experience out of which, or against the background of which, the argument has come to be formulated.

All but the most pedestrian and unpoetic of human beings must, at times, be impressed by the vastness, the grandeur, the beauty, and the order of the universe in which we find ourselves. There is a feeling of awe and wonder when one stands upon the shore of a stormy sea, or gazes upward on a starry night, or surveys the rugged beauty of a range of mountains. Here is power, restless and profound; here is vastness, staggering in magnitude; yet here is order, beautiful to behold.

Scientists in whom the sense of poetry is still alive tell us of a similar experience when they have penetrated some of the less obvious wonders of nature. To understand the structure of the atom is to marvel at its ordered complexity; to survey the course of evolution is to view a magnificent process unfolding through millennia of time; to grasp the genetic code is to possess a key by means of which yet further mysteries of nature may shortly be unlocked. Here, too, are wonders of the universe at which men may well marvel—and do. Here are phenomena capable of inspiring awe of which our ancient predecessors could not even dream; but the wonders they beheld—the starry sky, the mountains, and the sea—are ours as well. How very much there is, in the world as we perceive it, to inspire that sense of awe of which we have been speaking.

It seems very natural, when some feature or other of the universe impresses us in this way, to say that it could not be by chance or accident that the universe is the way it is. A beautiful poem, a great symphony, a particularly inspiring work of architecture, a remarkable engineering achievement—these are impressive and rightly cause us to give honor to those whose efforts brought them into being. But more wonderful still is the poetry, the harmony, the power, the beauty, the architecture, the structure of the universe itself. Surely it, too, has an Author, an Architect, a magnificent Craftsman, whose wisdom and power are commensurate with the mighty work which He has wrought. Every person living, at some time in his life—when these remarkable features of the universe were impressed upon him in some particularly overwhelming way —must have entertained sentiments such as these.

The Argument

It is against this background that we must try to understand and to appreciate the teleological argument, for the teleological argument is simply an attempt to extract, and to render conceptually precise, the argument that is implicit in the natural reflections to which this experience of wonder gives rise.

William Paley's formulation of the argument in *Evidences of the Existence and Attributes of the Deity* does not, unfortunately, lend itself to a brief summary statement. The argument, as he says, is cumulative; his whole book is the argument. I shall try to indicate the general course of his argument, however.

Paley begins by noting that whenever we come upon something of which it is apparent that "its several parts are framed and put together for a purpose"—a watch, for example—we conclude without hesitation that it has been designed for this purpose by some intelligent designer. Nothing that we may subsequently learn about the watch (for example, that it sometimes fails to work perfectly, or that it is capable of reproducing itself, or anything else) could ever dissuade us from believing that it (or, if it be the product of a "parent" watch, its most remote ancestor) is the product of an intelligent and skillful designer. Paley states:

There cannot be design without a designer; contrivance, without a contriver; order, without choice; arrangement, without anything capable of arranging; subserviency and relation to a purpose, without that which could intend a purpose; means suitable to an end, and executing their office in accomplishing that end, without the end ever having been contemplated, or the means accommodated to it. Arrangement, disposition of parts, subserviency of means to an end, relation of instruments to a use, imply the presence of intelligence and mind.[2]

---

[2] *Ibid.*, p. 10.

So much for the first part of Paley's argument. The second part of Paley's argument is to show that the universe abounds with phenomena which, like the watch, exhibit teleological order.

> Every indication of contrivance, every manifestation of design, which existed in the watch, exists in the works of nature; with the difference, on the side of nature, of being greater and more, and that in a degree which exceeds all computation. . . . The contrivances of nature surpass the contrivances of art, in the complexity, subtlety, and curiosity of the mechanism; and still more, if possible, do they go beyond them in number and variety: yet, in a multitude of cases, are not less evidently mechanical, not less evidently contrivances, not less evidently accommodated to their end, or suited to their office, than are the most perfect productions of human ingenuity.[3]

Paley's favorite example of design in nature is the eye, whose delicate and intricate mechanism he discusses in great detail. But countless other examples are to be found in nature.

The conclusion, Paley suggests, must therefore be drawn: design in nature points to the existence of an intelligent Designer of nature, just as design in a watch or other machine points to the existence of a designer thereof.

> Were there no example in the world of contrivance except that of the eye, it would be alone sufficient to support the conclusion which we draw from it, as to the necessity of an intelligent Creator. It could never be got rid of because it could not be accounted for by any other supposition, which did not contradict all the principles we possess of knowledge. . . .[4]

This, I am convinced, is a sound and convincing argument. I propose to reduce the argument to its barest essentials and to add a few comments by way of elucidating its fundamental structure.

---

[3] *Ibid.*, p. 13.
[4] *Ibid.*, p. 44.

Elucidation and Defense of the Argument

The teleological argument contains two premises, one straightforwardly factual and the other a general principle. The factual premise is: nature exhibits a number of instances of means ordered to ends. The general principle is: the ordering of means to ends presupposes the existence of an intelligent designer whose intelligence and power are sufficient to account for the product he has wrought. The whole argument, therefore, is as follows:

Nature exhibits a number of instances of means ordered to ends.
The ordering of means to ends presupposes the existence of an intelligent designer whose intelligence and power are sufficient to account for the product he has wrought.

The ordering of means to ends in nature presupposes the existence of an intelligent designer whose intelligence and power are commensurate with the magnitude of his product.

It is important to note, in attempting to assess this argument, that it does not say, or presuppose, that the whole universe is cooperating to achieve some single ultimate purpose. This may or may not be the case: the argument is neutral with respect to this question. Some critics of the teleological argument have unfortunately failed to grasp this point.

It should also be observed that the argument does not say, or presuppose, that the several "ends" toward which the various means are ordered are necessarily good, or such as human beings would always approve of, or such as tend to serve our needs. The ferocity of the tiger, for example, and the various endowments that make it such a dangerous animal, serve the end of *its own* self-preservation—sometimes, at man's expense. This is an "end" in the sense in which that term is used in this argument, human preferences in the matter notwithstanding. Numerous other examples could be given.

The factual premise in this argument seems to me to be simply beyond dispute. The evidence is all about us, and it is overwhelming. Animals have eyes in order to see, ears in order to hear, teeth in order to chew their food, digestive organs in order to utilize their food, lungs in order to breathe, and so on. In the plant world, too, we observe the adaptation of means to ends: root systems in order to draw nourishment from the soil, leaves in order to derive the benefits of the sunlight, and so on. Look where we will, the evidence is the same: every species of living thing known to us, every plant, every insect, every fish, every mammal, is endowed with those characteristics necessary to its existence and way of life.

We know, of course—as Paley did not—that this remarkable state of affairs has come about through a long process of evolution whereby the forms of life now found in nature have developed from other forms no longer extant. But this alters the argument not at all. Consider this process at any point you will: the sort of evidence we are now considering will abound in whatever state of the universe exists at that time. However far we press our inquiry into the remote past, we find not chaos but order: means subservient to ends; processes conducive to the emergence of life; circumstances conducive to the proliferation of life; powers adapted to the preservation of life. So much for the factual premise.

The second premise—that the ordering of means to ends presupposes the existence of some intelligent designer to "do the ordering"—is an inductive generalization well substantiated by experience. It is beyond dispute that in every such instance of which we have any reasonably certain knowledge, the principle holds true: we know of no watches without watchmakers, ships without shipbuilders, or planes without plane-builders. We would never allow, if we were to be shown one of these objects, that without the intelligent direction of any mind whatsoever the object in question (a watch, a ship, a plane, etc.) just "happened to happen." Where we find *means ordered to ends,* "chance" is as good as no answer at all; for in every such instance of which we do have knowledge, we find mind—intelligence—behind it. Every day we observe countless examples of this principle; we have never observed, or been offered, a counter-example. The principle would seem to be as secure, therefore, as it is possible for any inductive generalization to be.

If, then, the argument is to be attacked, it must be on the ground that the order which we find in nature is not sufficiently similar to the order which we find in human contrivances to justify applying the principle thereto. David Hume, for one, saw this clearly, and in his *Dialogues Concerning Natural Religion* (published posthumously in 1779) exercised, as he says, "all [his] sceptical and metaphysical subtilty" in an attempt to weaken the analogy. But after doing his best, or rather his worst, to find some alternative to intelligent design as a principle of explanation, even Hume is forced to conclude (in the words of Philo, his chief spokesman in the *Dialogues*):

> In many views of the universe and of its parts, particularly the latter, the beauty and fitness of final causes strike us with such irresistible force that all objections appear (what I believe they really are) mere cavils and sophisms; nor can we then imagine how it was ever possible for us to repose any weight on them.[5]

The order that we find in nature calls for some explanation. The analogy between it and the order that we find in contrivances known to be the product of intelligent purpose is infinitely stronger than any other analogy that anyone has been able to suggest. Against this objection, therefore, the teleological argument stands secure.

The Limits of Philosophical Argument

It is a mistake, extremely common in our day, to expect too little of philosophical argument; it is also a mistake, more common in the past, to expect too much.

The teleological argument by itself does not give us, and cannot be expected to give us, a rich, "full-blown theology," such as would satisfy the wishes of a religious community. For that is needed the images evoked and provided by religious literature, the sentiments that are nourished in various rites of worship, and the vocabulary and ideas that have life and meaning only in the context and the tradition of this or that worshiping community. Any philosophical attempt to "fill out" the concept of God in these essentially religious ways would be rightly resisted, both by philosophers and by non-philosophical adherents of religion.

The God whose existence is proved by the teleological argument

---

[5] David Hume, *Dialogues Concerning Natural Religion,* Norman Kemp Smith, ed. (New York: Social Sciences Publishers, 1948), 2nd ed., p. 202.

is not the Brahman of Hindu faith, the Yahweh of Jewish faith, or the Heavenly Father of Christian faith. The God of the teleological argument, strictly speaking, is simply an unknown Mind and Power, by virtue of whose workings we find order in the world about us. About this austere notion cluster the sentiments of awe and wonder at the marvels of nature—the natural precursors, perhaps, of that "sense of the holy" that is so distinctive of religious communities. Perhaps, too, the awareness of the beauty of nature and of the greatness of the privilege of being alive leads to some intimation of the goodness of God, so that He is conceived not only as Mind and Power, but also as Goodness. But beyond this—beyond the bare knowledge of God's existence, and the faint intimation of some few of His attributes—philosophical reflection on the awesome spectacle of order in nature cannot take us.

But—and this is, of course, the chief burden of this essay—it can take us this far. Having come this far, we may or may not turn to religion to enrich our concept yet farther: that is another matter altogether. Philosophy is not theology, and philosophical understanding is not religious faith; but the understanding that philosophy can give us, limited though it is, may—if we are so inclined—serve as a foundation for faith.

Study Questions

1. What relevance, if any, does the discussion of "the sense of wonder" have for the subsequent discussion of the teleological argument?
2. Look up St. Thomas Aquinas' "fifth way" (*Summa Theologica*, Part I, Question 2, Article 3), and compare it with the argument given in this chapter. What similarities do you find between the two arguments? What differences?
3. How does one go about identifying an instance in nature of "means ordered to ends"? What right have we to say, for example, that the "end" served by the ferocity of the tiger is the self-preservation of the tiger rather than the death of its prey? Is some criterion at work here that has not been made explicit?
4. Is the analogy between "order in nature" and "order in human contrivances" sufficiently close to support the second premise of the teleological argument? How important is this alleged analogy to the argument?

Chapter 45

THE NON-EXISTENCE OF GOD:
A NATURALISTIC REJOINDER

IT IS A fundamental tenet of philosophical naturalism that the whole of reality consists of objects and events occurring in space and time and that the system of spatio-temporal events that we call the "world" is self-dependent and self-operating. It is an obvious negative corollary of this view that there is nothing real that transcends this world—no gods, no values, no anything. To say that something "exists" is to say that it is, or is reducible to, some spatio-temporal event or events—events, moreover, that we can perceive, or could perceive under such-and-such circumstances, or (at a minumum) that are causally related to events of this kind. It makes sense to say that grasshoppers exist, because we can see them. It makes sense to say that mountains exist on the far side of the moon, because we know what it would be like to see them. It makes sense to say that electrons exist, because the event that we call the existence of an electron is causally related to other events that we perceive. It does not make sense, in any of these ways, to say that God exists.

But no sooner do we naturalists point out that the statement "God exists" is, at best, exceedingly odd (and at worst meaningless), than theists turn this very observation against us. "Quite so," they say, "but the reason is that the existence of God is a unique instance. Grasshoppers, mountains, and electrons exist only *contingently,* but God's existence—and this is the only one of its kind —is *necessary.* That is why the statement 'God exists' strikes us as being so odd." On this whole question of the existence of God I would like to make just one assertion and then be done with it: the statement "God exists" has no clear meaning; it is as senseless to deny it as it is to affirm it. But in view of the rejoinder ("This is a unique case") we have no choice but to go over the worn-out old arguments once again and show why they do not establish the proposition "God exists" in any meaningful acceptance of those terms. This will be, then, a *disproof of the proofs* for the existence of God.

The Ontological Argument

There is one very strong *prima facie* reason for doubting the soundness of the ontological argument and that is that practically everybody who has studied it carefully has in the end rejected it. St. Anselm, of course, who invented the argument, believed it to be sound; so also did Descartes and Leibniz. But Gaunilon in the eleventh century, St. Thomas in the thirteenth, Hume and Kant in the eighteenth, and nearly every major philosopher since then, has rejected it. If one can decide on the soundness of an argument on the basis of the consensus of those who are most competent to judge, the ontological argument must be adjudged a failure.

The critics of the ontological argument have rejected it principally for three reasons, all of which I consider valid.

First, if the reasoning contained in the ontological argument were sound, it should be applicable in other instances as well— namely, to the superlative instance of any positive quality. It should be possible, then, to prove (by a parallel argument) the existence of an island than which none more beautiful can be conceived (this was Gaunilon's example), a mountain than which none taller can be conceived, and so on. But this is clearly absurd. It seems evident, therefore, that something is wrong with the argument.

We begin to understand just what is wrong with it when we consider, in the second place, that it really is not the case that when anyone either affirms or denies the existence of God, a being than which none greater can be conceived "exists in the understanding." Let it be granted that we can utter the *words,* "a being than which none greater can be conceived"; but we have no *concept* of a being so described. St. Anselm's statement that, whether one affirms or denies the existence of God, a being than which none greater can be conceived "exists in the understanding," is an exceedingly odd statement; but if it means anything at all it must mean that he who affirms or denies the existence of God has a *concept* of a being than which none greater can be conceived. And this, I am saying, is highly questionable; indeed, I think it is false.

The third reason for rejecting the argument is the most decisive. Existence, as Kant said, is not a predicate. To assert that something is *red,* for example, is to make an assertion that requires us to alter our concept of that thing; "red," therefore, is a predicate. But the assertion that something *exists* in no way modifies our concept of that thing. The ontological argument hinges on an alleged contrast (Proposition 3 of the summary, see p. 396) between (a) a being existing only in the understanding and (b) an otherwise identical being existing both in the understanding and in reality. But this is a contrast, a distinction in thought, that it is not possible for us to make. Our *concept* of a real Dalmatian differs in no way from our *concept* of an imaginary one. The difference between the two does not consist in anything found in the concepts themselves but rather in the different ways in which the two concepts are related to our (actual or possible) perceptions. Hence, even if it were possible to form a concept of a being than which none greater can be conceived (and I have questioned this), it still would not be possible to conclude to the existence of God; for the crucial distinction upon which the whole argument turns is one that it is not possible to make.

The attempted reformulation of the ontological argument quite obviously does not succeed in overcoming these objections. If it is impossible to form a clear concept of "a being than which none greater can be conceived," it is equally impossible to form a clear concept of "the ground of being and value." Indeed, whatever plausibility the argument has depends entirely, I think, on its ambiguity. If you remove that, what remains is totally unconvincing. The presuppositions referred to in Proposition 2, for example, could only be (a) there is a physical world and (b) the world is capable of scientific description. We may grant that the statement

"God does not exist" makes these suppositions, but surely in making these suppositions we are not also presupposing "the ground of both," whatever that may mean. Hence, it does not follow that the statement, "God does not exist," is self-contradictory, nor does it follow that God exists. You cannot establish real existence by manipulating concepts, even if your concepts are extremely vague.

The Cosmological Argument

There are many forms of the cosmological argument, and it would be a tedious job to pass them all in review and criticize each in detail. In Chapter 43 the cosmological argument has been presented in the form which most contemporary supporters of the argument regard as its most persuasive form, and I shall restrict my remarks to this version. Anyone who understands what is wrong with the argument in this form will have no difficulty in detecting the weaknesses in any other form of the argument that he may happen to encounter.

The cosmological argument as stated, in any case, suffers from three very serious defects.

Let us begin at the beginning: the first premise ("Some contingent beings exist") is either unintelligible, or it is a truism. If it is unintelligible, it is not deserving of serious consideration. If it is a truism, nothing of importance follows.

I am at this moment looking at an ash tray. That, presumably, is one of the "contingent beings" that this premise says exists. Very well: what does it mean to say that this ash tray is "contingent"? I can think of three possibilities. It may mean that (a) there was a time when this ash tray did not exist, and now it does: it has "come into being" and will, presumably, some day cease to exist. Or it may mean that (b) the non-existence of this ash tray is conceivable. Or it may mean that (c) the continuation in existence of this ash tray is dependent on certain things without which it would cease to exist. If *a*, nothing of importance follows. You may, if you wish, argue to the existence at some time in the past of an ash-tray maker, but this is quite obviously beside the point. If *b*, again nothing of importance follows. One can conceive of the non-existence of anything simply by thinking of it as occupying space and then imagining that space to be empty. If *c* is meant, the situation is a little more complicated, but the result is the same. It is apparent, for example, that the continued existence of this ash tray depends on the continued validity of certain laws of physics—the cohesion of its parts, its tolerance of the temperature levels to which it is subjected, and so on. But this does not take us any distance at all toward establishing the proposition, "God exists."

If the proposition, "Some contingent beings exist," does not mean one of these three things, however, then I can only insist that I find it simply unintelligible. If there is something else that I am supposed to "see directly," I can only confess that I do not see it. And until the defenders of the cosmological argument tell us plainly and explicitly what they mean by the statement, I think we are justified in suspecting that they do not see it either. Either they mean one or more of the three things suggested above, or they mean nothing at all.

Let us, however, be as charitable as we can. Let us suppose that the supporters of this argument do mean something when they assert that "Some contingent beings exist." What might they mean? Option *c* would seem to be their most promising choice. "Something of significance does follow from this," they might insist, "for you cannot be satisfied with an infinite regress. If something *Z* (the ash tray, for example) is dependent on something else *Y* for its continued existence, then you can ask the same question about *Y*. Is it contingent or not? Eventually you must come to a *non*-contingent cause, and this is what we mean by God."

It is certainly evident that there is something phony about this argument from ash trays to physics to God. What is it? Just this: we know that by means of physical laws you can only reason to other physical laws or to some spatio-temporal event or events. Physical laws are passports that enable us to move from one range of phenomena to another range of phenomena *in the natural world*. They do not give us an exit visa to pass outside spatio-temporal reality. Moreover, what is wrong with a series of contingent causes, even an *infinite* series of contingent causes? In this case every member of the series is contingent in the sense defined above, and there is no first member. Is this any harder to conceive of than an infinite mathematical series, or infinite space?

Finally, the conclusion of the argument is so ambiguous that it seems quite impossible to either affirm it or deny it—impossible because it is totally unclear what one would be affirming or denying. How can anyone either affirm or deny that "a non-contingent ground of being exists"? What concrete difference would it make in your experience or mine whether this statement (if it is a statement) is true or false? None whatsoever. It is a meaningless combination of ponderous words, designed to intimidate rather than to elucidate. But one thing is clear: whatever these words are supposed to mean, the premises that precede them do not establish the existence of God. We may not like it, but it happens to be the case that this world and its laws are the only "reality" there is. Any attempt to reason from this or that feature of the world to some reality not of the world is sheer fantasy.

The Teleological Argument

The third, and by far the weakest, of the traditional arguments for the existence of God—though, oddly enough, it is popularly regarded as one of the most persuasive—is the teleological argument. Since the defects of the argument have only to be pointed out to be seen, I shall restrict myself to a very summary statement of them.

The statement that "Nature exhibits a number of instances of means ordered to ends" is subtly ambiguous. What nature exhibits is a high degree of *lawlike regularity*. If this is all that is meant by "means ordered to ends," all well and good; but one suspects that more than this is intended. The language suggests "purposiveness," or "ordering," and thus subtly suggests *in an allegedly factual premise* that we ought to look for a "purposer," or "orderer." We seem to have here, therefore, a case of syllogistic smuggling.

Furthermore, the alleged analogy between the lawlike regularity that we find in nature (to substitute for the offending terms) and that which we find in human contrivances is notably weak. We do indeed posit a human intelligence whenever we encounter an implement that (a) serves some conceivable purpose and (b) is evidently not altogether a product of nature. But neither of these characteristics applies to the regularities that we find in nature—not even to those offered by the author of Chapter 44 as examples of the sort of thing which he has in mind. On what basis, then, are we supposed to see an analogy?

It is quite beside the point to argue that "The analogy between (order in nature) and the order that we find in contrivances known to be the product of intelligent purpose is infinitely stronger than any other analogy that anyone has been able to suggest" (Chapter 44). This may well be. I am no more impressed than was Hume, for example, by the suggestion that the universe could be likened to a giant plant or to a spider web rather than to a machine. But why should it be likened to anything at all? A human contrivance, after all, utilizes in some way or other certain laws of nature that man, by careful inquiry or by good luck, has discovered. May not these laws be themselves the ultimate facts to which appeal can be made, and may not the universe itself be the model of regularity in relation to which every other instance of regularity is only a pale analogy?

Moreover, even if the argument were sound, the being whose existence it establishes would be nothing more than a finitely wise, finitely powerful, amoral (if not malevolent) architect. The inventor of a machine does not create the materials with which he works: he only shapes them. Hence the "orderer" whose existence is supposedly established by this argument is only a craftsman, not a creator. The argument, if it is sound, requires only that this cosmic "orderer" be very wise and very powerful: hence, it does not establish the existence of an infinitely wise and powerful being. And the argument requires nothing at all in the way of goodness; indeed, since there is evil in the world which he is supposed to have designed, it may be assumed that he is something less than perfectly good; at best he must be considered amoral, at worst malevolent. This is hardly a description of God in any religiously meaningful sense of the term.

Finally, even if the argument did establish the existence of this strange being, it would establish only his past, not his present, existence. The existence of a watch implies only the existence of a watchmaker *at the time the watch was made:* it does not in any way assure me of his *present* existence. Similarly, if the existence of an ordered universe implied anything at all (which I doubt), it would be that once upon a time, long, long ago, there was a world-maker. He may since have died, or changed his occupation.

The teleological argument, therefore, is not a good argument. It derives its prestige entirely, I suspect, from the fact that it unites the "natural wonder" of which we heard in the last chapter with the apparently kindred feeling of "reverence" in a way that is satisfying to religious people. It may even be that the feeling of reverence arose originally out of this feeling of natural wonder. Be that as it may, however, it is perfectly evident that the belief in the existence of God did not come about because of the cogency of the teleological argument.

A Final Word

None of the arguments for the existence of God is able to withstand careful scrutiny. Why, then, do so many people believe that God exists? The answer can only be that this belief is irrational—an illusion (Sigmund Freud), a personification of society (Émile Durkheim), or something else. The persistence of this belief in spite of the demonstrable fallaciousness of the arguments used to support it suggests that it must answer to some very deep emotional need of many people, and it may, therefore, be thought cruel to show, as I have done, how weak those arguments are. However, it is evident that people who believe in God did not arrive at this belief by means of rational argument; it is unlikely, therefore, that the removal of the arguments will by itself destroy that belief. Perhaps there are people who need this particular illusion. If so, they will probably keep it—with or without intellectual props. Second, we have addressed ourselves to this problem only in the interest of knowing the truth. Are there or are there not rational grounds for believing in the existence of God? As a convinced naturalist, I hold that there are not. I think that this is the truth. If the truth is painful, that is hardly my fault. Things are the way they are, and the best we can do is to try to see them that way, not the way we might like them to be.

Study Questions

1. What objections does Naturalist bring against the ontological argument? Are they all sound objections, in your opinion? (Compare Naturalist's third objection with the partial defense of Proposition 3 in Chapter 42.)
2. What are Naturalist's objections to the cosmological argument? Do they apply with equal force to Aquinas' "third way" and to the shorter formulation offered in Chapter 43?
3. What are Naturalist's objections to the teleological argument? Do they apply with equal force to Paley's argument and to St. Thomas Aquinas' "fifth way"? Do you think Naturalist is right in calling this "by far the weakest" of the arguments for the existence of God?
4. Select whichever of the traditional arguments you consider to be the strongest and attempt to defend it against Naturalist's criticisms.

Chapter 46

THE FAILURE OF THE ARGUMENTS:
A SYMPATHETIC APPRAISAL

IN THE DEBATE about the existence of God there would seem to be only two plausible positions: either (a) there is some sound argument for the existence of God, and everybody ought accordingly to believe that God exists; or (b) there is no sound argument for the existence of God, and everyone ought, therefore, to hold that the existence of God is improbable or, at best, highly problematic. The absence of an argument proving that something exists does not, of course, prove that the thing in question does *not* exist. It must be admitted, however, that the burden of proof rests with those who make the affirmative claim. (For example: I cannot prove that there are not little two-headed green animals on the far side of the moon, but sanity seems to require that I assume that there are none unless, or until, some evidence is produced to indicate that there are.)

I find myself in disagreement with both positions and therefore, I fear, in a position that must, at first, seem highly repugnant to common sense. I hold, with the author of the last chapter, that there is no sound argument for the existence of God; but I also hold, with the authors of the previous three chapters, that God exists, and that His existence can be known by us. It is this position which I shall try to elucidate. It represents, I think, the only possible way in which the impasse between theists and naturalists concerning the problem of the existence of God can be overcome.

Arguments and Rational Grounds

One way of stating the position which I should like to defend is: there are no sound *arguments* for the existence of God, but there are, nonetheless, valid *rational grounds* for believing in His existence. Naturalists are right in rejecting the arguments for the existence of God but wrong in denying His reality; theists are right in affirming the reality of God but wrong in insisting that His reality is capable of proof.

Strictly speaking, it is not possible to *prove* the reality of anything. Reality manifests itself to us, or it does not; only in the former case is it possible for us to know it. One cannot even prove the reality of the physical world, as the futile discussions between realists and phenomenalists over this very question show. Solipsism is the only consistent alternative to a direct cognition of the reality of that which manifests itself to us as real.

Few philosophers who have addressed themselves to the realist-phenomenalist controversy have realized, I suspect, that their reflections concerning that problem are intimately related to the question of our knowledge of the reality of God. But they are. The root question, in both cases, is: How do we cognize *reality?* How do we get beyond perception and feeling to an awareness of the reality of that which (as we say, in a solipsistic mood) seems to lie behind them? Upon our answer to this question depends the solution to both the realist-phenomenalist controversy and the problem of the reality of God.

The chief difficulty in the way of achieving a satisfactory solution to these and a number of other related problems is the very limited (and limiting) concept of *reason* which prevails in our culture at the present time.

In the great classical tradition of Western philosophy—and I include all of the major figures from the Golden Age of Greek philosophy down to and including the German Idealists of the nineteenth century—reason was conceived as the structure of the conscious self by virtue of which one is able both to grasp and to shape reality. It is one and the same reason, according to this view, that seeks to know the truth, to love the good, and to appreciate the beautiful. Man, it is evident, relates to his world in a variety of ways, each qualitatively different from the others: he knows (cognition), he feels (emotion), he appreciates (aesthetics), he loves or hates (conation), he acts (practice). Reason, in the classical view, is the ground and locus of all of these; it expresses the unity of the self even as it acknowledges the multiplicity of its relations to the world roundabout.

In our culture, however, this concept of reason has been lost. Reason is conceived by most people today simply as man's capacity for *reasoning*. Its function is conceived to be purely cognitive, and all the other functions formerly assigned to reason are therefore judged to be "irrational." Feelings may be appropriate or inappropriate, but they cannot be rational; acts may be discreet or indiscreet, but they cannot be right or wrong (consistent with or contrary to right reason). Even in its cognitive function, the scope of reason's competence has been radically narrowed: to espouse a moral or aesthetic value is no longer to cognize something but simply to express a private taste. The whole business of reason is, in short, to attain scientific knowledge, and what is not scientific knowledge is not knowledge at all: it is, in other words, irrational.

If any culture were absolutely consistent in maintaining this view, the consequences would be truly appalling. The outstanding characteristics of such a culture would be an impressive degree of technical competence, i. e., an ability to do an enormous variety of things exceedingly well, and a complete lack of conviction as to whether any of these things are really worth doing. People in such a culture would be (as F. Scott Fitzgerald once said of himself) like a little boy alone in a big house, who now could do anything he wanted to do, and who suddenly discovered that there was nothing he wanted to do. The whole life of man, on such a view, must be made up of technical knowledge and totally irrational feelings and inclinations; nor could techincal knowledge include a knowledge of the reality of the world toward which it is supposedly directed.

Fortunately, no culture—not even ours—has been absolutely consistent in maintaining this view; but ours has gone far in this direction. We are more than a little embarrassed about espousing values that cannot be defended "scientifically." We are reluctant to engage in public discussion of issues that do not admit of clear-cut factual answers—such as the responsible use of atomic power or the obligations of the industrialized nations of the world to those that are not.

No argument for the existence of God could be successful, for argument does not belong to the level of reason where the reality of God is manifest. Argument belongs to the level of "technical" or "scientific" reason; it cannot take us beyond this. On this point, naturalism is right. But neither is it possible, without making some gratuitous assumptions, to prove the existence of anything else. If we are to know of the reality of anything, reality must disclose itself to us; there is no other way.

Our knowledge of the reality of God might be described as "non-technical," "non-discursive," "non-argumentative," or even "non-scientific"; but it is not "non-rational." Too much of what is of value in human life belongs to the deeper levels of reason to allow scientific reason alone to determine what is rational and what is not. Scientific reason is and must be supreme in its own sphere: that is an important truth that was established only after a long and bitter struggle (witness the experience of Galileo). But the sphere of scientific reason is limited: that is also an important truth that our culture is dangerously close to forgetting. The penalty for ignoring the former was the temporary retardation of the progress of modern science, and that was most unfortunate; but the penalty for forgetting the latter is an overwhelming sense of the futility of life, and that—if it occurs—would be disastrous. Man can abide discomfort, but robbed of meaning he is reduced to nothing.

The Self-disclosure of God

Material reality manifests itself to us in sense experience. The reality of the tree that I see through my office window is disclosed in the very process by which I see it: I do not first have sense-data and then infer that there is something "real" corresponding thereto. Investigation, experimentation, reasoning may tell me much about *what* it is: it cannot tell me *that* it is. Either its reality is immediately evident to me, or I must remain ignorant of it. Scientific reason cannot persuade me of the reality of the tree; indeed, it is only as this reality is given that scientific reason can begin its work.

Human reality manifests itself in *interpersonal communication,* notably in conversation. Scientific reason cannot demonstrate the existence of other minds: this is the inescapable conclusion of the endless discussions of this topic carried on ever since Hume. In love, in friendship, even in the casual relationships that we sustain with countless people whose lives barely touch ours in various ways, the reality of other rational selves is manifest to us. Here we are more aware than in the case of material objects, perhaps, of the limitations of scientific reason, for we know full well that the richness of a human personality defies exhaustive description; we know —but sometimes we forget.

God manifests himself to us in the event called *revelation*. I do not mean by this anything odd or unusual—nothing in the way of an "ecstatic vision" or anything of that sort. I mean simply that our longing that our life shall have some significance, our desire that the future shall have some hope, and our anxiety over the transiency and insecurity of everything that we perceive, are somehow overcome. I do not think that any human being is without this experience. There is a need, a longing, an anxiety, a concern, an emptiness in human life. Somehow, from deep within ourselves as it were, these are overcome, the void is filled, and we find courage. This "finding courage," or "being grasped by meanings," or "being sustained in the conviction of the significance of life," is what I mean by revelation; the source or ground of these is what we are talking about when we use the term "God."

It should be noted that in stating what I have just stated I am emphatically *not* setting forth another argument for the existence of God. I reject all arguments for the existence of God, including the argument from religious experience. What I am saying is rather that we are all implicitly aware of the reality of God, that at a level of our selves far deeper than that at which reasoning and argumentation occur God discloses himself to us. We may choose to call the reality that is thus disclosed to us by some other name—that is a very trivial matter. Or we may turn away from this deeper dimension of our self and try to live without meaning and without courage. In no case are we attempting what is both foolish and impossible: to prove, by argument, the reality of God.

I have no serious quarrel with the definition of God suggested in the introductory chapter and adhered to with varying degrees of fidelity by the other writers. The reality that is disclosed to us in the way I have described does, indeed, disclose itself as the ground of being and value, and there can be little doubt that if and when we are moved to an act of worship, it is this reality that is the intended object of our devotion. But precisely because we are dealing with a reality that is apprehended by reason in its depth rather than by scientific reason, this concept is bound to be obscure. Theology is an attempt, among other things, to make the concept "God" more precise; but the best theologians know that you cannot give this concept scientific precision without robbing it of its deepest meaning. "The heart has its reasons, which reason does not know." [1] The "reasons of the heart" are not blind, irrational emotions: they are a function of reason itself in a dimension of itself more profound than that with which we engage in scientific "reasoning."

This matter of the inevitable obscurity of the concept "God" deserves to be emphasized more than it has been thus far. H. D. Lewis is right when he says:

> the skeptic and agnostic do not so much find themselves unconvinced that in fact there is a God as fail to see what is meant by "God"; and we cannot first tell them what we mean and then proceed to show that God is also real. If they can be induced to see what we mean when we speak of God they will at one and the same time be convinced of His existence . . .[2]

The chief difficulty in the way of acknowledging the reality of God is not the inescapable ambiguity of the concept; it is rather the fact that in popular religion the concept *has* been made precise, but in an absurd and childish way. People do not believe in the existence of a Bearded Father someplace off in space, and so (they think) they do not believe in the existence of God. But the God who is— the ground of being and value, whose reality is manifest to every man in the deepest reaches of his self—bears little or no resemblance to this Celestial Despot of popular fantasy. To deny the

---

[1] Blaise Pascal, *Pensées,* Fragment 277 (New York: Everyman's Library, 1932), p. 78.

[2] H. D. Lewis, *Our Experience of God* (London: George Allen & Unwin; London and New York: Macmillan, 1959), p. 44.

reality of the latter is to topple an idol and so to be on the side of God; to deny the reality of the former is impossible.

Another Look at the Arguments

If, now, we look at the traditional arguments from the perspective developed briefly in this chapter, it is not difficult to see why the debate concerning them has been so inconclusive. The critics of the arguments have, quite rightly, criticized their argumentative form; the defenders of the arguments have defended their implicit meaning. For reasons already given, the arguments cannot succeed *as arguments;* on this point the critics are right. But the arguments do express, albeit inadequately, the awareness of the reality of God that is imbedded deep in the consciousness of every man.

The ontological argument attempts to express this in one way. It tries, however, to put this fundamental awareness of the reality of God into a form acceptable to scientific reason: it affirms, accordingly, that *the proposition, "God exists," is self-evident.* This, as the critics of the ontological argument have pointed out, is not the case; hence, the argument is no good as an argument. But the self-disclosure of God to reason in its depth is not the same thing as the alleged self-evidence to scientific reason of the proposition "God exists." As an argument, the ontological argument is a failure; but the insight that it attempts to express in this very inadequate way is both true and important.

The cosmological argument attempts to express this same insight in a slightly different way. The truth of the cosmological argument is that we are aware, in the depth of our selves, of the reality of the ground of our being and of all being; but the cosmological argument distorts this fundamental insight by attempting to exhibit it to scientific reason as a bit of propositional knowledge that can be gotten by correct syllogistic reasoning. This, as the critics of the cosmological argument have correctly pointed out, cannot be done: the cosmological argument is no good as an argument. However, the insight that it is attempting to express, and that no argument can adequately express, is both true and important.

This insight is most weakly reflected, perhaps, in the teleological argument. The teleological argument, at least in the form made popular by William Paley and other writers in the eighteenth century, almost inevitably conjures up the image of a super-artisan going about the business of making a world; and this expresses little, if anything, of what is meant by the concept "God." There is indeed a sense of mystery that strikes one when one looks upward on a starry night, and I do not doubt that this sense of mystery is best understood as a momentary heightening of our awareness of the reality of the ground of all being; but very little of this sense of mystery carries over into the teleological argument itself. People who find the teleological argument impressive are not so much convinced by the argument itself, I suspect, for as an argument it is by far the weakest of the three; they respond to it rather, I would suggest, because it directs their attention to certain features of the world the consideration of which may tend to enhance the awareness of God which all men really do have. If the argument does do this for some people, then to that extent it is of value; but its value is that of poetry, not logic.

Harvard president Nathan M. Pusey once said, "It would seem to me that the finest fruit of serious learning should be the ability to speak the word God without reserve or embarrassment, certainly without adolescent resentment; rather with some sense of communion, with reverence and with joy." [3] But to do this, we must rid ourselves of concepts and images that make God into a thing among things, whose existence is accordingly open to question. Even our secular age knows, though it does not acknowledge, that there *is* a depth of reason and of reality; without this awareness there would be no sense of worth, of value, of destiny, or of hope. When we learn once again that it is at this level of our being that the reality of God is manifest, we shall learn "to speak the word God without reserve or embarrassment, . . . [but] with some sense of communion, with reverence and with joy."

Study Questions

1. How does the author of this chapter propose to overcome "the impasse between theists and naturalists concerning the problem of the existence of God"?

---

[3] Nathan M. Pusey, *The Age of the Scholar* (Cambridge: Harvard University Press, 1963), p. 145.

2. What, exactly, is the distinction drawn in this chapter between *arguments* and *rational grounds*.
3. What do you make of the discussion in this chapter of the various dimensions of reason? Is it true that there is a tendency today to limit reason to what is here called "scientific reason"? Are you at all persuaded by the suggestion that there are other dimensions of reason than the "scientific"?
4. Is it correct to say that existence is not capable of demonstration— that either we must cognize it directly or else be ignorant of it? Is this true, for example, of our knowledge of the existence of physical objects? of other minds?
5. What does the author of this chapter mean by "revelation"? Is this, in fact, another argument for the existence of God?
6. Is there, as this writer affirms, an analogy between this problem and the realist-phenomenalist controversy?

For Further Reading

Alston, William P., "The Ontological Argument Revisited," *The Philosophical Review,* Vol. 69 (1960), 454-474.

Anselm of Canterbury, *Proslogium,* in S. N. Deane, *Anselm,* 2nd ed. La Salle, Ill.: Open Court, 1962.

Aquinas, St. Thomas, *Summa Theologica.* Many editions. Part I, Question 2.

Brown, Patterson, "St. Thomas' Doctrine of Necessary Being," *The Philosophical Review,* Vol. 73 (1964), 76-90.

Ducasse, C. J., *A Philosophical Scrutiny of Religion.* New York: Ronald Press, 1953.

Ebersole, Frank B., "Whether Existence is a Predicate," *The Journal of Philosophy,* Vol. 60 (1963), 509-524.

Ewing, A. C., *The Fundamental Questions of Philosophy.* New York: The Macmillan Company, 1951. Chapter XI.

Harris, E. E. *Revelation Through Reason.* London: George Allen & Unwin, 1959.

Hartshorne, Charles, *The Logic of Perfection and Other Essays in Neoclassical Metaphysics.* La Salle, Ill.: Open Court, 1962.

——, and W. L. Reese, *Philosophers Speak of God.* Chicago, Ill.: University of Chicago Press, 1963 (paperbound).

Hawkins, D. J. B., *The Essentials of Theism.* London and New York: Sheed and Ward, 1949.

Hick, John, "God as Necessary Being," *The Journal of Philosophy,* Vol. 57 (1960), 725-734.

Hume, David, *Dialogues Concerning Natural Religion,* ed. Norman Kemp Smith. Indianapolis, Ind.: Liberal Arts Press, 1962 (paperbound).

Jack, Henry, "A Recent Attempt to Prove God's Existence," *Philosophy and Phenomenological Research,* Vol. XXV (1965), 575-579.

Kant, Immanuel, *Critique of Pure Reason,* trans. Norman Kemp Smith. New York: St. Martin's Press, 1965 (paperbound). See section entitled, "The Ideal of Pure Reason."

Lewis, H. D., *Our Experience of God.* London: George Allen & Unwin; New York: The Macmillan Company, 1959.

Martin, C. B., *Religious Belief.* Ithaca, N.Y.: Cornell University Press, 1959.

Mascall, E. L., *Existence and Analogy.* London: Longmans, Green and Co., 1949.

Malcolm, Norman, "Anselm's Ontological Arguments," *The Philosophical Review,* Vol. 69 (1960), 41-62.

McIntyre, John, *St. Anselm and His Critics*. Edinburgh: Oliver and Boyd, 1954.

Mill, John Stuart, *Three Essays on Religion*. New York: Henry Holt and Co., 1874.

Paley, William, *Evidences of the Existence and Attributes of the Deity*. London: 1802. Many editions.

Smart, Ninian, *Reasons and Faiths*. New York: Humanities Press, 1958.

Tillich, Paul, *Systematic Theology*. Chicago, Ill.: University of Chicago Press, 1951. Vol. I, pages 204-235.

Religious Language

PART IX

Religious Language

Chapter 47

THE PROBLEM OF
RELIGIOUS LANGUAGE

IT IS INDICATIVE of the preoccupations of contemporary philosophers that this introduction to philosophy both begins and ends with a discussion of language. Never before has language itself been made the object of so much painstaking study as it has in the past twenty or thirty years, and there can be little doubt that some of the conclusions that have been drawn about the nature of language by those who have studied it most carefully are of considerable philosophical interest and importance.

Nor is it surprising that the careful scrutiny of language by philosophers in our day should have raised anew the problem of the meaningfulness of religious language, for the affinities of most philosophers today are not with the humanities and theology, but with the natural sciences, particularly physics. Philosophers today tend to be empiricists in their epistemology, conventionalists in their view of language, and skeptics with respect to the claim that the language of religion is in some way descriptive of transcendent reality. As a result of this preoccupation with language, and more especially as a result of certain negative implications drawn from a theory of language widely held by contemporary British and American philosophers, the problem of religious language has become the most widely discussed issue in contemporary philosophy of religion.

Background of the Problem

Lest we become too myopic in our approach to this problem. however, it may be well for us to note at the outset that the problem is by no means a new one. It is well over two thousand years since Plato wrote:

> The father and maker of all this universe is past finding out; and even if we found him, to tell of him to all men would be impossible. . . . If, then, Socrates, amid the many opinions about the gods . . . we are not able to give notions which are altogether and in every respect exact and consistent with one another, do not be surprised. Enough, if we adduce probabilities as likely as any others. . . .[1]

St. Augustine, too, who wrote a great deal about God, was quite cognizant of the difficulty; he even went so far on one occasion as to suggest that we speak of God "not in order to say something, but in order not to remain silent." [2] Theologians of every age have on numerous occasions echoed St. Augustine's sentiments.

The problem achieved what might be termed its first classical, or definitive, formulation, however, in Part 1, Question 13, Article 5 of St. Thomas Aquinas' great *Summa Theologica*. The question as formulated by St. Thomas is: "Whether what is said of God and of creatures is univocally predicated of them?" Translation: Do terms normally applied to finite objects have the *same meaning* when they are applied to God? We cannot reply in the affirmative, says St. Thomas, for when we apply a given term (e. g., "wise") to, say, a man, "we signify some perfection distinct from a man's essence, and distinct from his power and being," whereas when we apply the same term to God "we do not mean to signify anything distinct from His essence or power or being." On the other hand, if we say that terms are predicated of finite objects and of God "equivocally," i. e., in such a way that the same *word* has a totally different *meaning* in the two cases, then "the reasoning would always be exposed to the fallacy of equivocation." We would, in short, be

---

[1] Plato, *Timaeus*, Book I. See *The Dialogues of Plato*, B. Jowett, trans. (New York: Random House, 1937), Vol. II, p. 13.

[2] St. Augustine, *To Simplician—On Various Questions*, II, 2, 1.

concealing our complete ignorance about God under a camouflage of words that *appear* to be meaningful only because they *are* meaningful in their ordinary application. St. Thomas' solution is to go between the horns of the dilemma. There is, he says, a third way, namely the way of *analogy:* "Whatever is said of God and creatures is said according as there is some relation of the creature to God as to its principle and cause, wherein all the perfections of things pre-exist excellently." [3] Thus, St. Thomas believed, the problem is solved.

Whatever one may think of this solution to the problem as posed by St. Thomas, it is important to recognize that the problem as revived by contemporary philosophers is much more radical than this. St. Thomas was making two assumptions that most philosophers today who are concerned about the problem of religious language are not able to make. First, although St. Thomas was remarkably cautious in his claims regarding our knowledge of God, he did assume that we know a good many things about the nature of God: the question for him was, therefore, how our language could express this knowledge. He also assumed that somehow or other our language about God is meaningful: the question was, *in what way* is it meaningful? The "way of analogy" is offered by St. Thomas not as a solution to the problem of how we can speak meaningfully about God at all, but as an account of the particular kind of meaning "God-talk" is supposed to have—it being assumed by everyone concerned (in St. Thomas' day) that talk about God has some kind of meaning.

The Problem Today

The problem of religious language was raised anew in the twentieth century by the formulation of what is called *the empiricist criterion of meaning.* According to this criterion, a proposition is factually meaningful if and only if some empirical facts are relevant to determining its truth or falsity. There are, according to philosophers who defend this criterion, just three kinds of linguistic ex-

---

[3] St. Thomas Aquinas, *Summa Theologica*, Part 1, Question 13, Article 5, Anton C. Pegis, ed., *Basic Writings of St. Thomas Aquinas* (New York: Random House, 1945), Vol. I, p. 120.

pressions: empirical statements, analytic truths, and nonsense. Empirical statements are factually meaningful according to the criterion. Analytic truths simply express certain meaning relations between the terms of which they are composed; they say nothing about any matter of fact. All other linguistic expressions, regardless of their "face value," are literally meaningless: they have no cognitive meaning whatsoever.

If one accepts this criterion, however, one cannot avoid asking, "Is it possible to speak meaningfully about God at all, and if so, how?" Statements about God do not seem to be either confirmable or disconfirmable on the basis of any empirical observations: they do not seem, therefore, to be factually significant. It seems evident (to most observers, at least) that they are not analytic truths. Are they, then, altogether meaningless—a particularly prevalent form of linguistic nonsense? So it seems to many philosophers—but not, as we shall see, to all.

Philosophers who hold that all sentences purporting to say something about God are literally meaningless do not mean to suggest, of course, that they are obviously so. Indeed, their point is precisely that the nonsensical character of such utterances is extremely *un*obvious—so unobvious, in fact, that well-meaning people have talked about God for centuries as if what they were saying were literally significant. It is only when we come to understand under what conditions language can be meaningful, they point out, that we can see that in the case of language about God some of those conditions are lacking; hence, they say, we are driven to a negative conclusion.

Nor do these philosophers deny that sentences purporting to say something about God may have certain sorts of "meaning" for some people other than descriptive significance. The linguistic expression, "God loves His people, and watches over them continually," may be emotionally comforting or aesthetically satisfying, or it may serve as a re-enforcement of one's moral commitment. In these senses, they will allow, it may be meaningful to one who utters it. But the utterance cannot be literally significant, say these philosophers, even to a believer; it does not assert anything that is capable of being either true or false.

Let us consider this example further. Philosophers who hold that sentences purporting to say something about God are meaningless frequently point out that in order for a linguistic expression to be factually significant, it is necessary that one be able to specify a state of affairs which, if it were the case, would render the statement in question false. I may or may not be able to actually determine whether the state of affairs to which I have reference obtains: that is purely a question of empirical possibility and does not affect the logic of my statement. But if I cannot specify any state of affairs which, if it were the case (whether or not I can ascertain if it is the case), would render my statement false, say these philosophers, then I am not really saying anything.

Suppose, now, that someone were to say to a person who affirms the above sentence about God, "What would have to be the case in order for you to withdraw your statement that God loves His people, and watches over them continually?" What could such a person say? One could imagine a conversation something like this:

Believer: I can't think of anything that would make me withdraw the statement. God just does love His people—we know that—and whatever happens, we have to go on believing that God loves us.

Critic: Let me see if I can help you. Surely the fact of human suffering—except, perhaps, for that inflicted by other men—counts against your statement?

Believer: No, not at all. Because, you see, God's love is not like human love. God's love is greater, more encompassing, more. . . .

Critic: Wait a minute! How can you say that God's love is *greater* than human love? When men are suffering, other men usually try to do something about it. God, apparently, does not do anything at all. I should think one might be justified in concluding that God's love is inferior to human love, or even non-existent.

Believer: You do not understand the infinite difference between God and man.

Critic: I see a difference, but the contrast, I must say, is not particularly flattering to God. And the "love of God" of which you speak seems to mean nothing whatsoever. With or without this love, there would be human suffering—no more and no less than there is now. With or without this love, the world would apparently be just the way it is now. Your alleged "assertion" about the love of God is no assertion at all.

This question about the *meaningfulness* of statements about God must not be confused with the quite different question as to how to determine whether this or that theological statement is *true*. Our question belongs to the logic of religious discourse, the other to the epistemology of religious truth-claims. The first question, moreover, is logically prior to the second: if the negative view on the significance of religious assertions should be sustained, religion could make no truth-claims, in which case the epistemological question could be simply ignored.

It is no answer to the present question, therefore, to say, "We know God loves His people, because it says so in the Bible." The question is: What if anything do sentences about God *mean,* whether or not they are authorized by any religious authority? Are they factually significant at all? Are they, can they be, assertions? And if so, how do they get their meaning?

Some Alternatives

It is very difficult to classify the many ways in which writers who have addressed themselves to this problem have attempted to deal with it, and it is impossible in principle to determine forever all of the possible ways of responding to it.

Many writers have taken the position that the empiricist criterion of meaning makes it evident that talk about God is and always was nonsensical: people may keep on using it, but if they think it is literally significant, or anything other than "emotive," they are deceiving themselves. For one who holds this view, the status of religious language is no longer a problem: he is satisfied that the empiricist criterion of meaning is correct, that it clearly rules out religious discourse, and that is the end of the matter.

Many others, however, have addressed themselves to the problem out of a desire to show that the empiricist attack on religious language need not be as fatal as the attackers seem to think it is. It is at this point that the picture becomes rather confused because several different lines of defense have been attempted.

We may distinguish, first, a group of writers who have accepted the empiricist criterion of meaning and have accepted the conclusion that religious language is devoid of literal significance, but they have argued (in a variety of ways) that this conclusion need not distress religious people since the meaning and importance of religious language lies in an entirely different dimension. Nor, these writers argue, is one saying anything to the point if one calls these utterances "emotive": that is simply a pejorative way of describing an utterance that is not factually significant. If we examine carefully how religious utterances are used by people who do use them, say these writers, we will find that they serve a useful and important function—though, to be sure, that function is not, as people may have once thought, factual description.

Chapters 48 and 49 represent two alternative ways of accounting for the nature of religious language along these general lines. The "ethical way," developed in Chapter 48, goes back to Kant, whose epistemological studies drove him to deal with this problem long before the empiricist criterion of meaning made its debut on the philosophical scene. The "existential way," developed in Chapter 49, is of more recent vintage; a fairly large number of contemporary writers tend to identify themselves with this position. In both of these cases, however, the claim is made that the referent of religious language is subjective rather than objective: talk about God, correctly understood, is just a very special kind of talk about ourselves.

Other writers have insisted on the more traditional view that religious language is descriptive of objective reality and have attempted to show how this position can be maintained in the face of the empiricist attack. Some (few) writers have attempted to maintain that the empiricist criterion of meaning need not force the conclusion that talk about God is meaningless: this position is developed in Chapter 50. Others have argued that the empiricist criterion of meaning is itself inadequate, and have attempted to affirm the factual significance of religious assertions in a way which, if accepted, would require one to reject the empiricist criterion. This approach is developed in Chapter 51. It has, as the writer points out, much in common with the "way of analogy" of St. Thomas Aquinas.

This attempt to provide some structure for the discussion of the problem of religious langauge has deliberately been more tentative than that suggested for many of the previous problems with which we have dealt. In part, this is a requirement of the problem itself: it does not admit of a definitive statement of all the alternative possible answers. More than this, however, it reflects the status of the problem at the present time: this problem constitutes (as a survey of a few contemporary philosophical journals will make evident) one of the "growing edges" of philosophy today. Perhaps, in time, some new consensus will be reached—possibly along one of the lines suggested here or along some line not yet suggested in the literature. The student who grasps the issues involved in this controversy may be confident, in any case, that in so doing he is familiarizing himself with a problem that is sure to be widely discussed in the years that lie ahead. He would do well, in the meantime, to keep his categories somewhat fluid and to be open to possibilities that up to this moment may not have been imagined.

Study Questions

1. What is meant by the terms "univocal" and "equivocal"? What are St. Thomas Aquinas' objections to saying that certain things are predicated of God and of creatures "univocally"? What are his objections to saying that certain things are predicated of God and of creatures "equivocally"?
2. What is the empiricist criterion of meaning? How does this create a problem so far as religious language is concerned? Is *all* religious language placed in jeopardy by this criterion or certain kinds only? Be specific.
3. Is the question about the meaningfulness of religious language separable from, and logically prior to, the question about the truth of religious truth-claims? Explain.
4. Formulate a concise statement of the problem of religious language as you now understand it. What do you understand to be the alternative ways of responding to this problem?

Chapter 48

THE LANGUAGE OF MORAL RESOLVE

The Empiricist Criterion

IT IS MORE than a little misleading to call the criterion referred to in Chapter 47 a criterion of *meaning*. The criterion, to speak more correctly, is a criterion of *factual significance*. To say that a certain statement is "devoid of factual significance" is one thing; to say that the same statement is sheer "nonsense" seems like quite a different matter. The prejudicial language in which the problem of religious discourse has been discussed in recent years has done much to add confusion upon confusion to an issue that is desperately in need of elucidation and, if possible, solution.

Although I regard the terminology in which much of the recent discussion has been carried on to be highly misleading, I do not think it can be denied that the empiricist criterion of factual significance (as I shall call it) is valid. No sentence can be significant—factually or otherwise—unless (a) its terms are understood and (b) it is in tolerable conformity with the syntactic rules of the language in which it occurs. ("Some drapples are snark pling" fails to meet the first requirement, "Pickle ostrich many seven" fails to meet the second.) If, however, a sentence is to be factually significant, in addition to fulfilling these two requirements it must also be the case that (c) it purports to describe some theoretically verifiable state of affairs: this, it would seem, is what we mean by calling it "factually" significant. If a person who claims to be uttering a factually significant statement can specify no state of affairs which, if it were the case, would render his statement false, it would seem fair to conclude that (despite his claim) he is not really uttering a factually significant statement. The criterion is nothing more than a definition of what we mean by "factually significant"; I do not see how we could reject it without blurring the rather obvious distinction between factually significant sentences and other sorts of sentences.

Nor can there be any doubt that according to this criterion religious language is not factually significant. The sentences, "God is three in one" or "God loves His people and watches over them continually," describe no states of affairs that are either confirmable or disconfirmable by any conceivable data. Such sentences are all right as far as their syntax is concerned. They may be all right as far as their terms are concerned. But they are not factually significant. They are descriptive of nothing. They are, therefore, neither true nor false.

This conclusion regarding the non-factual character of religious language is regarded by many people, including some philosophers, as seriously objectionable. "Certainly," it is sometimes said, "the religions of the world claim to be asserting some matters of fact when they utter sentences about God." Granted; this seems to be true, at least, of most religions (though Zen Buddhism appears to be an exception). But the pseudo-descriptions into which most religions seem to have fallen are, I would insist, a spurious element in those religions. These supposed assertions are not, *qua* assertions, essential to religion; their real significance lies in another dimension. It is to this "other dimension," in which the true (nondescriptive) significance of religious statements is to be found, that I wish to direct attention in the remainder of this chapter.

Religion and Morality

Construed as statements of fact, sentences about God are entirely vacuous; their true meaning, I shall argue, consists in the fact that they express the *moral resolve* of the person who sincerely utters them—his sincere intention, in other words, to act in certain ways. I propose to indicate some of the reasons for adopting this view. I shall then give a few examples showing how, on the view here developed, some very common sentences having "God" as their subject ought to be construed.

We may begin with the observation that, whatever the view on the question of religious language, it is evident that morality constitutes an exceedingly important *part* of religion. What would Judaism be without the Ten Commandments, or Christianity without the Sermon on the Mount and the moral precepts of St. Paul, or Buddhism without the Noble Eight-fold Path? There are, indeed, ceremonies of various kinds—baptism, communion, regular forms of worship, and so on. Practices such as the singing of hymns and praying are common in many religions. But at the heart of every religion is a system of *moral precepts:* rules for behavior which the adherents of that religion are expected (and frequently exhorted) to observe.

Every religious group, as a matter of fact, constitutes an ethical community. Corporate worship is a solemn act in which the ethical community is reminded of its moral duty and given an opportunity to deepen and reaffirm its moral resolve. In the Christian religion, baptism and communion are also easily explicable in this context: baptism is a rite in which the young are formally inducted into the ethical community, communion a rite in which the members of the local unit of the community affirm their identity with the larger community in the pursuit of a common ethical task. Indeed, one would not be far from the truth if one were to define religion as *the solemnizing of ethical commitment.*

Parables and Other Stories

Since, as we have argued, it is the chief function of religion to encourage certain kinds of moral behavior, it is to be expected that every religion would produce a body of linguistic materials that tend to support this function. This is precisely what occurs. There are, for example, numerous stories, some of which are told as if they were historical (like the crossing of the Red Sea, and the conquest of Jericho), others which are frankly fictional (like the parables of Jesus). The question as to whether a given story is really historical, however, is not of any great importance. Whether there ever was a "rich young ruler" who came to Jesus for advice is of no more consequence than the question whether there ever was a Good Samaritan who befriended the man who had been set upon by thieves. The point, in both cases, is to encourage a certain kind of behavior; the question as to the historicity of the story is inconsequential.

The genius of such stories consists in the fact that they make vivid, and thus lend powerful psychological support to, the ethical duty of the adherent. The injunction to "love your neighbor as yourself" is undoubtedly an excellent summary of the Christian ethic, but it is rather abstract; the story of the Good Samaritan reveals in a vivid and concrete way what it means to love one's neighbor as oneself. So also with the injunction to love one's enemies and to return good for evil: it is not the general precept, but the oft retold story of Jesus forgiving those who crucified him, even as he hung upon the cross, that moves Christians to act in a like manner. Countless additional examples could be given from the literature of man's religions.

If men are to be persuaded to act in the prescribed ways, however, it is not enough that they be shown how it is that they are to act: they must also be given some volitional support. Many of the stories with which religious literature abounds serve the purpose, therefore, of supplying motives that will encourage adherents to act in the desired way. Two sorts of motives seem, in varying degrees, to be promoted by these stories: gratitude, and fear. In some religious communities one motive seems to predominate, in others the other. But both are present in some degree in all religion. The people of Israel are to obey the law given at Sinai out of gratitude to the God who has delivered them out of Egypt "with a strong hand and an outstretched arm"; but this God is also a "jealous" God, who will tolerate no worship of other gods and will severely punish those who disobey Him. St. Paul appeals to his readers "by the mercies of God" to act in certain ways; but the New Testament also warns of "the outer darkness" and the "weeping and gnashing of teeth" that await those who disobey. Sometimes the Buddha smiles, and sometimes he frowns; but always he enjoins the extinction of desire as the key to a proper mode of life.

If one adds to these stories the poems and hymns that recount these self-same stories, that express the attitudes that the stories and the experience of the community have succeeded in creating, and encourage the further development of such attitudes, it is apparent that a very considerable amount of the linguistic materials of religion can be satisfactorily accounted for. Even prayers, perhaps, might be accounted for as verbal expressions of the community's (or the individual's) sincere desire to achieve more fully the ethical ideal of the community, though the fact that they are customarily addressed to God calls for further explanation. A great many things that are otherwise extremely puzzling about religion fall nicely into place as soon as one recognizes that a religious group is essentially an ethical community.

The Attributes of God

It is in this same context that language about God is to be understood. Sentences of the form, "God is ____," are not descriptions of an Absent Potentate, the truth of which depends on the veracity of certain esoteric sources of information. Sentences about God, like all of the linguistic materials of religion, are to be understood in terms of their function in relation to the moral resolve that is the very *raison d'être* of the community. The question that we must ask is: "How do sentences about God function in relation to the life of such a community?"

How, in fact, do religious people think of God? Chiefly, it would appear, as the giver and enforcer of the moral law. And because God is conceived to be the giver and the enforcer of the moral law, He is also conceived to be one who embodies within Himself all of the virtues enjoined in the moral law. *God is the personification of the ethical ideal of the religious community.* Every moral virtue espoused by the community, therefore, is *eo ipso* ascribed to God: love, mercy, wisdom, forbearance, and so on.

Every statement about God is in reality an assertion of some aspect of the ethical ideal of the community and an affirmation of the community's sincere intention to act according to that ideal. "God is love" means, in a Christian community, "We value self-denying love such as that enjoined and practiced by Jesus of Nazareth, and do firmly resolve to act in this way ourselves." The mercy of God, the wisdom of God, the compassion of God, the forbearance of God can easily be understood, *mutatis mutandis,* in the same way.

Let us return to the statement, "God loves His people and watches over them continually." This expresses, according to our view, the community's corporate concern for each of its members—its ideal, if you will, that every member of the community shall act in such a way as to serve the needs and the welfare of every other member. The concern of one person for another who is ill (or otherwise in need) *is* the "love of God" of which the statement speaks. The meaning of the statement consists precisely in the fact that it honors such concern and enjoins each and every member of the community to incarnate this concern in his everyday dealings with his fellowmen. Behind every statement about God is the implied injunction, "You shall be perfect as your Heavenly Father is perfect."

Is Some Religious Language Meaningless?

Although a great deal of discourse about God is, so to speak, "legitimized" in this way, it does not necessarily follow from what we have said that all of it is. There are, I should say, a number of sentences having "God" as their subject that cannot be construed in this way, and there would seem to be no alternative but to regard them as being absolutely meaningless. Examples of such sentences would be, "God is three persons in one," "God is able to do anything that He wants to do," and "God knows Himself perfectly and in knowing Himself knows the world."

It is to be noted, however, that sentences such as these are not the kind that would come naturally and spontaneously to the lips of a devout member of a religious community. They are not specimens of the language of living religion: they are the products of academic theology. Many sincere laymen have, in fact, a kind of instinctive "feel" for the irrelevancy of such sentences to the real life of the religious community: they are impatient with "theological abstractions," and prefer to hear their ministers talk about things that are "relevant to life."

Theologians, however, are not a completely unique species of human being, and it seems reasonable, therefore, to suppose that there must be some basis for such formulations in the conceptual frame-work within which the language of living faith occurs. Such a basis is to be found in the personification of ethical ideals that gives rise to the very idea of God. Once the notion of a supremely perfect Person is established, it seems natural to ask, "What is He like?" Much of what is said will faithfully express the ethical ideal of the community, and so the community will recognize in what is said a true description of "their God." Given the supposition that talk about God is talk about a personal being, however, certain other things will follow as logical consequences: God does not change (for the ethical ideal is constant); God does not alter his plans or feel either joy or sorrow (for such would involve change); and so on. How, then, can God be said to feel compassion (St. Anselm's problem)? Answer: He does not—but we experience the effects of divine compassion *as if* He really were compassionate. Immense efforts have been expended by theologians to achieve logical coher-ence in the concept of God, and innumerable things have been said about God in the interest of achieving such coherence which, ac-cording to our theory, are quite meaningless.

What our proposal really comes down to is this: the proper cri-terion for judging the meaningfulness of sentences about God is not the criterion of *factual* significance, but the criterion of *ethical* sig-nificance. No sentences about God are factually significant. But many sentences about God are, nonetheless, ethically significant: they express the ethical ideal of the religious community that as-serts them and record the community's resolve to act in ways con-sistent with this ideal. To construe statements about God in this way is to preserve everything that is of importance to a religious community. It is, at the same time, to acknowledge the indisputable validity of the empiricist criterion of factual significance. It seems, therefore, a completely satisfactory solution to the problem of reli-gious language.

Study Questions

1. What position does Moralist take with respect to the empiricist criterion? Does he endorse it? modify it? reject it? reinterpret it?
2. Moralist represents religion as "the solemnizing of ethical commit-ment" and interprets various things—rites, religious literature, etc.

—in terms of this definition. Is he right about this? Can you think of any elements that are constitutive of religion that cannot be interpreted in this way?

3. What concept of God does Moralist recommend as being closest to the view held by most religious people? Why? As far as you can judge, do you think he is right on this point?

4. How, exactly, does Moralist propose that we construe statements about God? Apply his proposal to several examples other than those which he himself offers.

5. According to Moralist, there are some things that religious people ought to stop saying since, in his theory, they are meaningless. Make a list of things that appear to fall in this category. Are they, as he suggests, superfluous to religion—"spurious elements"?

Chapter 49

THE LANGUAGE OF HUMAN EXISTENCE

BECAUSE I AGREE with Moralist about the validity of the empiricist criterion of factual significance and because I share his concern that religious language not simply be cast aside as meaningless, it is not surprising that I should find his account of religious language extremely attractive. For like Kant, from whom he evidently has learned much, he presents a very plausible account of religion and of religious language, and in so doing he preserves a kind of meaning for at least a part of our talk about God.

We ought not be surprised, nor hold it against this account of the matter, that it obviously leaves out much that religious people have always supposed that they were saying when they uttered sentences about God. Popular piety unquestionably *does* conceive of God as a kind of Absent Potentate, a Great-grandfather-in-the-sky, who is conceived to "have" his various attributes in the same way that Mr. Jones has red hair; and such literally "ascriptive" meaning clearly cannot be allowed by the empiricist criterion. Popular piety, and probably also academic theology, want our language about God to be objectively descriptive, and this it cannot be. Any dissatisfaction with Moralist's account that arises solely because of the fact that he does not allow this kind of meaning to religious language is, therefore, quite illegitimate.

Although I share Moralist's view regarding the non-objective character of religious language, I am not satisfied with his positive account of that language simply as an expression of moral resolve. Religion is more, I think, than simply a "solemnizing of ethical commitment," and the peculiar language of religion is more than the recording of the intention of some group of people to act in certain sorts of ways. It is my purpose in what follows to indicate what that "more" is and to suggest an account of religious language that takes proper cognizance of this.

Religion and the Human Situation

Religion is a product of man's response to what we may call "the human situation"—the existential conditions within which his life as an existing individual is and must be lived. To say that these are "existential" conditions is to say that they are implicit in the very structures that determine human existence: they cannot be removed by any improvement in man's external environment, by any increase in his wisdom, or by any advance in his understanding of himself. They are there. They profoundly condition his existence at its very center. They can be acknowledged and accepted, but they cannot be removed. They are a part of what it means to be an existing human being.

That every human life stands under the terrible threat of total personal non-fulfillment is the first "existential fact" relevant for a proper understanding of religion. To be a human being is to know that there is a way that one ought to go, a life that one ought to live—and to know, at the same time, that one may miss it altogether. This is the threat of being "lost" of which all religions speak. It is because all men know this threat, and because religion addresses itself thereto, that the appeal of religion is so universal.

The threat of personal non-fulfillment—the fear, deep within every man, of being utterly and irrevocably "lost"—expresses itself in a variety of ways. It expresses itself, for example, as a *horror of death*. What a mockery death makes of human life! Here a young man full of promise, there a mother of several little children, and there again a brilliant statesman in whom millions of people had placed their hope, is taken by death. And each such event reminds us: we, too, must die. Our hopes, our plans, our words, our works must one day come to an end. Does not this render absurd the hopes, the plans, the words, and works that occupy us now? To reflect upon this, to see death as the final absurdity in a life that is naught but "a tale told by an idiot, full of sound and fury, signifying nothing," is to feel at least something of the horror of death. It is one of the ways that the threat of non-fulfillment expresses itself in human existence.

It expresses itself also in a *sense of guilt* because of real or imagined wrongdoing. All men know this sense of guilt, whether or not it attaches itself to particular overt acts; for to be a human being is to experience the threat of non-fulfillment, to know that one may miss the way that one ought to go. The feeling of guilt is simply the recognition that one has "missed the way," that one's life has not measured up to what it might and ought to have been. The religious term for this is "sin." It denotes not naughtiness but a profound *lack* in human life.

The threat of personal non-fulfillment also expresses itself in a sense of meaninglessness that perpetually haunts human existence. If I have missed the way that I should be walking and if death has the last mocking word, then anything that I may set my hand to now must be utterly devoid of meaning. Nothing that I might do now can have any meaning unless there are at least some proximate values for me to pursue; and there can be no proximate values unless they, in turn, are steps toward the realization of some more ultimate values. But death robs me of the latter. I am left with drabness and weariness: an unlovely Chekhovian world in which "all is vanity and a striving after wind." [1]

This is only one side, however, of the dialectic within which we must try to understand religion. It accounts for the negative, or threatening, elements in religion: the wrath of God, the threat of Hell, the possibility of remaining bound to the cycle of re-births (Buddhism), and so on. Every religion exhibits some such elements, but no religion consists exclusively of these elements; it is precisely the claim of religion to point to a way in which this ultimate threat to human existence is overcome—a way, to use the religious term, of "salvation."

---

[1] Ecclesiastes. 1:14.

"Salvation" means the complete *fulfillment* of one's self—the overcoming, therefore, of the threat to self-fulfillment of which we have been speaking. There is, according to all religions, a grace in human existence, in which these threats are accepted and conquered. Grace, too, is experienced in many forms, of which we may pause to mention just three.

It is experienced, first, as the overcoming, the conquest, of the horror of death. There seems to be no distinctive word for this experience in our language, but religious literature abounds with references to such things as "deliverance from death unto life," "the conquest of man's last enemy," and so on. "O death," writes St. Paul, "where is thy sting? O grave, where is thy victory? Death is swallowed up in victory." [2] The doctrinal expression of this experience is the doctrine of personal immortality (and its many variants).

Grace is experienced also as *forgiveness*—as an acceptance of oneself despite one's having "missed the way" and a confidence in that continued acceptance of self into an unknown future. One could call this, really, simply a *sense of personal worth* that overtakes and sustains one; there is no particular reason for preferring the religious term "forgiveness." But it is this experience that religionists are talking about when they talk about "forgiveness."

Third, the experience of grace is manifest in human experience as a sense of meaning, a feeling that somehow the whole human enterprise is worthwhile and that one's part in that enterprise also shares in that worth. Somehow meaninglessness and despair do not have the last word in human life: values thrust themselves upon us, tasks really worth doing lie before us, and life itself seems eminently worth living. We know the threat of meaninglessness—but we know, too, the overcoming of this threat.

All religions are shaped and formed by the dialectic which we have been attempting briefly to describe. The several religions use an infinite variety of pictures, symbols, and ideas, but their function is always the same: to assist their adherents in achieving the "way of salvation" in which the threat to self-fulfillment is overcome in all its varied forms.

---

[2] Corinthians, 15:54, 55.

Our Language About God

It is correct, as far as it goes, to say that God is conceived by religious people as "the giver and enforcer of the moral law"; but it does not go far enough. More importantly, He is conceived as the giver of life and of salvation, the conqueror of death, the forgiver, the savior. *God is the supposed source of the grace that overcomes the "lostness" that threatens and oppresses human existence.* Of course, He is also conceived as giving and enforcing the moral law, but this is only because the moral law is thought to define in part the way that God would have His children walk.

What each religion sets before its adherents is not simply a distinctive moral code, but a concrete and all-inclusive *existence-possibility*. This includes, of course, a moral code of some kind, but it includes much more. It includes a distinctive set of symbols, through which adherents of this particular religion will be taught to conceptualize various dimensions of their experience. It includes certain rites, in which the peculiar religious needs developed in a religious group will find appropriate expression. A religious group is not only, or even primarily, an ethical culture society: it is a fellowship of human beings who are seeking the way of salvation together and who have learned to employ a common set of symbols to mark their progress on that way.

It is not at all difficult, against this background, to understand the ritual use of language that refers to God: God is addressed as a very exalted person not altogether unlike ourselves, and He is made the object of both prayer and praise. In prayer, the worshiper expresses both fear (which is never wholly overcome) and confidence that the Giver of salvation will supply his need. In praise, the worshiper expresses gratitude for blessings received, and most especially for the incomparable gift of salvation.

But what, according to the view here developed, can be the meaning of a theological assertion of the form, "God is _____ (good, wise, holy, just, etc.)"? According to the empiricist criterion of meaning, such statements cannot mean what religious people typically think they mean. What, then, is their meaning?

The answer seems to be as follows. Theological statements of this kind have, I should say, two elements: (a) they express the existential ideal of the community, and (b) they express also the gratitude of the community for blessings received. It is the intertwining of these two elements that gives to such statements their peculiar character.

Let us consider first the existential ideal. One is reminded at this point of St. Anselm's statement that "God is everything that it is better to be than not to be." [3] God is conceived by the faithful to realize in His own nature all of the goodness that He looks for in them—not only moral goodness, but also such non-moral qualities as wisdom and prudence. Much talk about God is, therefore, as Moralist says, a way of setting before the community the ideal to which the community is committed. But the ideal is not merely an ethical ideal: it is an ideal that encompasses the whole of life.

The picture is complicated by the fact that such talk about God also includes a great deal that is purely honorific. The feeling of gratitude that characterizes the life of religion leads the spokesmen of religion, the theologians, to ascribe to God, who is conceived as a very exalted person, all sorts of qualities that no mere human being could ever have or hope to have—power, majesty, might, ubiquity, and so on. Such statements have meaning not as an expression of the existential ideal of the community, but rather as an exaggerated expression of the gratitude of the community. The gratitude is real and legitimate, but the expression of it by the ascription to God of qualities such as "omnipotence" and "omnipresence" is very misleading.

Talk about God is meaningful not as a description of an unseen being, but as an expression of the existential ideals and the innermost feelings (of gratitude, etc.) of human beings. There may or may not be a Being who charts the way that we ought to go and gives forgiveness and salvation. But the way, forgiveness, and salvation are real components of our existence, and every moment of our existence is lived in relation to them. The meaning of our talk about God depends on the ways in which that talk reflects our experience of lostness, forgiveness, and salvation: that, at least, we have firsthand and can discuss as meaningfully as we can discuss anything else.

---

[3] St. Anselm, *Proslogium,* S. N. Deane, trans. (Chicago, Ill.: Open Court, 1962), p. 11.

Study Questions

1. What does Existentialist mean by "existential conditions"? What "existential conditions" does he suggest are relevant for a proper understanding of religion? To what extent does Existentialist's account of religion involve a rejection of Moralist's account, and to what extent could it be construed as simply supplemental to that account?

2. Is there some connection between (a) a view of the nature of religion, (b) a concept of God, and (c) a view regarding the meaning (or lack of meaning) of religious language? Illustrate your answer by reference to the theories discussed in this and the preceding chapter.

3. What does Existentialist suggest is the "peculiar character" of religious language? Does this strike you as a plausible suggestion?

Chapter 50

THE EMPIRICAL FOUNDATIONS
OF RELIGIOUS LANGUAGE

A PERSON WHO HAS gone through a substantial portion of his life complacently believing that his discourse about God is—at least in some respects—descriptive of a transcendent reality cannot but be taken aback by the suggestion that this is not so. Surely, he is inclined to think, there must be some relatively easy solution to the problem. But the empiricist criterion of factual significance is a very restricting doctrine. And so, in desperation, one is tempted to look for desperate solutions.

The two proposals that have just been presented are, I think, examples of this "strategy of desperation." There is no doubt that a "way of life," or a "pattern of existence," is an important element within the whole fabric of a religion. It is not surprising, therefore, that elements of "moral resolve," or "existential orientation," are to be found in the language of religion. There is equally no doubt, however, that religion is not simply a matter of moral resolve and/or existential orientation and that the language of religion cannot, as a consequence, be accounted for simply in those terms.

Suppose I say, "My grandfather was one of the kindest men I ever knew: would that I could be more like him." In speaking this way I am, of course, expressing a wish and an intention—recording my "moral resolve," if you wish—to act in a certain way. It may well be, further, that I have been taught from childhood to feel love and gratitude for grandfather—through being told stories of things he did for me when I was small and kindnesses he performed for other people whom I love, and so on. You may go on to embellish the tale as much as you wish, but my point is clear: under circumstances such as these my statements about grandfather would take on a certain "moral" or "existential" flavor. They would, *among other things,* record my own feelings, intentions, and aspirations.

However, my statements about grandfather would also, and primarily, still be statements *about grandfather.* Whatever it may say about my own intentions, the statement "Grandfather was a very kind man . . ." is a statement about grandfather. It may be true, or it may be false. It may also, incidentally, be quite beyond verification. But it is, in any case, a statement about grandfather. Whatever else it may express, it expresses primarily my belief that grandfather was a man of such and such a character.

Something of this kind must be said, surely, about religious language. No doubt it does express, among other things, the kinds of things that Moralist and Existentialist say it expresses. But this is not all. Language about God is, first and foremost, language *about God*—about a reality whose existence or non-existence is a matter of profound importance to us and whose real possession or non-possession of the attributes of love, mercy, compassion, and so on determines whether or not our language about Him is true. Religion is not purely a matter of moral resolve and/or existential orientation; it is also a matter of belief. Without belief, neither moral resolve nor existential orientation would be called "religion."

It seems clear, therefore, that those who today are content to adopt one or another of the "subjectivist" solutions to the problem of religious language are living on the capital of their forefathers. They revere the way of life exemplified by their elders and suppose that it can be preserved without the beliefs that created it. If this way of life should survive the rejection of the beliefs upon which it was based, however, it will not be a religion that has survived, but merely an ethic. Religion implies belief, and the language of religion is an attempt to express belief. And beliefs, all beliefs, are either true or false.

Religious Discourse and "Facts"

If we are persuaded of the validity of the empiricist criterion of factual significance, then there are only two alternatives: either to show that sentences about God are factually significant according to the criterion or to draw the unhappy conclusion that religious people are all mistaken in thinking that their language about God is expressive of beliefs. The latter alternative seems preposterous; I propose, therefore, to defend the former. I think that sentences about God are *factually significant*.

The empiricist criterion of factual significance, it will be recalled, requires that in order for a sentence to be accounted factually significant, some empirical data must be relevant to its truth or falsehood. That this is the case with respect to at least some sentences about God is evident, I would argue, from the fact that religious people are concerned about the problem of evil. The occurrence of evil in the world (a fact of empirical observation) is a problem for religious people precisely because it appears to be inconsistent with belief in the perfect wisdom, power, and goodness of the Creator. If God were limited in wisdom, He could be excused because of ignorance. If He were limited in power (as Plato held), He could be excused on the ground that He did the best He could. If He were limited in goodness, then the occurrence of evil together with good is just what might be expected. But if God is said to be altogether wise (omniscient), powerful (omnipotent), and good, then the occurrence of evil counts against the statement. It is, in the sense demanded by the criterion, relevant to the truth or falsity of the statement. If it were not, there would be no point in the concern over this vexing problem which religious people have always had.

Nonetheless, the occurrence of evil does not conclusively falsify the statement, "God is perfectly wise, powerful, and good." And in this fact we may see an important respect in which religious truth-claims (of the troublesome kind) are markedly different from scientific truth-claims. It is characteristic of scientific truth-claims that (a) they yield precise predictions regarding what will occur under such and such prescribed conditions and (b) the non-occurrence of what is predicted is allowed to falsify the truth-claim. In the case of religious truth-claims, however, the situation is different. A theological belief leads not to precise predictions, but to certain general expectations. Job believed that God, being just, rewards the righteous and punishes the wicked according to their desserts; and being a righteous man, he accordingly expected to experience health, long life, and prosperity. When expectations are disappointed, the result—as in Job's case—is not the *falsification of a theory* but the *calling in question of a belief:* it is what religious people call a temptation to unbelief. One may, in such a situation, cease to believe what one formerly believed; but when this occurs, what has occurred is not the refutation of a *theory,* but the collapse of a faith.

The difference between religious beliefs and scientific hypotheses does not consist in the alleged fact that the latter are factually significant while the former are not. The difference consists, rather, in the radically different ways, or attitudes, in which the respective beliefs are held. Scientific hypotheses are, quite properly, held in the tentative, provisional way with which we are all familiar: they are always open to revision, and every fact not explicable in the context of the hypothesis becomes a challenge to create a better hypothesis. Beliefs about God obviously are not, and cannot be, held in this way. The belief that God is powerful, wise, and good is not a hypothesis to be discarded as soon as some untoward event occurs: it is an article of faith, and as such it can be given up only through and with great anguish. The belief is part of a total and (ideally) unconditional *commitment*—what Friedrich Schleiermacher called "absolute dependence" and the late Paul Tillich called "ultimate concern." To be "absolutely dependent" on or "ultimately concerned" about anything other than God is what is called "idolatry"; but whatever be the object of ultimate concern, be it God or anything else, the beliefs that one holds about that object cannot be held in the mood of detachment appropriate to a tentative hypothesis. They can only be held in the passion that is the appropriate mood for faith.

Empirical Grounds for Theological Assertions

Thus far I have been content to argue only that acceptance of the empiricist criterion of factual significance does not necessarily force one to the conclusion that sentences about God are devoid of factual significance. The conclusion does not follow, I have argued, because empirical observations do in fact count against certain statements about God; but, I have said, it is implicit in the way that theological beliefs are held that such observations are not allowed to conclusively falsify them.

It may be protested, however, that this only takes us a very small part of the way toward solving the problem of religious language. It takes us beyond the empiricist criterion of factual significance—but does it not leave us with the problem that our language, though admirably suited to the description of ordinary objects, cannot be properly descriptive of God? And does it not leave entirely unanswered the question as to what, if anything, may be adduced as counting *in favor of* theological assertions? If nothing were to be said about this, there would be scant comfort in the knowledge that there are some empirical facts that appear to count *against* such utterances.

What makes this problem seem so utterly impossible of solution is, I submit, that those who concern themselves with it (both in defense and in criticism of theological language) commonly do so on the supposition that what demands to be proved is that language can be meaningfully descriptive of a *wholly transcendent* reality. To this question there is only one possible answer: it cannot; for by a "wholly transcendent reality" is meant a reality that is beyond the realm of all possible experience, and what is beyond the realm of all possible experience is, according to the empiricist criterion, also beyond the realm of factual significance. Of that of which we have no experience we are altogether ignorant, and of that of which we are altogether ignorant, we cannot speak.

There is, however, no good reason for such a one-sided emphasis on the transcendence of God. High religion, it is true, has always affirmed the transcendence of God—and has been healthily agnostic about our capacity to know anything about this aspect of God's nature. But it has also spoken of the *immanence* of God, and it is at this point that our language about God can be seen to have some intelligible meaning. To say that God is immanent is to say that He *is* present in human experience, and that our language can be descriptive of Him in the same way that it can be descriptive of any other reality encountered in experience.

The primary meaning of the term "God" is "a reality that saves man from the powers and processes that are destructive of his humanity, and (as a consequence thereof) is eminently worthy of his unconditioned commitment." Such a reality is encountered by us, I maintain, in the *creative intercommunion with other men* which characterizes interpersonal encounter at its best. Here, and here alone, do we encounter a creative power that truly transforms us, that overcomes the guilt, the meaninglessness and the triviality of our existence, and that enables us to fulfill our human potentialities. Here is salvation, in the only sense of that word that I can understand. Here, therefore, is God as He is experienced by us.

It is such creative intercommunion that creates and sustains the human mind and personality. It is this that saves and transforms him who gives himself to it without reservation. It is in this reality that we find that deep acceptance of ourselves in spite of ourselves that is the true meaning of forgiveness. To him who thus commits himself, this reality gives peace, courage, comfort, and renewal of mind. If this be God, then God is in very truth that omnipresent reality in whom we live and move and have our being.

How perfectly natural, then, and how profoundly meaningful (because so thoroughly interwoven in the very fabric of our experience) to say: "God creates," "God sustains," "God forgives," "God saves," "God transforms," "God loves." In this power of creative intercommunion—this power that is among us, and in us, and is infinitely more than simply the sum of our individual powers —we encounter a reality to which it seems natural and appropriate to ascribe the attributes of deity. And it is not surprising that it should be so: the true lovers of God have rarely been metaphysicians, but men deeply involved in the common life of man. "God" means "creative intercommunion among men"; it is to this that we offer our prayers and our praises, when we pray and praise.

What we experience is in very large part a function of what we have been trained to notice. A symphony is experienced as one thing by a novice and as quite a different thing by a trained musician; and even among trained musicians a given symphony may be experienced quite differently by a violionist and a clarinetist. The novice hears "a lot of sound," and he either likes it or he does not. The musician hears themes, harmonies, progressions, varying timbres, tempos and dynamics; he discerns structure and form in what he hears and compares the interpretation with others that he may have heard. He knows what to listen for, and because he knows, he hears (discerns) many things that the novice does not.

Most people today are not attuned, I think, to the kind of experience that I have been attempting to describe—the experience of God. God is a reality in our midst, but He is almost unknown; and the reason He is unknown is that we do not pay sufficient heed to that dimension of our experience in which He is manifest to us. We are novices in religious experience. What chiefly occupies our attention is things: how to get them, how to manipulate them, how to derive pleasure from them. We notice objects, we notice regularities, we notice mathematical relations—but we do not notice God. Hence, it is no wonder that our experience is shallow, and our talk of God is empty. We do not need an alternative to the empiricist criterion: we need a re-direction of our attention and an enrichment of our experience. Else all our talk of God, with or without the criterion, is empty.

Study Questions

1. Is Empiricist right in his contention that "religion implies belief"? Support your answer with specific illustrations.
2. What, exactly, is Empiricist's position on the problem of religious language? On what point or points is he in agreement with the previous two writers? On what point or points is he in disagreement with them?
3. What differences does Empiricist find between scientific truth-claims and religious truth-claims? Do you agree? Are there other differences as well?
4. What concept of God is suggested by Empiricist? Can one talk about God *thus conceived* in a way that is consistent with the empiricist

criterion? Would this solution to the problem be apt to satisfy most religious people? Explain.

5. What, according to this account, is the meaning of each of the following: "God creates," "God sustains," "God forgives," "God saves," "God transforms," "God loves"?

Chapter 51

THE SYMBOLIC CHARACTER OF
RELIGIOUS LANGUAGE

IT IS REGRETTABLE that so much of the philosophical discussion of religion in recent years should have been directed toward the solution of the problem posed by the empiricist criterion of factual significance. There can be no doubt that this unfortunate narrowing of the discussion has trivialized the philosophical interest in religion. In the all but unanimous endorsement of this vaunted criterion, and the resulting consternation of some philosophers (as well as theologians) about the apparent consequences for religion and theology, ancient insights of great and permanent importance have been overlooked. I shall attempt to redress the balance.

A Critique of the Criterion

Whatever the opinion regarding the status of our language about God, the empiricist criterion ought to be rejected as a general criterion of meaning (which is what its supporters usually claim it to be). Not only is theological language consigned by this criterion to the limbo of meaninglessness, but also (a) statements about events alleged to have occurred in the past ("The Battle of Gettysburg occurred in 1863"), (b) statements about other minds ("Mr. Jones is worrying about how he is going to send his son to college"), and (c) statements postulating the annihilation of all perceivers ("Should a full-scale atomic war occur, all life will be destroyed"). We do know what statements of these three kinds mean; yet none of them is meaningful according to the empiricist criterion.

Moreover, the status of the empiricist criterion itself is a matter of considerable embarrassment to its supporters. The most plausible account of it is that it is an *empirical hypothesis*—an inductive generalization about the conditions of meaningfulness, derived from careful observation of statements adjudged on other grounds to be meaningful. If this is the case, however, it is evident that the "criterion" is not really a criterion at all. It cannot determine what is or is not meaningful, since the method by which the theory is erected presupposes that one already knows, *on some other basis,* which statements are meaningful and which are not. It is only fair to say that the supporters of the criterion have by and large recognized this problem and have tried to deal with it. It is also only fair to say that their attempts so to do have not been very convincing even to themselves.

As a general criterion of meaning, the empiricist criterion is, therefore, grossly inadequate. What it defines is not the conditions of meaningful discourse in general, but the conditions of meaning commonly applied in the natural sciences. If we do assume that it is a correct description of the conditions of meaning required in the natural sciences (a question for the philosophy of science), it will follow that no statement which fails to satisfy this criterion will qualify as a *scientific* statement (in the narrow sense of "scientific" currently in vogue). It will by no means follow that the statement in question is completely meaningless.

A Deeper Problem

Although the preoccupation of philosophers with the problem posed by the empiricist criterion (construed as a general criterion of meaning) seems to have trivialized the philosophical interest in religion, it is not to be denied that the discussion of this problem has produced some valuable results. It has demonstrated, for example, that there are ethical and existential dimensions to the meaning of religious language, as previous participants in the present discussion have made clear. It has demonstrated, moreover, that the question of the meaningfulness of our *language* about God cannot be separated from the question of the meaning of the *concept* "God"—as even Empiricist's account makes evident. Consequently, the discussion has not been without value.

The older and much more serious problem that has been largely overlooked in all the excitement over the apparent consequences of the empiricist criterion, however, is: whatever may be the general conditions of meaningful discourse, how is it possible for a language whose form and structure are patterned after a world of finite objects to be descriptive of an infinite and transcendent reality? This was St. Thomas' problem, referred to briefly in the introductory chapter. It is an inescapable problem for any philosophy that seriously affirms the possibility of meaningful discourse about God.

St. Thomas' own proposal vis-à-vis this problem, as has already been pointed out, is the classical answer to it. God the Creator, said St. Thomas, stands as "principle and cause" in relation to the things He has created, and "all the perfections of things pre-exist excellently" in Him. Thus, said St. Thomas, it is permissible to ascribe the perfections that we perceive in creatures to God, provided that we bear in mind that in God they exist fully and perfectly, whereas in creatures they exist only fragmentarily and imperfectly. In the two sentences, "God is wise" and "Socrates is wise," the meaning of the predicate "wise" is neither absolutely identical (univocal) nor absolutely diverse (equivocal): it is analogical. Socrates is wise in the way that wisdom is appropriate to a finite and imperfect being; God is wise in the way that wisdom is appropriate to an infinite and perfect being. "In analogies," said St. Thomas, "the idea is not, as it is in univocals, one and the same; yet it is not totally diverse as in equivocals; but the name which is thus used in a multiple sense signifies various proportions to some one thing." [1]

The theory of analogical predication is both ingenious and profound, and it is worthy of great respect. It provides, as any adequate theory of theological language must, for both continuity and dis-

---

[1] St. Thomas Aquinas, *Summa Theologica,* Part 1, Question 13, Article 5, Anton C. Pegis, ed., *Basic Writings of St. Thomas Aquinas* (New York: Random House, 1945), p. 120.

continuity between God and the world. It allows one to affirm both the transcendence of God (by virtue of which our language is not *properly* applicable to God) and the immanence of God (by virtue of which our language has *some* meaning when applied to God). It permits us to say the kinds of things that we want to say about God (as none of the theories presented in the previous three chapters seem to me to do); yet it preserves a healthy agnosticism about the propriety of our language—reminds us, that is to say, that no description of God is really adequate to the reality of the divine mystery. It seems evident, therefore, that any theory which (a) presupposes that by "God" is meant an immanent-transcendent reality as conceived in classical theism and (b) affirms the possibility of meaningful discourse about this reality, must in the last analysis be something very similar to, or perhaps only a variant of, this theory.

Analogical predication consists, actually, in a very clever combination of positive and negative predication. It is evident that some statements about God are purely negative: they do not affirm that God is thus and so, but rather they deny that God is thus and so. It seems appropriate, for example, to say that God is not composite, not corporeal, not finite, and not subject to change, and these assertions are commonly expressed by saying that God is simple, incorporeal, infinite, and immutable. There is evidently no mystery about how such God-talk can be meaningful since the predicates employed are all being used in their proper everyday sense.

The "analogical way" of talking about God is in very large measure a further extension of this "negative way." To be sure, in analogical predication one is attempting to make a positive statement about God—to say something about what God *is* rather than about what He is *not*. But the negative way continues to function also in that one attempts to remove from the positive meaning of the predicate whatever it would not be appropriate to attribute to a being who is not composite, not corporeal, not finite, and so on. This is what is involved in saying that God is wise "in the way that wisdom is appropriate to an infinite and perfect being": by applying the negative way you are *ridding* the concept of those features which would make it inappropriate for a description of the divine reality.

Thus stated, however, the theory of analogical predication is open to one very serious objection. If the analogical meaning of a given predicate as applied to God is just its ordinary meaning minus those elements that render it incapable of describing the divine reality, does it not follow that the relation between a given term as applied to God and the same term as applied to creatures is in part equivocal and in part univocal? This would seem to be the case. Insofar as "wise" connotes finitude, corporeality, etc., it refers only to creatures: to this extent "wise" as applied to God and "wise" as applied to creatures are *equivocal* terms. But what of the meaning that remains once the objectionable elements have been removed? To that extent, it would seem, "wise" as applied to God and "wise" as applied to creatures are *univocal* terms. And so, it would seem, all of the objections to univocity apply with equal force to the analogical theory.

This is, in my opinion, a sound objection—though I would add that it touches only the letter and not the spirit of the theory of analogical predication. I think that the intention of the many philosophers who have supported the theory of analogical predication can be preserved in a way that gets around this objection. This can be accomplished through what I shall call the theory of *symbolic* predication. It is a kind of analogical theory, but with sufficient differences from the traditional theory to warrant a special name.

Symbolic Predication

The real purpose of the analogical way was to emphasize that (as well as to show how) our language about God is qualitatively different from our language about finite objects. The theory of analogical predication fails not because it does not recognize this important insight, but because it tries to express it in an inadequate way—namely, at the level of discursive meaning. At that level, however, there are just three formal possibilities: (a) the meaning of a term in each of two instances is absolutely identical (univocal); (b) the meaning of a term in each of two instances is absolutely different (equivocal); (c) the meaning of a term in each of two instances is partly identical and partly different (analogical). And to affirm that our talk about God is analogical, if this is what is meant by analogical, is not to escape the difficulties of "univocal" predication at all.

The kind of meaning that our language about God can have is, however, closely related to the kind of knowledge that we have of Him. If it were the case that we had some straightforwardly empirical knowledge of God, then there would be no problem at all in accounting for our language about God. This, however, is not the case. Our apprehension of God's reality, and our knowledge of His nature, do not occur at the discursive level. It is not "technical," or "scientific," reason that knows God but reason in its depth; hence, the language of scientific discourse (including the ordinary language of everyday experience) cannot adequately express this knowledge.

When we use language with reference to God, therefore, we are using it not in its ordinary literal meaning, but *symbolically*. When we say that God is good, wise, or merciful, we are not saying that He is these things in the same way that some men are good, wise, and merciful (only more so), nor are we saying that He is these things minus whatever elements of meaning connote finitude and imperfection. We are saying, rather, that God is *not* these things in the literal sense of "good," "wise," or "perfect" but that these terms point beyond themselves to realities in the ground of goodness, wisdom, and mercy—realities that cannot be grasped discursively but can only be acknowledged as dimensions of the reality of the divine mystery.

It is important to realize that in saying that our language about God is symbolic we are not saying that it is thereby inferior to literally descriptive language: on the contrary, we are saying that the mystery of the divine being so far surpasses our understanding that the descriptive language of everyday discourse is altogether inadequate to describe God. With St. Thomas Aquinas we say: he knows God best who acknowledges that whatever he thinks and says falls short of what God really is. Our language cannot describe God, even imperfectly: it can only point to Him. And this function of "pointing to" is precisely the function of a symbol.

The question may and should be asked, however: What is it that governs our choice of symbols? Why do we say (symbolically) that God is "good" and "wise," but not that He is "material" or "numerous"—for surely He is the ground of matter and number as well as of goodness and wisdom? It is our apprehension of the divine reality itself that governs our choice. Just as discursive reason learns the art of choosing terms to describe the realities with which it is conversant, so reason in its depth learns the art of choosing symbols to indicate the divine reality. Talk about God is, in the last analysis, an attempt to *make language revelatory* of the divine nature. It is the language that is adjudged successful in this effort that is retained as the language of theology.

The question as to whether or not it is possible to speak meaningfully about God, and, if so, what sort of meaning theological talk must have, cannot be decided on the basis of purely logical considerations. One must first take a stand on some very important ontological and epistemological problems: does "God" denote a reality, and do we have any knowledge of this reality? The theory of theological language here suggested presupposes an affirmative answer to both these questions. The view that theological language is meaningless—though it may claim to be nothing but the plain implication of a neutral principle of logic—just as evidently presupposes a negative answer to one or both of these questions. A theory of theological language that pretends to be neutral with respect to these questions only succeeds in confusing the issue.

This being the case, the recent uncertainty about the meaningfulness of theological language appears to be little more than a pale reflection of the waning awareness of the divine reality that is so frighteningly evident in the modern world. Men have always known that God is not a thing among things: hence, they have always known that there is something peculiar, something odd, something unique, about our language with respect to Him. But only men for whom God has altogether ceased to be—only men for whom, as Nietzsche said, God is dead—could seriously hold that our language about God is altogether devoid of meaning. Let the awareness of the divine reality be reborn among us, and our doubts about the meaningfulness of theological language will quickly disappear. Pending that, our talk about God must be empty, and our talk about that talk an exercise in futility.

Study Questions

1. Symbolist rejects the empiricist criterion as a general criterion of meaning. On what grounds? What more limited role does he assign to it? Do you agree with him on this?

2. Why, according to Symbolist, is the status of the empiricist criterion "a matter of considerable embarrassment to its supporters"? Can you think of any way by which an advocate of the criterion might get around this difficulty?

3. What is the "older and much more serious problem" to which Symbolist invites our attention? Is it in fact a different problem from the one discussed in the three preceding chapters?

4. What, exactly, is "analogical" predication? What does Symbolist have to say in support of this proposal? What objection does he raise against it? Is the objection, in your opinion, a sound one?

5. What is Symbolist's own proposal regarding the meaning of statements about God? Does it overcome the objection which he raised against the analogical theory?

FOR FURTHER READING

Aquinas, St. Thomas, *Summa Theologica*. Many editions. Part I, Question 13.

Ayer, A. J., *Language, Truth and Logic*, 2nd ed. New York: Dover Publications, 1946 (paperbound).

Braithwaite, R. B., *An Empiricist's View of the Nature of Religious Belief*. Cambridge: Cambridge University Press, 1955.

Carnap, Rudolf, "The Elimination of Metaphysics through Logical Analysis of Language," in *Logical Positivism*, ed. A. J. Ayer. New York: Free Press of Glencoe, 1957.

Christian, William A., *Meaning and Truth in Religion*. Princeton, N.J.: Princeton University Press, 1964.

Coburn, Robert C., "The Hiddenness of God," *The Journal of Philosophy*, Vol. 57 (1960), 689-712.

Ewing, A. C., "Religious Assertions in the Light of Contemporary Philosophy," *Philosophy*, Vol. XXXII (1957), 206-218.

Flew, A., and A. Macintyre, *New Essays in Philosophical Theology*. New York: The Macmillan Company, 1964 (paperbound).

Hempel, C. G., "Problems and Changes in the Empiricist Criterion of Meaning," in *Logical Positivism*, ed. A. J. Ayer. New York: Free Press of Glencoe, 1957.

Hick, John, *Faith and Knowledge*. Ithaca, N.Y.: Cornell University Press, 1957.

Lazerowitz, M., *The Structure of Metaphysics*. New York: Humanities Press, 1955.

Macintyre, A., ed., *Metaphysical Beliefs*. London: SCM Press, 1957.

Marhenke, P., "The Criterion of Significance," in *Semantics and the Philosophy of Language*, ed. L. Linsky. Urbana, Ill.: University of Illinois Press, 1952.

Mascall, E. L., *Words and Images*. New York: Ronald Press, 1957.

Miles, T. R., *Religion and the Scientific Outlook*. New York: Humanities Press, 1959.

Mitchell, Basil, ed., *Faith and Logic*. London: George Allen & Unwin, 1957.

Munz, Peter, *Problems of Religious Knowledge*. London: SCM Press, 1959.

Ramsey, Ian T., *Religious Language*. New York: The Macmillan Company, 1963 (paperbound).

Tillich, Paul, *Systematic Theology*. Chicago, Ill.: University of Chicago Press, 1951. Vol. I, pages 235-289.

Wieman, H. N., *Man's Ultimate Commitment*. Carbondale, Ill.: Southern Illinois University Press, 1958. Chapters 1-7.

Epilogue

Chapter 52

PHILOSOPHY AND LIBERAL EDUCATION

IT IS THE proper business of an introduction to make a beginning, to establish some basis upon which a deeper acquaintance may subsequently be developed. This is what we have been attempting to do in the preceding chapters of this book. It would be easy to continue indefinitely, for there are many problems in addition to those discussed that are of interest to philosophers, and some of them are of considerable importance. But a beginning must also come to an end.

Let us once again "back off" from our discussion of representative philosophical problems and try to take an objective look at it. Of what value has it been? How, if at all, has our philosophizing tied in with the rest of our academic work? What role might philosophy, of the type in which we have been engaged in the course of this study, be expected to play within the total context of a liberal education?

The Aims of Liberal Education

John Henry Newman once said:

A University training is the great ordinary means to a great but ordinary end. . . . It is the education which gives a man a clear conscious view of his own opinions and judgments, a truth in developing them, and a force in urging them. It teaches him to see things as they are, to go right to the point, to disentangle a skein of thought, to detect what is sophistical, and to discard what is irrelevant. It prepares him to fill any post with credit, and to master any subject with facility.[1]

Those words were written in 1852. At the time they were written they summed up, beautifully and accurately, the ideal "end product" of liberal education: a man of broad learning and culture, a conscious inheritor of the cultural riches of the past, an expert in the exercise of reason, a master of the art of conversation, a gentleman. Such a man, said Newman, is "at home in any society." He has "the repose of a mind which lives in itself, while it lives in the world, and which has resources for its happiness at home when it cannot go abroad." [2] He is, in short, a liberally educated man.

Much has happened since 1852 to make the university a very different place from that described by Cardinal Newman. The educated man of Newman's ideal was a generalist: the university graduate of today is expected to be a specialist. Higher education, as Newman conceived it, was supposed to be available only to the privileged few: today it is regarded as the right of the many. The university, as Newman described it, was aloof from society, a sanctuary of the mind well removed from the cacophony of the market place: the university of today is a mirror of society, highly solicitous of its support and responsive to its needs. The university of Newman's day functioned chiefly as conservator of the old: the university of today places a far higher priority on the discovery of the new. The "university" whose idea Newman so eloquently proclaimed has all but disappeared; in its place has appeared what Clark Kerr has aptly called the "multiversity." [3]

As the universities have changed, so also have liberal arts colleges. "Our Illiberal Liberal Arts Colleges," the title of an article

---

[1] John Henry Newman, *The Idea of a University,* Henry Tristram, ed., *Newman's Idea of a Liberal Education* (New York: Barnes and Noble, 1952), pp. 104-105.

[2] *Ibid.*

[3] Clark Kerr, *The Uses of the University* (Cambridge: Harvard University Press, 1963), Chapter 1.

published some years ago,[4] might well be taken as a description of the vast majority of the institutions that claim to be liberal arts colleges. As enrollments in these institutions have skyrocketed in recent years, the proportion of students who either desire or get a liberal education has steadily decreased. Students in so-called "liberal arts" colleges are also expected to become specialists, and specialists, in increasing numbers, they have become.

No doubt it would be both naive and anachronistic to suggest that this trend toward earlier and greater specialization at the undergraduate level is one that can and ought to be reversed. Ours is an enormously complex society, and such a society requires a multitude of specialists of all types simply in order to maintain itself. It is probably necessary to conclude, therefore—lamentable though it is—that the "liberally educated man" of Newman's ideal is a species of human being that is rapidly becoming extinct.

It cannot be denied, however, that these changes in the goals and structure of higher education have produced some rather acute problems. Educational leaders in colleges and universities all over the country are engaged in constant efforts to find some workable balance between the competing claims of general and special education, of the sciences and the humanities, of teaching and research —to mention just three areas of lively current controversy. Modernity has arrived with a vengeance, in the opinion of many.

The individual upon whom the various pressures thus generated converge is, of course, the modern student. He is told, perhaps, that the institution he is attending proposes to help him get a liberal education—but he soon discovers that most of his professors are specialists, as uninterested as they are incapable of discussing anything outside their "area of professional competence." He has been led to believe that the institution he is attending is primarily an educational institution and that the faculty is intensely interested in helping him get an "education"—but he discovers that many of the professors he would like to study with most are busy with research projects, and that the task of teaching has been largely turned over to graduate assistants. "The multiversity," as Clark Kerr has said,

[4] Paul A. Brinker, *Journal of Higher Education*, Vol. XXXI, No. 3 (March, 1960), pp. 133-138.

"is a confusing place for the student. . . . The casualty rate is high. The walking wounded are many." [5]

The Anatomy of Specialization

We have been speaking rather generally about certain recent developments in American higher education, one of which is a tendency toward greater specialization. What, precisely, is academic specialization? What are the evidences that this has in fact occurred?

We are concerned with academic specialization insofar as it is an indication of the de-liberalization of higher education. Thus understood, it may be seen that this specialization consists in the congruent emergence of three developments: the increasing isolation of the academic fields from one another, the decline of those academic areas traditionally committed to liberal education, and the tendency of even these latter fields to become narrow and somewhat esoteric specialties.

The growing mutual isolation of the several academic fields is a matter of common knowledge and hardly needs to be elaborated here. It is evident to some extent among, for example, the several natural sciences, where the concepts and nomenclature employed are in some instances becoming so specialized that representatives of one field can scarcely communicate with scientists in related fields—though here, it must be remembered, the universal language of mathematics is a powerful force for intercommunication. The problem is really serious, however, between the sciences and the humanities—the so-called "two cultures" of which C. P. Snow has written with such evident concern. [6]

The decline of the humanities has been going on apace since about the beginning of the present century. It is evident in a number of ways—in the declining proportions of students taking their baccalaureate degree with a major concentration in the humanities, in the declining proportions of doctorates in the humanities, etc. Consider, for example, the following statistics. During the years

---

[5] Kerr, *op. cit.*, p. 42.

[6] C. P. Snow, *The Two Cultures and the Scientific Revolution* (New York: Cambridge University Press, 1959).

1936-1945 (when, it must be remembered, only about 15 percent of college-age people went to college, as compared with well over 40 percent at the present time), 65 institutions produced five or more graduates who went on to earn a Ph.D. degree in foreign languages and literature; for the years 1946-1959 the corresponding figure is 40. For history, the figures are 88 institutions for 1936-1945 and 77 for 1946-1959. For English, the corresponding figures are 86 and 76; for philosophy, 24 and 20; and for fine arts and music, 19 and 12.[7] During the years 1938-1947, 17.8 percent of all the doctorates awarded in the United States were in the humanities; for the period 1958-1962 this figure had dropped to 13.2 percent.[8] Between 1901 and 1958 the proportion of undergraduates majoring in the humanities declined from 27.7 to 13.5 percent.[9]

As the humanities have lost ground numerically, so also have they tended to lose much of their vitality. Once the heart and soul of higher education, they have been increasingly consigned to a role on the periphery of the educational enterprise. The professors of literature, philosophy, history, and languages no longer set the pace in the modern college or university: the pace is set by others. One sometimes hears it said that the humanists are becoming demoralized.

One way by which some humanistic disciplines have sought to redress the balance—to prove their worth in the modern educational market—is by adopting, wherever possible, the quantitative-empirical methods of the sciences. Statistical techniques are being increasingly employed, for example, in linguistics and in textual criticism. The traditional concern of humanists with matters requiring taste and judgment (rather than measurement and demonstration) has not exactly disappeared, but many humanists have become a little embarrassed about it and have welcomed the "solid ground of empirical fact" whenever they have had the opportunity. The result is a series of subtle but important changes in the humanistic disciplines: a shifting of emphasis from qualitative to quantita-

[7] Figures compiled from Robert H. Knapp, *The Origins of American Humanistic Scholars* (Englewood Cliffs, N.J.: Prentice-Hall, 1964), Chapter 3.

[8] Allan M. Cartter, ed., *American Universities and Colleges* (Washington, D.C.: The American Council on Education, 1964), 9th ed., p. 54.

[9] Knapp, *op. cit.*, p. 58.

tive concerns, the slow but steady atrophy of traditional areas of study that do not lend themselves to quantitative techniques—in short, the gradual transformation of the humanities into quasi-sciences.

The Need for Integration

It is hardly necessary to insist that the consequences of this situation, both individually and socially, are most unfortunate and may yet prove disastrous. A culture in which major segments of the intelligentsia do not speak the same language, and at times give no serious indication of wanting to understand one another, is already in a fair way toward coming apart. This is occurring, moreover, at a time when the world is in the throes of multiple revolutions—the "revolution of rising aspirations" (as the late Adlai Stevenson once called the recent upsurge of the peoples of the underdeveloped countries), the technological revolution, and the anti-colonial and anti-white revolution of the peoples of Africa and Asia. At a time when history demands more than ever before that we combine a profound and perceptive ethical and human concern with the most exacting technical knowledge, we are retreating into our several specialties as though a concern for the *whole,* a quest for *unity,* were no one's proper concern.

It is precisely the business of philosophy to pursue this quest for unity. The great questions of philosophical controversy—such as those discussed in the preceding chapters—are by no means the rather odd and special preoccupations of just one more group of specialists, namely philosophers; they are, on the contrary, questions that cut across the artificial barriers of our academic specialties and compel us to *relate* our little pockets of specialized knowledge (and opinion, and conjecture, and even feeling) in some coherent way. A philosopher who refuses to make this effort, difficult though it is, has abdicated his responsibility as a philosopher; a student who knows philosophy only as one specialty beside others —as logic, perhaps, or as one rather queer strand of Western history—has missed the point of the whole endeavor.

I spoke a little earlier about the decline of the humanities in recent years. This decline has been particularly pronounced in philosophy, as evidenced by the fact that the proportion of undergraduates majoring in philosophy declined from just under 5 percent at the turn of the century to less than 1 percent in 1958.[10] The reason for this, surely, is not that students today do not feel the need for the kind of integrating educational experience that philosophy is supposed to provide. Quite the contrary: they feel it as never before. The reason is rather that philosophy as it is sometimes pursued today does not serve this integrating function. I think it should. Moreover, I think it can. No other effort is of more urgent importance at the present time. And no other effort deserves the name "philosophy," which means "the love of wisdom."

---

[10] Knapp, *op. cit.*, p. 58.

For Further Reading

Ardley, Gavin, "What Kind of Education?" *Philosophy,* Vol. XXXV (1960), 153-157.

Blanshard, Brand, "The Test of a University," in *Man, Science, Learning and Education,* ed. S. W. Higginbotham. Baylor, Tex.: William Marsh Rice University, 1963. Pages 21-40.

Hahn, Lewis E., "Philosophy as Comprehensive Vision," *Philosophy and Phenomenological Research,* Vol. XXII (1961), 1-25.

Kerr, Clark, *The Uses of the University.* Cambridge, Mass.: Harvard University Press, 1963.

Loewenberg, Jacob, *Reason and the Nature of Things.* La Salle, Ill.: Open Court, 1959.

Mure, G. R. G., *Retreat from Truth.* Oxford: Basil Blackwell, 1958.

Newman, John Henry, *The Idea of a Liberal Education,* ed. Henry Tristram. London and Toronto: George G. Harrap, 1952.

Snow, C. P., *The Two Cultures and the Scientific Revolution.* London: Cambridge University Press, 1959.

Supek, Ivan, "The Task of Philosophy Today," *Philosophy and Phenomenological Research,* Vol. XXIV (1963), 117-124.

White, Morton, *Toward Reunion in Philosophy.* Cambridge, Mass.: Harvard University Press, 1956.

Glossary of
Philosophical Terms *and*
Index

Glossary of Philosophical Terms

Note: Controversial issues can be fruitfully discussed only insofar as a neutral language—i. e., one acceptable to everyone discussing the controversy and understood in the same sense by all—is available for the discussion. Unfortunately, it is uncommonly difficult in philosophy to formulate neutral definitions of many key philosophical terms. The definitions that follow will indicate the usage observed throughout this book, and this in turn reflects the usage of a large number of English-speaking philosophers. The reader should be aware, however, that some philosophers have used and do use some of these terms in slightly different ways, and he should accordingly be prepared to modify his understanding of any term which he encounters being used in some other way.

Ambiguous: quality of a term which has different meanings when used in different contexts. (*Ex:* "line" means one thing to a painter, another thing to a mathematician, and yet a third thing to a plumber.)

Analogical predication: a mode of speaking about God, first advocated by St. Thomas Aquinas (1225–74), which is said to be a kind of mean between *univocal* and *equivocal* predication (see below). The idea is extremely complex, no less than three varieties of analogical predication having been distinguished by followers of St. Thomas.

Analytic: quality of a sentence, statement, or proposition which does not purport to say anything about reality, but simply explicates some part of the meaning of one or more of its terms. (*Ex:* "All circles are round.") Contrasts with *synthetic* (see below).

A posteriori: completely dependent on, and a product of, experience; mode of knowledge in which experience is the source as well as the occasion of knowledge. Contrasts with *a priori* (see below).

A priori: not completely dependent on experience; independent in the sense that experience, though it may be the occasion for one's coming to know, is not the source. Contrasts with *a posteriori* (see above).

493

Argument: (1) an attempt to show that certain considerations or alleged facts provide evidence in favor of the truth of some proposition. (2) A group of propositions concerning which it is claimed that the presumed truth of some (the premises) constitutes evidence for the truth of one (the conclusion).

Behaviorism: the view that man is constituted in such a way that every detail of his experience and behavior is the theoretically predictable consequence of causes lying outside himself.

Circumstantial freedom of self-realization: the opportunity to do what one wants to do; a situation in which neither one's own limitations nor external restraints prevent one from doing a given thing. (*Ex:* religious freedom, i. e., the opportunity to worship, or not to worship, as one wishes.)

Cognition: (1) the act or process of knowing (cognizing). (2) That which is known (cognized).

Common-sense realism: the view that the world as it really is does not differ in any important respect from the world as it appears to us; direct realism.

Connotation: see *intension.*

Consciousness: a center of awareness, feeling, and perception; mind.

Constructive empiricism: the view, with respect to the problem of induction, that induction is a legitimate logical procedure, and that its legitimacy can be established in a way that is consistent with empiricism, i. e., without invoking any *a priori* principles.

Contingent: (1) (in logic) quality of a proposition that is not necessarily true, i. e., the denial of which does not involve a self-contradiction. (2) (in metaphysics) Quality of a being that does not have the cause of its existence within itself; ontologically dependent. Contrasts with *necessary* (see below).

Contra-causal: incompatible with determinism.

Conventionalism: the view that language is a completely conventional system, i. e., it has no essential or intrinsic relation to reality. Contrasts with *essentialism* (see below).

Cosmological argument: (1) an argument for the existence of God which takes as its first premise some empirical or quasi-empirical observation about the world. (2) Some particular formulation of such an argument.

Cosmology: (1) the study of the origin and general structure of the physical universe. (2) A theory or system regarding the same. Most of the inquiries that once belonged to cosmology have now been taken over by the physical sciences.

Critical realism: any view which affirms that the world as it really is is in some respects similar to, and in some respects different from, the world as it appears to us.

Deduction: the act of drawing a conclusion from a set of premises; the act of inferring. In the case of a correct deduction, the conclusion (inference) must be true if the premises are true. In this respect *deduction* differs from *induction* (see below).

Defining characteristic: a characteristic which a thing must have in order to be a member of the class of things being defined. (*Ex:* being unmarried is a defining characteristic of bachelorhood; hence, all married persons are excluded by definition from the class of bachelors.)

Denotation: see *extension.*

Determinism: the theory that the universe is constituted in such a way that everything that occurs is the theoretically predictable consequence of antecedent causes; universal determinism; strict determinism. Contrasts with *indeterminism* (see below).

Direct realism: the theory that the physical universe is as it appears to be; common-sense realism.

Double-aspect theory: the theory, first advanced by the Dutch philosopher Benedict Spinoza (1632–77), that mind and body are simply two different aspects of a single underlying reality.

Dualism, mind-body: the theory that body and mind are ontologically distinct, neither being reducible to the other.

Dualism, ontological: the theory that reality consists of two different kinds of being (e. g., mind and matter) neither of which is reducible to the other.

Emotivism: a meta-ethical theory according to which moral utterances are held to be ejaculatory in nature, i. e., expressions of the feelings (of approval or disapproval) of the speaker; a form of *non-cognitivism* (see below).

Empirical: (1) derived from observation; *a posteriori.* (2) About the real world; capable of being exhibited in sense experience.

Empirical generalization: a general statement about a class of objects made on the basis of observation of some members of the class.

Empiricism: the epistemological theory that all knowledge of reality originates in and is a product of sense experience, i. e., that all knowledge of synthetic truths arises out of experience. Contrasts with *rationalism* (see below).

Epiphenomenalism: the theory that mind or consciousness is a mere by-product ("epiphenomenon") of physiological processes, and that it does not influence those processes in any way; the theory that mind is constituted by physiological processes, and is influenced causally by them, but that it has no causal influence on the body.

Epistemology: (1) a study of the nature and limits of human knowledge. (2) A theory concerning the same (e. g., "the *epistemology* of Kant").

Equivocal: quality of a term having different meanings in each of two or more applications.

Essentialism: the theory that language is not a completely conventional system, but that it has some essential or non-conventional relation to reality.

Ethics: see *normative ethics* and *meta-ethics.*

Existential: of or pertaining to existence, particularly human existence.

Extension: all of the individual things to which a given term is applicable;

denotation. (The *extension* of the term "man," for example, is Tom, Dick, Harry and all of the other individuals—living and dead and as yet unborn —to whom the term is applicable.)

Fallacy: an error in reasoning that makes it impossible to establish the conclusion in question on the given premises; a logical mistake. In the case of a deductive argument, the effect of a fallacy is to render the argument *invalid* (see below).

Freedom: (1) the opportunity to do what one wants to do. (2) The power to enact any of two or more genuinely open alternatives; free will. (3) The state in which "ideal manhood" is realized, in which one has become everything that man ought to be. (*Note:* This term is highly ambiguous. It is always important to try to determine the precise sense in which a given writer is using the term.) See also *moral freedom; natural freedom of self-determination; circumstantial freedom of self-realization; free will.*

Free will: power of the self to enact any of two or more genuinely open alternatives; contra-causal freedom; natural freedom of self-determination.

Hard determinism: the view that determinism is true, and that it is not compatible with moral freedom, and, consequently that man is not morally responsible.

Hedonism: (1) (analytic form) the theory that "good" (in the moral sense) means "pleasurable." (2) (synthetic form) The theory that pleasure alone is intrinsically good.

Heuristic principle: a principle which is not judged as to its truth or falsity (it is neither affirmed nor denied), but which is assumed for the purposes of some particular inquiry because of its demonstrated usefulness in raising fruitful questions.

Hyper-critical realism: the view that the world as it really is is highly dissimilar to the world as it appears to us; a radical form of critical realism.

Immanent: within; near; not transcendent.

Imperativism: a meta-ethical theory according to which moral sentences are held to be a species of directive language, i. e., implicit commands or recommendations to act in certain sorts of ways and not to act in other sorts of ways; a form of *non-cognitivism* (see below).

Indeterminism: the theory that the universe is constituted in such a way that some events are not the theoretically predictable consequences of antecedent causes.

Induction: the act of affirming a general statement about a class of things on the basis of observation of some members of the class; the act of making an empirical generalization.

Inductive skepticism: the view, associated with the Scottish philosopher David Hume (1711–76), that induction is not a legitimate logical procedure, i. e., that it is a procedure which is not capable of rational justification.

Inference: (1) a proposition which follows as a logical consequence of certain other propositions; that which is inferred; an implication. (2) The act of inferring, i. e., of deriving the actual or apparent logical consequences from a set of assumed premises.

Intension: the "sense meaning" of a term, such as would be normally stated in a formal definition of the term; the set of characteristics a thing must have in order to be included in the extension of a given term.

Interactionism: the theory that body and mind are ontologically distinct, and that they influence each other causally.

Introspection: the act or process of observing or noting one's own feelings, thoughts, or mental states.

Intuition: the act whereby, according to rationalists, the mind discerns non-empirical qualities and grasps *a priori* truths.

Intuitionism: a meta-ethical theory according to which "good" (in the moral sense) is held to denote a simple, non-natural quality; non-naturalistic objectivism; non-naturalism.

Invalid: quality of a deductive argument whose conclusion may be false even if all of its premises are true; not valid.

Legalism: an ethical theory according to which it is held that right and wrong are determined by one's adherence or non-adherence to a set of moral rules (laws) which are applicable at all times, in all places, and under any circumstances.

Libertarianism: the view that free will is a necessary condition of moral responsibility, and that man has this freedom, and, consequently, that determinism is not the case. Contrasts with *hard determinism* (see above) and *soft determinism* (see below).

Logic: (1) a study of the principles whereby one may distinguish correct from incorrect reasoning. (2) A system or theory regarding the same (*Ex:* "The *logic* of John Stuart Mill").

Logical connectives: words (such as "if," "and," "either," "or") which do not denote, but which are essential to the meaning of the sentences in which they occur; syncategorematic terms.

Materialism: the metaphysical theory that the whole of reality consists of matter and its determinations; a form of *monism* (see below).

Meta-ethics: a study of the logical structure of ethical reasoning and the logical characteristics of ethical discourse. The main effort of meta-ethicists to date has been directed toward the elucidation of the precise meanings of the key terms of moral appraisal ("good," "bad," "right," "wrong," "duty," "ought," etc.).

Meta-language: a language used for the purpose of talking about language, i. e., a language whose terms denote features of language rather than features of non-verbal reality; a language about language. (The language of grammar, for example, constitutes a meta-language.)

Metaphysics: (1) the study of the nature and structure of being (ontology) and of the origin and general structure of the universe (cosmology); first philosophy. (2) A theory or system concerning the same. (Some philosophers use this term simply as a synonym for ontology, excluding cosmology. Others use it pejoratively as a synonym for "nonsense.")

Monism: the view that the whole of reality consists of various determinations of some one ultimate substance, or kind of "stuff." The principal forms of monism are *materialism* (all is matter), *idealism* (all is mind), and *neutral monism* (all is some substance that is neither mind nor matter, but is the ground of both). Monism contrasts with *dualism* (see above) and *pluralism* (see below).

Moral freedom: the freedom (whatever be its nature) that is a necessary condition of moral responsibility; the freedom without which man is not, or would not be, morally responsible.

Morally responsible: answerable for one's behavior; a fitting subject of moral appraisal.

Multi-functionalism: a meta-ethical theory according to which moral sentences are held to serve a variety of functions, and are therefore not translatable without loss of meaning into sentences of any single logical type.

Naive realism: see *Common-sense realism.*

Naturalistic fallacy: the mistake, according to the non-naturalistic objectivism of G. E. Moore (1873–1958) of attempting to define "good" (in a moral sense), particularly in terms of some natural (empirically discernible) quality or qualities.

Natural freedom of self-determination: the power of the self to enact any one of two or more genuinely open alternatives; contra-causal freedom; free will. Libertarians affirm that man has such a power, determinists that he does not.

Naturalism: (1) any philosophical system which holds that the whole of reality consists of objects and events occurring in space and time. Contrasts with *transcendentalism* (see below). (2) (in meta-ethics) The view that "good" (in a moral sense) denotes some empirical quality or qualities; naturalistic objectivism.

Naturalistic objectivism: a meta-ethical theory according to which the key moral predicates are held to denote some empirically verifiable quality or qualities. A hedonist who affirms that "good" *means* "pleasurable," for example, would be affirming one very common version of this theory.

Necessary: (1) (in logic) quality of a proposition the denial of which involves a self-contradiction. (2) (in metaphysics) quality of a being which has the cause of its existence within itself; not ontologically dependent. Contrasts with *contingent* (see above).

Negative predication: see *Via negativa.*

Non-cognitivism: any meta-ethical theory which holds that moral sentences are not informative, i. e., that they assert nothing, and therefore are incapable of being either true or false. *Emotivism* and *imperativism* both qualify as theories of this type.

Non-naturalistic objectivism: a meta-ethical theory according to which "good" (in the moral sense) is held to denote a simple, non-natural quality, the presence of which in some things is what makes them good; intuitionism; non-naturalism.

Normative ethics: the quest for general principles of right and wrong; the attempt to determine what things really are good or bad, right or wrong, and to identify the general principles by virtue of which they are so.

Occasionalism: the theory that mind and body are ontologically distinct (therefore a *dualistic* theory), and that each operates according to its own laws, but that they appear to interact because of the fact that God from time to time does whatever is required in order to keep them synchronized.

Ontological: of or pertaining to ontology; having to do with being.

Ontological argument: a famous argument for the existence of God, devised by St. Anselm of Canterbury (1033–1106), in which the attempt is made to show that the denial of the proposition "God exists" is self-contradictory.

Ontological status: kind of being. To disclose the ontological status of something is to put it in some ontological category; it is to state in what precise sense it is true to say that that thing *is*.

Ontologically distinct: belonging to different ontological categories, neither of which is reducible to the other.

Ontology: (1) the study of the nature or structure of being. (Some philosophers use this term as a synonym for *metaphysics;* others use it as the name for one main branch of metaphysics, the other being *cosmology.*) (2) A theory or system put forward as a result of such a study.

Pan-psychism: the view that the whole of reality consists of minds ("psyches") of varying degrees of consciousness; one of the classical ways of attempting to overcome ontological dualism.

Paradox: an apparently self-contradictory assertion which is made nonetheless on the ground that to eliminate the apparent contradiction would allegedly involve denying some truth.

Parallelism: the view that mind and body are ontologically distinct (therefore a *dualistic* theory), and that each operates according to its own laws, the appearance of interaction between the two resulting from the fact that God has established a perfect harmony between them. This view was first advocated by the German philosopher Gottfried Wilhelm Leibnitz (1646–1716).

Percept: that which is "before the mind" in the act of perceiving; that which is immediately present to consciousness in perception.

Perception: the act or process of taking cognizance of the world by means of the senses.

Phenomenalism: the view that the reality of a material object consists in its being perceived by some perceiver, with the corollary that the physical world does not exist apart from the perceptions, actual or possible, of some perceiver. This view was formerly known as *subjective idealism.*

Pluralism: the view that reality is not reducible to one ultimate substance, or kind of "stuff," but that on the contrary there are several. Contrasts with *monism* and *dualism* (see above).

Premise: a proposition which, in conjunction with other propositions, supports a conclusion.

Primary quality: according to the critical realism of John Locke (1632–1704), a quality that belongs to an object in such a way that no particle of which the object is composed could be conceived to exist without it. Locke gives extension, shape, size, and mobility as examples of such qualities. Contrasts with *secondary qualities* (see below).

Private subjectivism: a meta-ethical theory according to which moral utterances are held to be statements about the personal likes and dislikes of the person making the utterance.

Proposition: that which is affirmed or denied by a declarative sentence; the meaning of a sentence which affirms or denies that something is the case. Propositions (and the sentences in which they are expressed) have the property of being either true or false.

Rationalism: (1) the view that some truths about reality are knowable in a way that is in some degree independent of experience, i. e., that some synthetic truths may be known *a priori*. (2) A European philosophical movement the most prominent representatives of which were René Descartes (1596–1650), Benedict de Spinoza (1632–77), Gottfried Wilhelm Leibnitz (1646–1716), Christian Wolff (1679-1754), and Immanuel Kant (1724–1804).

Reality: (1) the totality of the real, everything that is. (2) What truly or in actuality is the case, as over against what may appear to be the case. In this sense, reality is often contrasted with *appearance*.

Reason: (1) a proposition which, in conjunction with some other proposition or propositions, supports a conclusion not deducible from the other proposition(s) alone; a premise. (2) A statement which purportedly justifies a belief or act. (3) The faculty of knowledge. (4) The essential nature of the self.

Reasoning: the act or process of drawing conclusions from premises.

Res cogitans: literally, "thinking thing"; that which, according to René Descartes (1596–1650), man essentially is—in contrast to unthinking, extended being (i.e., material objects).

Secondary quality: according to the critical realism of John Locke (1632–1704), the capacity of a material object to produce in a percipient an impression (of color, sound, taste, etc.) unlike anything in the object itself. Such a quality is thus said to be "mind-dependent." Contrasts with *primary quality* (see above).

Self: that which one designates by the pronoun "I"; consciousness; mind. (Its status has long been a matter of philosophical controversy.)

Sense data: the immediate, uninterpreted objects of sense experience; the patches of color, geometrical shapes, etc., which one sees when looking at a material object, the vari-pitched noises which one sometimes hears (which may subsequently be interpreted as a melody on a violin), etc.

Societal subjectivism: a meta-ethical theory according to which moral utterances are held to be statements about the approval- and disapproval- tendencies of some social group of which the person making the utterance is a part.

Soft determinism: the view that determinism is true, but that the conditions of moral responsibility are such that man is nonetheless morally responsible whenever he has the opportunity to do what he wants to do.

Solipsism: the theory that oneself is the only mind or consciousness which exists, and that everything else exists only as a perception of this self.

Sound: quality of an argument which is formally valid and contains only true premises.

Subjective idealism: the view, associated with George Berkeley (1685–1753), that the being of material objects consists in their being preceived by some perceiver (*esse est percipi*), that they have no "independent" existence; phenomenalism. Contrasts with all types of *realism* (see above).

Substratum: that which, according to realist ontologies, underlies and supports the perceived qualities of material objects; that in which the accidents or attributes of material objects are said to inhere.

Summum bonum: literally, "highest good"; that which is worthy of being sought for its own sake.

Syncategorematic terms: a more or less obsolete term for what are now called *logical connectives* (see above).

Synthetic: quality of a sentence, statement, or proposition which purports to say something about reality. (*Ex:* "Some camels have two humps.") Contrasts with *analytic* (see above).

System: a comprehensive set of coherent and interdependent propositions in terms of which one attempts to understand and explain the phenomena within the range of its alleged relevance. An *ethical system,* for example, purports to provide a context for the understanding and explanation of all ethical phenomena. A *philosophical system* purports to provide a context for the understanding and explanation of all phenomena.

Teleological: of or pertaining to ends, goals, purposes (from the Greek *telos,* meaning "end" or "goal"). *Teleological* explanations (explanations in terms of ends), for example, are often contrasted with scientific explanations (explanations in terms of causes). The term is sometimes used to describe a kind of thinking, also to designate a very famous argument for the existence of God (see below).

Teleological argument: an argument for the existence of God made famous by William Paley (1743–1805). The argument begins with the allegedly empirical premise that there is order (means subservient to ends) in the universe, and by analogy with human contrivances asserts the necessity of positing a cosmic Intelligence to account for this order.

Transcendent: (1) (Kant's usage) beyond the categories of human experience. (2) (as commonly used in theology and philosophy of religion) Beyond the world of space and time; other. Contrasts with *immanent* (see above).

Transcendentalism: any philosophical system which holds that there are dimensions of reality in addition to objects and events occurring in space and time. Contrasts with *naturalism* (see above).

Univocal (applied to terms): having the same meaning in all instances in which it is used, or in all instances being considered. Contrasts with *equivocal* (see above).

Utilitarianism: (1) the theory that the goodness or badness of acts consists in their tendency to promote or hinder the realization of that which is intrinsically good. (2) The particular version of this theory advocated by the English philosophers Jeremy Bentham (1748–1832) and John Stuart Mill (1806–73). This view is more properly called "hedonistic utilitarianism."

Vague (applied to terms): imprecise in ordinary usage in such a way that any attempt at precise definition would render the term more exact than ordinary usage will allow. (*Ex:* "warm" is a vague term; it would be inconsistent with ordinary usage to define it precisely in terms of a definite temperature range.)

Valid: quality of a deductive argument whose conclusion must be true if its premises are true; logically correct.

Verbal: of or pertaining to words. Often applied to a given philosophical controversy to indicate that there is no "real issue" dividing the parties to the dispute, but simply a confusion or disagreement over the meanings of certain terms.

Via negativa: literally, "negative way." A mode of speaking about God wherein one attempts to say not what God *is* but what He is *not*. Thus "simple" (= non-complex), "incorporeal" (= non-corporeal), etc., are "negative predicates." Used by several medieval philosophers, including St. Thomas Aquinas.

Volition: (1) the act of exercising choice, of choosing among alternatives. (2) The power to exercise choice.

World-view: a comprehensive view of reality in terms of which one attempts to understand and "place" everything that comes before one's consciousness.

Index

A NOTE ON THE TYPE

The text of this book was set on the Linotype in a face called *Times Roman*, designed by Stanley Morison for The Times (London), and first introduced by that newspaper in 1932.

Among typographers and designers of the twentieth century, Stanley Morison has been a strong forming influence, as typographical advisor to the English Monotype Corporation, as a director of two distinguished English publishing houses, and as a writer of sensibility, erudition, and keen practical sense.